D1602691

A
CHEKHOV
COMPANION

A
CHEKHOV
COMPANION

Edited by
Toby W. Clyman

GREENWOOD PRESS
WESTPORT, CONNECTICUT
LONDON, ENGLAND

Library of Congress Cataloging in Publication Data

Main entry under title:

A Chekhov companion.

 Bibliography: p.
 Includes index.
 1. Chekhov, Anton Pavlovich, 1860-1904—Handbooks,
manuals, etc. I. Clyman, Toby W.
PG3458.A1C6   1985   891.72 '3   84-29024
ISBN 0-313-23423-X (lib. bdg.)

Library of Congress Catalog Card Number: 84-29024
ISBN: 0-313-23423-X

First published in 1985

Greenwood Press
A division of Congressional Information Service, Inc.
88 Post Road West, Westport, Connecticut 06881

Printed in the United States of America

10 9 8 7 6 5 4 3 2 1

CONTENTS

Preface   vii

Part I Background Material

  1. Chekhov's Russia: A Historian's View
     Ralph T. Fisher Jr.   3

  2. Chekhov: A Biography
     Toby W. Clyman   17

  3. Chekhov and the Literary Tradition
     Donald Rayfield   35

Part II Aspects of Chekhov's Fiction

  4. Chekhov's Major Themes
     Ralph Lindheim   55

  5. Chekhov's Cast of Characters
     Kenneth A. Lantz   71

  6. Chekhov's Humour
     Harvey Pitcher   87

Part III Chekhov's Literary Craftsmanship

  7. Chekhov's Dramatic Technique
     J. L. Styan   107

8. Chekhov's Narrative Technique
   Andrew R. Durkin   123

Part IV Chekhov's Impact

9. Chekhov and the Modern Drama
   Martin Esslin   135

10. Chekhov and the Modern Short Story
    Charles E. May   147

Part V Criticism

11. Chekhov at Home: Russian Criticism
    Victor Terras   167

12. Chekhov Abroad: Western Criticism
    John Tulloch   185

Part VI Chekhov's Works in Performance

13. Chekhov on Stage
    Laurence Senelick   209

14. Chekhov into Film
    H. Peter Stowell   233

Part VII Chekhov as Correspondent and Social Observer

15. Chekhov as Correspondent
    Thomas Eekman   255

16. Chekhov as Social Observer: *The Island of Sakhalin*
    Joseph L. Conrad   273

Part VIII Translation

17. Chekhov in English
    Lauren G. Leighton   291

Selected Bibliography
Leonard Polakiewicz   311

Index   333

Contributors   345

PREFACE

Chekhov's writings have changed the complexion of literature. A study of the short story and drama would be incomplete without a critical examination of his writings, and an anthology of modern short stories or plays would be lacking were it to omit selections from Chekhov.

The growing interest in Chekhov's works in the English-speaking world is apparent from the new editions and translations of his writings and from the increasing output of Chekhov scholarship. Chekhov's plays are in the permanent repertoire of all leading drama ensembles and are among the more popular productions of amateur groups. Yearly, new interpretations and adaptations of his plays can be seen in theatres throughout the world. His short stories have been adapted for the stage by the prolific playwright Neil Simon and successfully performed on stage and television. In recent years plays and books have appeared based on Chekhov the man, his life, and people with whom he had been close, such as James McConkey's *To a Distant Island*, Leonid Maliugin's *My Bantering Happiness*, Harvey Pitcher's *Olga Knipper, Chekhov's Leading Lady*, and, most recently, Michael Pennington's *Anton Chekhov*, shown on the London stage in the summer of 1984.

Most major colleges and universities offer courses on Chekhov, and every major Slavic department includes Chekhov in its curriculum. His works have long been required reading, not only in English, comparative literature, and theatre courses, but even in history and psychology departments.

Chekhov scholarship is considerable. Like every great writer, he is being discovered anew by each generation. *The Modern Language International Bibliography* lists under Chekhov's name over 150 titles published between 1980 and 1982 alone. In 1981 the International Chekhov Society was formed following a world conference of Chekhov scholars at Yale University, providing further impetus to Chekhov studies. A new 30-volume edition of his collected works, including 12 volumes of his letters, was completed in the Soviet Union in 1983. The volume includes some hitherto unpublished material and copious commentaries on his works.

The student seeking to gain a better understanding of Chekhov's art is thus confronted with a formidable body of scholarly works scattered in a large variety of sources. *A Chekhov Companion* brings together essays on major topics in Chekhov studies encompassing a wide spectrum of Chekhov scholarship. It provides the background and critical information necessary for more than a superficial knowledge of Chekhov's art.

The organization is straightforward. Part I includes background material: a chapter on the Russia of Chekhov's time, a biographical essay, and a chapter surveying the impact of Russian and European literary tradition on his writings.

Parts II and III examine Chekhov's themes, characters, and technique. Of course, these are interrelated, and a discussion of any one of these aspects of Chekhov's art invariably includes some reference to the others. This traditional division into theme, character, and technique is a practical one: it enables us to focus on each of these areas and to view Chekhov's art from different perspectives. Also included in this section is an essay that considers Chekhov's humour as manifested in his life and his writings.

Part IV examines the impact of Chekhov's writings on the modern short story and drama. Part V provides a chronological survey of Chekhov criticism in Russia, England, and America, noting the different trends at home and abroad.

Part VI treats Chekhov's works in performance. It includes a history of the stagings of Chekhov's plays and a list of annotated noteworthy productions. For teachers who wish to use Chekhov films in film courses or in connection with the study of a particular story or play, this collection provides a review of Chekhov films available for rental by U.S. 16 mm. distributors as well as an annotated filmography.

There are also chapters on Chekhov's non-fiction (Part VII): "Chekhov as Correspondent" focuses primarily on the letters to his brother Alexander and to Lidiia Mizinova, a woman with whom Chekhov corresponded for a considerable period of time. This essay complements the biographical chapter in Part I. The essay on *The Island of Sakhalin* looks at Chekhov, the writer and physician, as social observer. It considers how Chekhov saw the people and their lives on the penal colony.

Students and teachers have often expressed dismay when confronted with the large number of different English translations of Chekhov's works. *A Chekhov Companion* provides a chapter assessing the various English translations of his short stories and plays, as well as a bibliography of important collections and editions of Chekhov's works in English.

Those who wish to pursue the study of Chekhov's works in greater detail can avail themselves of the bibliographical sources in the notes and the bibliography provided in this collection.

The Library of Congress transliteration is used throughout, except, of course, when the original work cited uses different transliteration. Contributors who refer to the Russian editions of Chekhov's collected works provide their own translation from the Russian. The English titles of Chekhov's works in this collection adhere mostly to Magarshack's translations as given in his "Bibliographical Index of the Complete Works of Anton Chekhov," in his *Chekhov: A Life*; 1953 reprint, Westport, Conn.: Greenwood Press, 1970, pp. 393-423.

I am grateful to the State University of New York at Albany for the financial aid which enabled me to complete *A Chekhov Companion*. My special thanks to all those colleagues who graciously gave of their time to read and comment on the essays in this collection. I am particularly appreciative of my husband's sustained support and encouragement.

PART I

Background Material

1

Ralph T. Fisher Jr.

CHEKHOV'S RUSSIA: A HISTORIAN'S VIEW

Historians are among those who value Chekhov most highly. Bearing in mind how often he was working in haste, they marvel that he recreated so accurately the people and situations around him.[1]

On the other hand, descriptions that are in themselves precise cannot supply all of the background and are not necessarily representative. Chekhov, like other writers, chose topics because he thought they would attract, touch, amuse, or challenge readers rather than because he wanted to create a statistically exact model of the society of his time. The better we can picture the whole of Chekhov's Russia, in all of its variety, the closer we can come to full understanding and appreciation of his writings. So it is that even the reader whose interests are mainly artistic and aesthetic is, or should be, stimulated by love of Chekhov to rummage in the historical dust.

During Chekhov's lifetime, from 1860 to 1904, Russia despite its huge size and relative isolation was powerfully affected by what was happening in the rest of the world. Russians vividly remembered the humiliation of defeat in 1853-1856 on their own Crimean Peninsula at the hands of the British and the French. They felt further humiliated after the Russo-Turkish War of 1877-1878, when the other European Powers forced Russia, despite its victory, to renounce some of the terms it had gained from Turkey. The same Russia that, early in the century, had shared the glory of crushing Napoleon and building a new order in Europe could now not even pose as a protector of its smaller Slavic and Orthodox brethren in the Balkans. And behind such dramatic incidents lay the more fundamental fact of Russia's industrial backwardness. The leading countries of Western Europe had been industrializing faster than Russia, and by mid-century the differences were embarrassingly obvious.

From the Crimean War onward, the pace of change in Russia quickened. Many elements in the population promoted innovations in the economic sphere, acting sometimes through the central government and sometimes independently of it. Railroads were being built so fast that the total trackage increased from around 1,000 miles shortly before Chekhov's birth to about 40,000 miles just after his death. Russia's output rose spectacularly in coal, oil, and iron and steel, as well as in cotton textiles and beet sugar. Trade, both domestic and foreign, was growing. New technologies and new industries were appearing. The introduction of street cars and city lighting was transforming urban life.

New opportunities to make a living appeared not only in all kinds of businesses but also in such realms as education, law, medicine, and administration, both local and national. A country that had been undergoverned in comparison with France or England or the German states was acquiring a sizable bureaucracy. Military service, thanks to the reforms that followed the Crimean War, was embracing a much larger share of the population for much shorter terms of active duty, and was doing its part to teach people to regard themselves as part of a nation.

The older nobility with its base on farmland and forested land was having to adapt to new relationships after the abolition of serfdom. Landowning nobles were losing influence in comparison with those who achieved noble status without land through military or other government service, as well as those nobles or non-nobles who gained wealth and power through business, the professions, the sciences, and the arts.

Russian scientists were among the leaders in many fields. Those whose names are widely known by laymen, like Dmitrii Mendeleev, Aleksandr Popov, and Ivan Pavlov, are only a very small fraction of the many Russian scientists and mathematicians who contributed significantly to the worldwide advance of knowledge.

In music, the period of Chekhov is the period of Musorgskii, Rimskii-Korsakov, Borodin, and Chaikovskii. Similar richness emerged in the other arts, and most of all in the field of literature, where Chekhov was continuing a literary tradition that went back several generations and had recently produced such masters as Dostoevskii, Tolstoi, and Turgenev.

Such an economic and cultural flowering could not fail to involve the processes by which the society was governed. Just as old and new clashed in economic and social spheres, so too did they clash within the sphere of politics and administration. The educated and well-off were becoming not only more numerous but also more aware of the plight of the many who were not so favored, and more critical of conditions they saw as miserable, unjust, and unworthy of a proud nation. The possible causes for complaint were almost infinite, as were the possible remedies. The system provided more avenues for expressing grievances than is commonly supposed. Although the empire was nominally an autocracy, and although the tsars under whom Chekhov lived—Alexander II (1855-1881), Alexander III (1881-1894), and Nicholas II (1894-1917)—were encouraged to think of themselves as all-powerful, in practice the central government was far from monolithic, and by modern standards it was both weak and inefficient. All through the government, from the central offices in St. Petersburg down to local administrative units, practices and institutions were changing as people tried to cope with problems old and new. Many people had great expectations for solving these problems quickly, but solutions were not as easy as they seemed. Hope was mixed with frustration.

How successfully was the society adapting to new demands? For Chekhov's Russia that question is both especially interesting and especially hard to answer. All of our images of his era are unavoidably colored by our awareness that the tsarist system broke down within a few years after his death. Naturally, readers of Chekhov have often interpreted the sadness that pervades much of his writing as evidence that such a collapse was likely to occur soon even if war had not come in 1914. The task of evaluating that likelihood has been much complicated by the heavy reliance of Russia's post-1917 rulers on denigration of the tsarist system in order to justify their own authority. We must do the best we can to formulate our answers despite the political, ideological, and other obstacles that stand in our way.

It is clear that although Chekhov's Russia was modernizing fast—indeed, during the years of his adulthood it was industrializing faster than any other major country in the world except Japan—it had a long way to go. Even by 1905 about three-quarters of the population still lived by farming, lumbering, fishing, or hunting, as against only about one-tenth by mining, manufacturing, or handicrafts and less than 4 percent by trade or commerce. The *Statistical Yearbook* of 1905 also reported 1.8 percent living on pensions or investments, 1.6 percent in transport or communications, 1.4 percent in civil service or the professions, 1.0 percent in the armed forces, and 0.6 percent connected with religious institutions. The urban share of the Russian population, depending on how one counts, was only around one-seventh or one-sixth, as against shares three or more times that large in the leading countries of Western Europe. It is striking to realize that by the census of 1897, which reported the total population of the empire at some 126 million, only ten cities in European Russia outside of the Baltic and Polish provinces contained more than 100,000 people.[2]

Surveying that general picture, a historian is impressed by the many ways in which specialists' ideas on the Chekhov era have changed in the past few decades. A good gauge against which to measure the changes is Walter Horace Bruford's *Chekhov and His Russia: A Sociological Study*, which appeared in 1948.[3] Bruford's book is an ambitious attempt to understand the Russia of Chekhov's time on the basis of not only the collected writings of Chekhov but also many of the best scholarly works on Russia then available. We can use his book as an indication of historical interpretations that were current in Britain and the United States just after World War II.

Since that time the output of scholarly writing on Chekhov's Russia, even in the English language alone, has been truly enormous. The scale of growth is suggested by the fact that when Bruford wrote there were apparently in North America no more than a dozen universities that employed full-time specialists in Russian history. Now, full-time positions in Russian history may number as high as 200, and ten times that number of people may be doing research mainly in Russian history. The period from 1855 to 1914 has, of course, been especially important to those who were hunting for the origins of World War I and the roots of the Revolutions of 1917. It has been a central historiographical battleground between those who sought to prove the inevitability and legitimacy of the Bolshevik triumph and those who either attacked those claims or merely tried to figure out what really happened. In our own country an added factor has been that, under the cultural exchanges since 1958, many Americans who might otherwise have focused on the Soviet period have been prompted by Soviet restrictions to turn instead to the half-century or more before 1917. Fortunately, along with the flood of specialized publications in many languages on Chekhov's Russia have come textbook surveys, bibliographies, and other tools. Those are treated in an extended bibliographic note at the end of this chapter.

To sample changes in historians' interpretations, we may look first at the peasants who in Chekhov's time made up roughly three-fifths or more of the population. (If one adds other rural occupations, the share rises into the range of 70 to 80 percent, depending on definitions.) Among the many debated questions concerning the peasantry of this period is: Were they or were they not getting poorer? Bruford thought they were. He cited the increasing pressure of the fast-growing peasant population on the limited supply of land, the "impossible burden" of the tax by which the ex-serfs were supposed to pay for the land they got, and the peasant crisis of the late nineteenth century, including the famine of 1892 (pp. 30-75).

That view was shared by many scholars both before Bruford and since, including Geroid Tanquary Robinson, Lazar Volin, Alexander Gerschenkron, and the late Sergei Pushkarev. Pushkarev not only did research on the peasantry but also grew up on an estate in central Russia during Chekhov's lifetime.[4] Middle-of-the-road historians like those agreed that the Emancipation of 1861 had its drawbacks, including some overcharging of the ex-serfs for the land they got and the provisions for continuing the role of the peasant commune. They stressed that it was a remarkable accomplishment nevertheless, freeing over 20 million serfs through a legal and relatively peaceful change that was quite in contrast to the American emancipation of some four million slaves through a process that included a terrible war and other, longer-lasting forms of civil strife. Such historians pointed out that, moreover, the emancipated serfs constituted less than half of the peasantry, that both the state peasants and those formerly on estates of the imperial family had much more land per person than the former serfs, that altogether the Russian peasants of Chekhov's time had far more land per person than the farmers of Western Europe, and that despite the poor quality of much of the land and other obstacles to increasing productivity, over the ensuing decades the peasants both expanded their own numbers rapidly and bought a large amount of additional land, mostly from the nobility. But those moderate historians typically thought that nevertheless the peasants were getting poorer. On this point their outlook harmonized with that of many, if not most, educated Russians of Chekhov's time.

In recent years, however, several scholars have questioned that view. Raymond Goldsmith, restudying available statistics, concluded that, while Russian agricultural output grew only slowly in the period 1860-1913, it did apparently grow more than the total population, and the growth rate per head of the entire population was not very different from that in the United States and the United Kingdom. Goldsmith was careful to warn that he had not measured consumption and that the per capita increase in output might have been offset by exports and by industrial use. Paul Gregory followed up on that problem, examining the peasants' consumption of grain between 1885 and 1913. Using especially data on transportation of grains by rail and water, Gregory concluded that food grains retained in the village increased faster in the period 1885-1913 than either retail sales or the output of the economy as a whole. He suggested that agricultural production may have grown significantly faster than Goldsmith had estimated. He challenged the conventional idea that through oppressive taxes the tsarist government forced the peasants to pay more than their fair share of the cost of rapid industrialization.

James Simms reconsidered the data, too, looking at several indicators, including big increases among the peasants in the consumption of items subject to indirect taxation, such as tea, vodka, matches, and kerosene. He concluded that the growing arrears in redemption payments must have been based more on unwillingness to pay than on inability to pay; that the common view of a deepening poverty and an increasingly unbearable tax burden among the Russian peasantry toward the end of the nineteenth century was based on several misinterpretations; and that, although the data were admittedly far from adequate, such information as was available pointed not to a fall but rather to a rise in real income among the peasants in the late nineteenth century. Elvira Wilbur found evidence leading in a similar direction when she restudied data drawn mainly from a book published in 1900 that focuses on the central province of Voronezh, considered by many to have been one of the worst off at the time. The study examined the budgets of 232 rural households distributed among all the townships of the province. Over the 8-year period 1888-1896, a number of people collected information on some 677 items for each household. Wilbur saw three important errors, stemming from faulty methodology, that led analysts to exaggerate the poverty of the Voronezh peasants: Draft power was calculated counting only horses and omitting the very important bullocks; peasant leasing of land from others was considered a defensive measure to ward off disaster when in reality most of the leasing was done by the richer peasants to produce a surplus for the market; and reductions in the acreage that was allowed to rest and recover its fertility were interpreted generally as a desperate resort of the poor when actually much of the reduction was by prosperous farmers producing for the market.[5]

The traditional view of peasant impoverishment included references to the catastrophic famine of 1891-1892 and the government's mishandling of it. That question, too, has recently been reexamined. Richard Robbins has argued that the government managed the crisis surprisingly well, developing cooperation between the regular officials, the recently installed land captains, the *zemstvos*, and the peasant communes. It distributed food to over eleven million people, which was even more than the American Relief Administration served in 1921. It avoided a great potential loss of life far more successfully than the Soviet government did with American help in 1921-1922 or the British government did in India in 1899-1900. And, he recalled, in the famine of 1932-1933 in the Soviet Ukraine over ten times as many victims died as in 1891-1892. The criticisms of the government in the wake of the famine of 1891-1892, Robbins said, grew partly out of inade-quate publicity for the government's achievements, partly out of the tendency of many disaffected persons of the educated classes to blame the regime for any calamity, and partly out of frustrated hopes that the govern-ment would continue in the direction of expanding cooperation with those segments of the body politic whose help it had enlisted in the relief effort. James Simms followed up still more recently by looking at the after-effects of the famine. He concluded that the tsarist system coped so well with the famine that by 1893 the economy in general was operating as if there had been no famine at all. (This would not rule out pockets of continued suffering, as among the Volga Germans.) Yet many educated Russians continued to think of it as having a disastrous effect over the long term.[6]

In that connection, Esther Kingston-Mann, as a result of her analysis of the writings of early Russian Marxists concerning the peasants, has main-tained that a combination of an uncritical admiration of English rural development and a dogmatic interpretation of Marxism led these and other Russian radicals to ignore, misinterpret, or distort such information as was available on the Russian peasants, and thereby to see and to lead others to see conditions in the countryside as worse than they really were. Meanwhile, additional insights on the peasantry in Chekhov's time were emerging as byproducts of research on other topics.[7]

It is too early to say how far the prevailing view of the peasantry in Chekhov's time will be revised by the contributions mentioned here and others like them. It seems quite likely that if the continuing plight of the poorer elements among the peasantry loomed so large in the minds of

Chekhov and other educated, compassionate people of his period, it was less because of any real change for the worse among the peasantry as a whole than because the Emancipation, together with the other reforms and changes of the decades after the Crimean War, raised people's expectations so greatly. At the same time, many peasants were indeed poor, and many Russians, including many of the peasants themselves, *thought* the rural sector was getting poorer. That belief was in itself a political force.

Although this essay has dealt with only one limited aspect of the peasantry, and even that far from thoroughly, we should now turn to at least a few other social categories, recognizing that any treatment of them must be briefer still.

Concerning those who in Chekhov's time were already or were becoming industrial workers, one should at least mention a recent book by Robert Johnson, whose bibliography can serve as a guide to many earlier studies. Focusing on the Moscow workers of the period 1880-1900, Johnson finds that they, far more than workers in Western Europe, retained their attachments to their villages and continued to move back and forth, transmitting attitudes and ideas in both directions. One result was that their village base gave them a security cushion that increased their ability to endure strikes.[8]

In regard to the new class of industrialists and businessmen, Bruford, like others of his time, acknowledged their rapid growth (pp. 175-176) but dismissed as "insignificant" the "contribution of capitalistic free enterprise by 1904 to the general well-being" (p. 218). If he were redoing those passages today, he would have on hand a host of works providing a fuller understanding of the process. For example, John McKay has shown among other things how much foreign businessmen helped to inject a spirit of growth into Russia; how speedily Russian entrepreneurs emerged to share in the new opportunities and develop genuine partnerships with the foreigners and to use their superior technology; how soon local Russians, Jews, and Poles came to supplant the foreign managers and engineers; and how effectively the Russian state protected Russians against exploitation by foreigners. Thomas Owen has described the merchants in Moscow from 1855 to 1905, from small artisans to captains of industry, and has shown how Russian nationalism and the Orthodox faith together helped to produce government measures that protected Russian business against European competition. Alfred Rieber has explained how merchants and entrepreneurs, especially in Moscow, functioned politically outside of the court and imperial bureaucracies to promote their own interests as well as the development of the Russian economy. Rieber underscores the barriers to cooperation within the ranks of businessmen as well as between businessmen and such other categories as professional people.[9]

Entrepreneurs both inter-reacted with and overlapped to some extent with a category easy to laugh at and especially important for readers of Chekhov: the bureaucrats. Many Westerners of Chekhov's day, struck by the differences between government in Russia and in their own countries, assumed that the Russian bureaucracy was the autocrat's pliant tool. This attitude is recalled by Bruford's characterization of the policies of Alexander III's reign as "nothing but the blackest reaction" (p. 33). Such a view has now been widely discarded. Even at and near the top, the bureaucracy has been shown to have been astir with conflict among those who wanted to suppress development in order to preserve the traditional ways, those who wanted to industrialize while retaining strong state control, and the "modernizers" who wanted economic development along with reduced state control.[10] And it has become clear, for example, in Heide Whelan's book, that even the forceful Alexander III was readily blocked or frustrated by his bureaucrats.[11]

Another common misconception is that the Russian bureaucracy of Chekhov's era was unusually large. Complicating the matter is the fact that many employees of railways, banks, and the educational system could be counted as part of officialdom. But those who have tried to make accurate comparisons believe that Russia had far fewer government officials per capita than other European countries, perhaps only one-half to one-quarter as many as the leading Western powers. Russian officials as of 1897 included some 49,000 who had professional ranks in the civil, court, or diplomatic service, some 10,400 of similar rank in the police system, and some 4,500 in the service of the tsar's court. Beyond them were about 162,000 in the sub-professional categories embracing clerks, policemen, firemen, railway guards, and others. Russian bureaucrats of Chekhov's time seem to have been often regarded by the citizenry as incompetent, dishonest, or dictatorial. Although in such matters exact comparisons with other societies may be impossible, it seems likely that the relatively low numbers of officials, especially out in the provinces, could have given unusual room for petty tyranny. And the centralized nature of the tsarist system at the top made it hard for victims to get redress. There were plenty of tempting targets for a clever satirist.

From bureaucrats it is natural to move to nobles, provided we understand that the overlap was only limited. The nobility of Chekhov's time was a varied lot. As of 1897, about 1.2 million persons of all ages were classed as hereditary nobles. In addition, 630,000 or so adults had earned noble titles that were not transferable to their offspring. We must erase from our minds any notion that in this period nobility in itself connoted palatial estates and French governesses. Although over half a million nobles were members of households that owned farmland, the amount they owned had been dropping gradually since the emancipation of the serfs. In the 1860s nobles had owned about half of the cultivable land, but by 1905 their share had shrunk to around 30 percent. There were still a few hundred households with huge estates and a few thousand households that were quite well off, but the remaining hundred thousand or so noble landowning households lived on a scale ranging from modest to poor. As those landed nobles who could not succeed at farming either slipped into poverty or left the land for government service and other livelihoods, the number of people with noble titles was being swelled through the operation of the Table of Ranks. This system brought titles of either personal or hereditary nobility to those who rose to the prescribed ranks in either the civil or the military service. By the turn of the century over half of the hereditary nobles had no significant landholdings. At the same time, about half of the officers in the military had been non-nobles at birth, and in the civilian bureaucracy the percentage born as non-nobles was far higher. Even among the top four ranks of the civil service, where hereditary nobility came with the rank, some 70 percent either had no farmland or had holdings so small as to be more suited to summer residence than to production. One interesting trend, increasingly in the 1890s and after, was for those landowning nobles who really did live from agriculture to turn away from service in the capitals and involve themselves seriously in farm production and local public affairs.[12]

With regard to the military, reference should be made here to John Bushnell's articles arguing that the effectiveness of Alexander II's military reform has been overestimated. He finds the tsarist army of the 1880s and after to have been weak not only as a fighting machine but also as a force for education and modernization. The main debilitating factor among several, as he sees it, was the persistent emphasis on economic management rather than military skills. Army regiments right up through the Chekhov period, like those of a century earlier, had to procure a large share of their own food and clothing. Part they produced themselves; part they purchased with funds earned by soldiers sent out to work in the civilian economy. The officers were, says Bushnell, evaluated and promoted largely for their performance as managers and bookkeepers, and their units did very little true military training.[13]

No matter what other segment of the population one turns to, among those described by Chekhov and discussed by Bruford, one finds works published since 1948 that could have improved Bruford's basis for appraisal and can still enrich our own. For example, among the various categories of professional people, and having in mind Chekhov's own training, one should mention Nancy Frieden's recent examination of the medical profession, which as of 1897 embraced some 18,000 doctors and dentists. She shows how the conditions of the era prevented physicians from developing their own firm control of licensing, medical education, and medical ethics; how physicians acquired high prestige but relatively low pay in public service, especially in *zemstvo* medicine; and how a good many of them, owing partly to their dependence on the state, became involved in pressing for political change.[14]

For the legal profession, which as of 1897 included about 11,000 lawyers, Richard Wortman's book provides background on the great expansion of the judicial system in Chekhov's time and the continuing struggles between the administrative and the judiciary elements within the tsarist government. It was through this process that many high officials, including the tsar, became discredited in the eyes of the public. Samuel Kucherov's older survey gives us a useful description of the expanding judicial system and the extent to which it eroded the absolutism of the autocracy in the decades before 1905.[15]

The fateful process by which the theoretically absolute monarchy not only tolerated but even nourished the growth of a legal system that limited the autocratic power has been studied further by Marc Szeftel and William Wagner. They have sought to explain why the autocracy went to such lengths to preserve and even expand the autonomy of the reformed legal system in the civil sphere while at the same time interfering with its autonomy in criminal matters. At least part of the answer apparently lies in the government's desire to promote economic growth and its awareness that modern business required an impartial, predictable legal system.[16]

The same kind of tension between the desire for economic development and the desire to limit political change can be explored in another way by looking at the broad process of education. Patrick Alston's book on educational policy from 1855 to 1914 describes among other things the process by which controversies in the central government spread to local authorities, the ever larger educated class, and the general public. As a result, whenever the central bureaucracy tried to restrict educational opportunity, local institutions were often able to block those attempts and to press ahead with further expansion. Allen Sinel studied the policies pursued by the minister of public education from 1866 to 1880, Dmitrii A. Tolstoi. Without slighting Tolstoi's conservative aims, Sinel reveals Tolstoi's support for rapid expansion of the educational system as well as his refusal to raise fees to keep out the poor, with the result that during his tenure non-noble enrollments in secondary schools, on a percentage basis, grew about sixteen times as fast as noble enrollments.[17]

Literacy was spreading much faster than one would gather from reading Bruford (pp. 144-157). Certain parts of the population were sharply favored: males over females, young over old, urban dwellers over those in rural areas, and the people of the more urbanized western provinces over those of the remote fields and forests of the east. For example, among males called up for military service, only 22 percent were literate in 1874, but by 1884 the literate share had risen to 28 percent, by 1894 to 46 percent, and by 1904 way up to 71 percent. Gregory Guroff and Frederick Starr observe that in the large cities those who were learning to read were not just children in schools, but also working adults surrounded by a mushrooming assortment of signboards, posters, handbills, newspapers, magazines, and inexpensive books. Jeffrey Brooks, in his research on this topic, has pointed out that, in the last decades of the tsarist period, along with the fast growth of the reading public went a great diversification into distinct literary subcultures.

Various types of publications arose to meet their new demands. Informal schools emerged in the countryside, where self-appointed teachers supplemented the work of the regular school system. Admirers of Chekhov will be amused by Brooks's report that turn-of-the-century skilled workers in Khar'kov complained that Chekhov's writings overemphasized poverty and ignorance among the peasantry.[18]

Many of the items that might have been included in this essay remain undiscussed, works valuable for gaining an accurate understanding of the Russia Chekhov wrote about. The reader who wants to pursue any specific topic may turn to the surveys, bibliographies, and other tools mentioned in the bibliographical note.[19]

It is hoped that this short review has been enough to alert non-specialist readers of Chekhov to the risks of relying on some of the customary phrases used about Chekhov's era, including those that cite Chekhov's gloomier descriptions as signs that the tsarist system was predestined to an early and violent end. Recent scholarship has greatly expanded our knowledge. At the same time, there remains plenty of room for conflicting interpretations. The very thing that one specialist sees as a sign of healthy adaptation to new conditions may be seen by another as a portent of revolution.

But no matter which scholarly arguments prevail, Chekhov's works themselves will retain their worth for those who try to understand a period that, despite all its dark spots, was one of Russia's freest, most creative, and most exciting.

NOTES

1. Among the several friends who contributed valuable suggestions and comments during my work on this essay, I want to thank especially my former student, now colleague, Richard D. King.

2. Sergei G. Pushkarev, *The Emergence of Modern Russia 1801-1917*, trans. Robert H. McNeal and Tova Yedlin (New York: Holt, Rinehart and Winston, 1963), p. 278; Hans Rogger, *Russia in the Age of Modernization and Revolution 1881-1917* (New York: Longmans, 1983), pp. 125-126.

3. New York: Oxford University Press, 1947 (appeared in 1948), 223 pp. I am grateful to Carolina De Maegd-Soëp for first calling this book to my attention.

4. These and other versions of the traditional interpretation may be found in many textbook bibliographies as well as in the footnotes to the articles of Paul Gregory, James Simms, and Elvira Wilbur, cited below. There were some partially dissenting voices, based on alternative interpretations of essentially the same source material. See Petr I. Liashchenko, *Ocherki agrarnoi evoliutsii Rossii* (St. Petersburg, 1908), pp. 278-301, as cited in Paul R. Gregory, "Grain Marketings and Peasant Consumption, Russia, 1885-1913," in *Explorations in Economic History* 17 (1980): 154; also S. N. Prokopovich, *Krest'ianskoe khoziaistvo* (Berlin, 1924), as cited in Michael T. Florinsky, *Russia: A History and an Interpretation* (New York: Macmillan, 1953), II, 926. Florinsky himself did not question the general view.

5. Raymond W. Goldsmith, "The Economic Growth of Tsarist Russia,

1860-1913," *Economic Development and Cultural Change* 9 (April 1961): 441-475, especially 441-454, 474-475. Paul R. Gregory, "Grain Marketings," pp. 135-164, and *Russian National Income, 1885-1913* (Cambridge University Press, 1982), 359 pp. James Y. Simms, Jr., "The Crisis in Russian Agriculture at the End of the Nineteenth Century: A Different View," *Slavic Review* 36 (September 1977): 377-398. Elvira Wilbur, "Was Russian Peasant Agriculture Really That Impoverished? New Evidence from a Case Study from the 'Impoverished Center' at the End of the Nineteenth Century," *Journal of Economic History* 43 (March 1983): 137-144.

6. Richard G. Robbins, Jr., *Famine in Russia 1891-1892: The Imperial Government Responds to a Crisis* (New York: Columbia University Press, 1975), 262 pp., especially pp. 168-183. Robbins's estimate for 1891-1892 is between 375,000 and 400,000 deaths. For 1921-1922, he uses estimates of between 1 and 3 million, and for the Ukraine in 1932-1933, 5 million. Of course, different combinations of factors were at work in each case, including intentional deprivation in 1932-1933. See also James Y. Simms, Jr., "The Economic Impact of the Russian Famine of 1891-1892," *Slavic and East European Review* 60 (January 1982): 63-74. On the situation among the Volga Germans, see James W. Long, "Agricultural Conditions in the German Colonies of Novouzensk District, Samara Province, 1861-1914," *Slavonic and East European Review* 57 (October 1979): 531-551.

7. Esther Kingston-Mann, "Marxism and Russian Rural Development: Problems of Evidence, Experience and Culture," *American Historical Review* 86 (October 1981): 731-752. She has recently completed a book that carries this topic up into the Soviet period. For other related research on industrialization, see especially Paul R. Gregory, "Russian Industrialization and Economic Growth: Results and Perspectives of Western Research," *Jahrbuecher fuer Geschichte Osteuropas* 25 (1977): 200-218. Other items may be found in the bibliographies mentioned in note 19, for example, in the publications of Jacob Metzer on railroads, Hans Rogger on Jews and the peasantry, and George L. Yaney on governmental operations in the rural sector.

8. Robert Eugene Johnson, *Peasant and Proletarian. The Working Class of Moscow in the Late Nineteenth Century* (New Brunswick, N.J.: Rutgers University Press, 1979), 225 pp.

9. John P. McKay, *Pioneers for Profit: Foreign Entrepreneurship and Russian Industrialization, 1885-1913* (Chicago: University of Chicago Press, 1970), 442 pp. Thomas C. Owen, *Capitalism and Politics in Russia: A Social History of the Moscow Merchants, 1855-1905* (Cambridge: Cambridge University Press, 1981), 295 pp. Alfred J. Rieber, *Merchants and Entrepreneurs in Imperial Russia* (Chapel Hill: University of North Carolina Press, 1982), 464 pp. Many others are discussed in Paul Gregory's survey, cited in note 7.

10. For more on this point, see Gregory Guroff and Fred V. Carstensen, eds., *Entrepreneurship in Imperial Russia and the Soviet Union* (Princeton, N.J.: Princeton University Press, 1983), 372 pp., especially 347-360.

11. Heide Wölker Whelan, *Alexander III and the State Council: Bureaucracy and Counter-Reform in Late Imperial Russia* (New Brunswick, N.J.: Rutgers University Press, 1982), 258 pp.

12. Rogger, *Russia*, pp. 44-59, 88-95; Roberta Thompson Manning, *The Crisis of the Old Order in Russia: Gentry and Government* (Princeton, N.J.: Princeton University Press, 1982), 555 pp. Both books, as well as Whelan's, contain bibliographies, including recent works in English, on the bureaucracy and the nobility of Chekhov's time.

13. John Bushnell, "Peasants in Uniform: The Tsarist Army as a Peasant Society," *Journal of Social History* 13 (Summer 1980): 565-576; and his "The Tsarist Officer Corps, 1881-1914: Customs, Duties, Inefficiency," *American Historical Review* 86 (October 1981): 753-780. Among the many related studies Bushnell cites is Peter Kenez, "A Profile of the Prerevolutionary Officer Corps," *California Slavic Studies* 7 (1973): 121-158, which brings out the declining importance of the nobility in the army during this period.

14. Nancy Mandelker Frieden, *Russian Physicians in an Era of Reform and Revolution, 1856-1905* (Princeton, N.J.: Princeton University Press, 1981), 378 pp.

15. Richard S. Wortman, *The Development of Russian Legal Consciousness* (Chicago: University of Chicago Press, 1976), 345 pp. (dealing mostly with the period before 1870); Samuel Kucherov, *Courts, Lawyers, and Trials Under the Last Three Tsars* (New York: Praeger, 1953), 339 pp. See also Friedhelm B. Kaiser, *Die Russische Justizreform von 1864* (Leiden: E. J. Brill, 1972), 552 pp.

16. Marc Szeftel, "Personal Inviolability in the Legislation of the Russian Absolute Monarchy," *American Slavic and East European Review* 17 (February 1958): 1-24; William G. Wagner, "Tsarist Legal Policies at the End of the Nineteenth Century: A Study in Inconsistencies," *Slavonic and East European Review* 54 (July 1976): 371-394, and "The Civil Cassation Department of the Senate as an Instrument of Progressive Reform in Post-Emancipation Russia: The Case of Property and Inheritance Law," *Slavic Review* 42 (Spring 1983): 36-59.

17. Patrick L. Alston, *Education and the State in Tsarist Russia* (Stanford, Calif.: Stanford University Press, 1969), 322 pp.; Allen Sinel, *The Classroom and the Chancellery: State Educational Reform in Russia under Count Dmitry Tolstoi* (Cambridge, Mass.: Harvard University Press, 1973), 335 pp. Concerning the relative growth of primary, secondary, and higher education in Russia and other countries, see a review essay by Jeffrey Brooks in *History of Education Quarterly* 21 (Winter 1981): 509-514.

18. Arcadius Kahan, three chapters in C. Arnold Anderson and Mary Jean Bowman, eds., *Education and Economic Development* (Chicago: Aldine Publishing Co., 1965), pp. 3-10, 298-302, and 363-375; Ivan M. Bogdanov, *Gramotnost' i obrazovanie v dorevoliutsionnoi Rossii i v SSSR (istoriko-statisticheskie ocherki)* (Moscow: Statistika, 1964), 194 pp., citing pp. 55-56; Nicholas S. Timasheff, *The Great Retreat* (New York: E. P. Dutton, 1946), especially p. 35; Gregory Guroff and S. Frederick Starr, "A Note on Urban Literacy in Russia, 1890-1914," *Jahrbuecher fuer Geschichte Osteuropas*, New Series, 19 (December 1971): 520-531; Jeffrey Brooks, "Readers and Reading at the End of the Tsarist Era," in William Mills Todd, ed., *Literature and Society in Imperial Russia, 1800-1914* (Stanford, Calif.: Stanford University Press, 1978), pp. 97-150; the reference to Chekhov is on p. 142. While I was working on this chapter, Brooks completed a book manuscript that treats that and related subjects in much fuller detail.

19. Among the many broad surveys, the three that give fullest treatment to the years 1860-1904 are: Florinsky, *Russia*, 2 vols., 1511 pp.; Pushkarev's text (mentioned above), 512 pp.; and Hugh Seton-Watson, *The Russian Empire 1801-1917* (Oxford: Clarendon Press, 1967), 813 pp. More recent bibliographies, along with less complete sketches of the period, may be found in these newer or more recently revised texts, all published since 1981: W. Bruce Lincoln, *The Romanovs: Autocrats of All the Russias* (New York: Dial Press, 1981), 852 pp.; David MacKenzie and Michael W. Curran, *A History of Russia and the Soviet Union*, 2d

ed. (Homewood, Ill.: Dorsey Press, 1982), 689 pp.; Nicholas V. Riasanovsky, *A History of Russia*, 4th ed. (Oxford: Oxford University Press, 1984), 695 pp.; and Donald W. Treadgold, *Twentieth Century Russia*, 5th ed. (Boston: Houghton Mifflin Co., 1981), 555 pp. Among other fairly broad works especially useful to readers of this chapter are: Ronald Hingley, *Russian Writers and Society, 1825-1904* (New York: McGraw-Hill, 1967), 256 pp.; Richard Pipes, *Russia Under the Old Regime* (London: Weidenfeld and Nicolson, 1974), 361 pp. (up to ca. 1880); W. Bruce Lincoln, *In War's Dark Shadow: The Russians Before the Great War* (New York: Dial Press, 1983), 608 pp. (begins with 1891); and the already cited text by Hans Rogger, 323 pp.

Among the available specialized bibliographies, perhaps those three that would be most useful to readers of this chapter are David Shapiro, comp., *A Select Bibliography of Works in English on Russian History, 1801-1917* (Oxford: Basil Blackwell, 1962), 106 pp.; Paul L. Horecky, ed., *Russia and the Soviet Union: A Bibliographic Guide to Western-Language Publications* (Chicago: University of Chicago Press, 1965), 473 pp.; and Stephan M. Horak, comp., Rosemary Neiswender, ed., *Russia, the USSR, and Eastern Europe: A Bibliographic Guide to English-Language Publications, 1964-1974* (Littleton, Colo.: Libraries Unlimited, 1978), 488 pp. Beyond them is what has become an essential tool: the yearly *American Bibliography of Slavic and East European Studies*, which includes references to book reviews as well as articles in scholarly journals such as the *Russian Review* and the *Slavic Review*.

Individual articles on hundreds of topics in the Chekhov period are found in the still-in-progress *Modern Encyclopedia of Russian and Soviet History*, ed. Joseph Wieczynski, and *Modern Encyclopedia of Russian and Soviet Literature*, ed. Harry B. Weber. For explanations of many terms, see Sergei G. Pushkarev, comp., George Vernadsky and Ralph T. Fisher Jr., eds., *Dictionary of Russian Historical Terms from the Eleventh Century to 1917* (New Haven, Conn.: Yale University Press, 1970), 199 pp.

For primary sources of the period in English translation, see: Basil Dmytryshyn, ed., *Imperial Russia: A Source Book, 1700-1917*, 2d ed. (Hinsdale, Ill.: Dryden Press, 1974), pp. 270-378; George Vernadsky, Ralph T. Fisher Jr., Alan D. Ferguson, and Andrew Lossky, eds., Sergei Pushkarev, comp., *A Source Book for Russian History from Early Times to 1917*, vol. 3, *Alexander II to the February Revolution* (New Haven, Conn.: Yale University Press, 1972), pp. 587-766.

For geographical background, see W. H. Parker's *An Historical Geography of Russia* (Chicago: Aldine, 1969), 416 pp.

2

Toby W. Clyman

CHEKHOV: A BIOGRAPHY

Chekhov was a very private person. When asked to provide biographical information about himself, he was reluctant to comply. He left no memoirs. What we have are numerous valuable recollections of Chekhov by his family, friends, and acquaintances, and a voluminous Chekhov correspondence, especially fruitful to his biographers.

Anton Pavlovich Chekhov was born in 1860 in Taganrog, a port town on the sea of Azov in the Crimea, one year before the emancipation of the serfs in Russia. His grandfather was a former slave who bought his own and his family's freedom. It took Chekhov years, as he told in an often quoted letter, to overcome the slave mentality instilled by his early background.[1] Chekhov's father Pavel, a narrow-minded, recalcitrant man and a family tyrant, owned a small general merchandise store where, as children, Chekhov and his older brothers were forced to work long hours. A devout Orthodox Christian, Pavel insisted that his children attend church services and participate in the church choir. "The entire congregation envied his parents and looked on admiringly," Chekhov later recalled, "while he felt like a little convict." "For us," he said, "childhood was sheer suffering" (To Ivan Leontev, March 9, 1892).

Chekhov deeply resented how his father treated his family, a resentment that persisted through the years. "Do you remember," he wrote at age 29 to his brother Alexander, "the horror we felt each time Father made a scene at the dinner table because the soup was oversalted or called Mother a fool?" "Despotism and lies have destroyed our mother's youth. Despotism and lies mutilated our childhood." It sickened and frightened him to think about it (January 2, 1889). Echoing these memories of his early years, in his story "Difficult People" (1886), the son, provoked by his ill-tempered father's behavior, accuses him of ruining the lives of his mother and sister. Similarly, in "Three Years" (1895), Laptev blames his sanctimonious father for his children's physical and emotional ill health. Images of despotic fathers and husbands whose tyrannical behavior adversely affects the lives of their families persistently recur throughout Chekhov's works.

When Chekhov was sixteen, the family store failed. To escape creditors his father fled to Moscow where his two older sons, Alexander and Nikolai, had gone the previous year to attend the university. The mother and the two younger children, Masha and Michael, soon followed the father. Another son, Ivan, joined them shortly thereafter. Chekhov stayed behind to complete his education in Taganrog. Left to fend for himself he gave lessons to younger students, saving some money to send to his impoverished family. Already at that early age Chekhov showed the strong sense of responsibility toward his family that was never to leave him, as well as a penchant for the paternal role. The sixteen year old Chekhov wrote to his cousin in Moscow asking him to look after his mother and he sent advice to his younger brother Michael about what to read and how to behave.

When Chekhov arrived in Moscow in 1879, after his graduation from high school, he readily took over as head of the family. His father had taken a low-paying job in a warehouse outside the city and came home only on Sundays and holidays. Chekhov assumed his place. His brother Michael jestingly called him "our little father."

The same year that Chekhov joined his family, he enrolled at the medical school at Moscow University. When he had first told his mother of his plans to study medicine, she had heartily approved. "Without fail," she said, "apply to medical school . . . believe me it is the best kind of study. . . . If you work hard you will always find a way to make a living in Moscow."[2] Of course, she had no way of knowing that soon most of his income would come from his literary submissions rather than from his medical practice. Alexander, the older son who worked as a free-lance journalist in Moscow, was considered the writer in the family and, in effect, acted as Chekhov's first literary critic.

Chekhov's early literary endeavours date back to his Taganrog days. While still a student at the gymnasium, he was compiling a manuscript magazine *Zaika* (*Stammerer*) for which he wrote comic sketches about incidents from Taganrog life, and he adapted Gogol's "Taras Bulba" into a play. He also wrote his own play, *Fatherlessness*, which he subsequently destroyed, and two vaudevilles. His brother Alexander, who read his works, saw little merit in them. The anecdotes Anton had sent him were weak, he said, "except for one," and the pieces Anton had written for the *Stammerer* "lacked salt."[3] It would not be long, however, before the brothers' roles would be reversed and Anton would not only offer literary advice to his older brother Alexander but would also intercede with publishers on his brother's behalf.[4]

Chekhov began submitting pieces to a variety of low-brow publications during his first year at medical school. His intentions were not literary; he wrote to make some extra money to supplement his family's meager income. On December 24, 1879, he mailed a work titled "The Letter from the Don Landowner Stephan Vladimirovich N. to his Learned Neighbor Dr. Frederik" to the humour journal *Strekoza* (*Dragonfly*). A month later he was informed that the work was accepted for publication. Chekhov came to regard that date as the beginning of his literary career.[5]

Most of the pieces Chekhov submitted to various fly-by-night humour journals were accepted. In January 1883 Nikolai Aleksandrovich Leikin, the editor of *Oskolki* (*Fragments*), who subsequently claimed he had discovered Chekhov, invited him to be a regular contributor to his journal. Chekhov wrote fast and prodigiously, turning out large quantities of jokes, anecdotes, and potboilers under a variety of pseudonyms. His most favourite pen name was Antosha Chekhonte. In 1884 Chekhov's first collection, *Tales of Melpomene*, was issued. He included in this volume only 20 of the more than 200 pieces he had published by that time.

The same year, 1884, Chekhov also graduated from medical school and shortly thereafter hung out his doctor's shingle. His medical practice soon brought him into contact with a broad segment of different social strata and provided him with subject matter for his stories. In later years, speaking about his relationship with medicine and literature, Chekhov was fond of saying that medicine was his lawful wife and literature his mistress. When he tired of one, he told his publisher Aleksei Sergeevich Suvorin, he spent the night with the other, and each benefited from his association with the other. Commenting, in a more serious vein, about the importance of his scientific training for his literary works, Chekhov wrote: "I have no doubt that my studies in medicine have had a serious impact on my literary activities. They considerably broadened the scope of my observations and enriched me with a knowledge whose true value for me as a writer only a doctor can appreciate."[6] Chekhov continued to practice medicine for the rest of his life, but he never quite settled down to full-time practice. As time went on his interest increasingly shifted to literature.

The humour journals provided a laboratory for the nascent writer, but soon he began to complain about the strictures imposed by these fly-by-night humour magazines. By 1885 he began publishing more serious stories, such as "Grief" (1885), "The Huntsman" (1885), "Misery" (1886), and "Aniuta" (1886). These serious stories, written with the economy and precision of an accomplished artist, carry Chekhov's own inimitable signature. Themes that would persistently recur throughout his literary career, such as lack of communication, the irretrievability of time, the interrelatedness of man and nature, the conflict between the given and the desired, are already present in these early works. The rhythmic structure of "Grief," or

"Misery," foreshadows the musical construction of his later stories and plays.

Gradually, Chekhov's stories began to attract a larger reading public. On March 28, 1886, he received a letter from Dmitrii Grigorovich, an established novelist, praising his originality and talent. Grigorovich also introduced Chekhov to Suvorin, the editor of the popular and prestigious newspaper *Novoe vremia* (*New Times*), who invited Chekhov to contribute his longer pieces to his paper. Suvorin subsequently became Chekhov's trusted friend, editor, and advisor. The year 1886-1887 was Chekhov's most prolific; he published 166 titles during that year alone.[7] His name was now becoming known in literary circles. When he traveled to St. Petersburg, at the invitation of his publisher Leikin, he found he was well known in the editorial offices. Indeed, Chekhov was becoming somewhat of a celebrity.

But all this professional recognition did not afford him much satisfaction. He did not think his writings had sufficient merit; in ten years, he said, no one would read his works. While in public Chekhov was joyous and entertaining, his private letters showed a growing dissatisfaction with himself. He was irritable and complained of being overworked. "I need to change life radically," he wrote to Leikin (September 30, 1886).

Undoubtedly, Chekhov's ill health contributed to his irritability and darkening mood. When he was 24 he first began showing symptoms of tuberculosis. He had developed a chronic cough, and about twice a year he had prolonged bouts of blood spitting accompanied by severe chest pains. He was also plagued by hemorrhoids, which were a constant source of irritation. For years Chekhov the physician refused to be examined by colleagues. "I am afraid," he said, "to submit to an examination" (to Leikin, April 6, 1886). Like so many of his protagonists, Chekhov dealt with a reality he could not confront by denying it whenever possible. He was frightened and worried only when he was spitting blood, but otherwise he was not concerned that "he threatened Russian literature with a loss" (to Suvorin, October 14, 1888). At another time he would say that his blood spitting was probably just a burst blood vessel in the throat. If it were tuberculosis, he told Suvorin, he would have been dead a long time ago. Trying to keep the gravity of his illness from his conscious mind very likely exerted a considerable toll on his emotions, especially when, in 1886, his brother Nikolai, who suffered from advanced tuberculosis that mirrored Chekhov's own symptoms, moved in with him.

Evidently projecting his own feelings, Chekhov wrote about his protagonist Ivanov in the play by the same name, that he is irritable because "he has no place to get away" (*emu nekuda uekhat'*).[8] Travel, new environments always had a salutary effect on Chekhov. In April 1887 he left on an extended vacation south. He spent two weeks in his home own of Taganrog, visiting friends and relatives, and returned by way of the steppe country.

His letters from Taganrog describing the squalor, the cultural desert, the mindless vulgarity of its citizenry, found echoes in his many stories set in the provinces: "Lights" (1888), "The Teacher of Literature" (1889), "Big Volodia and Little Volodia" (1893), "My Life" (1896), "At Home"(1897), "Ionych" (1898). His journey through the steppe revived memories of his childhood visits to his grandfather, and inspired his symphonic story "The Steppe" (1888). The work was published in *Severnyi vestnik* (*The Northern Herald*), a literary monthly that printed works of established Russian writers. That same year, 1888, the Academy of Sciences awarded Chekhov the Pushkin prize for literature. Chekhov's place as a short story writer was now firmly established.

When Chekhov turned his attention to drama at this time, he was not entirely a novice in this genre. In addition to his high school attempts at playwriting, he had also written, during his first years at medical school, an overly long play, now entitled *Platonov* or *A Play Without a Title.*[9] In 1885 he had adapted the story "Autumn" (1883) into a one-act play, *On the High Road*. However, neither of these two dramatic endeavours was published or performed during his lifetime.

In September 1887 the impresario of the Kirsh Theatre invited Chekhov to write a play: two weeks later he had completed *Ivanov*. After an unsuccessful production at the Kirsh Theatre, in November 1887, Chekhov undertook to revise it and did not offer the play again for the stage until 1889. During that period Chekhov also began work on *The Wood Demon*, which he later reworked into *Uncle Vania*. He also wrote several one-act sketches, *The Swan Song* (1887), *The Bear* (1888), *The Proposal* (1888), *A Tragic Role* (1889), and *The Wedding* (1889). These one-act plays, written in the tradition of his earlier stories, were very popular with audiences. "*The Bear,*" Chekhov said jestingly, "should have been titled *A Milk Cow*, for it produced more income than any of his other stories." (To E. K. Sakharova January 13, 1889). However, his full-length play, *The Wood Demon*, staged in December 1889, was taken out of production after the first performance. Discouraged by its poor reception, Chekhov did not turn to serious drama again until 1895.[10]

During his late twenties, marriage was very much on Chekhov's mind. Many of his friends were getting married, and his mother and relatives repeatedly urged him to find a wife. He would consider it, Chekhov jestingly said, if they would find him a rich widow or a merchant's daughter. On February 1, 1886, he announced to his friend Viktor Bilibin that he had gotten engaged. His "one and only" was Jewish, but she would have to convert to Orthodoxy; otherwise nothing would come of it. A month later he wrote that he had broken the engagement for good (March 11, 1886). The woman to whom he alludes is supposedly Dunia Efros, a school friend of Chekhov's sister Masha.[11] How real was this engagement? Ronald

Hingley, in his biography, suggests that this was probably a private joke between two friends.[12] According to Simon Karlinsky, Chekhov had a "deep and meaningful involvement" with Efros.[13]

Chekhov did not share with anyone his thoughts about women with whom he had any romantic involvement. Except in the letter to Bilibin, Chekhov made no other reference to his engagement. The fact remains, however, that during 1886-1887, Efros was very much on his mind. He often mentioned her in letters to friends, and when writing to his sister he rarely failed to inquire about her or to send regards to Efros, or the "nose" as he sometimes called her. Significantly, during his acquaintance with Efros, Chekhov wrote two works in which Jewish women figured prominently: "Mire" (1886) and *Ivanov* (1887). Admittedly, his acquaintance with Efros and her milieu had provided him with material for "Mire" (to Mariia Kiseleva, December 13, 1886). If Chekhov harbored any ideas of marriage to Efros, such thoughts certainly provoked considerable anxiety and fear. Susanna, the young Jewish woman in "Mire," is one of Chekhov's most awesome, overbearing, and destructive female protagonists. Images of containment, entrapment, and death abound in "Mire," and are associated with Susanna. Moreover, Sokolski, the young man whom Susanna lures and entraps, is 26 years old, Chekhov's age when he wrote the story. In *Ivanov*, Ivanov's Jewish wife Sara had converted to Orthodoxy to marry Ivanov, who feels burdened and entrapped by this marriage. At the time Chekhov wrote *Ivanov*, he told his friend Kiseleva that he regarded the noose to be a fitting "symbol of love and marital happiness" (March 3, 1887). If Chekhov's remarks to Kiseleva are to be taken seriously, and if Chekhov's fictional characters such as Susanna, Sara, or, for that matter, the awesome Raisa ("The Witch," 1886) and the snake-like Ilovaiskaia ("On the Road," 1886) are any indication of Chekhov's perception of women and marriage, then indeed he was not ready to marry at that time.

Moreover, Chekhov had a family that was dependent on him, and he never questioned this obligation. "As long as I am alive and well my family will be taken care of" (to Grigorii Rossolimo, January 31, 1885). He did not think they could manage without him; "I have a family," he would say, "that will fall apart if I don't earn enough money" (to Ivan Leontev [Shchegelov] April 18, 1888). This strong sense of duty, however, often conflicted with Chekhov's equally strong desire to be free of all responsibility. The difficulties of being a family man "drained his energies" (to Suvorin, February 10, 1887). He would have liked to have had some solitude, but family obligations did not allow it (October 27, 1888). He would feel guilty when he did not meet his responsibilities to his family as fully as he thought he ought to. "I am conscience-stricken, deserting you again," he would say, after taking another trip soon after his return from Sakhalin (March 9, 1891). Chekhov often blamed himself for being lazy and not earning enough money. When his sick brother Nikolai moved in with him, he felt he should take Nikolai to the Crimea, but, as he told Leikin, he had "no money" (April 10, 1889). At the same time Chekhov resented being tied down in the care of his tubercular brother. He would willingly get away somewhere, he frequently remarked to friends, but he could not leave his brother. Once he wrote rather callously, "If it were not for the coughing next door, I would not be so badly off" (*zhilos' by ne skuchno*).[14]

Chekhov's feelings about his family and his sick brother are strikingly echoed in *Ivanov*. Commenting about the play, Chekhov notes: "There are certain givens in Ivanov's life (*zhiznennye uslovia*) which he cannot escape: his sick wife and his debts" (December 30, 1888). In the play Ivanov tries to escape from the oppressive atmosphere at home and from his tubercular wife, Sara; the self-righteous Dr. Lvov castigates him for leaving his sick wife alone at home and blames him for not taking Sara to the Crimea for her health. Ivanov protests that he has no money. Dr. Lvov, it would seem, is the voice of Chekhov's own internalized guilt.

Chekhov tended to his brother most of the fall of 1888 into the early spring of 1889. The atmosphere at home was oppressive, and Chekhov yearned to get away for a while. When his brother Alexander arrived, Chekhov left for what was to be a few days of rest, but the following day he received word that Nikolai had died. Several days later, in a letter, he wrote: "In punishment for having left . . . a cold wind blew . . . and the sky was completely overcast: it poured all the way" (to Aleksei Pleshcheev, July 26, 1889).[15] Chekhov was in a vile mood throughout that summer. Guilt over Nikolai's death and confrontation with his own mortality as he watched his brother succumb to an illness that mirrored his own no doubt contributed to Chekhov's depression. During that summer he completed "A Dreary Story" whose narrator, the dying professor of medicine confronting his own imminent death, bears a striking resemblance to Chekhov, as critics have convincingly shown.[16]

Chekhov's most despondent year was probably 1889. Seeing his works in print, he wrote to Suvorin, gave him "no pleasure. . . . My soul seems to be stagnating . . . everything suddenly seems so uninteresting. I must do something to rouse myself" (May 4, 1889). Characteristically, he sought to dispel his depression by travel, by getting away from familiar surroundings. This time, however, he chose a somewhat unusual destination.

On January 28 Chekhov gave his brother Michael a detailed outline of his proposed trip to the penal colony on Sakhalin Island, off the Pacific coast. For two months Chekhov totally immersed himself in detailed preparations. He studied the island's geography and the history of its inhabitants. His sister and brother Michael helped him compile a bibliography and provided him with reading material. On April 21, 1890, he embarked on the long and arduous journey that would have been difficult for a healthy person. He traveled by train, by horse-drawn carriage, and by boat, in all sorts of adverse conditions and weather. During the early part of the trip, he wrote to his family, the jolting on the train caused him to spit blood, but soon, he said, "his body got used to it" (May 16, 1890). When Chekhov reached the Amur region, his letters were ecstatic. "One longs to live there forever," he wrote home (June 27, 1890).

Critics still puzzle over Chekhov's motives for this journey. The reasons he gave were varied: humanitarian, scientific, and personal.[17] He needed to live differently for several months; he wanted to immerse himself in rigorous physical and mental work, for he had become lazy and needed to discipline himself; people should be made aware of the appalling conditions of the prisoners on the island; he wanted to write at least one or two hundred pages to pay off some of his debt to medicine. Undoubtedly, there is some validity to each of these reasons. But reading his letters one is also struck by Chekhov's many references to the possibility that he might never return from this trip. "We shall meet in December or perhaps never," he wrote to Golike (March 31, 1890). Chekhov even thought of making a will prior to his departure, "just in case" he might be "drowned or something of the sort" (to Suvorin, April 15, 1890). To his friends Natalia Lintvareva and Ivan Leontev he wrote half in jest that if some beast should dine off him or some runaway should cut his throat, they should not remember him badly (March 5, 1890/March 16, 1890). "I am leaving Russia for an extended period, perhaps never to return," he told the publisher, Vukol Lavrov (April 10, 1890).[18] Perhaps Chekhov needed to flirt with death, to rouse his "slumbering soul." Or did he have a need to be punished to assuage his guilt?

After a fatiguing 81-day trip, Chekhov finally arrived on Sakhalin on July 11. He spent three busy months traveling virtually throughout the entire island, gathering a population census and interviewing prisoners. For two months he worked strenuously, not sparing himself. By the third month, close to exhaustion and depressed by all the suffering he had seen, Chekhov was anxious to get home. He left Sakhalin in October, returning by way of Hong Kong, Singapore, Colombo, and Ceylon, arriving in Moscow in December. En route to Singapore Chekhov had witnessed a burial at sea, an experience he recaptured in the final passages in "Gusev" (1891). Memories from his Sakhalin trip are also evoked in "Murder" (1895), "Peasant Women" (1891), "In Exile" (1892), and "In the Ravine" (1900). He took three years to finish organizing and writing the material he had gathered. The resultant work, *The Island of Sakhalin*, was first serialized in *Russkaia mysl'* (*Russian Thought*) in 1893.[19]

Back in Moscow Chekhov's wanderlust soon returned. After Sakhalin, Chekhov complained, Moscow seemed deadly boring. Suvorin proposed they go to Europe. At first Chekhov refused: he did not think he could leave his family again. But on March 5 he wrote to Suvorin, "I agree to go wherever you like, wherever you want." On March 17, Chekhov set out on his first trip to Western Europe in the company of Suvorin and his son. He was enraptured by Vienna, by its cleanliness and apparent freedom. From Venice, he wrote home, "one longs to be there forever" (March 24, 1891). As for the landscape in Naples, "he had never seen anything like it before" (May 13, 1891). By the end of April, however, his enthusiasm had begun to diminish. Still, he continued on to Nice, Monte Carlo, and Paris. "So much time," he wrote from Nice, "is wasted abroad breakfasting, dining and sleeping" (April 29, 1891). Gone from home for almost a year, Chekhov was anxious to get back and settle down to work, though before long he would complain "he feels like being put in a fortress" (May 7, 1892).

He returned to Russia on May 2, 1891, and the following day joined his family at their rented summer dacha. On Mondays, Tuesdays, and Wednesdays he would work on *The Island of Sakhalin*, and the rest of the week, except for Sundays, he would work on "The Duel" (1891). Sundays, he devoted to several shorter pieces.

Chekhov also found time to spend with friends and relatives who came to visit. One guest that summer was Lika Mizinova, a colleague of his sister Masha and a friend of the family. Chekhov was very fond of Lika and enjoyed her company. However, she was far more involved emotionally with Chekhov than he was with her.[20] Mizinova subsequently began seeing the writer Ignatii Potapenko, a married man, whom she had met at the Chekhov's. In 1894, Lika and Potapenko went to Europe together; she had a child by him, but the baby died after she returned to Russia. In *The Seagull* Chekhov would fictionalize the Lika-Potapenko romance.

No sooner did Chekhov return to Moscow in September than he began feeling restless and felt a need for a change. Life in the city seemed confining. "If I am a doctor I ought to have patients and a hospital," he wrote to Suvorin. "If I am a literary man, then I ought to live among people instead of on Malaia Dmitrevka . . . this life within the four walls, without nature . . . without health and appetite; this is not life" (October 18, 1891). What he needed was a place of his own in the country. Besides, he thought, in the country his family could live more cheaply. He became so anxious to find a place that when he heard of an estate for sale in Melikhovo, about 50 miles south of Moscow, he sent his sister and brother to inspect it, and upon their recommendation, Chekhov bought it sight unseen. In March 1892, Chekhov and his family (his father was now retired) moved into their new home. It was to be his permanent residence until 1898.

A disastrous harvest in 1891 had spread famine to a large part of Russia that winter, bringing with it a cholera epidemic. Prior to his move, Chekhov spent considerable time organizing various private famine relief schemes, and then part of the summer and fall of 1892 he worked as the local medical inspector in charge of containing the cholera epidemic. He returned to his writing only after the epidemic subsided.

The years in Melikhovo were busy ones. Chekhov the landowner actively participated in local affairs: he served on jury duty and took part in planning and supervising the building of local schools. He also opened a clinic at his home where he gave free medical treatment to peasants from the outlying district and frequently traveled long distances to visit sick villagers.

In Melikhovo Chekhov wrote such memorable stories as "The Black Monk" (1892), "Ward No. 6" (1892), "A Woman's Kingdom" (1894), "The Student" (1894), "Three Years" (1895), "The House with an Attic" (1896) and "Peasants" (1897). The publication of "Peasants" was somewhat of a literary event because of its frank depiction of peasant life.

Chekhov was not one to stay put. From Melikhovo he took frequent trips to St. Petersburg and Moscow where he met with friends and publishers; he also traveled to Yalta and revisited parts of Italy. There was even some restless talk about more exotic voyages. In 1895 Chekhov had a chance to visit Iasnaia Poliana where he spent a day and a half with Tolstoi, whom he greatly admired. It was their first meeting. Although by the time of this visit the spell the older writer had held over Chekhov for some time had worn off and Chekhov had become openly critical of Tolstoi's doctrines, still their philosophic differences did not prevent them from forming a strong and continuing friendship.[21] Chekhov left exceedingly gratified by this visit.

In the fall of 1895 Chekhov began work on *The Seagull*. "Imagine, I am actually writing a play," he told Suvorin. "I am writing it with pleasure, though I sin much against the conventions of the stage . . . there is much talk about literature, little action and tons of love" (October 21, 1895). He finished the play a month later, and in December *The Seagull* was read in Moscow at the apartment of the actress Lidiia Iavorskaia.[22] Those present noted resemblances between the Lika-Potapenko affair and the Nina-Trigorin relationship; Kirsh, the impresario of the Kirsh Theatre, did not think the play was sufficiently dramatic. His *Seagull*, Chekhov later wrote to Suvorin, "has failed before it was even staged" (December 13). He shelved the play for a time, then began revising it. In October 1896 it opened at the Alexandra Theatre. The performance was a disaster.[23] Dejected, Chekhov left after the second act and walked the streets of St. Petersburg for hours. The following day he left for Melikhovo, vowing never to write plays again.

His health continued to be precarious. In March 1897 an incident occurred which no longer made it possible for him to ignore the seriousness of his symptoms. While dining with Suvorin at a restaurant in Moscow, Chekhov began hemorrhaging from the lungs. Three days later, after another severe hemorrhage, he was rushed to the clinic and diagnosed as having tuberculosis; by then both his lungs were irreversibly damaged. Among his many visitors during his two-and-a-half week stay at the clinic was Tolstoi who, Chekhov later recorded in his diary, "came and talked about the immortality of the soul" (Nina Gitovich II, 461).

The doctors advised Chekhov to spend the winter months in a warm climate. On September 1, he left for southern France where he stayed the greater part of eight months in Nice. There he wrote "In the Cart," "Visiting Friends," "At Home," and "Pecheneg," the last two works evoking memories of his journey through the Ukrainian steppes ten years earlier. While he was in Nice the Dreyfus case reopened, producing bitter controversy throughout Europe. Alfred Dreyfus, a French-Jewish army officer, had been accused of treason in 1894 and condemned to life imprisonment in a penal colony. Chekhov, who followed the case closely, became convinced that Dreyfus had been falsely accused and convicted. In Russia, Suvorin's paper, *New Times*, was waging an anti-Dreyfus campaign with clearly anti-Semitic overtones. Chekhov was incensed and tried to convince Suvorin of Dreyfus's innocence. Their disagreement over the Dreyfus affair caused a rift in their relationship, and for a time Chekhov stopped corresponding with Suvorin.

When Chekhov was still in France, Vladimir Nemirovich-Danchenko wrote to him asking his permission to stage *The Seagull* at the newly formed Moscow Art Theatre. Chekhov refused; he still remembered the fiasco of the play's first performance and wanted to spare himself another harrowing experience. But Nemirovich-Danchenko persisted. When Chekhov returned from Europe in May, he approached the playwright again. *The Seagull*, Nemirovich-Danchenko told Chekhov, was the only contemporary play that intrigued him as a director (Gitovich II, 506). This time Chekhov gave in. On September 9 he attended the first rehearsal of *The Seagull* at the Moscow Art Theatre where he met the entire cast; among them was Olga Knipper, whom Chekhov would marry in 1901. For Chekhov this was the beginning of a fruitful and lasting association with the Art Theatre. Not only his professional but also his personal fortunes were now to be linked with the Moscow Art Theatre.

Chekhov would have liked to stay in Moscow, but with the cold weather coming, he was again forced to seek refuge in a warmer climate. He left for Yalta reluctantly, expecting to be there only temporarily. In October his father died, and he began making plans to bring his sister and mother to Yalta where he would make his permanent home. It had become increasingly clear that he would have to spend the falls and winters in the south because of his "bacillus," as he referred to his illness. He bought a plot of land in Autka, a Tatar village within walking distance of Yalta, and proceeded with the construction of a house. He was able to finish payment on the construction of the dwelling from the sale of his works (past and future) to Adolf Marks.[24] Soon he began taking part in the town council, and he actively campaigned in the press for the famine victims in the province of Samara. He also gave much of his time helping destitute tubercular patients who had been sent to the Crimea. During his first years in Yalta he even kept up a practice of sorts.[25] But in time he came to detest his confinement in the Crimea. In Yalta he was "not living life," but "just waiting to get well," and that, he said, was indeed boring (to Suvorin, April 2, 1899).

Moscow now seemed so much more desirable. "It seems to me if I had stayed in Moscow or Petersburg this winter," he wrote wistfully, "I would have had a warm, comfortable apartment and I would have completely recovered" (to Lidiia Avilova, August 30, 1898). Even the landscape in Moscow now seemed more attractive. "In Moscow," he wrote, "the surrounding countryside is interesting and there are so many places to see" (to Mme. Suvorin, March 29, 1899). In the *Three Sisters*, which Chekhov began writing in February 1899, he parodies his own dreams of Moscow. Undoubtedly, he was as aware of the illusory nature of his dreams as were the audiences listening to the three sisters' persistent longings for Moscow. In October 1899, the Art Theatre staged *Uncle Vania*. Confined to Yalta, Chekhov could attend neither the rehearsals nor the opening night performance. For the dramatist this must have been indeed very frustrating. But in April of the following year, the Theatre, with its entire entourage, arrived for a month's tour of the Crimea, and Chekhov had a chance to spend time with the members of the Theatre and to see them perform his plays. It was a triumphant tour for the Art Theatre and a very gratifying, if exhausting, time for Chekhov.

Olga Knipper had come to Yalta a week earlier and traveled with Chekhov to Sevastopol, where the Theatre began its tour. Since Chekhov had first met Olga in September of 1898 at the rehearsal of *The Seagull* she had made friends with his sister Masha, and during Easter week of the following year he had visited her at her home in Moscow. In May she had been a guest of the Chekhov family in Melikhovo. Olga spent two weeks with Chekhov in Yalta, and when the Art Theatre completed its Crimean tour and returned to Moscow, Olga rejoined Chekhov several weeks later to take her vacation with him. Judging from the changed tone of their letters, Olga and Chekhov had become intimate during that visit. They married in a quiet ceremony in Moscow on May 25, 1901.

Theirs was not a traditional marriage. Olga and Chekhov lived apart most of the year; she had her career with the Moscow Art Theatre, while he continued to live in the south because of his health. They were together infrequently, which was what Chekhov wanted, "a wife that would not appear on his horizon every day." Several years before Chekhov had met Olga, he had told Suvorin, somewhat prophetically, that if he were to marry, his wife would have to live in Moscow and he in the country. "I will go visit her" he wrote. "I can not endure the kind of happiness that lasts from day to day. Give me a wife who, like the moon, does not appear daily on my horizon and I will marry" (March 23, 1895).

Perhaps Olga sensed what Chekhov feared in a marriage when she told him that if they lived together, without parting, he would grow as used to her "as to a table or chair."[26] After all, as Chekhov so often shows in his writings, habit and repetition numb feelings and desensitize people to each other and their surroundings. Evidently, Chekhov could not conceive of a love that could endure the familiarity that comes from sharing day-to-day life (*byt*). In "The Lady with the Lapdog" (1899), written during his courtship with Olga, Chekhov, for the first time, depicts romantic love that is not destroyed by time. But the two lovers, Gurov and Anna, do not share their daily life; they live separately and see each other only on occasion.

The fact that Olga Knipper was self-sufficient also suited Chekhov. For someone who saw matrimony "as a noose," marriage to an independent woman like Olga seemed less of an entrapment. "If Olga and I had to separate," Chekhov told his sister (who was jealous of Olga and threatened by his marriage), "I could do so without any hesitation, as if I had never married. After all, Olga is an independent woman and self-supporting" (June 4, 1901). Marrying someone like Olga also meant he could assure his mother that "everything will remain as before"; he could continue his commitment to his family, just as he had always done. As counterpoint one can recall the Olga of Chekhov's "The Darling" (1898) who had no life separate from the men she married. His fictional Olga drew her identity from her husbands, and while she became plumper and rosier, her husbands got thinner and eventually died.

What was Chekhov's attitude toward Olga? Was their marriage one of equals? Not entirely. Chekhov treated Olga with the same affectionate condescension he generally accorded to all women.[27] He was often patronizing toward Olga and frequently dismissed her emotional responses as the inconsequential fancies of an immature adolescent. Instructing Olga how to play the part of Masha in *Three Sisters*, he adds, "Do you understand? Of course you do, because you are a clever girl" (January 2, 1901). In the same letter he writes: "You describe how you cried when I went away. What an exquisite letter it is, by the way. You couldn't have written it, you must have asked some one else to write it for you. A wonderful letter." Another example: "You write," Chekhov tells Olga, "that everything seems so bewildering (*tak smutno*); it is a good thing it does, my dear actress, it is very good. It shows that you are a philosopher and a clever woman" (September 8, 1900). When Olga complained that she was feeling sad, he would generally tell her she would soon get over it. "It does not become you, be joyous" (December 18, 1901). In an earlier letter he wrote: "You will not be feeling sad for long, soon you will be sitting in the train eating lunch with a very good appetite" (March 26, 1900). If Chekhov's "own suffering increased his sensitivity to other people's pain, and . . . sorrows," as the writer Evgenii Zamiatin remarked,[28] then his sensitivity certainly does not show in Chekhov's attitude toward his wife. "I may be permitted to mope, since I live in the wilderness, since I have nothing to do, see no one, and am ill almost every week," he told her, "but you? Your life is full, anyway" (January 20, 1902).

Olga complained that Chekhov did not share his feelings and thoughts with her, but she was only partly right. In his letters to Olga, Chekhov, who was exceedingly sensitive to changes in weather, rarely failed to report the Yalta weather or to make some observation about it. Often, in these remarks he told her much about himself, his feelings, his moods, his inclinations. In a tone reminiscent of the poetic language of his stories, he wrote: "Today I feel much better but there is no rain, and it does not seem there ever will be" (September 6, 1902). Or, "It is cold in my rooms . . . it was ever so much warmer in Moscow" (December 12, 1900). Olga, however, took such "weather reports" literally and complained he was the only one who always abused the weather. Besides, she told him, she could read about it in the paper.[29] "What a pity," Chekhov once responded, "there is so much interesting in that department" (January 21, 1902).

Olga may not have been attuned to the poetic subtleties in Chekhov's letters, but she was responsive to his needs. She was a warm and caring person, and Chekhov looked to her for solace and comfort. It was to her that he showed the face that was hidden from the public; to her that he complained about his loneliness, his frustrations, and his ill health.

Chekhov's strength declined noticeably in the winter of 1902. "Today and yesterday," he wrote, "I was pruning bushes, and after every bush I had to sit down to rest" (to Olga, February 6, 1902). That winter and early spring Chekhov was completing his masterpiece "The Bishop" and had yet to write "The Bride" and his last major play, The Cherry Orchard. The very act of writing had now become an effort; after every few lines he had to lie down to rest.

Chekhov first referred to The Cherry Orchard in a letter to Olga in January 1902. The directors of the Moscow Art Theatre were impatiently awaiting the play, but he did not complete it until October of 1903. In December Chekhov arrived in Moscow (the doctors had told him he could spend the winter in Moscow) and soon began taking an active part in the production of the play. The first performance of The Cherry Orchard was scheduled for January 17, 1904, on Chekhov's forty-fourth birthday, and to honour the twenty-fifth anniversary of his literary activities. Chekhov, who singularly disliked public jubilees, showed up during the third act of the performance and was showered with applause, speeches, and flowers. He remained in Moscow another month and then left for Yalta, intending to return in the spring. His health steadily deteriorated; he was now in constant pain and was taking opium. Nevertheless, he returned to Moscow in May but immediately took to bed. On June 4, Chekhov, accompanied by his wife, left for Berlin to consult a specialist. From there they went to Badenweiler, a spa in the Black Forest area of Germany, where he and Olga settled. For a while his health seemed to improve, and Chekhov even talked about traveling to Italy from where he would return to Russia. In his last letter to his sister (June 28, 1904), he wrote inquiring about sea transportation from Trieste to Odessa, for he did not want to travel back home by train in the heat of the summer. He died four days later on July 2. In an ironic twist of fate that Chekhov would have appreciated, his body was shipped to Russia by train in a refrigerated car. He was buried at the Novodevichi Cemetery in Moscow, next to his father's grave.

NOTES

1. See letter to Suvorin, January 7, 1899, in A. P. Chekhov, *Polnoe sobranie sochinenii i pisem v 30-ti tomakh. Pisma* (Moscow, 1974), III, 133. All further citations from Chekhov's works and letters are from this edition. The letters (*pis'ma*) are identified by addressee and date only, and the works (*sochinenia*) by volume and page number in parenthesis in the text.

2. N. I. Gitovich, *Letopis' zhizni i tvorchestva A.P. Chekhova* (Ann Arbor, Mich.: University Microfilms International, 1977), I, 36. This two-volume edition contains a day-to-day account of Chekhov's activities.

3. Gitovich, pp. 25, 32.

4. Thomas Eekman, in "Chekhov as Correspondent," in this volume, examines Chekhov's relationship with his brother.

5. Many facts about Chekhov's early creative writings are still unknown. Evidently, this piece was not Chekhov's first published work. See Vladimir Kataev, "Understanding Chekhov's World," *Soviet Literature* 1 (1980): 172.

6. See Chekhov, *Polnoe sobranie sochinenii i pisem. Sochinenia*, XVI, 271. The citation is from a biographical entry Chekhov had written for an album which his fellow medical school classmates, class of 1884, were compiling. For the English translation of the entire text, see *Anton Chekhov's Life and Thought: Letters and Commentary*, ed. Simon Karlinsky (Berkeley: University of California Press, 1975), pp. 366-367.

7. After 1887 Chekhov's productivity had diminished considerably. From 1888 until his death in 1904 he published only 61 stories.

8. In a letter to Suvorin, December 30, 1888.

9. The Polish producer, Adam Hanushkievicz, claims that *Platonov* is the work of a more mature writer and that Chekhov had probably written the play the same year as *The Seagull. Soviet Literature* 1 (1890): 172-173.

10. Concerning the performances of these plays, see Laurence Senelick's, "Chekhov on Stage," in this volume.

11. The letter to Bilibin in which Chekhov writes of his engagement was first published in 1960 in I. Ansimov, et al., eds., *Literaturnoe nasledstvo* (Moscow, 1960), LXVIII, 163. The editors of this volume suggest that the "intended" was Dunia Efros, who subsequently married Chekhov's friend and publisher Efim Konovitser.

12. Ronald Hingley, *A New Life of Anton Chekhov* (New York: Alfred A. Knopf, 1976), p. 76.

13. *Anton Chekhov's Life and Thought*, p. 189.

14. Letter to N. N. Obolenskii, June 4, 1889.

15. "A Russian," Chekhov wrote to Suvorin on December 30, 1889, "whether someone in his family dies, or he becomes ill, or he owes money, or he lends it to another, invariably feels guilty" (December 30, 1889). Chekhov evidently projects his guilt not only onto his protagonist Ivanov, but also to the Russian people at large.

16. See especially Donald Rayfield's analysis of "A Dreary Story" in *Chekhov: The Evolution of His Art* (London: Paul Elek, 1975), pp. 87-92; see also Hingley, *A New Life of Anton Chekhov*, pp. 118-119.

17. For an interesting interpretation of the motive for Chekhov's Sakhalin journey, see Joanne Trautmann, "Doctor Chekhov's Prison," in *Healing Arts in Dialogue: Medicine and Literature*, ed. Joanne Trautmann (Carbondale: Southern Illinois University Press, 1981), pp. 125-137.

18. It is not likely that Chekhov was telling "an outright lie" when he told Vukol Lavrov "he may never return" (as Karlinsky claims in *Chekhov's Life and Thought*, p. 167), given the many instances in which Chekhov writes of the probability that he will never return from his trip.

19. For a study of and further references to works on *The Island of Sakhalin*, see Joseph L. Conrad's "Chekhov as Social Observer: *The Island of Sakhalin*" in this volume.

20. For an analysis of Chekhov's relationship with Lidiia (Lika) Mizinova, see Thomas Eekman, "Chekhov as Correspondent" in this volume. In 1889, the year Chekhov met Mizinova, he had also become acquainted with Lidiia Avilova, an aspiring writer. Avilova, in her memoirs *Chekhov in My Life: A Love Story*, trans. David Magarshack (Westport, Conn.: Greenwood Press, 1971), claims Chekhov was in love with her. However, his letters to her give no such indication. Ernest J. Simmons in *Chekhov: A Biography* (Boston: Little, Brown and Co., 1962) convincingly disclaims Avilova's assertions.

21. Tolstoi's influence on Chekhov is evident in a number of didactic stories written during 1886-1887: "Excellent People," "The Beggar," "The Meeting," "The Bet," and "The Shoemaker and the Devil."

22. Chekhov apparently was having an affair with Iavorskaia at the time he was writing *The Seagull* (1885-1886). See *Chekhov's Life and Thought*, p. 267. According to Avilova's memoirs, *Chekhov in My Life*, it was during this time that Chekhov was in love with her.

23. Concerning the staging of *The Seagull* at the Alexandra Theatre, see Senelick's "Chekhov on Stage" in this volume.

24. When Marks signed the contract with Chekhov, he did not realize how large a quantity of work he had purchased. Marks had originally planned to issue a three-volume edition, but between 1899 and 1901 published ten volumes, excluding the plays, which were not part of the sale. Chekhov carefully revised every story included in this edition.

25. For a study of Chekhov's activities as a doctor, see B. Khizhnikov, *Anton Pavlovich kak vrach* (Moscow, 1947).

26. See Chekhov's letter to Olga Knipper, September 20, 1902.

27. For a study of Chekhov's relationship with women, see Virginia Llewellyn Smith, *Anton Chekhov and the Lady with the Dog* (London: Oxford University Press, 1973). See also Hingley, *A New Life of Anton Chekhov*, pp. 184-201.

28. "A Biographical Note on Anton Tchekov" in *The Life and Letters of Anton Chekhov*, trans. and ed. S. S. Koteliansky and Philip Tomlinson (London: Benjamin Blom, 1925), p. 12.

29. See Chekhov's letter to Knipper, January 14, 1903, and *The Letters of Anton Pavlovich Chekhov to Olga Leonardovna Knipper*, trans. and ed. Constance Garnett (New York: Benjamin Blom, 1966), p. 161n.

3

Donald Rayfield

CHEKHOV AND THE LITERARY TRADITION

Literary tradition alone, whether Russian or European, does not account for Chekhov's originality and richness. A sub-literary tradition, in which the detritus of earlier modes—eighteenth-century informative literature, vaudeville farce, Romantic melodrama—coalesced into something of a folk culture for the urban masses of London, Paris, and Moscow, left a permanent impact on Chekhov's work. Writing for popular journals like *Budilnik* (*Alarm Clock*) and *Oskolki* (*Fragments*) gave Chekhov concision and nurtured his acute sense of time and place. It encouraged self-effacement and endowed his work with clarity and intelligibility, both born out of respect for the limitations of readers and censors. Chekhov's subject matter, as well as his technique and view of art, also owes much to this formative influence. A late work such as "Ionych" (1898), in which a girl gives her admirer an assignation in a deserted cemetery, is plotted around the same sort of farcical joke that served as the staple material for the early work. Chekhov's almost satirical treatment of schoolteachers and doctors in his mature plays recalls the mockery of pedants and quacks so typical of farce.

Most important, however, Chekhov's beginnings apparently inoculated him against any overwhelmingly infectious literary influence. Unlike Dostoevskii or Maupassant, Chekhov did not have to spend years working Gogol or Flaubert out of his system. While literary tradition played a very important part in shaping Chekhov's work, its impact was delayed until he was of an age to resist.

Chekhov's contemporaries did not regard his literary development as altogether wholesome. Readers and critics complained that he lacked self-assurance, that he refused to "lord it about" in other people's households.[1]

Chekhov, unlike his great predecessors, was reluctant to make moral judgments, to infringe on the philosopher's role, or to write confessions.

Although Chekhov as a writer entered the literary tradition late, he was not unlettered. While his reading was not as encyclopedic as Tolstoi's, or as intense as Dostoevskii's, it was both wide and continuous. His provincial education in Taganrog did not shut him off from literature. The theatres and opera houses of Taganrog, a half-colonial, half-Mediterranean town, exposed Chekhov to the world's dramatic repertoire. The curriculum of its *gimnazia*, severely classical though it was, gave Chekhov a viable grounding in European literature.

From what we know of Chekhov's library and education, from his letters, and from references in his stories and plays, we must first of all establish what Chekhov read. Although he had a working knowledge of Latin, French, and German, Chekhov clearly preferred to read in Russian translation. This, however, restricted his access only slightly, for few countries translated foreign literature as avidly and quickly as did Russia in the nineteenth century. Zola's novels sometimes appeared in Russian before the French edition was published.

Chekhov apparently missed nothing of his native literature; the references to the decadents in *The Seagull* suggest he knew the fringes of contemporary writing as well as the works of established writers. His reading of the French nineteenth-century novel was fairly comprehensive, but he covered little beyond the landmarks in other literatures. He knew the work of many contemporary dramatists, from Gerhart Hauptmann to August Strindberg, but he appears to have had little knowledge of German *naturalismus*, the English novel after Dickens, or European poetry of any description.

Yet more striking, while Chekhov readily accepted that Zola, Maeterlinck, and Maupassant had a great deal to offer Russia and Russian literature, he could not conceive that his own work might have relevance for Eastern Europe or America. While Turgenev's involvement with French literature was a two-way process, Chekhov's was most definitely not, a difference due partly to his self-deprecation and partly to his view that Russian culture had little that was analogous or important to other cultures. Conversely, even foreign contemporaries whom he admired extravagantly, Maupassant for instance, he admired more for their artistry and the *modus vivendi* they had struck between their art and their public than for any way they might speak to the needs and problems of a Russian reader.

The same reserve characterized Chekhov's attitude toward his Russian contemporaries: he admired them insofar as they solved the same predicaments he faced—compromising between artistry and philistinism. Only the Russian giants of the past, Tolstoi and Turgenev, inspired Chekhov with anything like reverence, precisely because Chekhov saw a fundamental difference between them and himself as great as between "alcohol" and "lemonade." "They," he wrote to Aleksei Suvorin, "have some goal like the ghost of Hamlet's father" (November 25, 1892).

Frequently, the writer as a person, rather than his books, affected Chekhov most deeply. He did not appear to compete with his contemporaries or feel the urge to rebel against his predecessors. Flaubert wrote out of impatience with Balzac; Dostoevskii emerged from disgust with Gogol. But not only was Chekhov at ease with his father-figures, he even sought them out. He deferred to Nikolai Leskov and Tolstoi and took a similarly respectful attitude toward Zola and Maupassant, whom he had never met. Although it was Leskov who approached Chekhov, Chekhov accepted his recognition rather than demanded it.

In the Russian literary tradition, great writers evolve by parricidal resistance: Pushkin, Lermontov, Turgenev, Dostoevskii, and Tolstoi, whose fathers were alienated, driven out, or murdered, all too naturally take up a parricidal stance in literature and are most indebted when they are most in revolt. Although Chekhov's life suggests parallels, for he supplanted his ineffectually tyrannical father, he treated his father-figures quite differently. His relationships with Nikolai Leikin, the editor of *Fragments*, and Suvorin, the owner of *Novoe vremia* (*New Times*), or with Dmitrii Grigorovich and Aleksei Pleshcheev, survivors from Russian prose of the 1840s, suggest that Chekhov needed a benign, paternal literary and personal influence.

Chekhov's attitude toward Nikolai Przhevalskii, the explorer of central Asia, fell little short of deification,[2] and Przhevalskii's writings, as well as his personality, left their mark on Chekhov's fiction. Przhevalskii's landscape portrayal in his *Journey in the Ussuri District* and his forthright arrogance of narrative in *From Kiakhta to the Sources of the Yellow River* set the tone for much of the description and characterization in Chekhov's "The Duel" (1891). More muted was Chekhov's admiration for Zola's intervention in the Dreyfus affair, an example which Chekhov, the most unpolitical of Russian writers, was to follow when he protested Gorkii's expulsion from the Russian Academy. But however extravagant Chekhov's admiration for the man's heroic example, his artistic reserve overcame it. He expunged Przhevalskii after "The Duel," and Zola's direct influence is largely confined to experiments with such new settings as the steel foundry in "A Woman's Kingdom" (1894), or the haberdasher's business in "Three Years" (1895).

Of all the Russian writers who influenced Chekhov, Tolstoi and Leskov stand out; much has been written about the relationship between Tolstoi and Chekhov,[3] but equally interesting for comparative criticism is Chekhov's interaction with Leskov. From 1886 on, Leskov influenced Chekhov's work. Like Leskov, Chekhov used characters, the clergy in particular, as models for the artist. Like Leskov, Chekhov endowed his ordinary priests with gifts beyond their understanding which unaccountably affect their listeners. Just as Leskov linked art and religious dedication inextricably in "The Sealed Angel," so Chekhov portrayed the drunken carver in "Art" (1886), the impoverished student priest in "The Student" (1894), and the bewildered dying bishop in "The Bishop" (1902), as men who are repositories of frightening powers to which their humanity is not quite adequate.

Leskov's extraordinary scope also appealed to Chekhov. His settings range from the monasteries of the Arctic to the Kalmyk steppes, and his experience of life came from the bewildering variety of jobs he held during his itinerant life. Likewise, Chekhov's medical and social work took him far outside literature and led him to explore Russia from the western marshes to Sakhalin, from Perm in the north to the colonial outposts of the Black Sea. Both Chekhov and Leskov use exotic settings to suggest the rich, semi-Asiatic nature of Russia and to emphasize the smallness of the individual: Leskov's "Enchanted Wanderer" and the Russian characters in Chekhov's "The Duel" are all pilgrims in uncharted landscapes.

Leskov and Chekhov developed in a parallel fashion. Both came under the influence of Tolstoi. Leskov moved from a conservative point of view; Chekhov from indifference to condemnation of Russia as a madhouse. When Leskov exclaimed in 1892 that Chekhov's " 'Ward No. 6' is Russia," he had found an echo of his equally horrifying vision in "Hare Park."[4]

Critics lay such stress on Chekhov as an ironic, detached observer that they fail to see the mystic, apocalyptic vision one can find in scenes such as the storm in "The Steppe" (1888), or in Iartsev's dream in "Three Years": "A terrible roar, clanging, shouts in an incomprehensible language, quite possibly Kalmyk; and some village, all engulfed in flames, and the nearby forests, covered in frost and soft-pink with the fire, can be seen all around" (IX, 71).

These moments recall the storm in Leskov's *Cathedral Folk* or the prophetic dreams of his "Enchanted Wanderer," and enable us to understand the fire in *Three Sisters*, or the cherry orchard in blossom or under the axe, as the irruption of irrational, un-European forces.

Even though Chekhov had no sympathy with Christian doctrines and no religious faith, he shared Leskov's love of church ritual and was equally fascinated by folk Christianity. The brooding religious feeling of "The Murder" (1895) and the peasants' evangelical identification with the meek and the oppressed in "Peasants" (1897) and "In the Ravine" (1900) stem from the same Old Believer faith Leskov incorporated into his work.

Although Turgenev died before Chekhov became famous, his influence on Chekhov was nearly as great as Leskov's. Clearly, the format of Chekhov's plays, from the juvenile *Platonov* to *The Cherry Orchard*, derives from Turgenev's *A Month in the Country*, written, and largely unnoticed, 40 years before Chekhov came to the theatre. True, Turgenev borrowed heavily from Balzac's *The Stepmother*, a play remarkable for bridging comedy and tragedy, for confining the characters to an explosive household, and for leaving absolutely no trace in European drama. The whole concept of the month in the country, during which the intruders irrevocably disturb the peace of the residents, is transmitted from Turgenev to Chekhov, as are the detached, almost comic impotence of the doctor and the tangles of unrequited love.

In the 1890s Chekhov became more skeptical about Turgenev's achievements. He compared the somewhat stylized and Delphic Turgenev heroines with the full-blooded and complex characterization of *Anna Karenina*.[5] In *The Seagull*, not just the consonants of Trigorin's name, but his lazy dependence on his mistress, his conservative artistic values, and his sense of style seem to parody Turgenev. But nonetheless Turgenev's influence remained constant. Turgenev showed Chekhov how to sketch, with maximum economy, landscapes that reflect the mood of the story. Very often Chekhov used an identical device, such as the reflection of a setting sun on a church spire.[6] Turgenev's miniaturization and dislike of prolixity were even stronger in Chekhov, who (with one early exception) refused even to use the sub-title "novel" for his fiction.

Turgenev, the most European of Russian writers in his technique, if the most Russian in his raw material, was a vehicle for a number of European influences. In his vacillating heroes, from Platonov to Treplev, Chekhov carried still further Turgenev's conviction that Hamlet was quintessentially Russian in his inertia and in his political and sexual predicaments, a conviction stated as a thesis in Turgenev's essay "Hamlet and Don Quixote" (1858). Turgenev's use of the classical tragic form to deal nemesis to the overweening hero (as in *Fathers and Sons*) taught Chekhov how to handle death; the influence is obvious even in a very late work such as "The Bishop." When Chekhov employs a European setting, Turgenev, rather than the locality, is the chief inspiration. In "An Anonymous Story" (1893), a revolutionary hero with tuberculosis (shades of Turgenev's Bulgarian in *On the Eve*) elopes with the heroine to Italy, a land whose clarity and vivacity mask disillusion and death, just as it does in Turgenev's work. "Ariadna" (1895) likewise takes hero and heroine to Italy, where, as in Turgenev's *Smoke* or *Torrents of Spring*, the positively arachnid heroine exsanguinates the Russian hero in alien surroundings.

Chekhov's heroines are psychologically more complex and convincing than Turgenev's; their inner monologues and reactions relate them closely to Tolstoi's. But Chekhov makes just as sharp a division between the predatory female and the victimized female as Turgenev does. Turgenev's "gynocratic" view of the world, which stems from Tatiana in Pushkin's *Eugene Onegin*, shows a heroine who graduates from being the plaything of the hero to becoming a more profound and moral creature than he. Turgenev and Chekhov continued, under the thinnest of fictional veils, what Schopenhauer and Leopold Sacher-Masoch had to say about women.

Chekhov also inherited the "superfluous man," the hero of Turgenev's *Rudin*. Likharev in "On the Road" (1886), very loquacious but about to end his career in the most inappropriate of jobs, as a mine manager, is reminiscent of Rudin, who moves from canal-digging to schoolmastering as middle age undermines him. But Turgenev's heroes were too classical and literary to satisfy Chekhov, in whose mature works the boundary between hero and environment is much more fluid. Turgenev, unlike Leskov, gave Chekhov an apprenticeship which once served could be left behind.

Every Russian writer is put to the ultimate test of "Pushkin or Gogol." Is the author an affirmer, a clarifier, Apollonic, like Pushkin? Or a negator, an obfuscator, Dionysian, like Gogol? Does Pushkinian acceptance or Gogolian indignation motivate Chekhov's work? No Russian writer escapes this classification. For his reticence and respect for craft Chekhov deserves the label Pushkinian, but he takes up few of Pushkin's themes. The transcendence of the male by the female in *Eugene Onegin* and in Chekhov's work (whether "Verochka," 1886, or "The Bride," 1903), the murderous resentment of a stranger who cannot find acceptance in his chosen world, in Pushkin's *Gypsies* (Aleko) and in Chekhov's *Three Sisters* (Solenyi), are the only strong echoes. Pushkin's verse, however, is frequently quoted or misquoted by Chekhov's characters and narrators. Take, for example, the lines from *The Hero*, "No/ Dearer to me than a thousand base truths/ Is a lie that uplifts us," echoed in "Gooseberries," (1898) (X, 61). The Pushkin quotations, of course, function more as epigraphs to sum up the stories than as material for development.

Gogol is another matter. As a personality and a writer nobody could be more alien, and yet Chekhov felt Gogol to be a precursor he had to outstrip. Parody, perhaps the one trait common to Chekhov and Gogol, was innate, even unconscious, in Gogol's hyperbolic world, while for Chekhov it was either deliberate satire or, as in Treplev's playlet staged within *The Seagull*, an experiment with unfamiliar modes. Only once does Chekhov draw directly on Gogol. When he wrote his masterpiece "Steppe," he consciously ventured into Gogol's southern territory and Romantic descriptive genre. Writing to Grigorovich (February 5, 1888), Chekhov said that Gogol, "the tsar of the steppes," would be envious. Chekhov's evocation of summer, the sweeping imagery of sky, birds, and earth, recall Gogol's "Sorochintsy Fair," and his loose construction around a traveling *brichka* carriage recalls the plot of *Dead Souls*. In this almost entirely male world, the female, represented either by dreamlike beauty or motherhood, has a Gogolian lack of sexuality. Chekhov's macrocosmic detail of the harvested fields and microcosmic detail of insect life, his tricks of focus, his Romantic apostrophes, the anthropomorphism of a kite meditating high in the sky, are all Gogolian in their technique.

Gogolian caricature occurs in two closely linked Chekhov stories, "The Man in a Case" (1898) and "Gooseberries." Galoshes and a hat worn in the hottest weather characterize the schoolmaster in "The Man in a Case," while in "Gooseberries" the hero fulfills his dream of becoming a landowner only to become indistinguishable from his pigs. Chekhov uses Gogol's technique of depersonalizing a human being by substituting the clothes for the person or the swine for the swineherd.

Tolstoi excepted, no other classical Russian writer left any strong imprint on Chekhov. Dostoevskii's plots, where concatenations of events led to catastrophic breakdowns of character or social order, resemble Chekhov's nonsequential plots not at all. Only a few works of the early 1890s—the first chapter of "A Woman's Kingdom," where the heroine's charitable action meets an offended and proud rebuff, the opening of "An Anonymous Story," where offended pride and forced submission again make for Dostoevskian tension, or "Ariadna," where the heroine enslaves the narrator—strongly remind us of episodes in *Crime and Punishment, The Idiot*, and "The Gambler," respectively.

Tolstoi's influence, however, was as much a moral as a literary phenomenon. Very often, Tolstoian philosophy provides the dramatic situation. A number of stories of the late 1880s explore what happens to Chekhovian characters when they attempt to put into practice Tolstoian theories of simplification and nonresistance to evil.

Stylistically, Chekhov owes no more to Tolstoi than he does to Dostoevskii, although he valued the lapidary, assymetrical awkwardness of Tolstoi's syntax for its strength. And while he shares Tolstoi's distrust of cliches and abstractions, Chekhov, unlike Tolstoi, is reluctant to substitute a new set of abstractions for those he has demolished.

When Chekhov entered literature, Tolstoi's most controversial views concerned female emancipation and sexuality. Already adumbrated in *Anna Karenina*, they became steadily more categorical until they reached absurdity in "The Kreutzer Sonata" (1889). Chekhov, naturally fastidious and self-contained, was at first more influenced by Tolstoi's treatment of sexuality than by any other aspect of his work; only Chekhov's own experience and sanity, together with his medical training, enabled him to renounce Tolstoi's outlook. In the stories of 1886, written for the sensation-seeking readers of Suvorin's newspaper, Chekhov makes sex one of his main themes. Tolstoi's influence comes out in stories like "Misfortune" (1886), where the married heroine uncomfortably realizes that she is encouraging a family friend to become her lover. Chekhov's asides on "the triviality and egotism of a youthful nature" have all the condescension of late Tolstoi.

Nearly as strong a force in Chekhov's early work is Tolstoi's "Paul-from-Saul" formula, the sudden inner revolt of *Resurrection*. A well-intentioned young man suddenly confronts the enormity of his own life as compared with the lives of others in "A Nightmare" (1886). Chekhov asserts, with a Biblical phrase which Tolstoi also uses, that the rich hero can no more right the wrongs of society than the camel can pass through the eye of the needle.

Then, like Tolstoi, he concludes by sermonizing: "His whole soul was filled with a feeling of oppressive shame at himself and the invisible truth. . . . Thus began and culminated a sincere impulse for useful activity" (V, 73).

By 1888, Chekhov had become far more critical and subtle in using Tolstoian formulas. Tolstoianism becomes the ideological fuel of the story. "Excellent People" lets the brother and sister take opposing sides to argue out nonresistance to evil. In the various versions of this story, the authorial stance shifts, but nowhere does Chekhov allow either side victory or defeat. He suggests that he has felt, but not succumbed to, the lure of Tolstoi's evangelism, and he implicitly criticizes both Tolstoi and his own characters for their arrogance in fields beyond their competence: "it is wrong to practice as a doctor if you don't know medicine . . . to lord it about in a field of thought in which you can only be a guest" (V, 586).[7] Yet Tolstoi's authorial arrogance takes an even stronger hold on Chekhov. "Name-Day " (1888), furthermore, has an embarrassingly high number of coincidences with *Anna Karenina*. In one scene the husband scythes hay, amazing the girls watching him, as Tolstoi's Levin amazes himself. The heroine talks with the gardener's wife about her impending childbirth, as does Tolstoi's Dolly. Chekhov's heroine hates the back of her husband's neck with Tolstoian suddenness. The satire on the guests is a Tolstoian satire on the Europeanized lawyers of the provinces. Even the word *tolstovets* (Tolstoian) springs to the heroine's lips, as do Tolstoian moralizing proverbs: "Lies are just like the woods, the further you go, the harder it is to get out" (VII, 173).[8]

Chekhov's critics noticed the similarities; they misunderstood the monologue of the dying professor in "A Dreary Story" because they compared it too closely with Tolstoi's "Death of Ivan Il'ich."[9] Although they correctly saw Chekhov adopting Tolstoi's structure of a meaningless life gaining value with the approach of death, they failed to see the gulf between Tolstoi's morality play and Chekhov's elegiac prose-poem. Their accusations of imitation only accelerated Chekhov's distancing of himself from Tolstoi, as did Chekhov's journey to Sakhalin, which persuaded him that evil lay not so much in individuals as in external circumstances, making Tolstoi's Christian sense of sin irrelevant. The disillusionment was most fully expressed when Chekhov choked on the idiocies of "The Kreutzer Sonata." "Tolstoi deals with what he doesn't know or what he refuses out of obstinacy to understand. Thus his arguments on syphilis, orphanages, the revulsion copulation arouses in women, etc., are not merely arguable, they simply reveal the ignoramus."[10] "Before the journey to Sakhalin 'The Kreutzer Sonata' was an event for me, while now I find it ridiculous and think it senseless. Perhaps I've matured."[11]

In the course of the 1890s he became more hostile to Tolstoianism. To Suvorin he wrote, "There is more love of humanity in electricity and steam than in being chaste and abstaining from meat" (March 27, 1894). The conflict became sharpest in stories such as "My Life" (1896). The narrator-hero "drops out" and offers no resistance to his oppressors; he tries for a while to work alongside the peasants, but the drunken, thieving peasants frustrate him. The best the narrator can say for them is that they are no worse than the bourgeoisie, and indeed are better in their thirst for justice. Chekhov's "Peasants" trod on Tolstoi's territory, but with none of Tolstoi's patriarchal order and Christianity. Savagely superstitious, brutalized, and terrified, Chekhov's peasants have only a residual affection for the language of the Gospels and sympathy for oppressed Biblical characters. To Tolstoi it proved that "Chekhov did not know the people"; the story was "a sin against the people."[12] Despite Chekhov's "woe to the rich and the well-fed" refrains in these late stories, his divorce from Tolstoian traditions seems complete.

Yet after the break with Suvorin over the Dreyfus case, Tolstoi once more became a father-figure for Chekhov. They disagreed about the immortality of the soul and about the theatre, but the affection Tolstoi inspired in his daughters and the power of his language infected Chekhov. We must read the opening paragraphs of Chekhov's unfinished story "The Letter" (1902-1903) as a tribute to Tolstoi:

What strength! The form is awkward to look at, but then what broad freedom, what a frightening, unlimited artist emerges from this awkwardness. You get "which" three times and "apparently" twice in one phrase, the phrase is put down badly with a mop, not a brush, but what a fountain spurts from these "which's," what a pliant, harmonious, profound thought, what stentorian truth is hidden under them.[13]

For Chekhov the contemporary literary world could never match such giants. Indeed, he felt threatened by the precarious sanity of writers of his own generation. Just as Peter Chaadaev's, Konstantin Batiushkov's, and Vladislav Ozerov's mental illnesses made Pushkin fearful for his own sanity, Vsevolod Garshin's plunge to death down a stairwell after he had written a number of stories about extreme mental anguish left Chekhov preoccupied by madness. Garshin's personality and fate, rather more than his work, inspired such stories of neurasthenia and madness as "An Attack of Nerves" (1888) or "The Black Monk" (1894).

For all his reticence, Chekhov could see that he had no equals among his own generation. For realists such as Gorkii, Chekhov was a teacher of style; for symbolists and decadents such as Sologub, he was a traditionalist who had to be wooed. We can sense that Chekhov succumbed a little to the influence of his contemporaries. After his first contacts with Gorkii, he abandoned his nonpolitical position in such works as "In the Ravine" (1900) and echoed Gorkii's critique of capitalism. Moreover, he adopted Gorkii's technique of introducing false prophets, this time sheep in wolves' clothing, to foment useless and purposeless rebellion. Ania in *The Cherry Orchard* and Nadia in "The Bride" (1903) are misled by the same tubercular misfits who provide false palliatives for the poor in Gorkii's work.

The decadents made little impact on Chekhov. He used some of their devices—Satanic lights, strange smells—in stories such as "A Doctor's Visit" (1898), but with much more disciplined effect. The nonverbal aspects of Chekhov's plays—offstage noises, music—are paralleled, not inspired, by the experiments of the symbolists, most of whom reinterpreted Chekhov according to their own preoccupations. Chekhov's sufficiently sour view of lyrical verse kept him a skeptical distance from the incipient symbolist movement, and precursors of symbolism, such as Semën Nadson, were simply figures of fun. Chekhov regarded lyrical poetry as the symptom of an incurable disease, the proliferation of poets proving his favorite adage that the more treatments available, the less curable the disease.

Chekhov had far more respect for his contemporaries in European literature, perhaps because he could perceive a continuity from Marcus Aurelius to the present day which was absent from Russian literary tradition. Some European literature (Shakespeare, Voltaire) had been so well assimilated as to be naturalized. Long before Turgenev's famous lecture, "Hamlet and Don Quixote," Hamlet had become an honorary Russian citizen in a dishonorable Russian predicament. His failed duty to the state and to Ophelia mirrored the failures of Russian intellectuals and Russian "superfluous men." Hamlet infects all of Chekhov's plays, from *Ivanov* to *The Cherry Orchard*. Ivanov and Lopakhin not only name him, they quote him: "Ophelia, nymph, in thy orisons / Be all my sins remembered."[14] Uncle Vania, infuriated but paralyzed by his mother's betrayal; Ivanov, unable to face his duty until the last moment; Treplev, staging a playlet to arouse his mother's wrath, are only a few of Chekhov's reincarnations of Hamlet. *The Seagull* takes homage further than any other play. Konstantin Treplev's resentment of his mother's lover and of her whole attitude toward life mingles with his touching dependence as she bandages his head; the rage and guilt his little play provoke and the lines from *Hamlet* that he and Arkadina exchange before this play begins, all show how crucial Shakespeare's influence was.[15]

Like Shakespeare, Chekhov was fascinated by actors as characters. When faced with the mystery of an actor submerging his self in another personality, Chekhov, like Hamlet, asks "What's Hecuba to him and he to Hecuba?"[16] There are shades of *Macbeth* in *Three Sisters*, where Solenyi stalks his victim Tuzenbakh and vainly perfumes his hands like Lady Macbeth. But the persistent fascination emanates from Hamlet, the tortured intellectual, bemused by art, tormented by sexuality, incapable of effective action. Shakespeare's influence did not extend to the natural world, for Shakespeare paralleled breaches of moral hierarchies with natural catastrophes, while Chekhov held that human turmoil had no connection with nature's eruptions and moods.

Like Shakespeare, Voltaire had become an honorary Russian writer. He had filtered into Russian literature through Pushkin, whose evolution from erotic lyricism to historical writing and moral quietism exactly mirrored

Voltaire's, so Chekhov could quite unconsciously write Voltairean moralities. Many of Chekhov's early jokes are Voltairean anticlerical spoofs: in "A Story Without a Title" (1888) a monk who returns to the monastery gives such a lurid picture of the sinful world outside that the other monks immediately desert their calling. Only when Chekhov was studying the Dreyfus affair did he come to appreciate the important precedent Voltaire set when he interceded on behalf of the Protestant Colas. Chekhov began to read his work in earnest and donated a complete set of Voltaire's works to the city library of Taganrog. The idea of "cultivating one's garden" occurs in Chekhov's correspondence and becomes part of the despairing morality in such late works as "My Life." The nurturing of private life in a public hell—the framework of Voltaire's *Candide*—and the idea that one cannot predict good or evil consequences from good or evil intentions—the conclusion of Voltaire's Zadig—occurs in such stories as "About Love" (1898) and "The Lady with a Lapdog" (1899).

French novels from the first half of the nineteenth century left Chekhov relatively untouched. Victor Hugo's plots and melodrama fueled a number of parodies in his *Oskolki* period, and Chekhov's relentless pursuit of *le mot juste*, as well as his growing hatred for the bourgeois, faintly echoes Flaubert. Popular French fiction, particularly the detective novels of Emil Gaboriau and the society novels of Fortune Hippolyte Auguste Duboisgobey, influenced Chekhov's highly ingenious early pastiches, "The Phosphorous Match" (1883) and "The Shooting Party" (1884-1885). But not until the appearance of Maupassant did any French writer make a great impact on Chekhov.

Maupassant, like Somerset Maugham, has been grossly underrated, since the perfection and ease of his technique imply a shallowness of thought and feeling. Critics all too easily forget that the modern European and American short story owes an equal debt to Maupassant and to Chekhov for its miniaturization, organization, and subtlety. Maupassant shows how a writer can cope when the great geniuses of the novel appear to have exhausted the possibilities of fiction. Maupassant offers no ideals, no revelations, and no fantastic worlds; he works within the limitations of his reader's language and experience, refining them to the greatest possible clarity. Despite his much stronger plotting—he is melodramatic at times—he taught Chekhov how to end a story without a denouement.

Maupassant's work first attracted Chekhov with its portrayal of sexuality, for Maupassant regarded sex with neither Romantic fervor nor ascetic distaste. Chekhov, who remained intrigued with sexuality, particularly sexual dominance, all his life, found Maupassant a congenial source. Such early stories as "Mire" (1886), in which the Jewish heroine entangles her male creditors with a fascinating but ugly sexuality, have the intensity of Maupassant's best stories. Later, Chekhov was not averse to copying Maupassant's best known subject matter, prostitutes. The heroine of

Maupassant's "Boule de Suif," who sleeps with a Prussian officer so that the bourgeois party she is traveling with can continue their journey, is clearly the model for Chekhov's unfortunate "The Chorus Girl" (1886), who is bullied by a client's wife into handing over all her hard-earned jewelry, and for the prostitute heroine of "A Gentleman Friend" (1886), who loses a tooth for no good reason because she is too shy to reveal her plight or her name to the dentist, a former client. As in Maupassant, the prostitute displays a far nobler character than her bourgeois exploiter.

After Maupassant's death, when his novels became available in Russian and the horrible suffering of his last years was publicized, Chekhov came to respect him far more. The stronger plotting of Chekhov's stories of the early 1890s owes something to Maupassant's sharp delineation. Louder still are the praises Chekhov's characters sing of Maupassant. For all his dishonesty, Lysevich, in "A Woman's Kingdom," convinces the reader with his adoration of Maupassant: "Darling, read Maupassant! One page by him will give you more than all the wealth of the earth. Every line is a new horizon. The gentlest tenderest impulses of the soul give way to strong stormy feelings. . . . The fury of the transitions, the motifs, the melodies" (VIII, 285). The hyperbole is Lysevich's, but the thought is Chekhov's.

Of all Maupassant's works it is his little-known book of sketches and essays, *Sur l'eau*, which most anticipates Chekhov's vision. Maupassant expresses a duality of nature and man which Chekhov delineates in "The Lady with a Lapdog" and "The Duel." Sailing past the ports of the Cote d'Azur, which Maupassant loathed as much as Chekhov did the Crimea for the hopeless disease that lurked in its sunny sanatoria, Maupassant states: "This delightful country is the world's hospital and the flowering cemetery of Europe."[17] Maupassant went on to write the paragraph in French literature that most anticipates Chekhov:

Certainly, some days I feel the horror of existence so much that I long for death. I sense with a hyper-acute suffering the unvarying monotony of landscapes, faces and thoughts. The universe's mediocrity amazes and disgusts me, the littleness of all things fills me with revulsion. . . . The touch of the water on the sandy banks or the granity rocks moves and softens me and the joy that comes over me when I can feel the wind pushing and the waves carrying me comes from my letting brutal natural forces take me over.[18]

In Maupassant's late novel *Pierre et Jean*, Pierre attempts to come to terms with his mother's infidelity. He is staring at the sea, "Then over the deep water, over the unlimited water, darker than the sky, he felt he could see stars. . . . He thought, 'If one could live on it, how peaceful one might be.' "[19] Peace likewise supplants turmoil in Gurov's mind as he stares at the sea in "The Lady with a Lapdog": ". . . and the monotonous muffled roar of the sea which came from below spoke of peace, of eternal rest awaiting us . . . Gurov thought how in effect, if you thought about it, everything was beautiful in this world" (X, 22).

In *The Seagull* Maupassant plays as important a part as Shakespeare. In Act 1, Treplev associates his own horror at his mother's vulgar ideas of art with Maupassant's insane horror at the Eiffel Tower that "threatened to crush him with its vulgarity." In Act 2, Doctor Dorn is reading aloud to Arkadina and Masha from *Sur l'eau*. Arkadina takes the book and reads: "And of course for people in society to cherish novelists and bring them into their houses is as dangerous as for a corn merchant to rear rats in his warehouse." Two sentences later Arkadina closes the book with indignation, for it reflects too painfully on her capture of Trigorin. What Maupassant wrote next, however, is relevant to Chekhov's play, for it predicts the eventual collapse of Trigorin's attempts to escape. "Like water piercing the hardest rock drop by drop, praise falls word by word on the sensitive heart of the man of letters. Then as soon as she [woman D.R.] sees him softened, moved, won over by this constant flattery, she isolates him, cuts bit by bit all links he might have."[20]

Chekhov not only quotes Maupassant, but he also refines him. In Maupassant's *Bel-Ami* the seduced, then discarded Mme. Walter takes to wearing black: "Dressed in black, she had powdered her hair, which made her look charming. 'Are you in mourning?' asked Madeleine. She answered sadly: 'Yes and no. . . . I've reached the age at which one is in mourning for one's life.' "[21] Chekhov opens *The Seagull* with a distillation of this exchange:

Medvedenko   Why do you always wear black?

Masha   I'm in mourning for my life. I'm unhappy.

Although Chekhov respected Zola, the scale and type of Zola's novels quite unsuited them to Chekhov's literary methods. Zola's work was notorious in Russia. His erotic novels, such as *Nana*, circulated freely, and his more revolutionary works, such as *Germinal*, were all the more popular for being proscribed. Chekhov began by imitating and parodying the erotic. "My Nana," a short sketch, appeared in 1883; in "The Shooting Party," the narrator murders his parrot in a scene of erotic spite very like the killing of the cat in *Thérèse Raquin*. A number of Chekhov's stories—notably "A Woman's Kingdom" and "Three Years"—employ a documentation, a naturalism, and a set of social attitudes that seem from Zola's work. Some argue that this accounts precisely for the weakness of these somewhat clumsy, limp, overlong stories.

Even more important than the meticulously medical and naturalistic technique of the novel, Zola's defense of his art in the second edition of *Thérèse Raquin* anticipates Chekhov's frequent counterattacks, beginning in 1886, on critics such as Maria Kiseleva or Nikolai Mikhailovskii, who accused him, as French critics accused Zola, of wallowing in filth, of mistaking extreme states for typical conditions. Zola's claims to be a disinterested scientist, trying to disentangle the sequence of human motivation and action, have a forensically Chekhovian ring. "I have simply carried out on two living bodies the analytical work which surgeons perform on corpses. . . . I say, 'this writer is just an analyst who has managed to forget himself in human rubbish but who has done so as a doctor forgets himself in theatre.' "[22]

When Zola undertook the defense of Dreyfus, Chekhov became so convinced of his sincerity that he overlooked the distance between their handling of form and language, seeing only the closeness of the moral stance. Chekhov sided with Zola against Paul Bourget, the author of *Le disciple* (which had been printed in Russia), in defending science against the accusations of materialism and immorality. Chekhov felt that analogous battles against anti-Semitism and against scientific detachment were about to be fought in Russia. Thus, Zola the journalist was probably of greater significance than Zola the author of *Germinal*, whose Satanic mines Chekhov tentatively recreated in the steel foundry of "A Woman's Kingdom" or in the factories of "In the Ravine."

Chekhov also felt a certain sympathy for the irrational stream in French literature. His symbolism of the world as a hospital, which dominates "Ward No. 6" (1892), may owe more than a little to the imagery of Baudelaire and other *poètes maudits*; in *The Seagull* Treplev's playlet has the exalted tone and the imagery of Maeterlinck's *Les aveugles*.

But the chief irrational influences on Chekhov came from German philosophical writers, Schopenhauer in particular. For want of great German novels in the nineteenth century we can rightly accept the prose of the German philosophers as one of the most powerful formative forces in European literature. Schopenhauer dominates both French symbolism and the Russian novel, the latter to such an extent that it is not easy to determine whether Chekhov took Schopenhauerian thought direct, through the translation by the poet Fet, via Turgenev's *Smoke*, or through Tolstoi's *Anna Karenina* and *Confession*.

We meet Schopenhauerian acquiescence in inevitable suffering and evil in Chekhov's "Ward No. 6": Dr. Ragin justifies his inertia and refusal to alleviate his patients' suffering with a closely argued stoical view of human life as an untoward incident in a dead cosmos. The doctor's fate and the opposition of his one vocal patient, Gromov, clearly show where Chekhov stood.

Schopenhauer's views on women, expressed in his *Parerga and Paralipomena* of 1851, include the following arguments:

. . . as the weaker sex, they are driven to rely not on force but on cunning: hence their instinctive subtlety and their ineradicable tendency to tell lies: for, as nature has equipped the lion with claws and teeth, the elephant with tusks, the wild boar with fangs, the bull with horns and the cuttlefish with ink, so it has equipped woman with the power of dissimulation as her means of attack and defence.[23]

Chekhov's "Ariadna" concludes with a similar diatribe: "The main, basic characteristic, as it were, of this woman was an amazing cunning. She was constantly plotting, every minute, apparently quite unnecessarily, but as though instinctively, on the same instinctual basis as a sparrow chirping or a cockroach twitching its whiskers" (IX, 126-127).

Similar concerns attracted Chekhov to the work of Leopold Sacher-Masoch, whose importance he noticed as early as 1883. Chekhov mentions Masoch by name in *Platonov*. As his plays testify, Chekhov was fascinated all his life by the dominant female and the voluntary emasculation of the male, a subject that found classic expression in the surrender of Masoch's hero to the masterful Wanda in *Venus in Furs*. Masoch's Jewish *novellen*, unjustly forgotten, probably lie behind Chekhov's own studies of Jewish life, such as "Mire."

The best known German writer whose work had close connections with Chekhov's was Gerhart Hauptmann. Hauptmann had seen Chekhov's *Ivanov* in German shortly before he wrote *Einsame Menschen*, and Chekhov probably read Hauptmann's play before he wrote *The Seagull*. Certainly the hero of *Einsame Menschen*, unfaithful, weak, guilty, and suicidal, destroyed by the morality of his seniors, seems to be the missing link between Chekhov's Ivanov and Treplev in *The Seagull*. Like Ivanov, Johannes Vockerat is paralyzed by his intellectual decay, falls out of love with his good, simple wife, and is attracted to a strong-minded, intellectual young Russian girl. Unable to bear his own degeneration, he drowns himself. In Hauptmann's work the morality of the parents still has something to say for itself, as it does not in Chekhov's *Uncle Vania* or *The Seagull*; but both Hauptmann's and Chekhov's plays conclude ironically, with the destruction of the younger generation and the survival of the old. In fact, of all the "new drama" in the last two decades of the nineteenth century, Hauptmann's is the only work that shows close links with Chekhov.

Critics have customarily linked Ibsen with Chekhov, and certainly *The Seagull* suffers from what one wisely called "unpleasant Ibsenism."[24] The stuffed seagull, so ludicrously forced on Trigorin's attention in Act 4, is surely a farcical allusion to Ibsen's *Wild Duck*. Nina's sudden reappearance, via the back door, after years of absence, is typical Ibsen, who likes to bring ghosts back from the past to wreck the present. But the fact remains that Ibsen's morality, and his sense of inexorable retribution, bear no resemblance to Chekhov's. Attempts to link them will always founder on the fact that Chekhov would have written just as he did even if he had never read Ibsen.

The same strictures apply to any comparison between Strindberg and Chekhov. Chekhov read a manuscript translation of Strindberg's *Miss Julie* at the end of his life, but Chekhov's interest in dominant women never soured into Strindberg's intense horror of them. And while Ibsen, Bjørnson, and Strindberg learned to discard much of the theatricality that had killed off theatre, Chekhov's theatrical innovations arose independently, inspired more by Turgenev and, perhaps, Nemirovich-Danchenko.

When we place Chekhov within the literary tradition, then, we have to look at the problem from two angles: first, what influences can we discern in Chekhov's work, and second, how did Chekhov view his own role in literature. The two angles are very different. Chekhov thought himself, like his dying bishop, part of a secondary movement, a temporary literature that would not survive a decade after his death. Chekhov's own view of his art was eclectic; he willingly took from tradition whatever he felt to be "talented, clever and noble," as his professor of medicine put it, wherever he found it. The peculiar genius he invested his borrowings with was something which he quite sincerely discounted as no more than craft. But for us today, Chekhov ranks with Flaubert and Tolstoi; he is both an innovator and a classic, a central figure in the world's literary tradition.

NOTES

1. See A. P. Chekhov, *Polnoe sobranie sochinenii i pisem v 30-ti tomakh. Sochineniia* (Moscow, 1976), V, 586. All citations from Chekhov's works are from this edition, unless otherwise specified.

2. "One Przhevalskii . . . is worth a dozen educational establishments and a hundred good books . . . heroes who personify a higher moral force . . . are as necessary as the sun." See *Polnoe sobranie sochinenii. Sochineniia*, XVI, 236-237.

3. Notably, Logan Speirs, *Tolstoi and Chekhov* (Cambridge: Cambridge University Press, 1971); *Tolstoi i Chekhov* (Moscow, 1958).

4. See *A. P. Chekhov v vospominaniiakh sovremennikov*, ed. A. K. Kotova (Moscow, 1947), p. 316.

5. See Chekhov's letter to Suvorin, February 24, 1893.

6. See Peter M. Bicilli, *Anton P. Chekhov: Das Werk und sein Stil* (Munich: Vilhelm Fink Verlag, 1966), pp. 29-31.

7. This passage from "Excellent People" (1888) was deleted from the version published in 1902.

8. Compare with the epigraph "A claw is caught, the whole bird is doomed" in Tolstoi's *Power of Darkness*.

9. The critic A. I. Vvedenskii noted that Chekhov had been unsuccessfully imitating Tolstoi, while Kign wrote that Chekhov showed an "affinity with Tolstoi . . . in his ability to show a person's soul from an unexpected, new and convincingly truthful angle." See *Polnoe sobranie sochinenii. Sochineniia*, VII, 679.

10. Letter to Pleshcheev, February 15, 1890.

11. Letter to Suvorin, December 17, 1890.

12. *Literaturnoe nasledstvo* (Moscow, 1960), LXVIII, 519.

13. A. P. Chekhov, *Sobranie sochinenii v 12-ti tomakh* (Moscow, 1962), VI, 476.

14. See *The Cherry Orchard*, Act II, and the variant from *Ivanov* in *Polnoe*

sobranie sochinenii. Sochineniia, XII, 251. See also Chekhov's *The Wood Demon*, Act IV.

15. In Polevoi's contemporary translation, Shakespeare lost the effusive ambiguity of the original English (which so dismayed Tolstoi) and made an immediate impact on Chekhov. The rejection of Ophelia by an impotent Hamlet, the conflict of generations, and the absurdity of actors who take their parts so seriously are among the many aspects of Shakespeare that can be traced even in such early stories as "The Wallet" as well as in the late plays. Only in *The Seagull* does the influence amount to pastiche.

16. See Chekhov's "The Princess."

17. Guy de Maupassant, *Sur l'eau, Oeuvres complètes* (Paris: L. Conrad, 1908), XXIV, 34.

18. *Ibid.*, pp. 62-64.

19. Guy de Maupassant, *Romans* (Paris: Edition de la Pleiade, 1959), p. 866.

20. See Maupassant, *Sur l'eau*, pp. 31-32.

21. See Maupassant, *Romans*, p. 525 (Bel-Ami).

22. Emile Zola, *Oeuvres complètes* (Paris: Edition de la Pleiade, 1979), I, 520. In a letter to M. Kiseleva, January 14, 1887, Chekhov reacts to her attack on "Mire" with a Zolaesque scientific disinterestedness: "For chemists, there is nothing impure on earth. A writer must be as objective as a chemist; he must renounce everyday subjectivity and know that dunghills play a very important part of the landscape, and evil passions are as essential a part of life as good ones."

23. Arthur Schopenhauer, *Sämtliche Werke* (Leipzig: Brockhaus, 1891), VI, 652.

24. See the report of the Teatral'no-literaturnyi komitet (September 14, 1890) in *Polnoe sobranie sochinenii. Sochineniia*, XIII, 364-365.

PART II

Aspects of Chekhov's Fiction

4

Ralph Lindheim

CHEKHOV'S MAJOR THEMES

Chekhov's earliest works were absolutely conventional. He either imitated fashionable fiction—detective stories, naturalistic studies of degeneration and brutality, erotic romances, exotic adventures, tearjerkers about the humiliation and exploitation of social or economic inferiors by their superiors —or he followed the practice of the low-brow comic press of travestying or parodying these popular forms. Yet what Chekhov copied with one hand and mocked with the other left an indelible mark on his work. His early writing made him aware of the conflicts engendered by a society in transition, and he began to show particular concern for the potentially disastrous consequences of social, economic, and cultural change. "Late Flowers" chronicles the decline and decadence of the upper classes, and shows how the ambition and drive of the children of serfs and domestics were crowned by empty, materialistic triumph. In "The Mistress" Chekhov graphically depicts the brutishness of Russian rural life among both peasants and provincial gentry. These themes remained constant, to be explored with greater precision and depth in his mature work.

Chekhov altered and reshaped the conventions of comic fiction far more quickly. Soon after his debut in the comic journals, Chekhov was writing more elegantly structured stories and his characters had become more archetypal rather than topical. He meant these stories to raise more thoughtful laughter, so he began to explore more profoundly the traditional comic conflict between mask and face, between appearance and reality, between illusion and truth. His characters were those whose images of themselves, their society, and their universe are false. Some strut as liberals, others represent law and order; some pose as sophisticates, others as virgins and paragons of piety and virtue; some believe themselves intelligent and experienced, others see themselves as innocents ready and anxious to learn.

All view themselves and their world as better, nobler, simpler, more flexible, more hospitable than is true or even possible. Eventually their masks fall, their pretensions slip, their illusions vanish. In the wonderfully funny story "Surgery," a quack orderly, disconcerted at bungling a simple dental extraction, and his patient, a deacon without the inner strength to endure the pain accidentally inflicted on him, drop their masks of confident professionalism and humble piety to give vent to their true feelings. They display not only their incompetence and ignorance, but also their prejudices and hatreds. Yet this modest work also points to the truth of these masks and the need for them at the proper time and place. What better time to show professional competence and religious fortitude than at a moment of crisis? If true knowledge and endurance are not available in an emergency, then a facsimile helps to maintain calm and inspire thoughtful action.

Later in his career Chekhov continues to explore the complex relationship between mask and face, and in many stories and plays the conflict between appearance and reality, between illusion and truth, is profoundly and generously illuminated. He consistently values truth—recall how he wrote to a friend about "Name-Day": "But doesn't the story protest about lying from start to finish?"—and so do many of his characters.[1] Laevskii, the hero of "The Duel," alters the course of his life when overwhelmed by the "mountain of lies" he has built, when he can no longer deceive himself or his lover about their moral decline or about the vacuity of their relationship. *Three Sisters* traces the loss of dreams and illusions and the gradual acceptance of the hard, cold, often painful facts of reality. In the third act, more than an heirloom clock is shattered. Masha's words to her sisters, just before she leaves to meet her lover, cut to the very core of the play's thoughts on truth and reality:

How are we going to live our life, what's to become of us? . . . When one reads some novel, all this seems old and all of it so understandable, but when you fall in love yourself, you begin to see that nobody knows anything and everybody must decide for himself. . . . My darlings, my sisters . . . I confessed to you, now I'll be silent. . . . I'll be now like Gogol's madman . . . silence . . . silence.[2]

Masha not only recognizes the disparity between life as lived and life as described in books, but her speech also suggests the insubstantiality of all general descriptions and prescriptions since they cannot encompass individual experience. When the old universals prove irrelevant, Masha insists that in a world of uncertainties each person must earn whatever modest, limited glimpse of the truth is attainable. "If only we knew, if only we knew!"—the final line of the play mourns our inability to know either the future or the truth, and this acknowledgment of perhaps the hardest fact of existence is the last in a series of similar statements that conclude a number of Chekhov works: "There's no understanding anything in this world," comments the narrator of "Lights"; "Nobody knows the real truth," say and think the protagonists in "The Duel"; and at the end of "Three Years" Laptev, astounded at the dramatic changes he has suffered over the past years, notes both the future he cannot predict and his desire to experience and perhaps learn from what will happen in the conventional yet also curiously moving cliche, "Live—and see."

But Chekhov, in both early frivolous pieces like "Surgery" and later masterworks, also explores the need for masks and illusions. The marvelous short story "Gusev" and his last play, *The Cherry Orchard*, suggest a necessary antidote to facts that endanger rather than promote survival. Both works glimpse the possibility that human beings are helpless puppets in a brutal, hostile universe of natural and unnatural forces. "Gusev" reveals the worst features of its doomed heroes, their physical infirmities and psychological deformities, while at the same time it exposes the worst features of the worlds they inhabit, the storm-tossed realm of nature and the violence of the modern technological order. But both men also display great moral strength and beauty. Pavel Ivanych, the ridiculous paranoid liberal activist, fears that without his small voice of protest the social system will remain unchanged and the strong will continue to exploit the weak and stupid. Gusev the peasant fears that without him the solid, traditional values of the past will be lost and the peasant family and agricultural community will disintegrate. In the face of all the facts that expose their ugliness and weakness, their impotence before the forces dooming them to extinction or superfluousness in Russia, the will and spirit of both men are not broken. Despite their perception of a reality that supports no human illusions, neither man will admit his helplessness or uselessness. With the beautiful sunset that closes the story and celebrates the best within the characters we get a sense of the need for human beings in this world and for the illusions that sustain them and inform their human and poetic visions of an ideal reality.[3]

Similarly, in *The Cherry Orchard* Chekhov graphically illustrates the total impotence of human beings in a senseless, alien, external world. Nature seems to delight in confounding the characters' expectations by not conforming to their emotions and moods. The sentimental warmth of homecoming at the beginning of the play is contrasted with the unnatural chilliness of the May morning, while the gloominess of departure dominating the end of the play is made even heavier by November's unseasonably warm, bright weather. The play shows, totally without sentimentality, the march of time as destructive. The characters become older, shabbier, paunchier; the orchard will be razed to permit a cheap housing development. Reality constantly flouts human dignity; people bump into furniture, sit on hatboxes, fall down stairs, fall asleep in the middle of a sentence, hit one another with sticks, fail to find the right word to express what they feel, and even have difficulty focusing their minds on and sustaining one topic of conversation for any significant length of time. Fortune favors most of the foolish, secondary characters with success while the main characters suffer one setback after another.

In *The Cherry Orchard* human beings, hovering as they must on the brink of despair, could all too easily abandon hope and retreat into a catatonic state; they could stop posing, strutting, talking, waiting for change, and dreaming. They could surrender all illusions. But the characters hold onto them. They continue to expect a miracle to happen when the only miraculous things are the shopworn tricks of Charlotta the governess. In the face of all the facts they persist in expecting the estate to be saved, Russia to grow and prosper, Lopakhin the merchant to propose to the poor ward Varia, and when some of these hopes fail to materialize, they are convinced that all is for the best. They do not discard their foolish poses, their impractical dreams, their illusions, because to give them up would be to surrender not just their pitiful camouflage, but also their most intense desires and aspirations to be better, different, higher. Their illusions keep them alive, and if we in the audience cannot fathom fully Chekhov's compassionate insight into the truth of illusion, perhaps we can appreciate Madame Ranevskaia's whistling in the dark in the third act: "It's the wrong time to have the band and the wrong time to give a dance. Well, never mind."[4]

When in the mid-1880s Chekhov turned to more serious writing, he brought with him features from his early comic fiction. Numerous characters in the later stories and plays resemble the title character of "Sergeant Prishibeev." Prishibeev is the archetypal small man, whom Chekhov reveals as a petty tyrant rather than a pathetic victim, as a rigidly inflexible maniac who upholds the *status quo* more than its traditional defenders. He is the first major figure in a long list of primitives, including the central male figures in "Peasant Women" and "Pecheneg," but he is also the progenitor of Chekhov's successful businessmen or civilized leaders of provincial society, who, like the fathers in "Three Years" and "My Life," seek to impose on others their limited values and sterile vision. Prishibeev exudes *poshlost'*, that self-satisfied mediocrity which Chekhov—like Nikolai Gogol before him and Vladimir Nabokov after—illuminated in all corners of his fictional and dramatic worlds.[5] But while it is easy to counter the comic threat posed by Prishibeev, *poshlost'* has more serious consequences in late stories such as "The Teacher of Literature," "At Home," and "Ionych," which describe the insidious allure of provincial philistinism and its corruption of young, energetic, and intelligent men and women.

Prishibeev is also the first significant representative of Chekhov's man in a shell, where the shell stands for anything that traps and confines individuals, anything that impoverishes rather than enriches, anything that enslaves rather than liberates. And in this particular comic fool are prefigured many future manifestations of a shell mentality: an inordinate legalism that prohibits uninhibited movement; a Puritanical seriousness that inhibits or denies frivolity; an excessive formalism that hampers spontaneity of expression; an ideological commitment that precludes freedom of thought and action. The vast implications of the shell theme, intimated in the early comic fiction, find expression in a range of images in later works suggesting frustration, aimless, reiterated activity, as well as actual incarceration. People often stare out windows or drum on the panes ("Name-Day"), or they live in isolation behind fences and ditches ("Gooseberries"), or they are associated with objects—Belikov's umbrella and galoshes ("The Man in a Case") which are perfect icons of the shell since these standardized and functional items lack all character and individuality. In "The Lady with a Lapdog" all of modern Russian life is denounced as debilitating, frustrating, and enslaving, both the provinces with their oppressive grey fences and the capital Moscow, which inspires the following tirade from the hero:

What savage manners, what people! What wasted evenings, what tedious, empty days! Frantic card-playing, gluttony, drunkenness, perpetual talk about the same things! The greater part of one's time and energy went on business that was no use to anyone, and on discussing the same thing over and over again, and there was nothing to show for it all but a stunted, earth-bound existence and a round of trivialities, and there was nowhere to escape to, you might as well be in a madhouse or a convict settlement.[6]

Another major thematic issue exhibited in "Sergeant Prishibeev" is lack of communication. The inability of people to talk to one another in the same language or to make themselves understood across differences in temperament, status, and values, produces a confusion in communication or even its breakdown, which frustrates the participants and amuses onlookers in the farcical stories. But the chaos no longer amuses when the characters are more pitiable than ridiculous, more battered than aggressive, more ordinary and human than freakish. In Chekhov's serious stories and plays the chasm separating people remains and continues to obstruct communication, but it now separates not just those of farcically contrasting natures (fat and thin) nor just those of conventionally conflicting groups (social and economic), but those related in blood, class, and humanity, those who should, but don't, share similar feelings, sympathies, priorities, and values. In his first significant serious tales, father and child find little to say to one another ("The Requiem" and "Difficult People"), brother and sister cannot overcome the ideological differences between them ("Excellent People"), a cabby can find no one other than his horse to whom he can convey his grief at the death of his son ("Misery"). In a number of stories of country life peasants from the same district share very little indeed ("The Huntsman" and "Agafia"). In later works lovers and spouses have little in common ("The Grasshopper," "Three Years," "My Life"), old friends must mumble inanities to conceal their true feelings and opinions (Astrov's remark about Africa in Uncle Vania), and intelligent, committed members of the intelligentsia cannot work together to attain morally worthy goals and to realize mutually desirable ends ("The Duel").

Human weakness is another significant theme adumbrated in "Sergeant Prishibeev." Like Prishibeev, Chekhov's heroes and heroines are fairly ordinary people leading rather prosaic lives. Even when portraying the intelligentsia, he does not select their most prominent, dynamic representatives. And these mediocre people find it difficult to believe in illusions when experience constantly demonstrates the barren and blighted quality of ordinary life. All their desired possibilities are undercut by painful inevitabilities, many of which are suggested in the lyric sketches and stories that are Chekhov's major achievement in the last half of the 1880s. Utilizing the poetic descriptions of a narrator, dialogue, and artfully created moods, Chekhov comments movingly on the indifference of human beings toward one another fostered by routine toil and strengthened by real or imaginary slights and humiliations ("The Post"); on the elusiveness and delusiveness of happiness ("Happiness"); on the ecological tragedy of the ceaseless depletion of a country's natural resources and on its repercussions in other areas of human experience ("The Shepherd's Pipe"); on people's dreams and of the obstacles, both natural and man-made, that frustrate their realization ("Dreams"); on the inevitable sadness which true beauty evokes in us because it is both rare and ephemeral ("The Beauties"); on the promise for human beings and the threat posed by nature ("The Steppe"). As Chekhov filled in with greater detail the rough outline provided in these sketches of unrealized and unrealizable potential, of opportunities limited and missed, of fleeting second-hand pleasures, of continual disappointment, and of unavoidable deterioration and decline, there appeared more subdued, melancholy studies of failing strength, dimmed aspirations, fading hopes, piercing regrets, vague resentment, and physical and spiritual enervation that project more the image of Chekhov so familiar outside of Russia.

The perception of human weakness and of the poverty and absurdity of life becomes the crucial moment for Chekhov's characters, many of whom are devastated by their new understanding. In "The Kiss," for example, the hero's pained awareness of his diminished and limited existence leads him against his better instincts to isolate himself from life, to protect himself against the recurrence of illusion and the inevitability of disappointment. Many more characters, however, experience ordinary pain and suffering instead of anxious epiphanies of human impotence. Certainly Chekhov's famous clinical studies, written at the end of the 1880s and the beginning of the 1890s, which carefully describe the effects of disease, exhaustion, pregnancy, depression, old age, and so on, on moods, emotions, thoughts, and actions, acknowledge the centrality of pain in human experience and suggest that his heroes and heroines are those who suffer physical and psychological stress. But, at the same time, these studies continue to demonstrate his awareness that pain is usually destructive. Thus, Olga Mikhailovna, the heroine of "Name-Day," suffers more than a miscarriage; her experience acutely affects her sensitivity and warps her judgment:

She was worried, too, by the people who were in the boat with her. They were all ordinary, good people like thousands of others, but now each one of them struck her as exceptional and evil. In each one of them she saw nothing but falsity. . . . Olga Mikhailovna looked at the other boats, and there, too, she saw only uninteresting, queer creatures, affected or stupid people. She thought of all the people she knew in the district, and could not remember one person of whom one could say or think anything good. They all seemed to her mediocre, insipid, unintelligent, narrow, false, heartless; they all said what they did not think, and did what they did not want to. Dreariness and despair were stifling her.[7]

Similarly, heroes in some of the other clinical studies react to physical and psychological pressures with febrile visions. Vasilev, in "An Attack of Nerves," is so shattered by his first encounter with prostitution, which fulfills none of his expectations, that he has psychotic visions of a fallen humanity and an indifferent universe. Nikolai Stepanovich, the scientist-narrator of "A Dreary Story," beset by the infirmities of old age and threatened by imminent death, is appalled not by the world's sinfulness but by its abysmal mediocrity. Few emerge unscathed from the painful realization of their inadequacies and limitations—biological, psychological, and moral. Unable to contemplate quietly that they have failed themselves and others, they ease their shame and guilt by holding others responsible. Some even retreat into a drug-induced shell. At the end of "An Attack of Nerves" Vasilev resorts to morphine to obliterate the reality that triggers his depression. Olga Mikhailovna's post-operative calm blunts the shock of losing her child, but it also blocks out her husband's sincere confession and repentance, effectively reducing the possibility of their reconciliation. Nikolai Stepanovich, believing that what holds true for him holds true for all, retreats in a different direction; he explains all failures everywhere by the absence of a true, high purpose that would guide people in the right direction, provide worthy ideals, and thus give life significance. Although critics frequently quote this final explanation and justification as the author's position, it is actually the narrator's last attempt to assuage his guilt for a self-centered life consistently insensitive to the desires and needs of others.

In his literary maturity Chekhov continues to explore these biological, psychological, and moral concerns, but in the social, economic, and cultural terms more acceptable to the committed critics of his time and more relevant to our day and age. He considers issues such as drug addiction; the definition of mental health and mental illness; the quality of life in institutions for criminals and for the mentally disturbed; the opportunities for liberation offered women by their society's economic and political modernization and the restrictions imposed on them by traditional stereotyped assumptions and values; the problem of aging—not only the physical process and the reduced role the elderly play in modern society, but also the spiritual process of aging that begins with the loss of youthful idealism and the growth of complacency and sloth.

Many of Chekhov's important works depict with merciless clarity the dangers of reckless and thoughtless change as well as the obstacles to progress of provincial Russia's economic and spiritual backwardness. As a committed conservationist Chekhov continues to expose environmental abuses: the constant depletion of natural resources that Astrov's charts reveal in *Uncle Vania*; the poisoning of the environment by industrial waste products ("Gooseberries" and "A Doctor's Visit"); the noise pollution in the constant aural background of shouts, cries, curses, yelps, growls, barked orders, snivelling pleas, drunken roars, that batter body and spirit in the supposedly idyllic calm of the Russian countryside ("Peasants"). Despite industrialization, provincial Russia remains a barbaric jungle and prehistoric swamp. "Peasants" reveals the long-term stultifying effects of poverty and ignorance, the exploitation of poor peasants by marginally richer peasants, and the indifference of both church and state to the plight of its poorest but most fervent supporters. "In the Ravine" indicates how the development of capitalist alternatives to the feudal tradition reinforces rather than eradicates physical and moral savagery. "In the Cart" and "The New Country House" show the backwardness of rural Russian life, turning energetic and enlightened members of the intelligentsia into zombies drained of all vitality and hope, and depressing well-intentioned reformers without the fortitude to endure the hostility of the poor whom they wish to help.

Change, of course, occurs everywhere—in the sophisticated cities and provincial backwaters, in the shops and factories, on the landed estates, in the schools and universities, in the civil service, in the arts and sciences. Businesses thrive and grow, new industrial complexes spring up on the old estates, the middle class prospers—change is everywhere, but progress is nowhere perceived. Trofimov, the "eternal student" of *The Cherry Orchard*, parts from the merchant Lopakhin with the following advice:

We'll probably never see each other again, so allow me to give you a piece of advice at parting: don't wave your hands about! Get out of the habit. And another thing: building bungalows, figuring that summer residents will eventually become small farmers, figuring like that is just another form of waving your hands about.[8]

In essence, he warns Lopakhin that material prosperity without concomitant improvements in the nation's intellectual, aesthetic, and spiritual life will prove clumsy and empty, a waste of time, since the arms must work together with the head and the rest of the body for true progress to take place. On this point, Vershinin in the last act of *Three Sisters* seems to concur:

Life is difficult. It presents itself to many of us as blank and hopeless, and yet, one must admit, it gets always clearer and easier, and the day is not far off, apparently, when it will be wholly bright. (*Looking at his watch*) It's time for me to go, it's time! Once humanity was occupied with wars, filling its whole existence with marches, invasions, conquests, whereas now all of that is outlived, leaving behind it an enormous empty space which so far there is nothing to fill: humanity is searching passionately and, of course, will find it. Ah, if only it were quicker! (*A pause*) You know, if culture were added to industry and industry to culture . . . (*Looking at his watch*) However, it's time for me. . . .⁹

People certainly benefit from socio-economic change, but many are deeply troubled and have difficulty accepting these benefits and the society that bestows them. Chekhov often parodied the Horatio Alger myth, a variant of the Cinderella rags-to-riches story, by illuminating the problems associated with quick or sudden success: the guilt of some heirs about the source of the wealth they inherit ("A Doctor's Visit" and "Three Years"); the social dislocation of those whose sudden prosperity catapults them from one class to another and from one familiar way of life to a higher but uncomfortable standard of living ("A Woman's Kingdom"); the limited control wielded by owners over assets that are managed much too often by relatives ("At Home") or by experienced middlemen serving the interests of the firm rather than those of the owners or the workers or the customers ("A Doctor's Visit," "Three Years," "A Woman's Kingdom").

Chekhov's later writings often focus on power (*sila*, meaning strength or force, is a key word). Some characters are mysteriously driven to dominate others sexually, such as the eponymous heroines of "Ariadna" and "Anna on the Neck." Others, such as Natasha in *Three Sisters* and Aksinia from "In the Ravine" and the miser Ionych, seek to acquire money, property, and all the other trappings of wealth. Finally come all those who, like von Koren in "The Duel," Lida in "The House with an Attic," and Belikov, clearly control or attempt to control the thoughts and activities of others. Most, however, learn they have no power; they lack control over others and even over their own lives. Suddenly roused from a state of torpor, complacent self-satisfaction, and indifference, they realize that their lives have been misspent, their potential wasted, their energies misdirected ("Rothschild's Fiddle" or *Uncle Vania*). Some have missed opportunities, both personal and social ("About Love"), or have chosen the wrong career ("The Bishop") or the wrong ideological commitment ("An Anonymous Story," "Gooseberries," "My Life"). Some even come to realize that they were wrong in failing to choose and act ("Ward No. 6"). Their deep frustration and bitter disappointment generate searing insights into human impotence. Of himself and his contemporaries Doctor Ragin in "Ward No. 6" offers the following hopeless diagnosis:

You can't do it. You just can't do it. We're weak, my friend. I was indifferent, I reasoned cheerfully and sanely, but the moment I felt the rough touch of life, I lost heart . . . utter prostration. . . . We're weak, we're worthless. . . . You too, my dear fellow. You're intelligent, honourable, you imbibed noble impulses with your mother's milk, but you'd hardly begun life when you got tired and fell ill. . . . We're weak, weak.[10]

And often the admission of impotence is accompanied by images of a coarse and brutal world, which the characters describe as a slaughter house, a prison, a torture chamber, an insane asylum, a garbage dump, or an infested swamp.

Such an inhospitable world can ravage its inhabitants, and a number of works suggest or actually show the process by which many lose their identity as human beings and become associated with or are transformed into objects ("In Exile" and "The Man in the Case"), animals ("Anna on the Neck," "In the Cart"), pagan idols or the walking dead ("Ionych" and "At Home"). But such appalling metamorphoses are not inevitable. Numerous works trace the dramatic recovery of human identity and the reclamation of moral being ("Three Years," "My Life," "The Lady with a Lapdog," and *Three Sisters*—which also contains the antithetical plot strain) in the midst of the same horrors that dehumanize others.

Whether the characters lose their human identity or recover their moral being depends on what happens when they glimpse the truth about themselves and the surrounding world. Too many, overwhelmed by humiliating truths or trends they cannot alter, panic, thereby accelerating rather than postponing or averting disaster. In what are probably the key lines of *Uncle Vania*, Astrov describes the entire process through which he and his friends pass:

We have here a case of degeneration that results from a struggle that's beyond men's strength for existence; degeneration caused by sloth, by ignorance, by the complete absence of any conscience, when a cold, hungry, sick man to save what life he has left, for his children, instinctively, subconsciously grabs at everything that might satisfy his hunger, or warm him, destroys everything, without a thought of tomorrow. Nearly everything is already destroyed and in its place there is nothing created.[11]

Other characters withdraw from society, horrified by the indifference of some in the community and by their obstinate blindness to the immorality or sterility of their lives. This horror of normal, insignificant lives, which develops into a raw hatred of the obtuse and obdurate who see no need for change, proves incapacitating. By the end of his story Ionych, who comes to despise the provincial intelligentsia, cannot even talk like a human being: his utterances to others are either commands or rhetorical questions. Ivan Ivanych frankly confesses in "Gooseberries" how oppressive it is for him to see contented people enjoy the simple pleasures of life, while at the end of "The Man in the Case" his bitter reflections on the limitations and petty hypocrisies of his provincial acquaintances and colleagues blind him to the beauty and consoling power of one of Chekhov's loveliest landscapes. No less debilitating is self-imposed quarantine. Fear of what has already happened to others or what will happen to them unifies the leading characters in Chekhov's trilogy, "The Man in the Case," "Gooseberries," and "About Love." Not just the satirized grotesques—Belikov and the owner of the dilapidated estate with a gooseberry patch—but also the characters with whom we sympathize, Ivan Ivanych and Alekhin, share a cynical, naturalistic outlook that precludes a belief in Providence, precludes a faith that people can resolve in their favor, even if only temporarily, the inescapable conflicts and crises they face. Ivan Ivanych thinks everyone should realize that to every happy man "life sooner or later will show its claws."[12] Alekhin can neither declare his love for a married woman nor urge her to leave her husband and live with him because they cannot be guaranteed a secure, happy, trouble-free future. In what substantial way, therefore, do these two men differ from Belikov, who hesitates to do anything that others could later misrepresent or misunderstand? All of them fear the vulnerability that hinges on visibility and seek the illusory safety of the shell.

Some works, however, illuminate a more productive, creative response to the poignant epiphany of human loneliness and weakness or to the shocked discovery of the ghastly deficiencies of the social order. Here the revelations are often much broader and more metaphysical in thrust. Human beings are more pitied than feared or hated because all, not just special groups or generations, are caught in a losing battle against time, perhaps the major concern of Chekhov's mature writings. Recognizing the inevitabilities of human existence need provoke neither hysterical panic nor debilitation. Instead, people can respond as Laevskii does at the conclusion of "The Duel" when he recognizes that human beings, though doomed to take two steps backward for every one forward, are not overwhelmed by this prospect and persist in their frequently frustrated quest for truth. Or they can perceive, with Laptev, that timidity and servility can prevent human beings from searching for freedom but cannot smother their yearnings for it. Even those who hate others for their mediocrity, apathy, and obstinacy can learn to moderate, to qualify, indeed to correct, an uncompassionate assessment. Thus, Gurov in effect disavows his previous tirade when at the end of the story he can regard without anger what had once enraged him:

He led a double life—one in public, in the sight of all whom it concerned, full of conventional truth and conventional deception, exactly like the lives of his friends and acquaintances, and another which flowed in secret. And, owing to some strange, possibly quite accidental chain of circumstances, everything that was important, interesting, essential, everything about which he was sincere and never deceived himself, everything that composed the kernel of his life, went on in secret, while everything that was false in him, everything that composed the husk in which he hid himself and the truth which was in him—his work at the bank, discussions at the club, his "lower race," his attendance at the anniversary celebrations with his wife—was on the surface. He began to judge others by himself, no longer believing what he saw and always assuming that the real, the only interesting life of every individual goes on as under cover of night, secretly.[13]

Imitating Gurov rather than the heroes of the clinical studies, neither Laptev nor Misail Poloznev in "My Life" withdraws from milieus that are mean and rigid, from occupations that are time-consuming and not very satisfying, from relationships that are official and oppressive. Instead, they continue their normal, everyday lives, which they use as a screen behind which they explore and develop their deepest feelings and express their truest sentiments and notions. Behind this facade of respectability Gurov commits himself to the love that he discovered so late in his life, while Poloznev's occupation as a painter and construction contractor gains him the social acceptance he needs to live privately according to moral principles not approved by others in his community. And as the new head of a pros-perous family concern, Laptev finally acquires, together with burdensome responsibilities he did not seek but will not shirk, greater experience and the leisure to reflect on his mature knowledge in an honestly critical and self-critical manner: he becomes a sadder but wiser and more compassionate man. Finally, Chekhov has found a use for the shell. No longer is it just a prison inside which characters thrash bitterly at others and moan in self-pity; instead, the shell can give characters the time and space to express and expand their capabilities without hurting or humiliating themselves and others.

A saner, more creative response is possible because insight into the ordinary and commonplace arouses as much wonder and admiration as horror and terror. Gurov can think better of himself and consequently better of others he hated months before because he happens to fall deeply in love with a very ordinary woman: "he knew in a flash that the whole world contained no one dearer or nearer to him, no one more important to his happiness. This little woman, lost in the provincial crowd, in no way remarkable, holding a silly lorgnette in her hand, now filled his whole life, was his grief, his joy."[14] And the appreciation of yet another ordinary woman, his wife, and of what she was able to accomplish in the course of three years, helps mark Laptev's transformation. For Poloznev it is not just one person who impresses him but the peasants he encounters. Although he does not live among them and cannot appreciate their life of backbreaking toil, and although he severely criticizes their backwardness and their childish refusal to accept responsibility for their own fate, he is deeply moved by their simple belief that truth will out and justice will eventually be done. Their faith and their knowledge of right from wrong do not alter him but do bolster his determination to live according to conscience. An encounter with ordinary peasants is also central to the experience of Maria Vasilevna in "In the Cart" and Ivan Velikopolskii in "The Student." The unexpected gratitude and respect the peasant parents of her pupils show Maria and the unexpected plagiarism of two peasant women, who cry when they are reminded of Peter's bitter weeping after he had thrice renounced Christ, spark the recovery of both the teacher and the seminary student, as well as rekindle in both a sense of purpose they had lost. Unlike those who are appalled or repelled by ordinariness and insignificance ("nonentity"— or "nobody"—is the worst insult in *The Seagull* and *Uncle Vania*), some of Chekhov's heroes retain their humanity precisely because they come again to appreciate the ordinary and to identify with it.

According to some memoir accounts, Chekhov enjoyed talking with people who were fully themselves, eager and willing to discuss the simple things that delighted them and to share with others both their interests, no matter how trivial, and the intensity of their commitments.[15] In his stories and plays, the ordinary interests and feelings of people—how they react to frustration, disappointment, and the failure of their intentions, as well as to their broader insights into human limitations and errors—prove refreshingly simple, appealing, consoling, and even inspiring. Ionych's initial response, when Kitty does not keep the assignation she had offered him, is bizarre and yet very human: after an intense moment of erotic fantasy he leaves the cemetery worrying about his weight. As long as he continues to convey his worries to himself and others, he remains alive; one of the first signs marking his moral demise is his inability or refusal to voice complaints. To complain, of course, is not a noble, heroic act worthy of great men and women, but it is not an unusual way to voice dissatisfaction and to suggest a desire for something different and better. Another natural response, more impressive than it first appears, is Ragin's sneaking envy, despite his avowed indifference, of doctors and scientists outside of Russia who are contributing to the advancement of medicine and science. His envy is a perverse way of appreciating the accomplishments of others, and therefore is a sign foreshadowing and motivating his last-moment conversion prior to death. The hero of "An Anonymous Story" counters the argument that his feckless generation will disappear without a trace and without a legacy simply with his inextinguishable desire to accomplish not a grand feat but a simple, worthy act that would make his existence known to those who will follow and would also inform them of his desire to be remembered by them. More profoundly moving is the deep regret characters feel for choices made and for opportunities missed ("The Bishop," "Rothschild's Fiddle"). And where a simple, natural expression of distress is inhibited by the assumption that nothing good, true, and beautiful can be attained on earth, human identity is lost rather than regained ("At Home"). But perhaps the most intense, natural, and yet common emotion whose effect can prove inspiring is grief. Chekhov often associates the unaffected display of sorrow with beauty, and true grief always dignifies those it touches. Whether one grieves for the dead ("Enemies"), for the horrors perpetrated by an absurd socio-economic order ("A Doctor's Visit"), for a life wasted (Ranevskaia in the second act of *The Cherry Orchard*), or for a climactic fall in which the best in all of us is betrayed (the weeping of Peter after the third crowing of the cock, in "The Student"), the very expression of grief publicly affirms the value of everyone and everything that is mourned.

In so many ways Chekhov writes for ordinary people. He writes of their physical and moral aches and pains and about their world, the primitive core of which civilization has not substantially altered. True progress, while certainly possible, is years away—sometimes 50, sometimes 200 to 300 years away—but before radical changes can be achieved, the people, like the Israelites under Moses, will have to spend years in the wilderness to develop a new, strong, dynamic, and free generation untainted by the habits and values of a nation of slaves.[16] But, of course, Chekhov's basic concern is for the present rather than the future, and for the unheroic generation in the wasteland rather than the heroic pioneers of the future. Uncle Vania, the spokesman of ordinary people, poses their basic question:

If—suppose I'll live til sixty—if so I still have thirteen years left. That long! How shall I live through these thirteen years? What will I do, what will I fill them with? . . . Do you understand, if I could only live through what is left of life somehow differently. To wake up on a clear, quiet morning and to feel that you have begun to live anew, that all the past is forgotten, faded away, like smoke. (*Crying*) To begin a new life . . . teach me how to begin . . . from what to begin . . .[17]

For his people the physician-writer has no cure that will heal their common complaints, cure their petty but shameful weaknesses and vices, ward off the bleak inevitabilities awaiting them. He does, however, warn them of the worst: that mental and moral death can precede extinction, that some become utterly complacent while others succumb to hysteria, hatred, and self-imposed exile. And he seems to suggest that the best in the future will only come about if helped by those in the present who will not enjoy its benefits. Without the obstinacy of those whose aspirations for truth and happiness cannot be dampened by the certainty of their own failure, without the recognition or appreciation of simple humanity's creative potential, humanity has no future.

Because of their limitations, not much more is asked of human beings but o endure what must be suffered and to protest that which can and should be hallenged. This, of course, is easy to say, and therefore Chekhov allows his critics to say it for him. He does not mouth moralistic pieties that are always easier to follow in theory than in practice. Life is too messy, too much of a "kasha," as Korolev discovers in "A Doctor's Visit," to be summed up in maxims and precepts. Generalities don't usually lead anywhere, and this is why we should appreciate even more simple, healthy, spontaneous human feelings. And why the issue of human identity, its loss as well as its recovery, but most of all its expression, is at the thematic heart of Chekhov's thought and writing.

NOTES

1. Letter to A. N. Pleshcheev, October 9, 1888, in *Letters of Anton Chekhov*, trans. Michael H. Heim in collaboration with Simon Karlinsky (New York: Harper & Row, 1973), p. 112.

2. *Best Plays by Chekhov*, trans. Stark Young (New York: Modern Library, 1956), p. 200.

3. My interpretation is indebted to the study by Rufus W. Mathewson, Jr., "Intimations of Mortality in Four Čexov Stories," in *American Contributions to the Sixth International Congress of Slavists*, ed. William E. Harkins (The Hague: Mouton, 1968), pp. 261-284. But my conclusions about the story are a shade less pessimistic.

4. *The Portable Chekhov*, ed. Avrahm Yarmolinsky (New York: Viking Press, 1955), p. 569.

5. For an amusing as well as good definition of *poshlost'*, see Vladimir Nabokov, *Nikolai Gogol* (Norfolk: New Directions Books, 1944), pp. 63-74.

6. *Anton Chekhov's Short Stories*, selected and ed. Ralph E. Matlaw (New York: W. W. Norton and Co., 1979), p. 229.

7. *The Portable Chekhov*, pp. 203-204.

8. *Ibid.*, p. 584.

9. *Best Plays by Chekhov*, pp. 218-219.

10. *Lady with Lapdog, and Other Stories*, trans. David Magarshack (Baltimore: Penguin Books, 1964), p. 183.

11. *Best Plays by Chekhov*, pp. 110-111.

12. *The Portable Chekhov*, p. 381.

13. *Anton Chekhov's Short Stories.* p. 233.

14. *Ibid.*, p. 231.

15. Maxim Gorky, "Anton Chekhov," in *Literary Portraits*, trans. Ivy Litvinov (Moscow: Foreign Languages Publishing House, n.d.), pp. 134-168.

16. See Eric Hoffer, *Working and Thinking on the Waterfront* (New York: Harper & Row, 1969), p. 179.

17. *Best Plays by Chekhov*, p. 126.

5

Kenneth A. Lantz

CHEKHOV'S CAST
OF CHARACTERS

> In my head I have a whole army of people asking
> to be let out and waiting for my orders.[1]

A Soviet scholar once conducted a census of Chekhov's characters and established their population at something over 8000—more, surely, than were created by any other Russian writer and enough to make up a sizable small town.[2] A reader can easily imagine such a town, an *uezdnyi gorodok*, its center marked by a few dreary yellow government buildings, its streets dusty in summer, muddy in spring and fall; the shops that line them try unsuccessfully to ape Moscow chic. Farther from the center huddle groups of grey wooden houses separated by leaning fences overgrown with nettles; farther away, on the bank of a polluted river, stand some grimy factory buildings; still farther, tucked into the gently rolling landscape beyond the town, lies a monastery whose gold crosses reflect the setting sun; and on the horizon telegraph wires vanish along a railway line.

Such an imaginary picture is no idle flight of Gogolian metaphor but a useful beginning for a survey of Chekhov's characters. They do inhabit such a landscape—not always a small town, of course, but a world so prosaic and familiar that his Russian readers at once recognized it as their own. And Chekhov gives us a remarkably detailed picture that takes in all the inhabitants of the town and its environs: children playing in the streets, cab drivers, factory hands and factory owners, monks, priests, a bishop, landowners, peasants, tramps, inmates of the hospital's mental ward, overworked country schoolteachers, even a stray dog. We see this huge cast of characters in their everyday environment, dealing with one another as they go about their daily affairs, living the "placid, uneventful, ordinary life, life as it is in reality" which Chekhov suggested as a fruitful subject for a "little novel" (letter to N. A. Leikin, May 11, 1888). Chekhov's town offers a panorama of Russian life of the last decades of the nineteenth century that rivals the portrait of France found in Balzac's *Comédie humaine.*[3]

To survey this enormous cast of characters means to categorize them, and the most logical criterion to use would seem to be social. Since Chekhov's characters function within their social context, we can establish with some precision where each fits into his or her world. It would appear, at first glance, that an examination of each of the social classes that constitute Chekhov's world should tell us something significant about the individuals who make up those groups.[4]

If we begin with the landowners who form the top of the social hierarchy, we see at once that the generalizations to be made about this group are few and not particularly meaningful. Chekhov's landowning gentry range from the barely civilized "savage" in "Pecheneg" (1897) to the prosperous and genteel Shelestovs in "The Teacher of Literature" (1889). Characters who fall between these extremes may struggle desperately against debt or exhaust themselves in frenzied, often futile labor ("About Love," 1898 and *Uncle Vania*, 1897). Most are impractical, and few manage to cope with the inexorable social change they face. Another factor common in the lives of many is the loneliness and boredom of life on an isolated estate. The realization that one is the only person of culture in the district can have a profound effect on character. As Chekhov remarked about his *Ivanov*:

Were Ivanov an official, an actor, a priest, a professor, he would have grown used to his position. But he lives on an estate, in the country. Those around him are either drunkards or card players or people like the doctor. . . . None of them care about his feelings. . . . He is alone. The long winters, long evenings, the empty garden, empty rooms, the cranky Count, his sick wife. . . . He has nowhere to go. Therefore every moment he is tormented by the question of what to do with himself (to A. S. Suvorin, December 30, 1888).

Aside from these few common traits, however, Chekhov's landowners are a very diverse group.

Another sizable group in Chekhov's world consists of civil servants and officials of all levels. The most striking common feature is their attitude toward authority. His early stories are populated by a host of petty clerks who tremble before their superiors and bully their underlings and families. "A Chameleon" (1884), "Two in One" (1883), "Fat and Thin" (1883), "The Death of a Government Clerk" (1883), and others are classic treatments of this slave mentality. The slaves and tyrants of the earliest stories never disappear, however; they merely metamorphose into subtler forms. The protagonist in "The Privy Councillor" (1886) is as mistaken in seeing his relatives as innocent rustics as they are in seeing him as a fire-breathing general. The heroine of "Anna on the Neck" (1895) quickly grasps her husband's civil service mentality and exploits this weak point with a vengeance. Belikov, in "The Man in the Case" (1898), plays on his fellow citizens' fear of authority to frighten a whole town into submission. In *Three Sisters* Masha's Kulygin is but a milder form of the Belikov-type. Awe before rank is not restricted to the civil service, however, as the dying bishop in Chekhov's penultimate story finds when he tries to penetrate the wall that his status has built between him and those who ought to be closest to him. Mindless deference to authority may be common among Chekhov's civil servants, but it has spread to other classes as well.

The largest and most amorphous group of Chekhov's characters are the intelligentsia, a group broadly defined as the educated classes generally, excluding clergy and civil servants. As the best educated members of their society the intelligentsia are most keenly aware of its problems and best equipped to solve them. But Chekhov's doctors, artists, lawyers, writers, and students either agonize about their impotence ("An Attack of Nerves," 1888, and "A Nightmare," 1886) or are censured, implicitly or explicitly, for failing to assume their social responsibilities ("Ward No. 6," and "Gooseberries"). As the most sensitive members of their society they are the most likely to be overpowered by the harshness of their environment. The daily grind of the overburdened village schoolteacher, Maria Vasilevna, in "In the Cart" (1897), shows vividly how the environment can erode a character:

It is all so uncomfortable, so unpleasant. Her quarters consist of but one little room with a kitchen close by. Every day when school is over she has a headache and after dinner she has heartburn. She has to collect money from the children for firewood and to pay the janitor, and to turn it over to the Trustee, and then to implore him— that overfed, insolent peasant—for God's sake to send her firewood. And at night she dreams of examinations, peasants, firewood. And from such a life she has grown old and coarse, become homely, angular, and clumsy, as though they had poured lead into her. (IX, 338-339)

Chekhov's "merchants" range from millionaire industrialists and entrepreneurs to shopkeepers and artisans. The literary stereotype of this class is the narrow-minded, sectarian-leaning obscurant of Ostrovskii or Leskov. While Chekhov depicts such characters in "The Murder" (1895), for example, he also has his Lopakhin, the "soft man" who has enough poetry in his soul to be carried away by the beauty of his poppy field (but not carried away so far that he forgets the handsome profit he reaped). Money is one common factor influencing the behavior of this group, but their attitudes to money differ widely. Wealth can enslave, as Laptev, the scion of the family learns in "Three Years" (1895) and as Varvara in "A Woman's Kingdom" (1894) and Liza in "A Doctor's Visit" (1898) come to realize. Yakov the coffin maker ("Rothschild's Fiddle") sees his whole life in terms of "losses"; the Tzybukin family in "In the Ravine" (1900) is destroyed by their lust for gain. But one cannot say that greed is a constant factor that shapes all of Chekhov's merchant characters.

Neither do Chekhov's clergy fit neatly into a homogeneous group. Some live in wretched poverty, others in relative comfort and security. The dying bishop ("The Bishop," 1902) has more in common with Professor Nikolai Stepanovich ("A Dreary Story," 1889) than he does with Father Christopher ("The Steppe," 1888), or even with his own housekeeper Father Sisoi. Chekhov's priests are generally kindly and sincere, but there is no obvious common denominator in their characters that arises from their being clergymen. The one factor we would expect to find common to them all—their religious faith—seems to play a small role in their lives.

There is more uniformity among Chekhov's peasants, due, no doubt, to their shared burdens—poverty, both material and spiritual; long hours of backbreaking work; and submission to the inevitable, whether famine, bad weather, or death. Nevertheless, there is a broad range of characters among the peasants: the saintly Lipa of "In The Ravine," the brutal Kiriak of "Peasants," the resigned Gusev, the absurd Iasha of *The Cherry Orchard*. Thus, even in his most homogeneous social group Chekhov is concerned with the flaws and virtues of his characters as human beings rather than their specific qualities as peasants. Olga's observations of her peasant relatives ("Peasants") bears quoting:

During the summer and winter there had been hours and days when it seemed that these people lived worse than beasts. Living with them was frightful—they were rough, dishonest, filthy, and drunken. They could not live in harmony and were constantly squabbling because they held each other in mutual disrespect, fear, and suspicion. Who keeps the pot-house and makes the peasant drunk? The peasant. Who squanders his village, school and church funds on drink? The peasant. Who steals from his neighbors, sets fire to their property and perjures himself in court for a bottle of vodka? Who is the first to run down the peasant at council and other meetings? The peasant.

Yes, they were frightful people to live with. Still, they were human beings, they suffered and wept like humans, and there was nothing in their lives for which an excuse could not be found: back-breaking work that makes you ache all over at night, cruel winters, poor harvests and overcrowding, with no help and nowhere to turn for it. (IX, 311)

Finally, there is a large and heterogeneous body of characters one might call the dispossessed. This group includes peasants forced to migrate to the cities to find work—Iona in "Misery" (1886), Vanka from the story of the same name, the Chikhildeev's from "Peasants"—various tramps, wanderers, and exiles ("Dreams," 1886, and "In Exile" 1892), and miscellaneous hangers-on like Charlotta (*The Cherry Orchard*) and Waffles (*Uncle Vania*). One factor common to most of them is a deep sense of alienation from their own society. Iona the cab driver finds that even those of his own class—a gate-keeper and a fellow cabbie—will not listen to him pour out his troubles. Charlotta does not know where she comes from and has no one to talk to. Vanka simply has no home. Yet much the same can be said of many others who have not been dispossessed—Nikitin in "The Teacher of Literature," Anna Akimovna in "A Woman's Kingdom," and Maria Vasilevna in "In the Cart." Alienation and loneliness are not the exclusive traits of any one section of the social hierarchy.

The social contexts of Chekhov's characters are unquestionably important; regarded in this light they constitute what Edmund Wilson has called "an anatomy of Russian society . . . at the end of the nineteenth century."[5] Yet as illuminating as such an anatomy might be for an understanding of Russian society, it is only an introduction to an understanding of the characters themselves. While knowledge of a character's social status helps us understand his or her behavior, it does not by any means provide a full explanation. Chekhov is very specific in his use of a character's "context" or particular situation within his social group, and that makes generalizing difficult. Every case is "individualized," and the individual social reality of one priest, say, may be quite different from that of another priest. Chekhov conveys not only the complexity of his characters but also the complexity and diversity of the world they inhabit. His approach to character is essentially scientific: just as a scientist could not hope to understand an organism examined in isolation from its environment so Chekhov shows us his people within the context of their daily lives.[6] Understanding a character's social reality may suggest how his or her immediate environment influences behavior, but there is no sense that behavior is totally determined by social status. Chekhov's peasants are certainly peasants and his priests are certainly priests, but their individual traits clearly outweigh any predetermined peasant or priestly characteristics.

Chekhov's characters cannot be readily labelled. As he once said:

Phariseeism, obtuseness, and tyranny reign not only in merchants' houses and police stations; I see them in science, in literature, and among young people. . . . Therefore I can harbor no special preference for gendarmes, butchers, scholars, writers or young people. Tags and labels I regard as prejudices (to A. N. Pleshcheev, Oct. 4, 1888).

While social status has only limited validity as a criterion for grouping characters, as the brief survey of social groups has suggested, the specific social reality of each character is of profound importance. Chekhov explained something of his philosophy of character in his letter to Dmitrii Grigorovich of February 5, 1888:

All the artist's energy ought to be concentrated on two forces: man and nature. On the one hand, physical weakness, nervousness, early sexual maturity, a passionate thirst for life and truth, a yearning, ranging as broad as the steppe, for activity, a dearth of knowledge along with a broad scope of thought. On the other hand, a boundless plain, a severe climate, a colorless, stern people with its difficult, bleak history, the legacy of Tatar domination, bureaucracy, poverty, ignorance, the rawness of the cities, Slavic apathy, and so on. . . . Russian life beats the Russian into a pulp, crushes him like a twenty-ton boulder. In Europe people perish because they find life too cramped and stifling; in Russia they perish because they find life too spacious. . . . There is so much space that the little man hasn't the strength to find his way.

The response of a character to his or her environment is thus the focus of Chekhov's attention and provides some measure by which his characters may be judged. Chekhov's statement to Grigorovich stresses not only the harshness and dreariness of the environment; he notes also that space itself can defeat his characters. What he has in mind is surely a cultural as much as a geographical expanse: the scope and sweep of Russian life itself, with its extremes of wealth and poverty, culture and barbarity, noble ideals and crude reality, all set within a world whose only laws seem to be that nothing is certain and that change is all-pervasive.

The most basic problem Chekhov's characters face is to cross this "boundless plain" of Russian life, to cope with their environment (broadly understood as the sum of all things they confront in their daily living). His "little man" is bewildered and disoriented and is desperately trying to find his way. Fright is the most common reaction in the face of this sweep of life, and Chekhov has a number of characters such as Gromov in "Ward No. 6" who are all but paralyzed by fears they cannot explain. Silin in "Terror" (1892) admits: "What frightens me most of all is our daily life which none of us can manage to escape" (VIII, 131). But his characters do try to escape from life, to take refuge, to find something to cling to, or to hide behind. They look for means to define themselves and their place within their bewildering world.

In the early stories particularly, the certainties of rank provide convenient but illusory means of orientation. One's position in the bureaucratic hierarchy offers a shortcut toward ordering one's experience and a set of ready-made guidelines on how to behave. Rank can give an identity to characters who otherwise might have none. The retired ensign Vyvertov in "Abolished" (1885) finds his world shattered when he learns that the rank of ensign has been abolished through a bureaucratic reform. "If I'm not an ensign any more, then who am I? No one? Nothing?" (III, 224).

One's context within society can serve a function similar to rank. "A Gentleman Friend" (1886) provides a good and highly ironic illustration. The prostitute Wanda, newly released from hospital and nearly penniless, thinks only of acquiring a new set of flashy clothes to reestablish her professional identity. She decides to borrow money from a "gentleman friend," the dentist Finkel, but without the trappings to give her a sense of self, she lacks her usual confidence. Furthermore, she is so intimidated by the luxury of the dentist's waiting room that she cannot bring herself to ask him for money. Finkel, now in his everyday context, has assumed a professional identity that Wanda sees for the first time. Formerly, in the cafes where they had met, he was usually a bit tipsy, had a free-and-easy manner, and patiently bore Wanda's and her friends teasings; but in his own office he is "sullen . . . pompous and cold, like the head of a department" (V, 118). In their previous meetings he had been the non-professional consulting the professional, but now the tables are turned. Finkel does not even recognize her, pulls a perfectly healthy tooth, and takes her last ruble for his fee.

Chekhov's characters resort to many other means to find direction in life. In a world of uncertainty, laws and regulations serve as an infallible guide for characters such as Sergeant Prishibeev, in "Sergeant Prishibeev" (1885), and Belikov, in "The Man in a Case." Not only regulations but also principles, sometimes even the noblest of principles, can be invoked to create barriers against a hostile world. In "The House with an Attic" Lydia walls herself behind her single-minded devotion to the peasants' welfare, using her apparent selflessness to intimidate those closest to her and to reconstruct her world on her own terms. Her approach to life is narrow and dogmatic; she "never shows any sign of affection" (IX, 181); her mother and younger sister are afraid of her; she even carries a whip. In "Ward No. 6" Ragin's high-minded quest for the meaning of life represents a similar wall erected to shield him from the horrors of his daily reality.

Work itself, usually a virtue in Chekhov's world, can also serve as a box into which characters retreat. Silin in "Terror" admits: "So as not to think I divert myself with work and try to exhaust myself so as to be able to sleep soundly at night" (VIII, 132). In "A Dreary Story," Professor Nikolai Stepanovich's assistant is a happy, hardworking man utterly in love with science but oblivious to all else. "I think if Patti sang right in his ear," the professor says, "if Chinese hordes invaded Russia, or if an earthquake struck, he'd not move a muscle; he'd just go on squinting into his microscope, unperturbed as usual" (VII, 260).

Immersion in domestic affairs can serve as a similar retreat from life. In the early stories Chekhov laughed at the Korobochka-type who could see no farther than her kitchen cupboard. In "An Inadvertence" (1887), for example, Strizhin returns home late and somewhat tipsy, decides to have a nightcap, and in the dark drinks from a bottle of kerosene which he has mistaken for vodka. His housekeeper ignores his pleas for help and scolds him for rummaging in her cupboards and drinking up expensive kerosene ("Do you know what kerosene costs nowadays?" VI, 67). He survives, but on the following day she complains that the shopkeeper must have passed off some poor quality kerosene. In later works this subject is treated seriously, but the narrowness of attitude is still the issue. Varia, in *The*

Cherry Orchard is inseparable from her bundle of keys and is obsessed with her household accounts and her empty larder. To be sure, the burden of managing the house and feeding the servants has fallen on her alone; but she becomes mired in this domestic routine. Her fate at the play's end—to remain the old-maid housekeeper rather than marry Lopakhin—is appropriate. Likewise the lyrical romance between Nikitin and Masha ("The Teacher of Literature") founders on the rocks of domesticity as suggested by Masha's fascination with jam, pots of sour cream, and jugs of milk.

A frequent avenue of retreat from a hostile environment is what Frank O'Connor has called the creation of "the false personality."[7] A character builds up an identity or is given one by those around him, but this personality is ultimately shown to be specious. Many Chekhov stories turn on this gap between the real and the assumed personality. Three examples taken from different periods of his career illustrate this point. "An Actor's End," written in 1886 toward the close of Chekhov's humor magazine period, represents a somewhat serious treatment of what had been one of Chekhov's staple comic themes, the incongruity between an actor's stage persona and the real character beneath it. Shchiptsov, "a noble father and simpleton," becomes ill while on stage, returns to his hotel room, and, convinced he is dying, ponders his career as an actor. He realizes his life has been wasted; his years on the stage have been nothing but a long series of false identities and false emotions; better, he thinks, to have remained in his native town, married, had children, and led an ordinary life. His actor colleagues try to console him, but they can only see him and themselves in terms of their stage roles; not surprisingly they fail to make any meaningful contact with him. The comic actor is full of strained humor; the *jeune premier* tries, and fails, to mask his shabbiness with smart clothes and scent; the tragic actor is appropriately solemn. They are all baffled to see for the first time that Shchiptsov has a different and much deeper personality than the one he played on stage; they cannot comprehend that he can shed real tears and have real sufferings. The story is not a great one even by standards of Chekhov's early fiction, but like so many of his early works it provides a vivid example of a theme that recurs, further refined, in later works.

The false personality is depicted with more subtlety and depth in "Name-Day" (1888). Petr Dmitrich's function as a judge spills over into his private life, corroding his relationship with his wife. He will not confide in her that he is desperately worried over an impending legal action—an action that itself arose out of the "false part" (VII, 173) he was playing—because his own view of a judge's role will not permit any such admission of weakness. His strident but apparently insincere conservatism is another by-product of his profession. Beneath Petr Dmitrich's self-importance is an essentially simple man who longs for a simple life. His wife would be delighted to share that life, but outside forces drive her to play a false role as well. An heiress and a university graduate, she is keenly aware that these facts influence others' expectations of her. Her wealth and education also alter her relationship with her husband, making her less spontaneous and open; like him she feels she ought to be a "serious person," above mundane concerns. In this story the pressures that distort the personality are not merely those of education or profession: they are built into the very fabric of society. Olga must act the gracious hostess, pressing her guests to stay even though their presence is almost unbearable. Her uncle flaunts liberal ideas to prove that he "still retained his youthful spirit and freethinking" (VII, 168). Even the students who arrive late and are obviously hungry decline to eat out of politeness. Such petty but universal social hypocrisies accumulate, leading the characters to form false images of themselves and of each other, creating confusion, dissension, and ultimately tragedy.

"The Bishop" presents yet another treatment of the same theme. Bishop Petr is not much impressed by his own status, but it influences the behavior of others toward him.

He simply could not become accustomed to the awe which, through no wish of his own, he inspired in people in spite of his quiet, modest manner. All the people in this province seemed to him small, frightened, and guilty when he looked at them. Everyone was timid in his presence. . . . The whole time he had been here, not one person had spoken to him sincerely, simply, as to a human being; even his old mother, it seemed, was no longer the same, not the same at all! (X, 194).

But the bishop's problem is more than a matter of status. The circumstances in which he must live every day—the quirks and crankiness of Father Sisoi, the trivial conversations, the endless cups of tea, the taxing round of official services—constrain the freedom of his personality. He escapes from the pressure of his environment for brief moments into vivid memories of his past, when he, a barefoot peasant lad, could follow the icons in a religious procession with a smile of simple faith, "infinitely happy." In his final vision he not only cast off the weight of his office, but also the burden of everyday routine. At last he can be himself. "And he imagined he was now a simple, ordinary man, walking quickly and cheerfully through the fields, tapping with his stick, while above him was the open sky bathed in sunshine, and that he was now free as a bird and could go where he liked" (X, 200). What we see in these three stories, then, is a steady multiplication of the environmental factors that limit the freedom of the personality: from the specific conditions in which the actors work, to the more general social niceties which Petr Dmitrich and his wife must observe, to the very fabric of the bishop's daily existence.

Chekhov depicts characters from all levels of society whose response to life is to fall into a routine. Some, like Bishop Petr, are aware of what has happened to them; others, even those of considerable talent, are not. In *The Seagull* (1896) both Arkadina and Trigorin have acquired complete technical mastery of their respective arts through years of experience, but this apprenticeship has taken a toll. Although Arkadina can summon up a whole range of emotions at will and Trigorin can create a moonlit night in only a few phrases, the art of each lacks feeling; it has become routine and almost mechanical. Their younger counterparts, Nina and Treplev, may have far to go to achieve the technical skills of their elders, yet their art expresses more passion, sincerity, and spontaneity—more life, in short— than that of Arkadina and Trigorin.

Chekhov's stories of children feature a similar contrast between the spontaneous, sensitive attitude of the child and the rigidity of the adult. Chekhov's children have not yet become numbed to life; their personalities have not yet become frozen into fixed identity; they have no preconceived structure on which to order their experiences and so must be guided directly by their feelings. A charming example of the child's response to life is found in "Grisha" (1886). Here, the little boy, not yet three years old, is taken for his first walk through the city. The world he perceives is beautiful, frightening, confusing, and endlessly fascinating. At the end of the day, feverish and "bursting with impressions of this new life which he has only just tasted" (V, 85), he is unable to sleep; his mother, unaware of his emotional turmoil, assumes he is ill and doses him with castor oil. A child's encounter with life is the subject of "The Steppe" as well. For Egorushka the journey across the steppe is filled with images of beauty, terror, and mystery. Open to the new experiences offered by his environment, Egorushka continually listens, sees, smells and learns, but his Uncle Ivan and Father Christopher, immersed in their workaday worlds, are closed to new impressions.[8] For Uncle Ivan the steppe is only an obstacle to be crossed as quickly as possible so that he can make a profitable business deal. Even Father Christopher, more kindly and sensitive than Ivan, regards the journey not as an end in itself but in terms of its ultimate purpose, to bring Egorushka to school in the city. The scene in Chapter 2 when Ivan and Christopher sleep while Egorushka explores his surroundings neatly sums up the difference between the child's and the adults' attitudes. The story "Home" (1887) also shows a child whose response to life is open and direct. A lawyer, a sensitive and affectionate father, ponders the difficulty of communicating with his seven-year-old son Serezha after he fails to convince him that the drawing the boy has done is illogical because it shows a house smaller than a man.

Daily observation of his son had convinced the lawyer that children, like primitives, have their own artistic visions and distinctive aspirations which are inaccessible to an adult's understanding. Under close scrutiny Serezha might seem abnormal to an adult. He found it possible and reasonable to draw people taller than houses, to render with his pencil not only objects but also his feelings. (VI, 103)

Serezha, like Chekhov's other children, has few preconceptions about his world and so can respond spontaneously to it. In his view people should be taller than houses because he feels that they are more important.

The suggestion that a character has become deadened to life and closed to new experiences is often conveyed by Chekhov's technique of characterization. One of his common techniques is to repeat a certain detail of physical description or action or to have a character repeat a pet phrase. In "At Home," for example, Vera's aunt is described as *always* wearing a fashionable dress and *always* putting on a pince-nez to speak to the peasants or the estate manager. Vera's suitor, Dr. Neshchapov, is *always* silent at social gatherings and *always* wears his white waistcoat. Her aunt repeats the same phrase "I'm your obedient slave" (IX, 314; IX, 315; 320). Vera's grandfather's life seems to consist only of frequent meals and fits of temper. When Vera, in a rage, finds herself repeating his pet phrase "Flog him!", we know that she has fallen victim to the same mindless routine that rules the lives of those around her. In *The Seagull* Sorin's frequent repetition of the phrase "And that's all" (*i vse, vot i vse*) suggests the same thing, as does Gaev's billiard jargon in *The Cherry Orchard*. "Ionych" (1898) provides the most brilliant example of this technique. The story's last chapter omits nothing from its portrait of a man whose soul has so shrivelled that his empty life can be fully described in a page. Chekhov uses the present tense here, stressing the repetitive nature of his daily existence:

While having dinner he sometimes turns and breaks into someone's conversation: "What are you on about? Eh? Who?"
And when the conversation at a near-by table turns to the Turkins, he asks: "What Turkins do you mean? The ones with that daughter who plays the pie-ano?"
And that is all that can be said about him. (X, 41)

Ionych's unhappy love has taught him that feelings can be painful. He has retreated into a safe, enclosed world of routine where he can cultivate an indifference that need not put his feelings at risk. Indeed no more need be said about him.

More often than not we have only the sketchiest notion of the externals of Chekhov's characters; what we do know of them, and know in detail, we learn from their thoughts, their reactions to their surroundings. And clearly this suggests that their inner rather than their outer lives are what is of real significance about them. Their feelings matter more than their actions, and habit deadens feelings. V. Ia. Linkov has expressed this notion succinctly:

The Chekhov character exists so long as he feels; when there are no feelings the hero is no longer alive. When he relates the story of Ionych the writer passes over whole years; but he describes in detail the journey to the cemetery which has no consequences whatever and which does nothing to reveal the character of the hero. The years in which Ionych amassed his money have passed without a trace; his life during this time was dreary and uninteresting. And when he does not linger to describe this period Chekhov thus expresses its significance for the hero. Whole years amount to nothing; a trip to the cemetery by night contains real feeling, a sense of life. The story ends with the hero's spiritual death: Startsev no longer remembers the single authentic moments of his life, his love for Kotik.[9]

We know *how* Chekhov's characters react; the question of *why* they feel as they do is not easy to answer. In "The Lady with a Lapdog" (1899), we gradually learn some of the external facts of Gurov's life: he is securely, if not entirely, comfortably immersed in his routine of unrewarding work and egotistical pleasures; his responses to situations are fixed and predictable, so that when he meets an attractive, available woman he immediately sets out to seduce her. We are perhaps as surprised as he is to watch him gradually lose his heart and find his soul in his encounter with Anna, a woman he himself describes as "utterly unremarkable" (X, 139). There seems to be a whole "submerged" part of his personality that he, and we, discover as he moves from a mechanical approach to life to a more human and much more painful way of living.

"Ionych" provides a contrasting example. The submerged side of his personality slowly but relentlessly pulls him down, transforming a bright, enthusiastic doctor into a cranky, overweight miser. But why Gurov moves upward and Ionych slides downward is difficult to explain. Did Ionych suffer from some weakness of character that let him give up on life so easily? The text hints at this: early in the story Ionych cautions himself to watch his weight, a sure Chekhovian signal of potential spiritual flabbiness; likewise, he is quickly drawn in by the general admiration for the vulgar Turkins. Gurov, on the other hand, has had some urge to seek fulfillment in life: even though he now works in a bank he had once studied literature and trained to be an opera singer. Still we do not sense that the actions of either character are *determined* wholly by their personalities or their environments. Chekhov never provides a full explanation of their motivations, although a good deal may be inferred from various hints. Chekhov's technique of characterization is akin to the famous subtext or undercurrent of his plays: we catch occasional glimpses of deeper motivations and may be able, on consideration, to explain some of the reasons why they act as they do. But what is truly significant in their natures goes on "behind the scenes." The submerged side to their personalities is, however, a token of their freedom: they do have the potential to develop further.

Chekhov's approach to his characters is like Tolstoi's, as described by Boris Eikhenbaum:

These are not types, limited by the narrow confines of their social milieu and professions; nor are they personalities somehow encased in a set of feelings and experiences assigned to them by a psychological norm. They are individuals who move freely in and among their feelings and thoughts and who are not isolated from each other by any complicated barriers. They are "in flux" as Tolstoy was fond of saying of people. This principle of "fluctuation" takes us back first and foremost to Pushkin.[10]

Character, in the sense of a fixed set of permanent qualities that make a person what he is—character as identity—is problematic in Chekhov's world. Those characters who are truly alive are "in flux"; but those who have a distinct identity and thus a set of fixed responses to situations are, although they breathe, dead or dying. Do we know Ionych's character? We do at the end of the story when his personality has atrophied and he has become crabby, greedy, and selfish; but he was not always so easily characterized. And we can describe Gurov at the beginning of the story, but when we leave him we find that his personality has expanded and grown more complex. Likewise we can easily sum up Belikov, or Olga in "The Darling" (1898), but Maria Vasilevna of "In the Cart" or Lopakhin of *The Cherry Orchard* or Nadia of "The Bride" (1903) do not have this sort of fixed, limited, and easily defined character. They are alive, they respond to their surroundings, they feel and react, they have hopes and dreams, they are unpredictable, and they can develop. In short, they are "in flux." But when they are characterized as "always" doing, saying, or wearing something, when they have accepted a fixed role and a permanent identity, then they become spiritually moribund.

The life of a Chekhov character, at least of those who live, is one of continual evolution. In Chekhov's last story, "The Bride," Nadia does manage to escape from the prison of life her family and fiance have prepared for her. But even here her new "identity" as a free woman is problematic. Consider the final line of this, Chekhov's final, story: "She went upstairs to her room to pack, and the next morning she said farewell to her family: happy and full of life she left the town—*as she supposed*—forever" (X, 220 [emphasis added]). Even here, where she seems to be turning her back on the stultifying small-town environment to move to something much more promising, Chekhov refuses to make her future settled and final.

Chekhov's approach to character is decidedly non-deterministic. He shows the enormous pressures life exerts on his characters and how they are often broken by these pressures. But environment is by no means all-powerful, and submission to it by no means inevitable; characters do resist and triumph over it. Laevskii, in "The Duel" (1891), is fond of justifying his weakness by claiming his environment made him what he is, a child of the 1880s, "crippled by civilization." Yet he, more than anyone else in the story, manages to patch together the untidy remnants of his life and work toward something better. Even von Koren, as dogmatic a character as any Chekhov created, is, if not "reformed," at least brought toward a more tolerant view of his fellow humans. Nina Zarechnaia, in *The Seagull*, loses her family, her innocence, her lover, and her illusions; yet even within the tawdry and unrewarding milieu of the provincial theatre she finds the strength to endure and to maintain her faith in herself and in life. At the end of "In the Ravine" Lipa has not descended into the moral ravine in which the others live, even though she continues to share their physical setting. These and many other characters triumph over their environment, but none of their victories is won without great cost. Chekhov's characters can surprise us and themselves. The freedom to develop exists in their world, but Chekhov makes it abundantly clear how painful it is to take on the burden of even a small measure of that freedom.

Chekhov's characters can best be understood not by sorting them into precisely defined categories but by imagining them arranged on a continuum that stretches from the lackey to the free man, from the barbarian to the person of genuine culture, from spiritual deadness to sensitivity to life. At one end of the scale are those who believe they have found their "truth"— whether it resides in their social status, their daily routine of life, or in some slogan or ideal—and so have closed themselves to any further development. At the other end of the scale are those who are still seeking direction in life. They may seem bewildered or weak and may feel enormous guilt over their doubts, but they have retained something of the child's wonder at life and openness to new experience. But Chekhov's characters cannot be readily pigeonholed: most frequently they move along this scale, either because they have been jarred out of their complacency or because they sink unthinkingly into indifference and spiritual death.

In that sense Chekhov's characters are "all alike," as a number of critics have charged.[11] They are all human beings trying to cope with the difficulties of their lives in ways we quickly recognize since they are our ways. What we know of them are their feelings about life—boredom, terror, hope, or despair. Chekhov chooses not to emphasize those quirks that set people apart but to focus on traits shared by all, no matter how much the conditions that provoked them may differ. He is concerned first and foremost with examining the humanity of his characters by depicting those qualities —apart from the more or less accidental ones of education, profession, social class, or political outlook—that make them more or less human. As he said: "When I portray such types or talk about them, I'm not thinking about their conservatism or liberalism but about their stupidities and their pretenses" (to A. N. Pleshcheev, Oct. 9, 1888). His works are an affirmation of the supreme value of the free individual. And his hopes for humanity rest firmly on the individual human being: "I believe in individuals; I see salvation in individual personalities, scattered here and there all over Russia, whether they are educated men or peasants—they may be few, but they are a power" (to I. I. Orlov, February 22, 1899).

NOTES

1. Letter to A. S. Suvorin, October 27, 1888, in *A. P. Chekhov, Polnoe sobranie sochinenii i pisem v 30-ti tomakh. Pis'ma* (Moscow, 1974-1984), III, 47. All citations from Chekhov's works and letters are from this edition. References to *Pis'ma* (Letters) are noted by addressee and date only. References to *Sochinenia* (Works) are given in parentheses in the text by volume and page number.

2. M. P. Gromov, "Povestvovaniia Chekhova kak khudozhestvennaia sistema," in *Sovremennye problemy literaturovedniia i iazykoznaniia k 70-letiiu so dnia rozhdeniia Mikhaila Borisovicha Khapchenko,* ed. N. F. Bel'chikov (Moscow, 1974), p. 314.

3. As noted by I. Gurvich, *Proza Chekhova (chelovek i deistvitel'nost')* (Moscow, 1970), p. 6.

4. Chekhov's characters have in fact been discussed intelligently in this way by W. H. Bruford, *Chekhov and His Russia: A Sociological Study* (London: Routledge and Kegan Paul, 1948).

5. Preface to Anton Chekhov, *Peasants and Other Stories.* (Garden City, N.Y.: Doubleday, 1956), p. ix.

6. Chekhov devotes far less attention to heredity, the other factor that influences character. This seems less a matter of his discounting it than a result of the limitations of the short story form: unlike the novel, there is simply not enough space to follow the destinies of several generations of a family. Still, in his longer works like "Three Years" and "My Life" we do have a clear sense of the heroes' struggle with their own heredity.

7. "The Slave's Son," in *The Lonely Voice: A Study of the Short Story* (Cleveland and New York: World, 1962), p. 88.

8. The notion of the journey as Egorushka's learning process is developed at some length in Jerome H. Katsell's "Cexov's 'The Steppe' Revisited," *Slavic and East European Journal* 22 (Fall 1978): 313-323.

9. "O nekotorykh osobennostiakh realizma A. P. Chekhova," in *Russkaia zhurnalistika i literatura XIX v,* ed. E. G. Babaev and B. I. Esin (Moscow, 1979), p. 141.

10. Boris Eikhenbaum, "Pushkin i Tolstoi," in *O proze: sbornik statei* (Leningrad, 1969), p. 176.

11. See, for example, I. P. Lyskov, *A. P. Chekhov v ponimanii kritiki* (Moscow, 1905), p. 53; Somerset Maugham, *The Summing Up* (Garden City, N.Y.: Doubleday, 1938), pp. 208-209; D. S. Mirsky, *A History of Russian Literature From Its Beginnings to 1900,* ed. Francis J. Whitfield (New York: Vintage Books, 1958), p. 377.

6

Harvey Pitcher

CHEKHOV'S HUMOUR

Chekhov told his last comic story on the evening before he died. He was staying with his wife, Olga Knipper, in a hotel at Badenweiler in the Black Forest. "That evening," writes Knipper,

> while we were talking, I missed the gong for dinner, and a servant brought me up something to eat. It was then that Anton Pavlovich began to invent a story of how the guests at a well-to-do health resort gather one evening, tired out after a day spent on various kinds of sporting activities, rich, well-fed Englishmen and Americans, all greedily looking forward to a satisfying dinner, when—horror of horrors—it turns out that the chef has disappeared. . . . And what an effect this blow to the stomach would have on all those well-fed, spoilt people.[1]

This is a story that comes readily to mind when one is trying to pinpoint the distinctive qualities of Chekhov's humour. He was not an Oscar Wilde figure striving to think up witty things to say which other people remembered and wrote down for posterity. He was not a raconteur, smoothly delivering the set story of the kind that begins: "A Russian, an American and an Englishman were standing one day outside the Moscow Kremlin . . ."; and we have it on Gorkii's authority that "coarse anecdotes never amused him."[2] Abstract humour—the verbal and logical gymnastics of a Lewis Carroll—seems not to have amused him either, although he did indulge a mild taste for puns ("I've now become a Marxist," he explained to everyone after selling the copyright of his works to the publisher A. F. Marks in 1899). No, Chekhov's humour, as on that occasion at Badenweiler, was much more improvised, more spontaneously inventive, and very much *person*-oriented.

The story of the disappearing chef is helpful, too, as a reminder that

Chekhov did not lose his sense of humour as he grew older. It would be odd, one might think, if he had; but the obvious contrast between Chekhov's writings in the 1880s and the 1890s, taken in conjunction with the steady decline in his health, may tempt one to think otherwise. Reading Knipper's account of Chekhov's last story, one is transported straight back to the comic world created by the "Chekhonte" stories of 1880-1888. Ivan Bunin, who knew him well only during the last five years of his life, recalled that an atmosphere of "jokes, laughter and even pranks" surrounded the sick Chekhov, and that even when they were alone together Chekhov "frequently laughed in his infectious way, loved joking, making up all manner of things, inventing ridiculous names; as soon as he was feeling better, he was tirelessly resourceful in that department."[3] There is an obvious continuity between the schoolboy Chekhov who was "renowned for his skill in making fun of the masters" and whose popular turns included "comic lectures by aged professors,"[4] and the adult Chekhov who so thoroughly undermined the teaching profession in his portrayal of Serebriakov in *Uncle Vania* (1897), Belikov in "The Man in a Case" (1898), and Kulygin in *Three Sisters* (1901)—just as Chekhov the practical joker and comic master of ceremonies of the mid-1880s is obviously the same person as the post-1900 Chekhov of whom Bunin tells the following story. The two of them were walking home together one evening from Yalta to Chekhov's house at Autka. Chekhov had been ill and was walking very slowly with his eyes shut.

We were walking past a balcony. Behind the canvas awning there was a light and female figures were silhouetted. Suddenly he opened his eyes and said very loudly: "Have you heard? Isn't it terrible? Bunin's been murdered! At the house of a Tatar woman in Autka!" I stopped in amazement and he quickly whispered: "Not a word! Tomorrow the whole of Yalta will be talking about Bunin's murder."[5]

Where does one find the comic Chekhov? One finds him in his works: very obviously and directly in the comic stories of 1880-1888 and the one-act farces or vaudevilles of 1888-1891; rather less obviously and directly, as this essay will show, in the later plays and stories. One finds him in his letters, some of the liveliest and wittiest ever written in Russian, especially those of the "middle" years, when he was traveling widely and meeting many different people. One might expect to find him also in the vast number of memoirs about Chekhov, but a deadly seriousness seems to have settled like a shroud on all but a handful of his contemporaries when they sat down to commit their recollections of the Great Writer to paper. From a general study of his life Chekhov emerges as someone who preferred the company of people who were lively and amusing, unpredictable and good fun, and who were not inclined to take themselves too seriously or to attach great importance to their own celebrity; someone who enjoyed comic banter and was forever inventing comic nicknames for himself and other people, assigning them comic roles and weaving comic fantasies around them; and who seems to have had his own distinctive conversational style: a somewhat un-Russian style, since he was not rambling and verbose, but laconic, with an offbeat, understated sense of humour.

Like the painter whose eye is always attracted to certain scenes, Chekhov the writer-observer could not help being drawn to certain comic elements in people and situations. He was especially attracted to the odd and incongruous. Physical incongruities caught his eye. One can be sure that the writer in whose fiction a spreading waistline is always the first sign of spiritual degeneration would not have missed the opportunity of describing to Knipper in loving detail the bulging tummies of all those "rich, well-fed Englishmen and Americans." Of a lady doctor he once wrote: "She's an obese, bloated lump of flesh. Strip her naked, paint her green, and she'd be a marsh frog." [6] The lady happened to be Nabokov's great-aunt, a person of impeccable character and good works, and Nabokov never forgave Chekhov for his "incredibly coarse outburst." [7] Chekhov could not have foreseen that his letter would one day become public property, but it is worth commenting that he could be very caustic about people behind their backs, while maintaining a facade of polite friendliness.

If Chekhov's humour is usually more subtle than that, it still has very much to do with people. In Yalta he was amused to hear of an old Tatar who had died at the age of 127—having married at the age of 125; [8] or to read in the newspaper (he was an avid newspaper reader) of a certain merchant Babkin, living in the provincial town of Samara, who had left all his money for a monument to be erected to the German philosopher Hegel. [9] In the summer of 1902 Chekhov was delighted to make the acquaintance of an English governess, Lily Glassby, who is thought to have been the prototype of Charlotta Ivanovna in *The Cherry Orchard* (1903). According to K. S. Stanislavskii, she was

a small, thin creature with two long girl's pigtails and wearing a man's suit. . . . She was on hail-fellow-well-met terms with Anton Pavlovich, much to the writer's delight. They would meet every day and tell one another the most outrageous nonsense. For example, Chekhov would assure the Englishwoman that in his youth he had been a Turk, that he had his own harem, that he would be returning shortly to his native country to become a pasha, and would then summon her to join him. As if to show her gratitude, the agile English gymnast would then jump onto his shoulders, and settling herself there would greet all the passers-by on Anton Pavlovich's behalf, i.e., she would take his hat off his head and doff it, adding in clownishly comical broken Russian: "Gut mornink! Gut mornink!" (*zdlas'te! zdlas'te! zdlas'te!*) Then she would give Chekhov's head a jerk as a sign of greeting. [10]

With Lily Glassby, Chekhov was in his comic element.

The story of the chef would have been very much at home, then, among the vast output of stories Chekhov wrote between 1880 and 1888. These

early writings are a rag bag, a lucky dip. Apart from stories and sketches—
often, but by no means always, comic, since the young Chekhov was
nothing if not versatile—you may come up with literary parodies, comic
calendars, diaries, questionnaires, aphorisms, advertisements, and captions
to cartoons. You must be prepared to find yourself clutching items for
which even the adjective "schoolboyish" seems charitable, like the one
from "Problems of a Mad Mathematician" (1882): "If my mother-in-law is
75 and my wife is 42, what time is it?" (I, 125). The graduate writing a
doctoral thesis on the importance of the "Hamlet" theme in Chekhov's
works will have to take due note of this little space-filler from 1881:

A performance of *Hamlet* is taking place.
"Ophelia!" yells Hamlet. "O nymph! in thy orisons . . ."
"Your right moustache has come off!" whispers Ophelia.
"In thy orisons . . . What?"
"Your right moustache has come off!"
"Blaaaast . . . be all my sins remembered." (I, 104-105)

If Chekhov's early writing has so far received less critical attention than it
deserves, this is partly because of its uneven quality and partly because of
the sheer volume of material for consideration. Yet clearly this is where one
must look to find the origins, serious as well as comic, of Chekhov's mature
art. At their best, moreover, the early comic stories still stand up very well a
hundred years later. The following draws attention to four different kinds
of comic story, briefly outlining one or two outstanding examples of each,
and attempting to suggest by illustration something of their comic quality.

Let us suppose that Chekhov had not died at Badenweiler but had
recovered and said to himself: "that idea about the chef disappearing
wasn't a bad one. I shall write it up in the style of one of my stories from the
1880s." How might he have done it?

He might have taken the basic comic situation and elaborated on it with a
wealth of comic detail. What made Knipper laugh so much was not presum-
ably the simple fact of the chef's disappearance, but how Chekhov
described the varying reactions of all the diners. He would certainly have
been tempted to indulge his taste for inventing comic names, though even
his invention might have faltered at the prospect of finding comic names for
Englishmen and Americans. This is comedy of *situation*.

A good example is the story "Orator" (1886), an original variation on the
theme of comic mistaken identity. The hero has a typical Chekhovian comic
name, Zapoikin (from *zapoi*, drinking bout/orgy). Zapoikin "possesses a
rare gift for making impromptu speeches at weddings, anniversaries and
funerals. . . . He always speaks eloquently and at great length, so that
sometimes, particularly at merchant weddings, the only way to stop him is
to summon the police." On this occasion he is delivering a graveside oration

when he realizes half-way through that he has got the wrong man, and the man he is talking about is standing right opposite him (V, 431).

Another example is "From the Diary of a Violent-Tempered Man" (1887). This is a sophisticated version of by far the most common kind of Chekhov comic story—the story of Mock Romance. In these stories Chekhov (or Chekhonte) gives the impression of a man bent on undermining single-handedly the whole concept of romantic love. The foolishness of his young men is matched only by the silliness of his young girls. Chekhonte explores every comic possibility of such themes as broken engagements and abortive proposals (typically, the hero ruins his chances by hiccupping at the opera).[11] Mothers, mothers-in-law, and matchmakers loom large in this world. Once married, however, these Chekhonte wives and husbands lose no time in striving to be unfaithful to their partners. Everyone wonders how a fat, red-nosed old husband has managed to keep his pretty young wife faithful for so long. The answer is simple: he has spread the rumour that she is sleeping with the dreaded local chief of police.[12]

What distinguishes a story like "From the Diary of a Violent-Tempered Man" from, say, "The Orator," is that the comic situation is used more as a vehicle for comedy of characterisation. The hero is not quick-tempered at all, although he would like to be. He describes himself as "a serious person with a philosophical turn of mind." An accountant by profession, he is writing a thesis on the dog-tax, so that whenever he hears a dog barking he is reminded of his thesis. He is spending the summer with his mother in a dacha and is being hotly pursued by all the marriageable girls (referred to as "the variegated young ladies") and their mothers from the surrounding dachas. To the quick-tempered man the young ladies all seem so much alike that he cannot tell Nadenka from Varenka or Varenka from Mashenka. Worried by the quick-tempered man's silence, Nadenka (or Varenka) begs him to say something to her: "I tried to think of some popular topic she might be capable of understanding. So after much thought I said: 'The felling of forests is causing enormous havoc in Russia.' " (VI, 296). And here is Chekhov's violent-tempered man's description of a romantic summer evening: "The revolting moon was creeping up from behind the shrubbery. The air was still, with an unpleasant smell of fresh hay" (VI, 297). Almost caught by one of the variegated young ladies, the quick-tempered man decides that he will have to explain to her that he does not believe in marriage.

To avoid going too deeply into the subject and in order to be as concise as possible, I put things briefly into their historical perspective. I spoke about marriage among the Hindus and Egyptians, then came on to more recent times with a few of Schopenhauer's ideas. Mashenka listened attentively, but suddenly she felt obliged to interrupt me with a curious *non sequitur. "Nicolas*, give me a kiss!" I was so embarrassed I didn't know what to say to her. She repeated her demand. So there was nothing else for it—I got up and put my lips to her elongated face, experiencing the same sensation I had as a child when I was made to kiss my dead grandmother's face at her funeral. (VI, 301)

A second possibility is that Chekhov might have developed the chef's story in a more serious, satirical way. He might have concentrated the reader's attention on the contrasts and relationships between the rich tourists and the hotel servants. New characters might have been introduced: an obsequious head waiter, for example, whose manner changes according to the social status of the person he is addressing, whether it be a hotel guest or one of his subordinates.

This is comedy of *subversion*, in the sense that it exposes and holds up to ridicule the whole authoritarian, hierarchical arrangement of society.

Tsarist Russia, of course, was a hierarchical society *par excellence*, with its Table of Ranks whereby all civil servants—army and navy officers as well as government employees—were graded from 1 to 14, with corresponding ranks and special titles to be used when addressing them. After stories of Mock Romance, stories satirising the huge Tsarist bureaucracy are the most common among Chekhov's early stories, particularly in evidence in 1883 and 1884. Chekhov satirises the absurd outward conventions—the wearing of official decorations, the ritual paying of courtesy calls, and the signing of the departmental chief's visitors' book at Easter and the New Year. He satirises red tape—the needless exchange of official letters which benefits no one except the paper manufacturers,[13] the difficulty an ordinary citizen experiences in transferring a single rouble by post.[14] More seriously, he satirises the inner defects of the bureaucracy—the perennial Russian temptation, familiar from Gogol's *The Inspector General*, to ask for and to accept bribes ("You seem to have left something behind in my hand," says the official in "Mayonnaise," 1883, to a petitioner when his chief appears at an awkward moment), the patronage and time-serving and the absence of self-criticism. In a rank-conscious situation, individuals quickly slip into the roles that are expected of them: the departmental chief can scarcely believe his eyes when he sees on a tram a man holding forth loudly and belligerently about politics to his fellow passengers—and recognises in him a member of his staff, a poor spineless creature whose only role in the office is to pick up handkerchiefs and to wish his chief the compliments of the season.[15] Rank-consciousness inevitably breeds arrogance toward those below and servility toward those above in the social hierarchy. As the hero of "The Professional Pianist" (1885) explains, "while you're free or studying or loafing about, you can have a drink with a Russian, pat him on the stomach and pay court to his daughter, but as soon as you're in the slightest degree subordinate to him, then you've got to know your place" (IV, 208). If anyone *is* moved to protest, the attempt is likely to end in bathos. The "office spokesman" becomes so tongue-tied in the presence of his chief that he utters not a word of protest and instead is bullied into buying five lottery tickets for twenty-five roubles.[16] Here is the end of a very typical, if unremarkable, story of this kind in which comedy of subversion is combined with a comic twist: the young men from a government department are having a celebration lunch on a public holiday, and one of them is making a fiery speech about the ills of society:

Everywhere there is theft, embezzlement, pilfering, plundering, extortion. Drunkenness is universal. Oppression is rife. And the suffering, the innocent victims! Let us take pity on them, let us shed a tear. . . ." (The orator's voice begins to quaver.) "Let us shed a tear and drink a toast to . . ."

At that moment the door squeaked and someone came in. We looked around and saw a very small man with a large bald patch and an avuncular smile on his lips. We'd have known that figure anywhere! On entering, he paused to hear the end of the toast:

"—Let us shed a tear and drink a toast," continued our orator, raising his voice, "to the health of our guardian and benefactor, to the dearly beloved Head of our Department! Hurrah!" (II, 81)[17]

Several stories in this "subversive" genre have become well known. "The Fat and Thin One" (1883) tells how two schoolboy friends meet by chance in middle age in a railway station. All goes well until the No. 8 discovers that his friend is now a No. 3. In "The Chameleon" (1884) the attitude of the police inspector to the stray dog changes constantly according to who he thinks the owner is, while "Sergeant Prishibeev" (1885) depicts a retired staff-sergeant who subscribes to the curious philosophy that rules are not there to stop you doing things; you can only do things if a rule says you can. Both characters have acquired literary immortality in Russia. These last two stories in particular are not so much comic anecdotes as psychological studies in miniature, studies in the hierarchy mentality. They are very subversive, and they certainly do not apply only to Russia in the nineteenth century, nor indeed only to Russia.

A third possibility is that Chekhov might have taken the plot and given it an unexpected ending, a comic twist. Thus, it turns out that the chef has not disappeared at all but is lying dead drunk under the kitchen table, an empty brandy bottle by his side. This is comedy of *surprise*. You lead the reader in a certain direction, you build up expectations, then suddenly you turn everything on its head.

Between 30 and 40 Chekhov stories fit this category, some more original and successful than others. In "A Case from a Lawyer's Practice" (1883) a brilliant defence counsel is defending an obvious crook. His eloquence is so moving that he reduces everyone to tears, including the jury, the judge, and even the prosecutor. "Members of the jury," he winds up in his closing speech, "can you dare as human beings to say that this man is guilty?"

At this point the accused himself could bear it no longer. Now it was his turn to start crying. He blinked, burst into tears and began fidgeting restlessly. "All right!" he blurted out, interrupting the defence counsel. "All right! I *am* guilty! It was me done the burglary and the fraud. . . ."(II, 88)

A more sophisticated example is "A Story Without a Title" (1888). Like the defence counsel and like Zapoikin in "The Orator," its hero, the abbot of a remote monastery, possesses a marvelous gift of eloquence which gives him limitless power over his monks. He decides to go alone on a visit to the town in the hope of saving souls. Three months later he returns, looking a broken man, gathers all the monks around him, describes to them with his usual eloquence all the unspeakable vices that he has come across in the town, and retires to the cell for the night. Next morning, the story concludes, when he came out of his cell, "there was not a single monk left in the monastery. They had all run away to the town" (VI, 458).

A fourth possibility is that Chekhov might have developed the chef's story in an absurd manner. This is less easy to imagine, but let us suppose that the chef is some kind of eccentric and has gone off for some wildly improbable reason of his own. Within this comedy of the *absurd* one is subsuming a whole cluster of rather similar adjectives, ranging from "incongruous" and "ridiculous" to "bizarre" and "grotesque."

A well-known example is "The Daughter of Albion" (1883). She is the very superior English governess who has lived in Russia for ten years but still does not speak a word of the language. There is a grotesque physical description of her: her nose looked like a hook, "she was wearing a white muslin dress, through which her yellow, scraggy shoulders showed quite clearly," and according to her employer, there was "a kind of rotten smell about her." She is fishing in complete silence with her Russian employer on the river bank when his line becomes entangled. The only way to free it is to take off all his clothes and plunge in. He tries to persuade the Daughter of Albion to disappear from sight by pointing toward the bushes, but she concludes that he is making improper advances. She is not in the least embarrassed, however, by the sight of her employer standing there "in a state of nature." On the contrary, "a haughty, contemptuous smile passed over her yellow face" (II, 198). The implication seems to be that this is no more than she would have expected from these barbaric Russians.

This story is apt to provoke conflicting reactions. I have known English readers who find it deeply offensive and accuse Chekhov of caricaturing and slandering the English governess in a most shameless and shameful way. Gorkii, however, took the opposite view. The unfeeling public might laugh when they read the story, but what they failed to see was that Chekhov's real target was the Russian landowner, who had behaved so abominably "towards a lonely, alienated human being."[18] Neither of these views seems to me remotely tenable. Both characters are unsympathetic: it's a case of "six of one and half a dozen of the other." It is true generally of absurd comedy that it is unsentimental, even brutal: it eliminates the element of human sympathy. What appealed to Chekhov in the story was the grotesque absurdity of the situation, which is presented in very striking and memorable terms.

Finally, let us consider another famous little story, "The Death of a Government Clerk" (1883) in which comedy of subversion is combined with comedy of the absurd. A minor civil servant sneezes over a general's bald head at the opera and pesters him with apologies until finally the general throws him out of his office. So far this is comedy of subversion, but the ending moves the story on to the level of the absurd: "Without seeing anything, without hearing anything, he staggered backwards to the door, reached the street, and wandered off. He entered his home mechanically, without taking off his uniform, lay down on the sofa, and . . . died" (II, 166).

This reminds one of a passage in the reminiscences of Chekhov's friend, Tatiana Shchepkina-Kupernik. She and Chekhov were returning from a walk when they were overtaken by a storm and had to take shelter in an empty barn.

Holding his wet umbrella, Chekhov said: "One ought to write a vaudeville in which two people are waiting in an empty barn for the rain to pass. They laugh and joke, dry their umbrellas, declare their love for one another—then the rain passes, the sun comes out—and suddenly he dies of a heart attack!"[19]

Shchepkina-Kupernik threw up her hands in predictable horror at this suggestion, but it does seem as if a streak of "black" humour was one element in Chekhov's comic make-up.

It is usual to think of 1888 as a watershed in Chekhov's literary development. Almost overnight, it seems, the "immature literary apprentice" of 1880-1888 is miraculously transformed into the "serious mature artist" of 1888-1904. That 1888 was a watershed in Chekhov's literary career is indisputable, but whether the year is particularly significant in his development as a *writer* is another question. The more interesting, mysterious turning-points seem to have occurred in the years 1885-1887. The accepted division between "early" and "mature" Chekhov is too neat and artificial: it absolves the critic from the need to look for the continuities in Chekhov's writing and to see his work as a whole. Its effect is particularly unfortunate in the case of Chekhov's comic stories. These are too easily dismissed as little more than an expression of youthful high spirits, as something he soon outgrew, although it would be more accurate to say that he outgrew the kind of journals that would have been willing to publish them. Comic touches, it would be agreed, can often be found in Chekhov's later work, but the convenient assumption is that in 1888 Chekhonte died a natural death. In the following an argument is made in favour of greater continuity, and it is suggested that the early comic stories do feed his later work at several points and in unexpected ways.

Let us consider in turn the four kinds of comedy outlined above, starting with comedy of situation. In one particular area, of course, Chekhonte remained very much alive after 1888. In February of that year Chekhov sat down to write *The Bear*, the first of his very popular one-act farce-vaudevilles. This was followed by *The Proposal* (1888), *A Tragic Role* (1889), *The Wedding* (1889), and *The Anniversary* (1891). Although they contain an assortment of comic ingredients—parody, slapstick, misunderstandings, the absurd, the grotesque, irony, and social satire—the vaudevilles still belong to the genre of "comedy of situation." This is because, as Vera Gottlieb comments on *The Wedding*, the emphasis for an audience is "not on mystery and surprise, but on the working-out of a known situation . . . not so much on *what* will happen next, as on *how* it will happen."[20] In the most successful farces, *The Bear* and *The Proposal*, as in the best of the comedy of situation stories, the situation itself opens the door to comedy of characterisation. There is a comic psychological inevitability about the way Smirnov in *The Bear* fails to live up to his misogynistic principles and Popova abandons the role of the faithful widow. Popova's curtain-line, "Tell them in the stables—Toby gets no oats today," neatly echoing the opening scene in which the mere mention of Toby's name was enough to send Popova into floods of tears because her husband had loved him so, is not an unexpected comic denouement but rather an extremely effective way of rounding off this psychological process.

By rights the post-1888 Chekhov should have turned his back on the broad humour of the vaudevilles; but although they undermine any simple division of Chekhov into "early" and "mature," "frivolous" and "serious," it is hard not to see the vaudevilles more as an extension of the early stories than as forerunners of the later stories and plays. From comedy of situation stories in which the dialogue predominated it was but a short step to the vaudevilles; *A Tragic Role*, *The Wedding*, and *The Anniversary* are in fact all dramatised adaptations of earlier stories.[21] It is in the elements of irony and the absurd that the greatest continuity is to be looked for.

Nor is it easy to find in Chekhov's fiction of 1888-1904 a strong line of development from the early comedy of situation stories. It is possible to think of "Anna on the Neck" (1895) and "The Man in a Case" (1898) as comedies of situation/characterisation, but in both stories the satirical edge is uncomfortably sharp for comedy; only "The Darling" (1898) seems a permissible candidate. Yet there is an important line of continuity to be traced here: not, however, with Chekhov the man. Chekhov the writer may have given up comic fantasising and mock romancing; Chekhov the man certainly did not.

Nowhere is this more evident than in his relations with Lika Mizinova. The beautiful Lika was nineteen when Chekhov first made her acquaintance in the autumn of 1889.[22] In his letters to her, Chekhov can be serious when giving advice on health matters or begging her to stop smoking, but where feelings are concerned—we are back in the familiar world of Mock

Romance. "I love you passionately, like a tiger, and offer you my hand." "Lika, it's not you I love so ardently! In you I love my former sufferings and my vanished youth." "As soon as you wrote that my letters do not bind me to anything, I breathed a sigh of relief, and here I am writing you a long letter without any fears that some auntie will read these lines and force me to marry a monster like you."[23] Chekhov/Chekhonte embroiled Lika in a web of imaginary suitors of whom he was supposedly jealous. To one, Trofim, he even addresses a letter. Hasn't Trofim heard that Lika belongs to him and they already have two children? If Trofim does not stop running after Lika, he will shove a corkscrew up an unmentionable part of Trofim's anatomy. The letter is signed "Lika's lover" (November 1892).

What did Lika feel when she read a letter like that, knowing how far Chekhov was in fact from being her lover, let alone the father of her children? When Chekhov does very occasionally express himself with apparent sincerity—when he writes, for example, that Lika has turned his head so much that he's "even prepared to believe twice two are five" (November 23, 1892)—what weight can be attached to his words? Here Chekhov's sense of humour leads us straight to a very central problem— perhaps *the* central problem—in interpreting Chekhov the man: what kind of relations did he have with people close to him, especially his "women"? In inventing comic relationships and mock romances, was he deliberately avoiding "straight" emotional relationships? Was he using his sense of humour, in other words, as a means of distancing himself from other people?

When one turns to comedy of subversion, one can see a much stronger line of continuity within Chekhov's fiction itself. At their best, as in "The Chameleon" and "Sergeant Prishibeev," the early subversive stories make a psychological point: that within an authoritarian, hierarchical system both individuals themselves and the relations between individuals become absurdly and harmfully distorted. In the later Chekhov this theme broadens out into one of his most distinctive preoccupations, his concern for freedom. Chekhov points a sharply critical finger at all those characters who interfere with the freedom of others. Such people are self-centered, self-satisfied, and self-important. Not only are they themselves warped as individuals; they are also apt to make life extremely unpleasant for the people around them.

Take Belikov, the teacher of classics in "The Man in a Case." Of all Chekhov's later stories this is the one which in Ronald Hingley's opinion "shows most resemblance to *Chekhonte*, especially in everything which concerns the central character."[24] Simon Karlinsky describes Belikov as "a companion figure" to Sergeant Prishibeev. He is "both the reverse of Prishibeev's coin and his Siamese twin in the universal political landscape. Where Prishibeev needs to run other people's lives, Belikov requires that he be guided by rules and regulations devised by others. Not only does he require it for himself, but he also needs to force everyone around him to conform to restrictions imposed from the outside, no matter how useless or nonsensical these restrictions may be."[25] Belikov is more of a figure of fun than Prishibeev, deriving absurd pleasure from mouthing the Greek word *antropos* and insisting on carrying an umbrella at all times of year. He is apprehensive where Prishibeev is openly aggressive; yet with his authoritarian, repressive attitude to life he succeeds in terrorising the local town community just as thoroughly as Prishibeev does the neighbouring peasants.

An umbrella is symbolically associated with two more of these "anti-freedom" figures: the father in "My Life" (1896) and Serebriakov in *Uncle Vania*. When first seen returning from a walk on a hot day, Serebriakov is still clad in an overcoat, gloves, and galoshes, and is carrying an umbrella. Not for a moment does he doubt that his academic status, his former academic status, gives him the right to reorganise other people's lives. The professor, at least, is thwarted in his plans, whereas Natasha in *Three Sisters* succeeds brilliantly in reorganising other people's lives to suit her own selfish schemes and ambitions.

Particularly interesting is the case of Lida Volchaninova, the elder sister in "The House with an Attic" (1896). In contrast to all the characters so far mentioned, Lida's activities appear much more useful and unselfish: she is helping to organise better medical facilities for the peasants, and she herself teaches peasant children. Yet she, too, interferes with the freedom of others, bullying her mother and younger sister, and breaking up the love affair between her sister and the narrator. Does it matter very much if Lida is responsible for saving the life of just one peasant mother in childbirth? To Chekhov, clearly, it does matter. "Good" actions are worthless—and may in the long run become positively evil—if they are not accompanied by the right motives. Lida, as Karlinsky suggests, is well on the way to becoming a political fanatic.[26]

In his treatment of these later characters, Chekhov was more daringly subversive than he had been in his early stories. There the context was the Tsarist bureaucracy, which had long been a permissible target for mild social satire. In his depiction of the schoolmaster Belikov, the architect father in "My Life," Serebriakov the retired university professor, and Natasha the successful social climber, Chekhov was undermining the kind of solidly respectable middle-class people who form the backbone, and shape the values, of any educated society. Particularly daring was his treatment of Lida, the kind of figure whose "good works" would automatically have received the seal of approval of contemporary progressive liberal opinion. It would be wrong, however, to see these subversive portraits in purely social or political terms; Chekhov's target is more the authoritarian, hierarchical tendency to be found in each one of us, the tendency to feel that we have a right to organise other people and to tell them what to do.

Chekhov's early subversive stories have a brittle, heartless quality: he is not so much amused as exasperated by these downtrodden civil servants with their complete lack of self-respect. He sees them entirely from the outside, without compassion. The same is true of Belikov and his like. They are denied the right that Chekhov grants to many of his characters—some of them, on the face of it, far more disreputable, like the protagonists of "Horse Thieves" (1890)—the right, that is, to be seen from their own point of view. Belikov, after all, had a life of his own; to him everything he did seemed plausible and natural. But Chekhov makes no attempt to enter into his world. When Belikov is pushed downstairs by his fiancée's brother, his reaction reminds one immediately of the ending of "The Death of a Government Clerk." Returning home, he first removed his fiancée's portrait from his desk, "then got into bed and never rose from it again." So Belikov is unceremoniously bundled out of life and the narrator comments that it is really "a great pleasure to bury people like Belikov."

Turning now to comedy of surprise, one can find another interesting line of continuity between the early and later stories. Of course, the surprise ending as such, the comic twist, has disappeared. This is an obviously contrived literary effect; the later Chekhov would have dismissed it, saying: "That's not how things happen in real life." On the other hand, what you do find in the later stories is a very highly developed sense of irony. Story after story turns on some kind of ironic reversal—often the plot seems to have suggested itself to him in that way.[27] One can choose examples at random. In "The Grasshopper" (1892) Olga Ivanovna spends all her time collecting "remarkable" people, only to discover—too late—that the one truly remarkable person in her life was her very "ordinary" doctor-husband. Dr. Ragin in "Ward No. 6" (1892) finds himself incarcerated in the very ward that he has presided over with such calm indifference for so many years. In "Anna on the Neck"—the title itself is ironical—the young wife who has been so scared of her pompous careerist husband turns the tables on him when she realises that she is in a position to tell *him* what to do. From the plays one can point to Natasha, the diffident visitor of Act I of *Three Sisters* who becomes the domestic tyrant of Act IV, and to Lopakhin in *The Cherry Orchard*, buying the estate on which all his ancestors had been serfs.

As well as ironic reversals of plot, there are ironic shifts in the sympathy we feel for Chekhov's heroes and heroines. Some characters, like Belikov or Olga Ivanovna in "The Grasshopper," enter his fiction "ready-made," and the degree of sympathy, or rather non-sympathy, which we feel for them develops predictably; but often this is not so. From the neutral opening description of Matvei Savvich in "Peasant Wives" (1891) as "a serious, business-like man who knows his own worth" one could not guess that this character will slowly be revealed as one of Chekhov's most odious villains; Chekhov here is deliberately holding something back. At the start of "Ionych" (1898) the Turkins are described as "the most educated and talented family" in the town. True, this is no more than the general opinion, but it sounds like a genuine recommendation and we accept it at face value; only later do we come to revise our judgment. Or the process may work in reverse. We are not likely to feel any sympathy for Gurov at the start of "The Lady with a Lapdog" (1899), but by the end of the story he has become a sympathetic, if not a pathetic, figure. In "Ionych" there is a double shift of sympathy. The reader warms at first to the idealistic young country doctor, who desperately wants to experience love and blinds himself to the heroine's shortcomings, whereas she forfeits sympathy by frivolously rejecting him out of an artificial belief that she should devote her life to music. Four years later the positions have been reversed. The heroine has changed for the better: she sees the true value of the love she turned down and the unimportance of her own musical ambitions; but the hero is no longer the man he once was, and his idealism has been replaced by a complacent materialism.

To find the origins of this complex use of irony one would need to trace a line of continuity back through the vaudevilles to those early comic stories in which Chekhov deliberately set out to surprise his readers, misleading them and setting up false expectations in their minds.

Finally, we come to comedy of the absurd. This surfaces again unexpectedly in Chekhov's four major plays, especially in *Three Sisters* and *The Cherry Orchard*. There is a curious and striking link between Chekhov's very early writing and *Three Sisters*. In March-April 1882 he compiled a weekly comic *Calendar* for the Moscow magazine *Budil'nik* (*Alarm Clock*) (I, 143-158). For each day he composed two entries. The first was devoted to "outstanding events, meteorology, prophecies, world history, commercial information, useful advice, prescriptions, etc."; the second offered the reader a comic menu of the day (such items as "stewed Adam's apples," I, 150). Among the events and prophecies, one encounters the following: "In Tambov [a well-known provincial railway junction, a place of extreme ordinariness] a volcano is going to erupt" (I, 148); "In Berdichev [an important commercial centre in the Ukraine] the refraction of light will take place" (I, 148); "On the island of Borneo [here the place is exotic, the event ordinary] there's an outbreak of diptheria" (I, 144). Anyone who is familiar with *Three Sisters* will be reminded of the highly distinctive contributions, or non-contributions, that are made to the dialogue by the old army doctor, Chebutykin. When he first wanders onto the stage, he is copying down in his notebook a prescription from the newspaper to stop hair from falling out. In Act II, still carrying his newspaper, he announces that "Balzac was married in Berdichev," and he follows this up soon after with the information that "in Tsitsikar they've got a smallpox epidemic."

How consciously the 40-year-old Chekhov was recalling the kind of comic item he wrote at the age of 22 would be hard to say. What can be said is that had it not been for his early experience of comic-absurd writing, it is unlikely to have occurred to him to make a character, for example, read out irrelevant scraps of information from a newspaper. Of course, it needed a touch of genius to perceive how dramatically effective this might be. The unexpectedness of this entrance at once fixes the doctor in the audience's mind, while the very incongruity of his comic irrelevancies makes them stand out so sharply that we remember where Balzac was married long after more serious lines have been forgotten.

One might go further and speculate that the unconventional approach to dialogue which Chekhov perfected in his four major plays could only have occurred to someone in whom a taste for the comic-absurd was highly developed. Faced by conventional stage dialogue, so neat and rational and orderly, Chekhov said: that's not what human conversation is like. It's haphazard and unpredictable; people are having a serious discussion, then someone else reads out something totally irrelevant from a newspaper. Natasha remarks innocently of Bobik: "He's an exceptional child." Solenyi replies: "If that child were mine, I'd fry him in a pan and eat him." Or the old servant Ferapont starts telling ridiculous stories about a rope stretched right across Moscow, or about some merchants eating pancakes. "They say one of them died after eating forty. Maybe forty, maybe fifty."

It is as if Chekhonte had been given *carte blanche* to wander through the play and liven things up at odd moments. The timing of his appearances can be breathtakingly unexpected. Masha is distraught after Vershinin's departure. Then Chekhonte in the person of Kulygin puts on the false beard and moustache that he had confiscated in school and pretends to be the German master. Masha even manages a smile. To moments such as these, when the serious and the absurd are daringly juxtaposed, the overworked adjective "Chekhovian" seems for once appropriate.

If Chekhonte appears only at odd moments in *Three Sisters*, in *The Cherry Orchard* he is seldom absent for long. He is the obvious inspiration behind Simeonov-Pishchik and Epikhodov. The improbable name Simeonov-Pishchik is a combination of the very ordinary, respectable Simeonov and the absurd Pishchik, "Squeaker," a name that occurs in a comic Chekhonte sketch.[28] Pishchik is farcically obsessed by money. He describes himself as "an old horse": his constitution and his appetite are horse-like, and his father used to joke that the ancient stock of the Simeonov-Pishchiks was descended from the horse that Caligula made into a senator. When Epikhodov first appears, he drops the bunch of flowers he is carrying and is unable to stop his new boots from squeaking. One morning he wakes to find a huge spider sitting on his chest. Though prone to such accidents—"I'm used to it. I can even raise a smile"—he also has pretensions to culture which Chekhonte comically deflates. It is Chekhonte who creates the memorable image of the governess Charlotta, reminiscent of the strikingly visual portrayal of the Daughter of Albion, with her man's peaked cap, her shot-gun, and the cucumber that she takes out of her pocket and starts to munch. He has also had a hand in creating Gaev, with his sweets, his speeches, and his imaginary billiard shots, and Firs, muttering to himself and answering questions no one has asked.

Chekhonte is responsible, too, for all the comic stage business in *The Cherry Orchard*. He makes Pishchik pour out the pills from Ranevskaia's medicine bottle onto the palm of his hand, blow on them, and wash them all down with kvass. When Epikhodov is not dropping something, he is knocking something over or squashing something flat. Chekhonte presides over the comic love triangle formed by Iasha, Duniasha, and Epikhodov. He stage-manages Charlotta's conjuring tricks and her ventriloquism. He is the instigator of lost galoshes and of sticks that come down over the wrong person's head.

Chekhov himself, of course, called *The Cherry Orchard* a "comedy." He was prompted to do so by fears that Stanislavskii would make the play too lachrymose. These fears were amply justified, since Stanislavskii decided at once that the play was not a comedy but a tragedy. It is part of the fascination of *The Cherry Orchard*, however, that it resists all attempts to give it a simple label. Like the moment when Masha is confronted by Kulygin in false beard and moustache, the play as a whole is a wonderfully daring mixture of the serious-moving and the comic-absurd. For that we have Chekhonte to thank. It is fitting that in Chekhov's last play the wheel has turned full circle and the irrepressible humorist of the 1880s has once more come into his own.

NOTES

1. V. Ia. Vilenkin, ed., *Ol'ga Leonardovna Knipper-Chekhova* (Moscow, 1972), I, 65-66.

2. S. N. Golubov et al., eds., *A. P. Chekhov v vospominaniiakh sovremennikov* (Moscow, 1960), p. 509.

3. *Ibid.*, pp. 532, 534.

4. Ronald Hingley, *A New Life of Anton Chekhov* (London: Oxford University Press, 1976), pp. 15, 24.

5. Golubov, pp. 526-527.

6. Letter to the Chekhovs, July 22, 1888, in A. P. Chekhov, *Polnoe sobranie sochinenii i pisem v 30-ti tomakh. Pis'ma* (Moscow, 1974), II, 299. All subsequent references to Chekhov's works are from this edition and are noted in parentheses in the text by volume and page; references to letters are by addressee and date.

7. Vladimir Nabokov, *Speak, Memory: An Autobiography Revisited* (London: Weidenfeld and Nicolson, rev. ed., 1967), p. 68.

8. Letter to A. S. Suvorin, December 27, 1898.

9. Golubov, p. 523.

10. K. S. Stanislavskii, *Moia zhizn' v iskusstve* (Moscow, 1962), pp. 325-326.

11. "Confessions, or Olia, Zhenia, Zoia" (1882).

12. "At the Post Office" (1883).

13. "A Lot of Paper" (1885).

14. "My Talk with the Postmaster" (1886).

15. "Two in One" (1883).

16. "The Deputy, or a Story About How Dezdemonov Lost 25 Roubles" (1883).

17. "A Story for Which It Is Hard to Find a Title" (1883).

18. Golubov, p. 503.

19. A. K. Kotov, ed., *Chekhov v vospominaniiakh sovremennikov* (Moscow, 1952), p. 260.

20. For a recent study of the vaudevilles, see Vera Gottlieb, *Chekhov and the Vaudeville: A Study of Chekhov's One-Act Plays* (Cambridge, London, New York: Cambridge University Press, 1982), p. 170.

21. *A Tragic Role* is based on "One of Many" (1887); *The Wedding* on "A Wedding with a General" (1884), "Marriage Season" (1881), and "A Marriage of Convenience" (1884); and *The Anniversary* on "A Helpless Creature" (1887).

22. Their subsequent friendship has been sensitively analysed by Virginia Llewellyn Smith in *Anton Chekhov and The Lady with the Dog* (London: Oxford University Press, 1973), pp. 108-120.

23. See letters to Mizinova, June-July 1891; March 27, 1892; June 28, 1892.

24. Ronald Hingley, *Chekhov: A Biographical and Critical Study* (London: George Allen and Unwin, 1950), p. 215.

25. "Introduction: The Gentle Subversive," in *Anton Chekhov's Life and Thoughts*, trans. Michael H. Heim and Simon Karlinsky (Berkeley: University of California Press, 1975), p. 25.

26. *Ibid.*

27. See Chekhov's notebook entries for "Anna on the Neck," "Gooseberries," "The Man in a Case," etc. For an index of the notebook entries for the various stories see, *Polnoe sobranie sochinenii i pisem*, XVII, pp. 520-524.

28. "Visiting Cards" (1886).

PART III

Chekhov's Literary Craftsmanship

7

J. L. Styan

CHEKHOV'S
DRAMATIC TECHNIQUE

As the years pass and as Chekhov's plays are given different treatments and exposed to new and larger audiences, it grows increasingly clear that Chekhov was the complete playwright. In his awareness of the needs of the stage and its actors it might be said that he was also a complete man of the theatre. He held to a minimum of rules for writing a play, and he ruthlessly abandoned others that had been sanctified by centuries of tradition, but he could only do this because he enjoyed a full sense of the theatre. A sense of the theatre embraces not so much its *mechanics* of acting and staging, plotting, and character-drawing as the way a playwright may exactly manipulate an *audience* for its strongest, yet its subtlest and most rewarding, response. This account of the method by which Chekhov put his major plays together, therefore, will emphasize how he made them work in performance. Only once before in the story of the theatre, in the plays of Shakespeare, do we find such a bold sequence of experiments to secure an audience's maximum participation in the workings of the stage. On these grounds alone it is arguable that not only is Chekhov Russia's greatest dramatist and the consummate realist of the modern theatre, but also that he must rank with the two or three best the theatre has known.

We cannot know the limits of Chekhov's skills of the stage, nor exhaust his secrets. As with Shakespeare, the unknown remains constantly to be discovered: each play is worth seeing again, and new insights are possible each time it is played. One reason for this phenomenon may be that Chekhov always works with a multitude of the most delicate details of human behavior, the finely perceived elements of speech and action, and compounds them in so infinite a variety of ways that the dramatic imagination of the spectator is unpredictably expanded. Thus, like the actor and the director, the student of Chekhov's plays must begin to approach them through those details and elements.

His first major play, *The Seagull*, is by no means his most subtle, and it is introduced by two lesser characters, Medvedenko the schoolmaster and Masha the girl he wishes to marry. Yet this play captures its audience immediately on the rise of the curtain with two challenging lines:

Medvedenko   Why do you always wear black?
Masha   I'm in mourning for my life.[1]

The lines catch the audience by surprise, and in performance they echo in the mind through the scene. When, later in the first act, we see Arkadina in light summer clothes, we will be reminded of Masha's dress and Medvedenko's question. Meanwhile, the first decision for the actors must be how to speak the lines. Is Masha tearful and sad, or angry and sarcastic?—two quite opposed notions, and either of them possible. It is especially necessary to see the characters in their setting, in the garden, having returned from a walk on a hot evening. It is a quite romantic setting: this part of Sorin's park near a lake in the moonlight will seem enchanting and beautiful. Does this pair of lovers therefore enter with their arms about one another, and when they sit on the bench do they sit side by side? The ambiguity in the opening lines hardly permits such romantic behavior. In the production of the play at the Moscow Art Theatre in 1898, Konstantin Stanislavskii had Medvedenko and Masha stroll about the stage, the man smoking and cracking nuts. But this too could be wrong, since, although he has been wooing Masha for some time, he surely must not seem to be indifferent to her. How far is their entrance a comic one? Is it intended that they enter with Masha walking a little ahead of Medvedenko, as if she were trying to escape his attentions? He certainly is a bore who complains constantly about his life as an underpaid schoolteacher. In any case we soon learn that Masha has her eye on another man, Konstantin Treplev. Thus, if she is in fact running from him, her remark about being in mourning for her life may be spoken as an irritated rebuff or with a teasing laugh, depending on the degree of comedy perceived in the scene. The truth is that we cannot be sure, in their uneasy relationship with each other and their enigmatic relationship with the spectator, that any of these treatments is intended. Yet none can be ruled out.

Something of each approach is implied, and the audience is intended to be left in tantalizing uncertainty. The element of doubt is characteristic of the basic ingredient with which Chekhov works as a playwright in matters large and small. He sustains an ambiguity in tone and mood, character and incident, for as long as he dares—chiefly to engage his audience in the effort of participation, which will ensure that we have reexperienced as closely as possible the life of his stage, but also to strike a note of indeterminacy that we cannot easily identify as tragic or comic, but that certainly captures the ironic feeling of real life. In the first act of *The Cherry Orchard*, Lopakhin pops his head round the door and moos like a cow at Varia. With no more than this brief signal, Chekhov indicates the miserable situation that spinster finds herself in, aware that the family is in debt and unable to get Lopakhin to make the proposal of marriage that would solve her problems. At the same time, the trick undercuts with our laughter the solemn news that the orchard will be sold that very August. In the next act Ania and Trofimov separate for their "love scene" in the moonlight, but while the romantically inclined Ania waits in anticipation of a kiss, the inept "eternal student" can only make an irrelevant speech to an imaginary crowd of fellow Trofimovs, "Forward! Do not lag behind, friends!", a speech that quite passes over the girl's head; "How well you speak!" (Act II) is all she can say. Again the audience laughs, for she can think only of pleasing him; yet it also recognizes that another hope of saving the family's fortunes has been dashed. "God defend you from generalizations," wrote Chekhov in a letter to his brother Alexander (May 10, 1886).[2] His effort to avoid stereotypes of character or situation, to achieve a fresh observation of true human relationships, repeatedly required him to work for a particular effect that did not admit simple classification. He did this by a hundred and one touches in which the very process of our interpretation called for a new effort of understanding of a character in its situation. The pretty girl Natasha, who makes a late entrance into Irina's party in Act I of *Three Sisters*, is wonderfully young and shy—embarrassed at being late, checking in a mirror that her hair is in place after hurrying, uncertain of the right color to go with her dress, ready to burst into tears. We forgive her everything, even her lack of taste, although we may remember that Masha thought her cheeks were rosy because she had resorted to the Victorian practice of pinching them to make them red. Perhaps we forgive her this too, until we see her evolve into the ruthless little *hausfrau* of Act II. Even then we may excuse some of her treatment of the sisters, who in their pretensions must have been difficult to live with.

By such minutiae of ordinary life Chekhov controls the response of his audience. He eschewed the traditional methods of critical and satirical comedy, like the exaggeration of character and the eccentricity of behavior, even though he had mastered this kind of stagecraft in the five short "vaudevilles" he had written between 1888 and 1891, *The Bear, The Proposal, A Tragic Role, The Wedding*, and *The Anniversary*. In the mature plays there is no Gregory Smirnov to fly into a rage when thwarted by a pretty widow with dimples (*The Bear*) and no Ivan Lomov to clutch at his heart and fall into a faint when insulted (*The Proposal*), unless we except the obsequious Waffles and his pathetic history in *Uncle Vania* or the lovelorn Epikhodov with his bookishness and his squeaky boots in *The Cherry Orchard*. Yet even these caricatures enjoy a three-dimensional quality that would satisfy many realists. Chekhov makes a point of creating every character, major or minor, with a complete life history. No two are alike, so that every line of dialogue contributes to the imagined whole, although the final character is unpredictable until we have pieced it together at the end of the play. Thus, the maidservant Duniasha in *The Cherry Orchard* has just sprung from young girlhood, so much so that Mme. Ranevskaia only just recognizes her after a five-year absence. At the beginning of that momentous summer in which the family is broken up, she cannot resist excitedly telling everyone of the proposal of marriage she has received from Epikhodov. When Iasha's pseudo-Parisian sophistication magnetizes the girl, she promptly forgets Epikhodov and tries to impress Iasha by aping the ladies with a powder-puff and a pretense to refined ways, "I'm going to go faint. I'm fainting!" (Act I). She is overwhelmed when the post office clerk calls her a "flower," and she offers herself to Iasha as someone "grown sensitive and delicate" (Act III). Thus, before the summer is over, we have the strongest suspicion that Iasha has seduced her and is leaving her pregnant. Duniasha's little drama is slight indeed, but it is complete and woven subtly through the stronger warp and woof of the play, one more illustration of the breaking up of the social structure represented there.

Character, however deceptively realistic, is in this way part of a guiding pattern. It is first a pattern of checks and balances achieved by carefully setting one character off against another. In *Three Sisters*, the reticent, doomed Baron Tuzenbakh is placed in contrast with his voluble Colonel Vershinin, who will survive his troublesome marriage and his tour of duty in the provinces. Natasha the intruder slowly gains ascendancy over the family as Olga's authority and security slip. In *The Cherry Orchard*, Mme. Ranevskaia's fecklessness is brilliantly in parallel with the landowner Pishchik's empty optimism, and while she loses everything he at the last moment has a stroke of sheer good luck when the Englishmen "come along" and find on his land "some sort of white clay"; or the vapid idealism of Trofimov, the son of a chemist, is in nice counterpoint with the practical, but equally inappropriate, thinking of Lopakhin, the son of a peasant. In *Uncle Vania*, the plain Sonia's unselfish altruism sits in pathetic contrast with the self-serving of the beautiful Helena who apparently can whistle up any man she chooses; and Telyegin supplies a bleak image of miserable dependency for Vania, who himself is shortly to recognize his powerless slavery to the professor. This device of implicit character comparison and contrast both undermines and controls the sentiment and emotionalism in each play, and encourages a subtle ambivalence in the action played out before the audience.

A powerful dramatic strategy came of Chekhov's decision never to allow us a simple or comforting moral response to a character's actions. He accepts unreservedly that the human personality is complicated, and he demonstrates his point again and again. At the time of writing the early *Ivanov* (1889), he wrote to Alexander,

Present-day playwrights begin their plays solely with angels, villains, and buffoons. Now, search for these characters in the whole of Russia. Yes, you can find them, but not such extremes as are necessary for a playwright. . . . I wanted to be original; I have not introduced a single villain nor an angel, although I could not refuse myself buffoons; I accused nobody, justified nobody. (October 24, 1887)

He is particularly careful to prompt contradictory, impersonal feelings about those who might otherwise have served him powerfully as villains. In *The Seagull*, the famous author Trigorin is the man who is responsible for the seduction of the aspiring young actress Nina, but we are never to see him as the elderly *roué*, or as the matinee idol of modern melodrama. From the start he is shown wearing old shoes and checked trousers, dissatisfied with his own success, trying to flee his responsibility to Arkadina by, of all things, going fishing, finding in Nina at best some copy for his next story. When Nina so romantically offers her life to him by drawing his attention to a line in one of his own books, he is arguably more the seduced than the seducer. In *The Cherry Orchard*, the merchant Lopakhin is the son of a peasant who has the opportunity to buy the very estate on which his ancestors were serfs, "where they weren't even admitted into the kitchen." What a sensational avenger this character could have been, and what a strongly satirical point Chekhov could have made! But Lopakhin is no stereotype. If he has made his money by hard work, it is a sensitive man who regrets the loss of the fields of poppies he must harvest for their oil. If it is his destiny to be the one to dispossess the family, he has always loved Ranevskaia like a mother, from the time when she comforted him as a little boy with a bloody nose. He buys the orchard almost reluctantly, as if unintentionally, even protectively, from under the nose of Deriganov—the unseen villain.

We think of Chekhov's characters before his plots, not because their dialogue is easy to read, but because they so readily come alive and are so rewarding to actors in the many submerged hints and suggestions of psychological depth with which their author has endowed them. As a result, each character, like Shakespeare's, is wholly individualized, never interchangeable, and in a good performance quite unforgettable. Nevertheless, Chekhov probably did not construct a play by elaborating his characters first. With the objectivity of a true comedian, he envisioned them as a group in a realistic situation, not so much a plot as a set of circumstances. It is a commonplace that Chekhov's plays present us with families, in which even the servants are part of the group. From the start he works for the conflicts and contradictions of a group reaction, one that embodies the same principles of balance and control in order to command his audience's unemotional, but not unfeeling, understanding and judgment.

In all this he was working determinedly against the theatricalism of the nineteenth-century stage—hence his frequent clashes with his director Konstantin Stanislavskii, who was essentially a product of his period, albeit an outstanding and intelligent actor and manager. But Chekhov was demanding and far ahead of his time. Along with the star system and the flamboyant style of speaking and acting, the "well-made" ordering of events, and the overdramatic scene, which Stanislavskii and his partner Nemirovich-Danchenko had themselves rejected when they agreed on their plans for the Moscow Art Theatre, Chekhov also found himself disapproving of the stage practice of Henrik Ibsen. The Norwegian playwright's major contribution to stage realism was to require a more natural prose dialogue and to choose subjects that illuminated more honest human problems, those unencrusted with melodramatic characters and incident; but he was largely unable to avoid building his plays as a series of duelling duologues, and dealing in big conflicts and obligatory scenes of crisis. Chekhov does not have much to say about his famous counterpart in the naturalistic movement, but when he saw *The Wild Duck*, probably Ibsen's most Chekhovian drama, he declared he found it "uninteresting"; *Ghosts* was a "rotten" play; and the suicide in *Hedda Gabler* was for him too sensational.[3] Chekhov's increasing impulse was to outlaw the obligatory scene and contrive to undercut what was potentially sensational, always moving closer to an ideal of balanced realistic theatre.

It is true that we can find certain Ibsenesque moments in the earlier Chekhov. The quarrel between Arkadina and Treplev, mother and son, in Act III of *The Seagull*, with explosive lines like "You are nothing but a Kiev shopman! . . . You miser! . . . You ragged beggar!" may be considered to have been written in the older tradition, as may the quarrel between Arkadina and her lover Trigorin later in the same act ("You won't abandon me? . . . I have no will of my own. . . . Now he is mine!"). But when a comparable scene between Mme. Ranevskaia and Trofimov surfaces in the third act of his last play, *The Cherry Orchard*, when the student accuses the older woman of having led an immoral life, the incident is neatly turned for comedy, so cooling the emotionalism and distancing the audience. As Trofimov storms out of the room, crying, "All is over between us!" Chekhov adds the reductive stage direction, "There is a sound of somebody running quickly downstairs and suddenly falling with a crash. Ania and Varia scream, but there is a sound of laughter at once":

Liubov	What has happened? (Ania runs in.)
Ania (laughing)	Petia's fallen downstairs! (Runs out.)
Liubov	What a queer fellow that Petia is!

As a result of this ambiguous encounter, Liubov and Trofimov are seen to be no less fond of one another, since she dances with him immediately after, while the incident has served to illuminate the weakness of both characters in a purely comic way and to keep the moral issue of Liubov and her French lover in critical perspective. The exchange follows the perfect pattern of anticlimax: the building of dramatic tension is swiftly undercut for laughter, but without wholly destroying the basic purpose of the heated confrontation when the excitement is defused. A residue of deeper feeling and a fuller understanding of the difference between the two generations are subtly carried over into the next segment of the play.

It would not be too much to say that the characteristic device in Chekhov's mature plays is indeed that of anticlimax, implying his deliberate refusal to allow the pathos beneath his scenes to dictate the response of his audience for very long. He was not always successful. At the end of *The Seagull*, he aimed to undercut the sensationalism of Treplev's suicide by arranging that it should take place offstage, but in so doing Chekhov found himself inadvertently building up a sensationalism by default. The very absence of direct comment on the sound of the offstage shot, and the careful underplaying of Dr. Dorn's information to those who heard it on the stage ("It must be something in my medicine-chest that has gone off"), followed by his aside to Trigorin ("The fact is, Konstantin Gavrilitch has shot himself"), called for the audience itself to supply the missing emotional response. The rule that "a writer has to be just as objective as a chemist," as proposed in Chekhov's letter to M. V. Kiseleva (January 14, 1887), would not serve in all cases in the theatre. The effect of the next shot fired in a Chekhov play, that of Vania's attempt on the life of Professor Serebriakov at the end of the third act of *Uncle Vania*, is more precisely regulated. The gun is now visible; but not only does the bullet miss its target, but also the ridiculous behavior of the principals to the affair is fully written in, so that little of the intended effect is left to chance. Serebriakov has run in "staggering with terror" and Vania has run in looking for him: "Where is he? Oh, here he is! (Fires at him) Bang! (a pause) Missed! Missed again! (Furiously) Damnation—damnation take it. (Flings revolver on the floor and sinks on to a chair, exhausted)" With the professor running in panic and ducking the shot, possibly behind a chair, in an uncharacteristically undignified fashion, and with Vania childishly crying "Bang!" before he flings his gun down in a tantrum of frustration, Chekhov guaranteed that a scene which carried a potentially tragic explosion of feeling must create a decisively comic image of Vania's ineffectuality.

As a naturalistic dramatist concerned to reveal the forces of the environment and the circumstances of ordinary people working on their lives, Chekhov's greatest achievement was this controlled objectivity. Nowhere does it prove its worth more than at the crisis of *The Cherry Orchard* in Act III. During the ill-timed party flung by Mme. Ranevskaia at the time of the sale of the orchard, both the audience in the theatre and that on the stage are awaiting confirmation of what is a long foregone conclusion, that the orchard has been lost. To look again at Lopakhin's "triumph": insofar as this representative of the peasant class will buy the estate, he could have been used to make a powerful political point, one that a lesser playwright might have exploited. Not so Chekhov. Here was to be no triumph for the forces of "justice," only an occasion, long anticipated, that would bring sorrow to everyone concerned, and Chekhov used it to mark the uneasy end of an era. The ironic moment of Lopakhin's entrance into the party fore-shadows the whole anticlimactic treatment of the end of the play. Varia, who as housekeeper holds the keys to the family and who still cherishes the hope of marrying him, offers a blow with Firs's stick at Epikhodov, but almost hits Lopakhin on the head. The incident is turned for a joke at which everyone laughs, but it ensures that the new owner is to make no grand entrance. Instead, it touches the edge of symbolism. While the gesture with the stick reminds Lopakhin and us of his peasant boyhood and shows him more as an intruder than as a tyrant, it releases for comedy all the tension of the auction. The moment is laughable and fleeting; it is lightly done, yet it is full of meaning.

From total anticlimax to the persistent undercutting of fine detail, Chekhov's method as a comedian was consistently deflationary. *The Seagull* was composed of many aborted affairs between the sexes (I try to avoid the term "love-affairs"), those between Treplev and Nina, Nina and Trigorin, Trigorin and Arkadina, Masha and Treplev, Masha and Medvedenko, Polina and Dorn: so many, indeed, that they would seem to identify the play as a farce as they proliferate and cancel one another out. "How hysterical they are," says Dorn at one point, "and what a lot of love" (Act I). Yet the general tenor of these affairs, felt through the realistic inter-action between each pair of lovers, teases us with tragedy. In *The Cherry Orchard*, eight years later, Chekhov again compounds his love-affairs, between Ania and Trofimov, Charlotta and Pishchick, Epikhodov and Duniasha, Duniasha and Iasha, Varia and Lopakhin, but of these not one allows a true pathos. Even in the case of Varia and Lopakhin, Chekhov was careful to avoid building sufficient sympathetic feeling to color with any sense of disaster that delicious moment when Lopakhin bolts from Varia's presence rather than propose to her. If Nina of *The Seagull* can be admitted as a pathetic figure, the cry-baby Varia can never be.

Communication from stage to audience by a host of fleeting but sugges-tive details was a method that Chekhov learned in the hard school of short story writing, and it served him well in the theatre where an economy of means is *de rigueur*. For the writer of fiction, Chekhov's well-known *mot* occurs in a letter to Alexander on May 10, 1886: "You will get the full effect of a moonlight night if you write that on the mill-dam a pin-point of light flashed from the neck of a broken bottle." This statement in part explains the brevity and immediacy of his glancing, impressionistic style of prose. On the stage, the smallest and simplest element of voice, or pause, or gesture, can in its context have a momentous impact, and the slightest hint on the surface of the dialogue can plumb a profound subtext. *Three Sisters* is particularly rich in little lines that guide the listener toward the hidden life of the family. The following unforgettable touches are presented here without comment:

Natasha	I was saying to your sister this morning, "Take care of yourself, Irina darling," said I. *But she won't listen* (Act II).

and

Olga	Whoever proposed to me I would marry him, if only he were a good man. . . . *I would even marry an old man.* . . . (Act III)

and in Act IV

Masha	Did you love my mother?
Tchebutykin	Very much.
Masha	And did she love you?
Tchebutykin	*(after a pause) That I don't remember.*[4]

On the stage the technique also appears in Chekhov's choice and use of props and costume. In Act I of *The Seagull*, Masha's defiant little habit of taking a pinch of snuff (evidently used to keep Medvedenko at bay) subtly descends to become her new drinking habit in Act III; by then she has married him, and her slight tipsiness neatly understates her resignation to her new condition. In the same play, the decline in old Sorin's health is marked out by his progress from a limp and a shuffle with a stick in Act I, to his appearance followed by Medvedenko pushing a wheelchair in his wake in Act II, to his attack of dizziness in Act III, until in Act IV we finally see him confined to his chair. Thus have the two years passed for him. In *Uncle Vania*, we note the hypochondriacal professor's inability or unwillingness to make the adjustment when he leaves the city for the heat of a rural summer: Vania reports, "It's hot, stifling; but our great man of learning is in his greatcoat and galoshes, with an umbrella and gloves too" (Act I). Through those summer months the old nurse Marina's endless knitting of woollen stockings against the arrival of the Russian winter warns us, as they grow in length from scene to scene, of the relentless cycle of the seasons which govern the lives of Vania and Sonia. In *Three Sisters*, it is the silence and soft whistling of Masha, together with her attention to her hat, which tells us how her mind is working in Act I: at one point she puts it on to indicate her boredom with the company and her intention of leaving in the middle of Irina's party, then, long after the appearance of the new Colonel Vershinin with the information that he has come from Moscow ("TUZENBAKH: Aleksandr Ignatevitch has come from Moscow. IRINA: From Moscow? You have come from Moscow?"), Masha suddenly takes off her hat again as she makes a quiet decision that no one seems to hear,

"I'll stay to lunch." By such oblique indications does Chekhov tell his story.

The technique brings the feel of actual life to the stage, almost a "documentary" touch, in which the actuality of speech and behavior seems to dictate what happens, and the pursuit of its authenticity becomes for the dramatist almost an imperative in itself. Indeed, with *Uncle Vania*, which Chekhov subtitled "Scenes from Country Life" after Aleksandr Ostrovskii, he seems to aim at an ideal of realistic objectivity in which he promotes his balance of compassion and detachment by letting actuality speak for itself. This play above all his others presents a group of trivial people in order to show the dullness of life in provincial Russia. The challenge for the playwright is to prove that even if they are dull, an audience need not find them uninteresting. *Uncle Vania* takes the first important step toward a "documentary" representation of life, and this, in the memorable words of the Scottish documentary film pioneer, John Grierson, implies "the creative treatment of actuality."[5]

A critical crux in *Uncle Vania* may well be resolved by reference to the latent principles of documentary in the play. At the end, when Vania and Sonia must patch together their former lives after the visitors of the summer have departed, the girl tries to comfort her uncle with a moving speech which nevertheless remains wickedly ambiguous, and any director of the play must decide whether or not his actress will play for a rousing and optimistic ending. Such lines as "We shall rest, we shall rest!" must be tested by performance: is Sonia expressing the hope of all downtrodden people in need of courage to face the future, or are her words to be heard as painfully ironic, mere pieties that offer hope only in the next world? As usual, Chekhov is careful to leave the matter in doubt. Yet the student of the stage should not overlook the fact that Sonia and Vania are not alone. Chekhov once said that it is the day-to-day living that wears you down, and at the end of *Uncle Vania* he arranges that four others besides Sonia and Vania will contribute to the uncertain spirit of his curtain scene. The Watchman resumes his tapping offstage, Maria takes up her pen again and begins to scratch her notes, Marina continues to click her knitting needles, and Telegin quietly tunes and strums his guitar. These four are all making the faint sounds that are to form a dry, melancholy background to Sonia's speech, pacing and commenting on the scene as a whole—like Andrei who aimlessly pushes his baby-carriage across the back of the stage at the end of *Three Sisters*, or like the noise of the axe that falls with monotonous regularity on the trees at the end of *The Cherry Orchard*. The "silent" characters at the end of *Uncle Vania* represent the day-to-day living and provide a chilling perspective on Sonia's innocence.

Uncle Vania is "about" the socio-economic conditions in rural Russia at the end of the nineteenth century, but the toll paid by the human mind and spirit is conveyed as a sensory experience constructed out of noises heard in counterpoint with words, and neither words nor noises can be escaped by their audience. Chekhov's social criticism thus remains tangential and elusive, and properly so, and thus documentary becomes drama. *Three Sisters* exactly documents the nature of provincial life in a small town many miles from the great metropolis of Moscow. Its fragile cultural life depends on the presence of the officers from the regiment of artillery stationed nearby. It is easy to recognize that the chorus of voices crying for a return home to Moscow is ineffectual, and it is even easier to pass some sort of judgment that the three women should apply themselves and take a more positive attitude to life. It is Chekhov's purpose to show how the weight of trivial living bears down on the three of them remorselessly. While Irina clings hopelessly to her romantic notions of love, Masha settles for a shabby affair with the colonel of the regiment and Olga sacrifices herself to play the double role of breadwinner and mother to the family. As the audience comes to acknowledge the sisters' limitations as human beings and theatrically reexperiences, as it were, the increasing pressure of their circumstances, its criticism will be muted.

The general framework of Chekhov's balanced comedy admits a remarkable variety of muffled, but subversive, social criticism, and at unexpected moments he will disrupt the apparent calm of his scene. In that balmy summer afternoon of Act II in *The Cherry Orchard*, for example, Firs expresses his disapproval of the Emancipation in his longing for the past, and Lopakhin catches us with a throwaway line, "Those were fine old times. There was flogging anyway." Or Chekhov contrives to insert an oblique reminder of the Jewish persecution under Nicholas II when the pathetic Jewish orchestra is heard faintly and is then later hired for the ball in the next act by Mme. Ranevskaia, suggesting her sense of guilt and obligation. Or he introduces the disagreeable image of the drunken beggar who comes upon the family group sitting in the dusk, frightening Varia and affording them and us an ugly glimpse of what could happen to them all. In the same letter to Kiseleva mentioned above, Chekhov had insisted that "To chemists there is nothing unclean on earth," and with no jot of sensationalism his comedy admitted both the ugly and the painful. When near the end of the play Gaev volunteers that he has taken a job as a bank clerk, "I am a bank clerk now—I am a financier—cannon off the red" (Act IV), Chekhov's intention is more than to provoke a facile laugh. Gaev's line fits into the pattern of the play's constant reference to money and points to a devastating change in the social order: "How am I going to feed the servants?" demands Varia.

The fabric of Chekhov's drama is thus slyly interwoven with an acute commentary on the times. In his foreword to *Miss Julie* in 1888, Strindberg outlined an appropriate method for writing the dialogue of naturalism when he described how in his own play "the dialogue wanders, gathering in the opening scenes material which is later picked up, worked over, repeated, expounded, and developed like the theme in a musical composition."⁶ If this sounds altogether too deliberate to describe Chekhov's way of working, it nevertheless implied that writing realistic dialogue was a matter of great discipline. The commonplace that Chekhov offered his audience "a slice of life" was always inadequate, since what appears to be an image of desultory and humdrum existence in fact carried a purposeful and meticulously designed "subtext" that moved relentlessly to a point. In another of Chekhov's famous assertions, "In life people don't shoot themselves or fall in love every minute. . . . They spend more time eating, drinking and talking nonsense, and while they're doing it, their lives may be shattered."⁷ The method deceived Tolstoi, who thought of him as an impressionist painter for whom "it is all only mosaic without a governing idea," but it should not deceive the spectator in the theatre.⁸ If there is no obvious "hero" on whose fortunes it might have been possible to focus attention, if there is no discernible issue of right or wrong in the representation of events on the stage, and if there is no "plot" in the Aristotelian sense, Chekhov achieves the dramatic unity these classical concepts all imply. If there is little plotting, there is much planning.

The unity of a Chekhov play arises when all its parts come together to form an experience greater than their sum. We look for this unity, therefore, in those elements that determine the rhythm of the experience and control the processes of the play in performance. They are the elements that can be seen to regulate both the actors on the stage and the responses of the audience. They can be found in every stroke of character and incident, but let us conclude this essay by indicating what may be most easily missed in reading the text of the plays.

Chekhov was well aware that the *setting* on his stage could speak powerfully to the spectator, who could not avoid seeing it, and he perfected a way that drew a partly realistic, but equally symbolic, visual pattern from act to act. In *The Seagull*, the scene changes from the romantic to the almost sordid: from Sorin's glorious park with its setting sun and rising moon. reflecting the youthful idealism of Treplev and Nina in Act I, to the pretty croquet lawn bathed in sunlight outside the house, the domain of Mme. Arkadina and her little social circle in Act II; Act III takes us inside the house for the first time, and we see it disordered by the preparations for leaving; and Act IV moves still further into the heart of things, into the world of books and careless furniture that Treplev miserably inhabits. *Uncle Vania* follows a comparable pattern, beginning outside the house, but this time set on the edge of a plantation that lacks all romance; thereafter, Acts II and III move each time deeper into the house, until Act IV finds out Vania's own room, his bed and his personal jumble of account-books, scales, and papers, together with a starling in a cage and a map of Africa on the wall, all lightly suggesting the clutter of his mind and his ineffectual longing for escape.

The setting for *Three Sisters* is different by beginning inside the house and embracing us with its main public room for the first two acts. Columns suggest a former grandeur, and the partly seen dining room hints at the scale of the house. However, in Act II the evidence of Natasha and her baby is everywhere, and many subtle changes in the scene tell us of the passage of time. Act III continues the process of dispossession by confining us to Olga's bedroom, now shared with a displaced Irina, so that the confusion of beds and screens looks and feels uncomfortable. With Act IV, the sisters are finally found outside the house, with Natasha and her lover Protopopov inside, so that the visual symbolism of exclusion is complete. *The Cherry Orchard* dares a circular pattern of scenes in order to symbolize the cycle of life. It begins in the nursery, the one room where every member of the household has a rooted memory. It then passes to a spot beyond the orchard which manages to include in one composition a little of the rural estate and a glimpse of urban and industrial growth, with the family caught between the past and the future as it lolls about in a disused graveyard: the set seems required to bear too heavy a weight of meaning. Act III returns us nostalgically to the ballroom of the house as a background for the incongruity of the party, and Act IV comes full circle to the nursery of the first act, although it is now a scene of desolation: bare trees, furniture covered over, heaps of luggage—a setting that holds out no hope.

In parallel with each visual setting, mood and atmosphere are precisely adjusted, and Chekhov makes use of the seasons, the weather, and the time of day to regulate our changing image of the action. *The Seagull* begins in the twilight of a hot summer's day—"How stifling it is!", says Masha—and the heat seems to provide an excuse for the ruffled feelings which next afternoon explode in ill-temper and direct confrontation. In the last act, the final pathos of Treplev and Nina is set against a dark, wild night of wind and rain. *Uncle Vania* also begins sluggishly in the sultry heat of summer and proceeds through a restless night until the storm breaks, all to prepare the audience for the shock of the professor's announcement that he is planning to sell the estate which precipitates Vania's brainstorm. The last act dips down anticlimactically to the painful time when autumn is changing to winter in a characteristically Chekhovian going-away scene of bitter reflection and regret.

Three Sisters makes some use of the seasons, beginning in spring sunshine with the optimism of an impending party in the air; but in Act II the mood is utterly different as reality begins its advance with the gloom of a winter evening. In Act III, we feel the tensions and hostility arising from the sleeplessness and exhaustion of the fire in the night. For Act IV, Chekhov tries a new device: he ends his play in midday sunshine, although there is a touch of autumn in the air (Stanislavskii had leaves falling throughout the act), the better to capture the sisters' regret at the departure of the regiment, ironically colorful in dress uniforms and marching to the spirited music of a military band. In *The Cherry Orchard*, Chekhov falls back on the cycle of the seasons, which extend from the last frost of May to the first of the winter, matching the cycle of the orchard itself all in white blossom, in the brilliant light of the early morning sun as it rises in Act I, to the time when the trees are glimpsed standing starkly through the bare windows of Act IV. So the summer months of the calendar are quietly marked off as the sale of the estate approaches in Acts II and III, until the cold returns in Act IV—"three degrees of frost," remarks the practical Lopakhin. The story of the family's fortunes seems to be told by the changes in the cherry trees themselves, as if they were sentient creatures.

By such devices of setting and atmosphere Chekhov unifies his play and focuses on a central theme. The dramatic surface of *non sequiturs* and brilliant pauses, of centrifugal incidents and tangential comments, is misleading, like much else of his dramatic method. He suddenly fills his stage with people and as quickly empties it in the first acts of *Uncle Vania* and *The Cherry Orchard*—against all the "laws" of drama. Indeed, he works with an empty stage as effectively as with a full one. He appears to give as much time and attention to "minor" characters as to "major" ones. He scatters his scenes with distracting cues for music and song, some twenty or so in each of his last two plays. He loads his lines with two or three times as many unseen characters as are in the cast itself, and until one counts them it is hard to believe that there are 50 or so "offstage" characters in each of *Three Sisters* and *The Cherry Orchard*. So Chekhov's picture of humanity is infinitely extended by offstage mothers and fathers, sisters and brothers, grandfathers and aunts, friends and acquaintances, servants and workmen, porters and peasants, musicians and nurses, and cooks and gardeners. Who can ever forget Telegin's courageous wife, who ran away from him the day after their wedding "on the ground of my unprepossessing appearance" (Act I). Or Natasha's persistent lover Protopopov, or Kulygin's intimidating headmaster, or Pishchik's long-suffering daughter Dashenka?

This rich abundance in Chekhov's world of people is part of his illusion of reality, providing family backgrounds, giving depth to the lives of the few we see. Yet his most deceptive technique may be that of arranging for his characters to fall into patterns that indicate order in what otherwise seems to be at random—a kind of dramatic *Gestalten* awaiting the perception of an audience watching a performance. In *Uncle Vania*, each of the eight principals falls into a category of what might be thought of as a master-and-slave relationship. There are those who exercise a power over others without thought: Professor Serebriakov through his position in society and his ownership of land, and Ielena through her sex and her beauty. There are those who are as yet unreconciled to their servitude and see some possibilities of change: Vania, Sonia, and Astrov. And there are those who have succumbed to the dead hand of routine and the pressures they have no control over: Maria, Marina, and Telegin. In *Three Sisters*, the fortunes of the family change as the self-centered ones, Natasha, Solenyi, and perhaps Vershinin, prevail over the weaknesses of others, particularly the sisters and their brother Andrei.

It is with *The Cherry Orchard* that Chekhov perfects his magical technique of character patterning, and, had he lived, he would no doubt have explored further. In this play twelve characters appear to make ten times that number as each serves as a representative of more than one aspect of society. Thus, each is a richly individualized composite of many elements, while being at the same time one of a group identified by social or economic class, or sex, or age, and more, as each group is affected differently by the sale of the orchard. As members of the landowning class, Gaev and Mme. Ranevskaia lose their place in society, and pull down with them their immediate dependents, Ania and Varia. Meanwhile, the former peasants, Lopakhin and Iasha, acquire new economic and social responsibility, so that the financial distress of some is seen to be to the advantage of others; two generations after the Emancipation, the results of the upheaval on the changing structure of society are still being felt. If the cast is divided by sex, the loss of the orchard places a marital urgency on the spinsters, Varia, Duniasha, and Charlotta, and introduces a human need that Lopakhin, Iasha, and Pishchik cannot understand and to which they cannot respond; Ania and Trofimov still move in an unreal, romantic fog where they are as yet content to remain "above love"; and Liubov, now a rather desperate lady, is thrown back on the resource of her Paris lover. If the cast is divided by age, those of the older generation whose lives are locked in the past view change as the loss of a whole way of life too precious to be contemplated; for those of the youngest generation, Ania, Trofimov, Iasha, and Duniasha, the sale of the orchard is a necessary break with the past and an opportunity for a new life; and those of middle years, Lopakhin, Varia, and Charlotta, are the realists who must face the demands of the moment, take stock of their financial position, find work. Such differences between the generations bring time alive on the stage. Only Firs, aged 87, is beyond class, sex, and time: he is the near-absurd chorus who is able to survey all the others, unaffected by events, and even as those he has loved forget him at the last, so the play ends on a crashing irony.

By Chekhov's dramatic techniques the audience is placed in the classic comic role of objective observer. It is finally academic to ask whether these plays are tragedies or comedies when their fugitive methods in performance call at one moment for the audience's compassionate understanding of the human condition and at the next for its unemotional judgment. Faced with the mass of detailed evidence, we the jury must temporarily withdraw and calmly try to reach a verdict. Our ambivalent, tragicomic response to the multitude of Chekhov's signals from the stage, apparently all at odds like the contradictions of life, reflects a process at the heart of his dramatic method and amazingly corresponds to the actual experience of living. In his

Preface to Shakespeare, Samuel Johnson recognized that "the real state of sublunary nature . . . partakes of good and evil, joy and sorrow, mingled with endless variety of proportion and innumerable modes of combination,"[9] and thus justified the dramatic mixture in Shakespeare. In the world of his plays, Chekhov, like Shakespeare, generously embraces human life and does so with a little of the same impulse toward creative variety.

NOTES

1. Anton Chekhov, *The Cherry Orchard, and Other Plays*, trans. Constance Garnett, Phoenix Library Edition (London: Chatto and Windus, 1935). Further quotations from *The Seagull, The Cherry Orchard*, and *Uncle Vania* are from this edition.

2. S. S. Koteliansky and Philip Tomlinson, eds., *The Life and Letters of Anton Tchekhov* (London: Benjamin Blom, 1965). All subsequent citations from Chekhov's letters are from this edition.

3. See Ernest J. Simmons, *Chekhov: A Biography* (New York: Little, Brown, 1962), p. 542; S. S. Koteliansky, ed. and trans., *Anton Tchekhov: Literary and Theatrical Reminiscences* (London: Routledge, 1927), pp. 156, 161; Anton Tchekhov, *The Letters to Olga Leonardovna Knipper*, trans. C. Garnett (New York: Benjamin Blom, 1966), p. 368.

4. Anton Chekhov, *Three Sisters and Others Plays*, trans. Constance Garnett, Phoenix Library Edition (London: Chatto and Windus, 1935), pp. 30, 68, 80, emphasis added. Further quotes from *Three Sisters* are from this edition.

5. *Grierson on Documentary*, ed. Forsyth Hardy (London: Collins, 1946), p. 11.

6. August Strindberg, *Six Plays*, trans. Elizabeth Sprigge (Garden City, N.Y.: Doubleday, 1955), p. 69.

7. Quoted in David Magarshack, *Chekhov the Dramatist* (London: John Lehmann, 1952), p. 118.

8. Quoted in Dmitri Chizhevsky in *Anton Čechov: 1860-1960: Some Essays*, ed. T. Eekman (Leiden: E. J. Brill, 1960), and reprinted in *Chekhov: A Collection of Critical Essays*, ed. R. L. Jackson (Englewood Cliffs, N.J.: Prentice-Hall, 1967), p. 53.

9. Samuel Johnson, *Johnson on Shakespeare*, ed. Walter Raleigh (London: Oxford University Press, 1908), p. 15.

8

Andrew R. Durkin

CHEKOV'S NARRATIVE TECHNIQUE

Chekhov is aware of hackneyed nineteenth-century literary conventions when he first begins writing for the humour magazines. In one of his earliest works, the parodic "What Does One Most Find in Novels, Short Stories, Etc." (1880), he enumerates the clichés of standard fiction: fixed epithets in style ("faces which are not handsome, but sympathetic and appealing"); stock characters ("a rich uncle," "an aunt in Tambov"), whose personalities and actions are merely predictable adjuncts to their plot functions; standardized settings, and automatic descriptions of them ("The heavenly heights, the impenetrable, the unembraceable . . . the incomprehensible distance, in a word: Nature!!!. . . . A dacha near Moscow and a mortgaged estate in the south"); hackneyed plot devices ("Inadvertent eavesdropping as the source of major revelations"), and, perhaps least typical of Chekhov's own later practice, predictable closure ("The seven deadly sins in the beginning and a wedding at the end").[1] The significance of this piece lies not so much in Chekhov recognizing these clichéd features so early in his career as in his locating clichés at every level of a work, from its surface of style to its core of structure. Chekhov rejected the automatic and sought new techniques that would involve the reader in new and unexpected ways.

If we take his rejection of standard techniques of previous fiction as programmatic, what then seems to be the distinctive feature of Chekhov's fiction that he created in the course of the next twenty years? First of all, Chekhov avoids the predictable on the level of style, thus forcing the reader into new perceptions and awareness. He achieves this in a number of ways, but perhaps his most frequent technique is what has been termed Chekhov's laconicism.[2] However, this term is not entirely adequate; it usually implies deliberate understatement or withholding of nonessential information motivated by a certain stoicism or indifference, whereas Chekhov intentionally "fails" to describe a situation fully so as to draw the attentive reader into more imaginative participation than would be the case if Chekhov were to state explicitly all implications. An extreme example of such compression, verging on mystification, occurs in the first paragraph of "Gusev" (1890). The paragraph in its entirety reads: "It had already gotten dark, soon it would be night." The scantest information with regard to time, in the total absence of any reference to place or character, draws the reader into the story, forcing the reader to search for other data to fill out this minimal picture.

Similarly, stories often end with brief statements that close the narrative without concluding it: "Outside, he stood about for a while, thought a bit, and, saying good-bye to his friends, slowly made his way to the university" ("An Attack of Nerves," 1889, VII, 221). "A minute later the wayfarers were already trudging along the muddy road. The tramp had stooped over even more and put his hands further into his sleeves. Ptakha was silent" ("Dreams," 1886, V, 403). In both, only brief statements describe the characters' physical actions. The one verb dealing with inner experience—"he thought"—does not specify the content of that thought. Adjectives and adverbs, which might provide clues to authorial attitude toward the events described, are practically nonexistent. In both endings the reader may infer the inner state of the characters from the events of the preceding narrative, but this can be only conjecture, perhaps differing slightly in the mind of each individual reader. We are not told, we are shown, and we must draw our conclusions, tentative as they may be.

Openings and endings in Chekhov's stories provide particularly striking examples of Chekhov's tendency to avoid the full exposition characteristic of much nineteenth-century fiction precisely because traditionally these two points were heavily laden with information. This technique is prevalent throughout Chekhov's texts. For example, in "The Darling" Olenka's mourning for her husband is reduced to a few lines: "Kukin was buried on Tuesday, in Moscow, at Vagankovo. Olenka returned home on Wednesday, and as soon as she entered the house, she fell on the bed and began to sob so loudly that it could be heard on the street and in the houses nearby" (X, 105). Nothing more is said about Olenka's reaction. Such compression, of course, heightens the impact of what is actually said. By metonymy, her sobbing conveys more strikingly the intensity of her grief than lengthy authorial statements could. Similarly, "In the Ravine" (1900) presents the horror of an infant deliberately scalded to death through a secondary effect, the mother's scream, even though the cause is very specifically described: "Aksinia grabbed a basin of boiling water and dashed it on Nikifor. After that a shriek was heard, the like of which had never before been heard in Ukleevo, and it was unbelievable that a small, weak creature such as Lipa could shriek like that" (X, 172). Chekhov's avoidance of clinical detail increases the horror of Aksinia's action; it makes it seem literally unspeakable. This emotional intensity is the reverse of the detachment generally associated with laconicism.

Chekhov's prose is not uniformly Spartan in style. On the contrary, part of its subtlety lies in its variability. As has often been noted, Chekhov typically enhances the illusion of reality by including "accidental" or "unnecessary" information (accidental or unnecessary from the perspective of earlier Realism), details that seem unconnected with action or character development, which a strictly laconic style would exclude. Two frequently cited examples are the platter of ham and peas that the waiter Chikildeev drops at the onset of his incapacitating illness in "Peasants" (1897)—it hardly matters to the plot what the platter contains—and the missing leg of Olenka's deceased father's chair in "The Darling."[3] Indeed, since the chair leg is merely absent, the detail is not only "unnecessary" but deliberately enigmatic, a ghostly trace of what once was but now leads nowhere.

Similarly, the use of such superfluous details can also be seen on the level of action, as in the story "Gooseberries" (1898). Chekhov describes at length the characters bathing and swimming. One has not washed in so long that the water around him is discolored, but neither the bathing nor this graphic detail has anything to do with the core of the story, the tale that one of the characters tells about his miserly brother. Such apparently pointless details not only intensify the illusion of reality within the confines of a short work, but also help to engage the reader who cannot assume that all the elements in the story have been "preselected" because they are significant or directly pertinent to the plot. The reader's task is to distinguish the essential from the peripheral or nonessential. His judgment must be actively involved in these small matters and in larger ones as well.

The apparent randomness in the mixture of "essential" and "nonessential" in objects and actions is matched by similar variability of narrative tonality. For instance, the final paragraph of "Gusev" consists of a highly poetic description of the sun setting in the Indian Ocean:

Meanwhile, up above, in that part of the sky where the sun is about to set, clouds are massing, one resembling a triumphal arch, another a lion, a third a pair of scissors. A broad shaft of green light issues from the clouds and reaches to the middle of the sky; a while later, a violet beam appears alongside of it and then a golden one and a pink one. . . . The heavens turn a soft lilac tint. Looking at this magnificent enchanting sky, the ocean frowns at first, but soon it, too, takes on tender, joyous, passionate colors for which it is hard to find a name in the language of man. (VII, 339)

Not only does the visual beauty and poetic tone of the paragraph contrast with the earlier prosaic, even naturalistic, burial at sea of a common soldier (where a voracious shark is about to rip into the sinking corpse), but within the passage itself the cloud forms yield no traditional metaphorical or allegorical "meaning." They share no common feature or quality, and the scissors, a mundane tool, adds a note of absurdity to otherwise elevated diction. Such interplay of the poetic and the prosaic is strikingly evident in "The Steppe" (1888), Chekhov's first major prose work, in which highly poetic extended descriptions of the South Russian plain alternate with much more prosaic presentations of the characters as they move across the steppe.

This juxtaposition of styles very easily leads to their interpenetration, so that the boundaries between them become imperceptible. This subtle blending of the real and the metaphoric or poetic is particularly evident in and characteristic of Chekhov's openings. For instance, the opening of "Misfortune" (1886) suggests the world of imposed order and fixity from which the heroine will break free at the end of the story when she turns her back on her conventional marriage for an affair (perhaps equally conventional). Seemingly objective but potentially metaphoric objects (stifling heat and silence, trapped stagnant clouds, railroad embankments with pacing armed guards blocking the view, a church with a rusting roof) not only orient the reader in a specific setting, but also subtly align him or her perceptually and emotionally with the central character. Other psychologically colored landscapes include the depressing southern steppe in "At Home" (1897) or the slightly tawdry resort town of Yalta in "The Lady with a Lapdog" (1899).

In particular the qualities of light and dark in many of Chekhov's settings take on metaphorical significance. Many stories, "Dreams," "Enemies" (1887), "Sleepy" (1888), "Lights" (1888), "The Student" (1894), to name a few, depend on crepuscular lighting and the contrast of light and dark to reinforce themes of confusion and illumination. The titles of Chekhov's first significant collections, *Motley Tales* (1886) and *In the Twilight* (1887), draw attention to the importance of such chiaroscuro techniques.

Chekhov's descriptions are thus not simply poetic or metaphoric, as those of Turgenev often are, but also serve a psychological function in that the character rather than an omniscient narrator perceives them; the reader's perception thus depends on the character's. This close identification with and emphasis on interior experience make psychological rather than physical events the crucial action in Chekhov stories, a shift with important implications both for characterization and for the typical patterns of Chekhov's plots.

With regard to characterization, the inner experience of a character becomes the focus in Chekhov's stories. Thus, the perceiving and experiencing individual often occupies center stage in Chekhov's fictional world. In a story such as "The Name-Day," the entire text is filtered through the consciousness of the main character. Setting and mental state, the physiological and psychological, the character's perceptions and the reader's, interpenetrate and intensify to the point of inseparability. Since what the character perceives is very often the incongruity between his or her previous notion of the nature of reality, especially social reality, and the true state of affairs, the perceiving character also typically plays the role of victim, one whose greater perception leads directly or indirectly to suffering and anguish. Such characters are often contrasted to non-perceiving egoists, characters who lack the capacity to empathize or suffer. Many stories are built on the direct confrontation of two characters, one of each type; stories structured in this way appear relatively early in Chekhov's career. In "A Chameleon" (1884), a police officer deals with a stray dog according to his shifting assumptions concerning the dog's presumed owner. The officer, encased in his uniform, embodies the security, blindness, and cruelty of social forms; the uncomprehending, trapped, and helpless dog is an extreme version of the victim that recurs throughout Chekhov's works. In contrast to the philanthropic tradition of Russian fiction, in Chekhov these two types, the established egoist and the defenseless outsider, are not determined sociologically but psychologically. The closed, indifferent egoist may be an official ("Sergeant Prishibeev," 1885), in conformity with the tradition, but he may as easily be a writer ("Excellent People," 1886), in clear exception to the Russian intelligentsia's image of itself, or a sexually exploitative peasant ("Agafia," 1886), in violation of assumptions about the positive qualities of the Russian peasant. The victim may be an animal or child ("A Chameleon" or "Vanka," 1886) but may as easily be a village priest ("A Nightmare," 1886), a character generally treated with contempt and disdain, as, indeed, the self-defined "liberal" official in "A Nightmare" treats him until he realizes the priest's true desperate predicament.

"An Upheaval" (1886) clearly juxtaposes the unfeeling egoist and the perceptive victim: the tyrannical, intrusive mistress of the house so offends the sensitive young governess (the search of her belongings for a missing brooch belonging to the mistress is a metaphorical rape) that the governess resigns and leaves. As is often the case in Chekhov, the egotistic character is associated with food and satiety; much exposition of her character takes place at the dining room table, where she uses her finicky tastes to terrorize and manipulate the entire household. The victim is often either hungry or unable to eat; here the governess does not eat at the table but does hide small treats. Despite her emotional and moral shock at having been suspected of theft, the governess, unlike many of Chekhov's victims, including the weak-willed husband in this story, has the fortitude to flee, despite the unknown dangers of a new, uncharted life.

No sooner had Chekhov developed these fundamentally contrasting types, however, than he began to modify and adapt this basic dichotomy, exploring its possibilities. In "At the Mill" (1886), he presents a hermetically closed egoist in the figure of the miller, a bearish misanthrope at odds with his neighbors and indifferent to his mother's pleas on behalf of his destitute brother. But Chekhov is no longer interested merely in creating such a character. The story ends with the miller begrudgingly giving his mother the smallest coin he has, perhaps out of guilt, perhaps out of shame before the audience (two monks and a hired hand) who witness, along with the reader, his confrontation with his mother. The miller seems to desire desperately both to cut himself off from all human communion and yet at the same time to maintain this last tenuous link with the human community and with his own human self. Chekhov, in true laconic fashion, shows us only the outward signs of this internal struggle, avoiding any direct presentation of the miller's consciousness or any overt evaluation by the narrator (although the monks provide a moral barometer by their reactions). Monstrous as the miller may be, the hints of other emotions in him, which he himself ruthlessly suppresses, make him an object of horrified sympathy rather than of easy condemnation, a creature trapped in the coils of his own self.

Chekhov's focus on the experiences of an individual psyche enmeshed in the particularities of its specific immediate environment leads him to use a distinctive type of symbolism. Objects take on additional value only because of their significance for the character as an individual and consequently for the reader who alone has access to the character's inner life. Thus, symbols in Chekhov tend to be contextual and private, in the sense of being meaningful only for the character. This close link between the symbol and the workings of the individual mind intensifies the symbol's power while at the same time reducing the communicability of its meaning or effects; even the reader can only approximate the full impact of a symbol for the character who experiences it directly. In "The Lady with the Lapdog" the grey fence in the town of S——— sums up stultifying convention for Gurov. In "Three Years" (1895), an ordinary umbrella becomes a symbol of love first for the central character Laptev and later for his wife Iuliia, but neither can tell the other what the umbrella means, nor could the other share that meaning fully. Such problems of communication, particularly with regard to the intensely individual experience of symbols, are constant and thematic in Chekhov.

At times such symbols "break down," but such counter-examples are illuminating. "A Work of Art" (1886) depends on the disparity in the value assigned to an object; a doctor disposes of an unsightly candelabra given him by a grateful patient only to have the patient retrieve the eyesore from the second-hand market as a mate to the (supposed) first one. The result here is comic, but similar disjunctions in perception and value underlie many of Chekhov's stories. In "The Black Monk" (1894), the central character Kovrin experiences hallucinations that are in effect powerful private symbols with no signifier in the real world to anchor them or make them even partially communicable. In "Gooseberries," the berries become a symbol for the central character of the ultimate satisfaction in life, but neither the narrator of the story nor the reader can see their value or share this symbol. The gooseberry-craving bureaucrat becomes a *reductio ad absurdum* of Chekhov's closed egotistical feeders, and the gooseberries come to symbolize for us the exact opposite of what they mean to the character (disgust versus bliss). But this radically ironic treatment of symbol can be seen as an experiment in which Chekhov's usually careful presentation of the character's subjective world is deliberately and totally reversed.

On the level of plot, Chekhov's interest in psychological experience rather than events per se leads to an elimination of plot in favor of incident. Such stories as "A Chameleon" or "At the Mill" exemplify this tendency; the events described lead to no real change in the order of things. The characters and their social relationships at the end of the story are those that obtained at the beginning. The only difference lies in the fact that the reader has gained insight into this order. Even in stories where the causal sequence of events could be termed a plot, Chekhov eliminates or telescopes the traditional exposition of the various stages of the plot.

Stories often end before all the consequences of an act have been presented, leaving continuation of the causal chain to the reader's imagination. For example, "A Misfortune" ends with the wife fleeing a conventional marriage for the uncharted territory of an affair. The reader accustomed to the detailed plot of a novel such as *Anna Karenina*, may find such an interruption and avoidance of definite resolution disconcerting, as many of Chekhov's first critics did. The more modern reader, formed in part by the tradition Chekhov himself inaugurated, recognizes that a crucial psychological shift in the character has occurred; the practical implications, whatever shape they may finally take, are all contained in that shift and thus in some sense are predictable and redundant. In "Sleepy" (1888), Chekhov relates the essential plot incident, the smothering of an infant by his exhausted, thirteen-year-old nurse, to a subordinate phrase of the final sentence of the story. This reduction of plot serves two purposes; it shifts the reader's interest to atmosphere and psychological state, and it also intensifies the impact of the final action by leaving its aftermath undescribed.

With the change of focus of attention away from plot and toward the character's experience, particularly his or her inner suffering, Chekhov replaces traditional plot with the process by which the character gains insight into his or her situation and its effects. Such stories, which have been termed "stories of discovery,"[4] dramatize through the character's struggle toward illumination the assumed effect of reading a Chekhov story. The reader realizes that accepted modes of thought and judgment do not hold, that apparent universal truths and fixed rules, especially moral certitudes, break down under the impact of unique facts as they are immediately perceived. Characters (and readers) in Chekhov do not discover "the truth," a proposition buried under a crust of falsehood but self-evident and incontrovertible once apprehended, as is the case in Tolstoi. Rather, they discover that supposed truths are limited, not universally valid. They come to recognize, often through painful disillusionment, that the truth lies not in propositions but in sceptical distrust of any dogmatic assertion or belief. Truth exists more in methods of discovery than in conclusions, which are always liable to revision in the light of new experience. The purpose of a Chekhov story is not so much to establish the truth or to convince the reader as to eliminate falsehood, making it possible for the reader to approximate the truth more closely, if never attain it fully. Even a non-fictional work which marshalls such meticulous factual evidence as *The Island of Sakhalin* (1893-1894) was intended to dispel public ignorance of a complex problem and to cut through official rhetoric that had obscured the reality of Russia's penal colonies. The book presents no definitive solution, of the sort Tolstoi was wont to write; it simply collects and analyses the facts necessary to attempt ameliorating the situation. "No one knows the real truth"; "If only one could know!"—these lines, from the end of "The Duel" (1891) and *Three Sisters* (1901), respectively, are not cries of epistemological despair as some critics have thought, but the start of a journey to an elusive goal.

The tendency of many Chekhov stories to end in tentative insight, a fleeting apprehension of an ever elusive truth, is reflected in a structural pattern typical of his fiction. Journeys are frequently used as organizing principles, but in contrast to the traditional conclusion of a journey structure where the characters return to the starting point or achieve rest at their destination, Chekhov's stories end with a departure or the continuation of a journey. "On the Road" (1886) consists of a brief intersection of the two characters' separate journeys in a snow-bound inn; at daybreak, both continue their separate ways, although each has profoundly affected the other. In "Dreams," the story ends with two constables and their prisoner resuming their plodding course through the dark, mist-shrouded landscape, their momentary reverie of a different, free life evaporating. At the end of "The Duel," von Koren departs, his moral and social axia shattered by the tawdry drama in which he has been a principal player. In "Beauties" (1888), the narrator's evanescent glimpses of human beauty occur during journeys, indeed can probably only occur in such fleeting contexts. "The Bride" (1903), Chekhov's last story, ends with the heroine setting out for a new life in St. Petersburg, her ties with her previous, stultifying provincial life severed irrevocably. *The Cherry Orchard* (1904), Chekhov's last work in any genre, fittingly devotes its last act to leave-taking. Even when a work concludes with the end of a journey, it is not a static conclusion or true resolution. In "Steppe," Egorushka's entire life lies before him as he begins school in the city after his travels across the steppe. For Chekhov, each step is a new departure; forms with marked closure are untrue to the very life they aspire to reflect.

Fiction that seeks not to establish or validate truths but rather to question assumptions believed on insufficient grounds to be true (and the possibility of a real ending is one of these assumptions) must be termed ironic.

Chekhov's irony, like Pushkin's before him, has as its goal not the destruction of belief for its own sake but rather the elimination of facile conventions as a necessary preliminary to recognition of the complexity of life (as well as of the freedom and unpredictability of valid literature). Thus, in a major work such as "The Duel" the assumptions of each of the characters, and of the reader, about themselves, about one another, and about essential values (Laevskii the fashionable pessimist, von Koren the Social Darwinist scientist, the humanist Samoilenko, and the mystic deacon all fit the pattern) are, through the crisis of the duel, overturned, and each character is left, liberated and humbled, to begin the search for "the real truth." The story has upset the reader's preconceptions as well: instead of a tragic denouement, the duel leads to moral regeneration and reconciliation among the characters. In "Ward No. 6" (1892), however, Dr. Ragin's moral indifference, justified through his abuse of philosophy, leads to his incarceration in the mental ward of his own hospital and to his death. His certitude is crushed and illumination comes, but only when it is too late for him, if not for the reader. In other stories, such as "The Grasshopper" (1892), "A Woman's Kingdom" (1894), or "The Darling" (1898), the ironic disparity between character and reader is greater; the character never achieves insight or glimpses it only briefly, while the reader's perception exceeds that of the character through most of the text. In late stories such as "The Lady with the Lapdog," "Three Years," "At Home," or "The Bride," reader and character share insight, and as the text ends both enter into an existence that is ambiguous but free of the restrictions of literary illusions or social conventions.

This sense of a potential world beyond the text becomes increasingly important in Chekhov's fiction, as does the necessity of the reader's active participation. The reader's collaboration (in the etymological sense of working together) in discovering the form and meaning of a given story increases as the range of Chekhov's experimentation and his freedom from predictable strategies grow. In fact, this encouragement of a new kind of reader and new modes of reading may be Chekhov's boldest and most fundamental experiment. Chekhov's ideal reader develops from an audience to be entertained to a close observer of events, particularly the subtle workings of the character's inner lives, to a searcher, together with the author and the character, for a new sort of truth. Although we cannot place exact chronological boundaries on these phases, the first coincides with Chekhov's years as a writer for the humourous journals such as *Oskolki* (*Fragments*), the second with his years of emergence as a serious author in the St. Petersburg newspapers and *Novoe vremia* (*New Times*), and, after 1888, in the serious journals. The final phase includes the last ten or twelve years of Chekhov's career, when his established reputation freed him from the constraints of the demands of a given paper or journal. In the last phase, rather than formulating "the real truth," Chekhov seeks only to point the way, to search for truth by eliminating those misperceptions that hinder the quest. In his insistence on the provisional nature of truth and on the reader's autonomy and free cooperation in the process of discovery, Chekhov was one of the founders of modern literature and remains our contemporary.

NOTES

1. A. P. Chekhov, *Polnoe sobranie sochinenii i pisem v 30-ti tomakh. Sochinenia* (Moscow, 1974), I, 17-18. Subsequent citations from this edition will be identified in the text in parenthesis, by volume and page.

2. Peter M. Bitsilli, *Chekhov's Art: A Stylistic Analysis,* trans. Toby W. Clyman and Edwina J. Cruise (Ann Arbor, Mich.: Ardis Press, 1983), discusses this quality of Chekhov's work. Bitsilli's study originally appeared in Russian in Bulgaria in 1942.

3. A. P. Chudakov, *Poetika Chekhova* (Moscow, 1979).

4. V. B. Kataev, *Proza Chekhova: Problemy interpretatsii* (Moscow, 1979).

PART IV

Chekhov's Impact

9

Martin Esslin

CHEKHOV AND THE MODERN DRAMA

Anton Chekhov was one of the major influences in the emergence of a wholly new approach to the subject matter, structure, and technique of dramatic writing at the end of the nineteenth century. It can be argued that he, in fact, occupies a key position at the point of transition between a millennial convention of "traditional" and the emergence of "modern" drama.

What was it that the "modern" drama replaced? What was it that the multifarious types of traditional dramatic fiction, however different they might appear, had fundamentally in common—from Greek tragedy and comedy to the well-made play of the nineteenth century; what were the characteristics that all these shared that were so decisively displaced by the new elements of the "modern"?

It was not what had so long been regarded as the hallmarks of the truly correct and classical form of drama: the Aristotelian unities of time, place, and action. After all, medieval drama, the Elizabethans, and the Romantics had superseded those by constructing rambling, epic plot-lines. But Greek drama and the French classical tradition, the medieval mystery plays and the Spanish theatre of the "siglo d'oro," Shakespeare and commedia dell'arte, Restoration comedy and the well-made play, do have a number of characteristics in common. Foremost among them is the assumption that the audience must be explicitly and clearly told what the principal characters' state of mind is at any given moment in the play, whether through the monologues of Shakespeare and the Elizabethans that are directly addressed to the audience, or the use of confidants in French classical drama, or, indeed through "asides" uttered in the presence of other characters who, by convention, were assumed to remain unaware of them.

Even more important perhaps was another basic assumption that underlay all language used in drama: that what a character said was not only what he or she meant to say, but that he or she was expressing it as clearly and eloquently as possible. Dramatic speech was deeply influenced by, and obeyed the rules of, the classical tradition of rhetoric as practised and formulated by Demosthenes, Cicero, and Quintilian, and as it was taught in the schools from the time of Socrates to the nineteenth century and beyond (in the United States, in public speaking courses in some colleges and universities to this day).

Similar ideas of a clear, transparent structure (derived from the rhetorical rules of statement of theme, development, and conclusion) also governed the construction of the plot from exposition through complication and reversal to a definite and conclusive ending.

That the theatre should attempt to present a picture of the world as it really is never occurred to the theoreticians or practitioners of pre-modern drama. The theatre was an art—and art was artifice, quite apart from the practical impossibility of creating a true facsimile of human life under the technological conditions of a stage in the open air, or lit by candles, with painted scenery, or no scenery at all. The theatre could only present the essential aspects of the human condition, compressed and idealised, according to a firmly established set of conventions (just as, for example, painting eliminated pubic hair in nudes and showed crowds of people in neatly stylised groupings).

It was the great change in the technology of theatre (with gas and later electrical lighting, hydraulic stage machinery, and so on) which, combined with the rise of the scientific world view, led to the idea that the stage could not only reproduce an accurate image of "real life," but should also become like an instrument of scientific inquiry into human behaviour, a laboratory in which the laws governing the interaction of human beings and social classes could be studied.

Yet Zola who first formulated the theoretical concept of the theatre of Naturalism and Ibsen who was the first to gain gradual acceptance for it— through scandal and the violent partisanship of radicals—found it very difficult to liberate themselves from some of the old conventions. Although Ibsen did away with the soliloquy and the "aside," although he tried to create, in his socially oriented drama, stage environments of the greatest possible realism—rooms with the fourth wall removed—structurally, he tended to adhere to the convention of the well-made play. Ibsen's analytical plots developed toward a climax with the relentless logic and compressed time-scale of French classical drama. Even so, his failure to let his characters explain themselves to the audience mystified even intelligent playgoers. As Clement Scott, in reviewing a performance of *Rosmersholm* in 1891, put it:

The old theory of playwriting was to make your story or your study as simple as possible. The hitherto accepted plan of a writer for the stage was to leave no possible shadow of doubt concerning his characterisation. But Ibsen loves to mystify. He is as enigmatic as the Sphynx. Those who earnestly desire to do him justice and to understand him keep on saying to themselves, "Granted all these people are egotists, or atheists, or agnostics, or emancipated, or what not, still I can't understand why he does this or she does that."[1]

It was Chekhov who took the decisive step beyond Ibsen. He not only renounced the convention of characters who constantly explain themselves to the audience, but he also discarded the last remnants of the plot structure of the well-made play. As a natural scientist and physician, Chekhov rebelled against the artificiality of the conventional dramatic structure. As early as 1881, when he was embarking on his first full-length play, which he discarded (the untitled manuscript, usually referred to as *Platonov*) after it had been rejected by Ermolova, he formulated his ideas as follows:

In real life people do not spend every minute in shooting each other, hanging themselves or declaring their love for each other. They don't devote all their time to trying to say witty things. Rather they are engaged in eating, drinking, flirting and talking about trivialities—and that is what should be happening on stage. One ought to write a play in which people come and go, eat, talk about the weather and play cards. Life should be exactly as it is, and people exactly as they are. On stage everything should be just as complicated and just as simple as in life. People eat their meals, and in the meantime their fortune is made or their life ruined.[2]

It took Chekhov some fifteen years before he himself succeeded in bringing this theoretical program to full practical realisation and fruition with *The Seagull*. For it was not easy to work out all the implications of the endeavour to present real "slices of life" on the stage. It meant, for one, that the action on stage would have to get as near as possible to "real elapsed time," that is, that an hour on stage would have to correspond to an hour of "real life." How could one tell a story with a scope larger than that of one-acts (such as Chekhov's own *The Proposal* and *The Bear*) by adhering to this principle? The solution that emerged was to present a number of significant episodes showing the characters and their situation in detail and in as near to "real time" as possible in widely separated segments extracted from the flow of time (usually four acts)—so that the events of months and years became visible by implication through the way in which the situation in each vignette differed from the previous one. Thus, the relentless forward pressure of the traditional dramatic form was replaced by a method of narration in which it was the *discontinuity* of the images that told the story, by implying what had happened in the gaps between episodes.

Even more decisive, however, was the demand that the characters should not be shown in unnaturally "dramatic" and climactic situations but pursuing the trivial occupations of real life—eating, drinking, making small talk, or just sitting around reading the newspaper. The state of mind of the characters, the emotional tensions between them, the subterranean streams of attraction and repulsion, love and hate, now frequently had to be indicated indirectly, so that the audience would be able to apprehend them by inference. In other words, the playwright had to supply the signs from which the spectators, having been turned into equivalents of Sherlock Holmes, would deduce the meaning of seemingly trivial exchanges, and, indeed, the meaning of silences, words that remained unspoken. This, after all, is what happens in real life: we meet people and from the cut of their clothes, the accents of their speech, the tone of voice with which they address remarks to us about the weather, we have to deduce their character or their intentions toward us. In our small ways each of us has to be a semiotician decoding the signs supplied to us by our fellow human beings and the environment.

Another consequence of this program for a new drama was the abandonment of the central figure—the hero—of the drama. There are no subsidiary characters in real life, no Rosencrantzes and Guildensterns whose presence in the play is merely dictated by the requirements of the plot and who therefore remain uncharacterised. In the traditional drama such characters were emotionally expendable. It was the hero or heroine alone with whom the spectator was meant to identify, from whose point of view he or she was supposed to experience the action, living through, vicariously, the emotions felt by such central characters. The new drama required a far more detached, clinical attitude that would allow the audience to look at all the characters with the same cool objectivity.

Characters viewed objectively, from the outside rather than through identification, tend to appear comic. If we identified ourselves with the man who slips on a banana peel we would feel his pain; if we viewed him from the outside we could laugh at his misfortune. The characters in Chekhov's mature plays, in which he succeeded in putting his program into practice, are thus essentially comic characters, even if what happens to them (frustration in love, loss of an estate, inability to move to Moscow) is sad or even tragic. Thus, Chekhov's program for a new approach to drama implied the emergence of tragicomedy as the dominant genre.

Chekhov's conflict with Stanislavskii about the production of his plays centered around this demand for a cool, sharp objectivity that would preserve the essentially comedic form of the tragic events, while Stanislavskii wanted to milk the tragic elements to produce an elegiac and as Chekhov felt "larmoyant" effect.

The demand for absolute truth, full conformity with the randomness and triviality of "real life," from which Chekhov started out, was clearly inspired by the same positivist, scientific ideas that had led Zola to proclaim the program of Naturalism. But, paradoxically, the resolve to reproduce the casualness and triviality of ordinary life led to a higher rather than a lesser degree of "artificiality." For, if meaning was to emerge from the depiction of people pursuing commonplace activities, if the spectator was to be enabled to deduce significance from the multitude of signifiers offered by decoding what they revealed, every move, every word, every object had to be carefully planned and designed as a bearer of such meaning. In other words, as real randomness would be totally meaningless, it was merely the *appearance* of randomness and triviality that had to be evoked by creating a structure of which every element contributed to the production of meaning. This type of drama thus required a far greater degree of skill in weaving an intricate texture of great complexity which could, nevertheless, add up to the intended effect and meaning.

This also was the reason why Chekhov so strenuously objected to Stanislavskii's overloading his productions with a clutter of details not indicated in the text. The proliferation of off-stage sound effects and other naturalistic detail brought in for the sake of mere "reality" smothered the structure of the signifiers Chekhov had carefully written into his scripts.

The dense texture of signifying detail within each segment of seemingly "real time" and the building of a sense of larger time-spans through a discontinuous four-act structure require a very high degree of control over the expressive means at the disposal of the playwright, a sense of rhythm and orchestration that would unify the seemingly casual and disconnected elements and transform the text into a texture as complex as that of the counterpoint of an orchestral score. Thus, the program that started from a rejection of "the poetic" on stage paradoxically led to a new kind of more complex poetry. Chekhov himself, in his acrimonious discussions with Stanislavskii, repeatedly insisted that the theatre was an art, striving to produce the appearance of reality, but it was never to be confused with reality.

On the other hand, the cold, objective nature of this art makes it impossible for the playwright to take sides or to offer solutions to the problems posed in his or her work:

You are right to demand that an author take a conscious stock of what he is doing, but you are confusing two concepts: answering the questions and formulating them correctly. Only the latter is required of an author. It is the duty of the court to formulate the questions correctly, but it is up to each member of the jury to answer them according to his own preference.[3]

Chekhov's drama thus rejects all moralising, just as it eschews the neat solutions that were required by the playwrights of traditional drama. With him "open form" entered the theatre.

It took a long time for Chekhov's revolutionary innovations to be recognised, let alone generally accepted outside Russia, where the successful production of his plays by Stanislavskii's and Nemirovich-Danchenko's Moscow Art Theatre (however much Chekhov himself disagreed with them) had established him as a major playwright.

In Russia Gorkii was deeply influenced by Chekhov's technique, although his plays were far more partisan and explicitly political than Chekhov's. But it was only after the discomfiture of the revolutionary avant-garde and the introduction of socialist realism as the leading aesthetic doctrine in the Soviet Union in the 1930s that the Moscow Art Theatre was elevated into the model for Soviet drama, and Chekhov became the official model, at least as far as the superficial and external aspects of his "realistic" technique were concerned. In spirit the stereotype of the contemporary Russian "realistic" play, with its openly propagandistic message, is far removed from Chekhov.

Western Europeans found it difficult at first to understand Chekhov's intentions. Early performances of *Uncle Vania* in Berlin (1904) and Munich (1913), *The Seagull* in Berlin (1907), Glasgow (1909), and Munich (1911) and *The Cherry Orchard* in London (1911) remained without lasting echo. There was one major exception: Bernard Shaw was so deeply impressed that he modeled his own *Heartbreak House* (1919) on *The Cherry Orchard*. He clearly saw the parallel between the death of the Russian upper classes and the inevitable decline of English society.

After World War I, tours by the Moscow Art Theatre to Germany, France, and the United States spread the Russian playwright's fame. In France the Pitoeff family, exiled from Russia, consolidated his reputation, but there too they only gained general acceptance for him after World War II.

It was in England that Chekhov first achieved recognition as a classic and one of the great innovators of drama. A production of *The Cherry Orchard* by J. B. Fagan (with the young John Gielgud as Trofimov) at the Oxford Playhouse in January 1925 was so successful that the play was transferred to London and ran there for several months. Yet the real breakthrough for Chekhov came with a series of productions of his late plays by the Russian emigré director Theodore Komisarjevsky at the small Barnes Theatre in London in 1926. By the end of the 1930s Chekhov had become a recognised classic in the English theatre. Since then Shakespeare, Ibsen, and Chekhov have been regarded as the standard classics of the English repertoire. No British actor or actress can lay claim to major status without having successfully portrayed the principal parts created by these playwrights.

The reasons for Chekhov's spectacular rise to the status of a classic in Britain are complex. The fact that pre-revolutionary Russia and England were both societies in which the upper classes spent a great deal of their time in country houses populated by a large cast of family members and guests may well have something to do with it. In these plays theatre audiences in England recognised their own way of life. Similarly, Chekhov's use of "subtext" has its affinities with the English penchant for "understatement."

English audiences may thus have been more skilled than those of other countries in the art of decoding subtle nuances of utterance. The fact remains that actors like Gielgud, Laurence Olivier, Peggy Ashcroft, Ralph Richardson, Michael Redgrave, and Alec Guinness made Chekhov their own and that he has remained one of the most performed standard authors over a period of 50 years.

That an author so favoured by major actors would have an influence on the writing of plays in Britain was inevitable. Among the many direct, if shallow, imitators of the Chekhovian style are playwrights like N. C. Hunter (1908-1971) whose *Waters of the Moon* (1951) scored a big success by providing fat parts for "Chekhovian" actors; Enid Bagnold (1889-1981); or Terence Rattigan (1911-1977) who used Chekhovian techniques in plays like *The Browning Version* (1948) and *Separate Tables* (1954).

In the United States Chekhov's influence spread indirectly through the success of Stanislavskii's approach to the technique of acting, not least through the efforts of Chekhov's nephew Michael Alexandrovich Chekhov (1891-1955) who had emigrated to England in 1927 and moved to America in 1939. Undoubtedly playwrights like Tennessee Williams, Arthur Miller, William Inge, or Clifford Odets absorbed at least some of Chekhov's ideas about the "subtext" and the emotional overtones of seemingly trivial conversation.

Yet to look for the direct influence of Chekhov on individual playwrights is perhaps futile. His real influence, though mainly indirect, goes far deeper and is far more pervasive. For he was one of the major innovators who changed the basic assumptions upon which the drama of our time (and "drama" nowadays includes the dramatic material of the cinema, television and radio) is founded.

Many influences, often of a seemingly contradictory nature, have shaped present approaches to drama. George Buechner (1813-1837), also a physician and natural scientist, but almost certainly unknown to Chekhov as he was only being rediscovered at the turn of the century, in many ways anticipated the technique of discontinuous plot development and the use of a type of dialogue that was both documentary and poetically orchestrated. The Naturalists—Ibsen, Strindberg, Gerhart Hauptmann, Arthur Schnitzler —eliminated the conventions of the soliloquy and aside; Frank Wedekind was a pioneer of dialogue in which people talked past each other, neither listening nor answering their interlocutor's points; the German Expressionists, following the lead of Strindberg in the last phase of his career, shifted the plane of the action from the external world to the inner life of the leading character so that the stage became a projection of his or her fantasies and hallucinations; Bertolt Brecht rebelled against the theatre as a house of illusions, the tight construction of continuous plot-lines and developed his own, discontinuous "epic" technique of storytelling; Antonin Artaud tried to devalue the word as an element of drama; and the "Absurdist" playwrights of the 1950s and 1960s (Samuel Beckett, Jean Genet, Arthur Adamov, Eugene Ionesco) created a non-illusionistic theatre of concrete stage metaphors.

Many of these tendencies seem to be in direct contradiction to Chekhov's program of a theatre that would faithfully reproduce the appearance of real life, its casualness and its seeming triviality. Yet, paradoxically, his example and his practise contributed a great deal to developments that, at first sight, may seem very far removed from his ideas and intentions.

Above all, Chekhov, more than any other innovator of drama, established the concept of an "open" form. By putting the onus of decoding the events on the stage on the spectators, by requiring them to draw their own conclusions as to the meaning as well as the ultimate message of the play, and by avoiding to send them home with a neatly packaged series of events in their minds, Chekhov anticipated Brecht's "Verfremdungseffekt" (which he may well himself have inherited from the Russian formalists' concept of "defamiliarisation," in turn directly related to Chekhov's practise). And at the other end of the spectrum a play like Beckett's *Waiting for Godot* carries Chekhov's technique of characters in apparently idle and trivial chatter to its extreme, creating a dramatic structure without action and completely open-ended. Here the trappings of Realism have fallen away, but the Chekhovian principle remains triumphant.

Chekhov's renunciation of high-flown poetic language and rhetorical explicitness (which went much further than Ibsen's attempts at realistic dialogue) produced another paradoxical consequence: the need to orchestrate the seemingly casual conversations, and the silences and hesitations in the characters' speech produced a new kind of poetry, a lyricism in which the rhythms and pauses coalesced into a new harmony. This created an emphasis on mood, on atmosphere, that was very different from the conscious lyricism of Symbolists like Maurice Maeterlinck or Neo-Romantics like the young Hugo von Hofmannsthal, a texture of often bitter ironies and counterpoints between the overt meaning and the subtext. Chekhov's practise opened the way for a new concept of the "poetic" in the theatre, what Jean Cocteau has called the "poetry of the stage" as against mere "poetry on the stage": the formally prosaic statement that acquires its poetry from the context in which it is pronounced, its position within the rhythmic and semantic structure of a *situation*.

The new type of "lyricism" has become the main source of "the poetic" in contemporary drama, not only in stage plays but also in the cinema, where a host of great directors, from Jean Renoir and Marcel Carné to Antonioni and Robert Altmann have extracted poetry from the trivial dialogue and objects of real life situations.

By reducing the importance of overt action and "plot" Chekhov created a new focus of attention: the situation itself, the conjunction of characters, the subtle use of seemingly incongruous detail (like the map of Africa on the wall of Uncle Vania's study), the sparing use of sound (like the strumming of a guitar) put the emphasis on the complex audiovisual *image* of the stage and made the stage itself into a poetic metaphor. Chekhov was one of the pioneers in moving the theatre away from putting its main emphasis on action in the simple, literal sense. A great deal is still happening in the seemingly static stage images of Chekhov, behind the apparently trivial dialogue. But it is complex and covert rather than on the surface and direct. Much of contemporary drama derives from this use of ambivalence and irony. Sonia's last words in *Uncle Vania* in a seemingly idyllic situation, with Maria Vassilevna working on her pamphlet, Marina knitting, Telegin softly playing his guitar, and Sonia herself kneeling before Vania, "We shall rest!" seem hopeful and the situation idyllic. Yet, at the same time, Sonia may not really believe what she is saying, and the idyllic situation enshrines, in reality, the horror of endless boredom and futility. Compare this with the last line of *Waiting for Godot*: "Let's go," followed by the stage direction "(They do not move)" to see a much reduced, almost minimalist, version of the same technique.

Chekhov's refusal to depart from the mere objective delineation of people and events in their inherent inner contradictions and ambivalences made him the pioneer of another main characteristic of contemporary drama: the emergence of the *tragicomic* as its prevailing mode. That the "death of tragedy" derives from the loss of moral certainties and metaphysically grounded principles is clear enough. Chekhov was one of the first to see this and to embody its consequences in devising a new genre of drama. As Friedrich Duerrenmatt has argued, modern people are far too deeply enmeshed in society's organisational framework ever to exercise the heroic privilege of assuming full and proud responsibility for their acts, to allow their misfortunes ever to be more than mere mishaps, accidents. Chekhov was the first to cast his drama in this mode of tragicomic ambivalence; the three sisters' inability to get to Moscow, the ruination of their brother's talents, the death of Tuzenbakh—all are prime examples of just such socially determined inevitabilities, such mishaps and accidents. Vania's failure to hit the professor is comic, although the situation is tragic. But even if Vania did shoot the professor it would still not be tragedy, merely a regrettable incident. If Harold Pinter speaks of his plays as being meant to be funny up to that point where they cease to be funny, he was formulating a perception of the tragicomic that directly derives from Chekhov.

There is only a small step from Chekhov's images of a society deprived of purpose and direction to the far more emphatic presentation of a world deprived of its "metaphysical dimension" in the plays of Beckett, Genet, Adamov, or Ionesco. Admittedly, the dramatists of the Absurd have left the solid ground of reality behind and have taken off into dreamlike imagery and hallucinatory metaphor. Yet it can be argued that Chekhov himself, by his very realism, blazed even that trail. In creating so convincing a picture of the randomness and ambivalence of reality, he, more than any other dramatist before him, opened up the question about the nature of reality itself. If every member of the audience has to find his or her own meaning of what he or she sees by decoding a large number of signifiers, each spectator's image of the play will be slightly different from that which his or her neighbour sees, and will thus become one's own private image, not too far removed from being one's own private dream or fantasy. The Theatre of the Absurd merely builds on that foundation by posing, less subtly, more insistently than Chekhov, the question: "What is it that I am seeing happening before my eyes?"

The Brechtian theatre, insisting as it does on the solid material basis of the world, also requires the audience to decode the signifiers of its parables by themselves. It also derives its poetic force from the ironic juxtaposition of ambivalent and contradictory signs to produce an ultimately tragicomic world view. While it is almost certain that Brecht was not consciously or directly influenced by Chekhov, his ideas pervaded the atmosphere of theatrical and literary modernism and, indeed, more complex lines of inter-connectedness can be traced. Brecht's "Verfremdungseffekt," as has already been mentioned, owed a great deal to the Russian formalists' concept of *ostranenie* (defamiliarisation). Moreover, Brecht was a great admirer of Vsevolod Meierkhold, who, before he broke away from Stanis-lavskii and the Moscow Art Theatre had been the first Treplev in Stanislavskii's *Seagull* and the first Tuzenbakh in the *Three Sisters* (it is said that Chekhov had written the part for him). Meierkhold's modernism thus derives indirectly from, and is an extrapolation into more daring innovation of, the demand for ruthless objectivity and open forms in the theatre. Meierkhold once sent Chekhov a photograph of himself, inscribed: "From the pale-faced Meierkhold to his God."

The greatest and most directly discernible impact of Chekhov's innova-tion on the modern theatre, however, is undoubtedly to be found in the field of dialogue. The concept of the "subtext" has become so deeply embedded in the fabric of basic assumptions of contemporary playwriting and acting that, literally, there can be hardly a playwright or actor today who does not unquestioningly subscribe to it in his or her practise.

Chekhov's ideas have not only been assimilated, but they have also been further developed by dramatists like Harold Pinter, whose use of pauses, silences, and subterranean currents of meaning clearly derives from Chekhov but goes far beyond him in the exploration of the implied signifi-cance of a whole gamut of speech-acts, from the use of trade jargon to that of tautology, repetition, solecisms, and delayed repartee.

Pinter's linguistic experiments, so clearly derived from Chekhov, have engendered a host of followers in Europe and the United States (where perhaps David Mamet is the foremost practitioner of this type of linguistic exploration).

The concept of the "subtext" has also led to attempts to bring onto the stage characters whose linguistic ability is so low that they are unable to express themselves clearly. Here the playwright, through the rudiments of a vocabulary they may still possess, has to show what goes on in their minds and emotions. The English playwright Edward Bond, in a play like *Saved* (1965), made extremely successful use of a technique clearly derived from Chekhov, by making fragments of illiterate speech and silences reveal the characters' thoughts and feelings.

In the German-speaking world the Bavarian playwrights Franz Xaver Kroetz and Martin Sperr, the Austrians Wolfgang Bauer and Peter Turrini, have also become masters of this type of highly laconic dialogue in which silences and half-sentences are used to uncover the mental processes of tongue-tied individuals.

It is only since the end of World War II that Chekhov has been received, by general consensus, into the canon of the world's greatest dramatists that extends from the Greek tragedians to Shakespeare, Lope de Vega, Calderon, Racine, Corneille, Moliere, to the great moderns—Ibsen and Strindberg. Today Chekhov may well be regarded as being even more important and influential than Ibsen and Strindberg.

His output of only four major, mature plays may be much smaller than theirs, but, in the long run, its originality and innovative influence may well prove much greater.

Chekhov's determination to look at the world not merely with the cool objectivity of the scientist but also with the courage to confront the world in all its absurdity and infinite suffering (without flinching or self-pity and with a deep compassion for humanity in its ignorance and helplessness) led him to anticipate, far ahead of all his contemporaries, the mood and climate of our own time. That is the secret of his profound and all-pervading influence on the literature, and, above all, the drama of the century that opened so soon after his early death.

NOTES

1. *Daily Telegraph*, February 24, 1891, quoted in Michael Egan, ed., *Ibsen: The Critical Heritage* (London and Boston: Routledge and Kegan Paul, 1972), p. 168.

2. Quoted in Siegfried Melchinger, *Tschechow* (Velber bei Hannover: Friedrich Verlag), p. 68.

3. Chekhov's letter to Suvorin, October 27, 1888, in *Letters to Anton Chekhov*, trans. Michael H. Heim and Simon Karlinsky (New York: Harper & Row, 1973).

10

Charles E. May

CHEKHOV AND THE MODERN SHORT STORY

Anton Chekhov's short stories were first welcomed in England and America just after the turn of the century as examples of late nineteenth-century realism, but since they did not embody the social commitment or political convictions of the realistic novel, they were termed "realistic" primarily because they seemed to focus on fragments of everyday reality. Consequently, they were characterized as "sketches," "slices of life," "cross-sections of Russian life," and were often said to be lacking every element which constitutes a really good short story. However, at the same time, other critics saw that Chekhov's ability to dispense with a striking incident, his impressionism, and his freedom from the literary conventions of the highly plotted and formalized story marked the beginnings of a new or "modern" kind of short fiction that combined the specific detail of realism with the poetic lyricism of romanticism.[1]

The primary characteristics of this new hybrid form are: character as mood rather than as either symbolic projection or realistic depiction; story as minimal lyricized sketch rather than as elaborately plotted tale; atmosphere as an ambiguous mixture of both external details and psychic projections; and a basic impressionistic apprehension of reality itself as a function of perspectival point of view. The ultimate result of these characteristics is the modernist and postmodernist focus on reality itself as a fictional construct and the contemporary trend to make fictional assumptions and techniques both the subject matter and theme of the novel and the short story.

CHARACTER AS MOOD

The most basic problem in understanding the Chekhovian shift to the "modern" short story involves a new definition of the notion of "story" itself, which, in turn, involves not only a new understanding of the kind of "experience" to be embodied in story but a new conception of character as well. Primarily this shift to the modern is marked by a transition from the romantic focus on a projective fiction, in which characters are functions in an essentially code-bound parabolic or ironic structure, to an apparently realistic episode in which plot is subordinate to "as-if-real" character. However, it should be noted that Chekhov's fictional figures are not realistic in the way that characters in the novel usually are. The short story is too short to allow for character to be created by the kind of dense detail and social interaction through duration typical of the novel.

Conrad Aiken was perhaps the first critic to recognize the secret of Chekhov's creation of character. Noting that Chekhov's stories offer an unparalleled "range of states of consciousness," Aiken says that whereas Poe manipulates plot and James manipulates thought, Chekhov "manipulates feeling or mood." If, says, Aiken, we find his characters have a strange way of evaporating, "it is because our view of them was never permitted for a moment to be external—we saw them only as infinitely fine and truthful sequences of mood."[2] This apprehension of character as mood is closely related to D. S. Mirsky's understanding of the Chekhovian style, which he described as "bathed in a perfect and uniform haze," and the Chekhovian narrative method, which Mirsky says "allows nothing to 'happen,' but only smoothly and imperceptibly to 'become'."[3]

Such a notion of character as mood and story as a hazy "eventless" becoming is characteristic of the modern artistic understanding of story. It is like Conrad's conception in *Heart of Darkness*, for to his story-teller Marlowe, "the meaning of an episode was not inside like a kernel but outside, enveloping the tale which brought it out only as a glow brings out a haze." More recently, Eudora Welty has suggested that the first thing we notice about the short story is "that we can't really see the solid outlines of it—it seems bathed in something of its own. It is wrapped in an atmosphere."[4] Once we see that the short story, by its very shortness, cannot deal with the denseness of detail and the duration of time typical of the novel, but rather focuses on a revelatory break-up of the rhythm of everyday reality, we can see how the form, striving to accommodate "realism" at the end of the nineteenth century, focused on an experience under the influence of a particular mood and therefore depended more on tone than on plot as a principle of unity.

In fact, "an experience" phenomenologically encountered, rather than "experience" discursively understood, is the primary focus of the modern short story, and, as John Dewey makes clear, "an experience" is recognized as such precisely because it has a unity, "a single *quality* that pervades the entire experience in spite of the variation of its constituent parts."[5] Rather than plot, what unifies the modern short story is an atmosphere, a certain tone of significance. The problem is to determine the source of this significance. On the one hand, it may be the episode itself, which, to use Henry James's phrase, seems to have a "latent value" that the artist tries to unveil.[6] It is this point of view that governs James Joyce's notion of the epiphany—"a sudden spiritual manifestation, whether in the vulgarity of speech or of gesture or in a memorable phase of the mind itself."[7]

On the other hand, it may be the subjectivity of the teller, his perception that what seems trivial and everyday has, from his point of view, significance and meaning. There is no way to distinguish between these two views of the source of the so-called "modern" short story, for it is by the teller's very choice of seemingly trivial details and his organization of them into a unified pattern that lyricizes the story and makes it seem natural and realistic even as it resonates with meaning. As Georg Lukács has suggested, lyricism in the short story is pure selection which hides itself behind the hard outlines of the event; it is "the most purely artistic form; it expresses the ultimate meaning of all artistic creation as *mood*."[8]

Although Chekhov's conception of the short story as a lyrically charged fragment in which characters are less fully rounded realistic figures than they are embodiments of mood has influenced all twentieth-century practitioners of the form, his most immediate impact has been on the three writers of the early twenties who have received the most critical attention for fully developing the so-called "modern" short story—James Joyce, Katherine Mansfield, and Sherwood Anderson. And because of the wide-spread influence of the stories of these three writers, Chekhov has thus had an effect on the works of such major twentieth-century short story writers as Katherine Anne Porter, Franz Kafka, Bernard Malamud, Ernest Hemingway, and Raymond Carver.

THE MINIMAL STORY

The most obvious similarity between the stories of Chekhov and those of Joyce, Anderson, and Mansfield is their minimal dependence on the traditional notion of plot and their focus instead on a single situation in which everyday reality is broken up by a crisis. Typical of Chekhov's minimalist stories is the often-anthologized "Misery," in which the rhythm of the old-cab driver's everyday reality is suggested by his two different fares, a rhythm Iona himself tries to break up with the news that his son is dead. The story would indeed be only a sketch if Iona did not tell his story to his uncomprehending little mare at the end. For what the story communicates is the comic and pathetic sense of the incommunicable nature of grief itself. Iona "thirsts for speech," wants to talk of the death of his son "properly, very carefully."[9] He is caught by the primal desire to tell a story of the break-up of his everyday reality that will express the irony he senses and that, by being deliberate and detailed, will both express his grief and control it. In this sense, "Misery" is a lament—not an emotional wailing, but rather a controlled objectification of grief and its incommunicable nature by the presentation of deliberate details.

The story therefore illustrates one of the primary contributions Chekhov makes to the modern short story; that is, the expression of a complex inner state by presenting selected concrete details rather than by presenting either a parabolic form or by depicting the mind of the character. Significant reality for Chekhov is inner rather than outer reality, but the problem he tried to solve is how to create an illusion of inner reality by focusing on external details only. The answer for Chekhov, and thus for the modern short story generally, is to find an event that, if expressed "properly," that is, by the judicious choice of relevant details, will embody the complexity of the inner state. T. S. Eliot later termed such a technique an "objective correlative" —a detailed event, description, or characterization that served as a sort of objectification or formula for the emotion sought for. Modern short story writers after Chekhov made the objective correlative the central device in their development of the form.

Like Chekhov, whom she greatly admired, Katherine Mansfield was often accused of writing sketches instead of stories because her works did not manifest the plotted action of nineteenth-century short fiction. The best known Mansfield story similar in technique and theme to "Misery" is "The Fly." The external action of the story is extremely slight. The unnamed "boss" is visited by a retired friend whose casual mention of the boss's dead son makes him aware of his inability to grieve. The story ends with the boss idly dropping ink on a fly until it dies, whereupon he flings it away. Like "Misery," the story is about the nature of grief; also like Chekhov's story, "The Fly" maintains a strictly objective point of view, allowing the details of the story to communicate the latent significance of the boss's emotional state.

However, Mansfield differs from her mentor, Chekhov, by placing more dependence on the symbolism of the fly itself, regardless of whether one perceives the creature as a symbol of the death of the boss's grief, his own manipulated son, or the trivia of life that distracts us from feeling. Moreover, instead of focusing on the inarticulate nature of grief that goes deeper than words, "The Fly" seems to emphasize the transitory nature of grief —that regardless of how much the boss would like to hold on to his grief for his son, he finds it increasingly difficult to maintain such feelings. Such an inevitable loss of grief does not necessarily suggest that the boss's feelings for his son are negligible; rather it suggests a subtle aspect of grief—that it either flows naturally or else it must be self-consciously and artificially sought after. The subtle way that Mansfield communicates the complexity of the boss's emotional situation by the seemingly irrelevant conversation between the boss and his old acquaintance and by his apparently idle toying with the fly is typical of the Chekhovian device of allowing objective detail to communicate complex states of feeling.

Chekhov's "Aniuta" also depends on a rhythm of reality being momentarily broken up by a significant event, only to fall back once again. The story opens with the medical student walking to and fro cramming for his anatomy examination, repeating his lessons over and over as he tries to learn them by heart, while Aniuta silently does her embroidery to earn money to buy him tea and tobacco. The fact that she has known five others before him who left her when they finished their studies indicates that the story depicts a repetitive event just as his sounding out his lines is repetitive. When the young medical student tries to learn the order of ribs by drawing them on Aniuta's naked flesh, we have an ironic image of the typical Chekhov device of manifesting the internal as external. After she is used for the sake of "science," she is then used for the sake of "art" when the artist borrows her for his painting of Psyche.

The fact that the story ends as it began with the student walking back and forth repeating his lessons seems to reaffirm the usual charge against Chekhov—that "nothing really happens" here. But what has happened is that by the means of two objectifications it is revealed that Aniuta is used both body and soul. The doctor tries to "sound" Aniuta's body, just as the artist tries to capture her soul, but neither is able to reveal her; only Chekhov can "sound" her by his presentation of this significant episode. We know nothing about Aniuta in any realistic detail, nor do we know the workings of her mind, but we know everything we need to know about her to understand her static situation.

Many of the stories of twentieth-century writers after Chekhov depend on this same use of objective detail and significant situation to reveal subtle moral and emotional situations. For example, in Joyce's "Clay," it is not through introspection that we know Maria, but rather by the seemingly simple details and events of the story itself. However, Joyce goes beyond Chekhov's use of simple detail to reveal a subtle emotional state by making all of his apparently "realistic" references to Maria ironic revelations of her manipulated and lonely situation. Joyce, like Mansfield, also depends more on the use of a central symbol than Chekhov does, in this case, the clay itself, which is an objective correlative not only of Maria's malleable nature, but of the decay of her possibilities. Similarly, Joyce's "Eveline" depends solely on homey details such as dusty curtains, the photo of a priest, and the sound of an organ-grinder's song to objectify Eveline's entrapment by the paralysis of the past.

One of the most reticent of Chekhov's stories, a story so pure and clean that it presages the lucid limitations of Ernest Hemingway, is "The Lady with a Lapdog"—a paradigm for the story of the illicit affair. It is never clear in the story whether Gurov truly loves Anna Sergeevna or whether it is only the romantic fantasy that he wishes to maintain. What makes the story so subtle and complex is that Chekhov presents the romance in such a limited and objective way that we realize that there is no way to determine whether it is love or romance, for there is no way to distinguish between them. Although Gurov feels that he has a life open and seen, full of relative truth and falsehood like everyone else, he knows he has another life running its course in secret, a true life, and the false only was open to others. "All personal life," he feels, "rested on secrecy."[10]

However, there is no way to determine which is the real life and which is the false. At the end of the story, Gurov and Anna wonder how they can free themselves from their intolerable bondage, but only Chekhov and the reader are aware that there is no way to free themselves, for the real bondage is not the manifest one, but the latent bondage all human beings have to the dilemma of never knowing which is the true self and which is the false one. Although it seems to the couple that they would soon find the solution and a new and splendid life would begin, at the same time it is clear to them that they had a long way to go and that the most complicated part of it was only just beginning. Indeed, what seems so simple is indeed complicated. This device of presenting a seemingly simple external situation in such a way as to suggest emotional complexities beneath it is typical of the best of Hemingway's short stories.

Hemingway's debt to Chekhov lies in the radical limitation of authorial comment and the complete dependence on situation, a situation often so limited, with so much of what we usually expect in narrative left out, that all we have is dialogue and description. "Hills Like White Elephants" is perhaps the best example of Hemingway's use of the Chekhov device of allowing the bare situation to express a complex emotional dilemma. Beneath the surface level of "Hills Like White Elephants," a story made up mostly of silences, lies a complex emotional conflict between what the man thinks is "reasonable" and what the girl wants emotionally. The key to the silences of the story is the seemingly irrelevant detail announced at the beginning that the train will arrive in forty minutes. If delivered dramatically, the actual dialogue of the story would actually take only about fifteen minutes. Consequently, the story contains approximately twenty-five minutes of silence, a silence more telling in many ways than the dialogue itself. Moreover, the exposition of the story—that is, what the couple's life is like, what the girl wants, and what the man wants—is communicated by simple details, such as the man looking at their bags which have labels from all the hotels where they had spent nights and the girl looking at the dry hills and the fertile hills on the two sides of the valley. The bare situation and the seemingly trivial dialogue reveal a complex moral and emotional problem about the girl's proposed abortion which cannot be talked about directly.

Hemingway's focus on radically realistic events and his minimal description of such events seem obviously influenced by Chekhov. In his famous iceberg analogy, Hemingway echoes the typical Chekhovian idea about limiting his stories: "If a writer of prose knows enough about what he is writing about he may omit things that he knows and the reader, if the writer is writing truly enough, will have a feeling of those things as strongly as though the writer had stated them. The dignity of movement of an ice-berg is due to only one-eighth of it being above water.''[11] Hemingway's seemingly inconclusive stories such as ''Hills Like White Elephants'' and his highly detailed stories such as ''Big, Two-Hearted River'' are Chekovian in their use of concrete details to reflect complex states of mind. What critics have referred to as Hemingway's ''objective magic'' and his creation of stories that seem like ''nightmares at noonday'' derive from Chekhov's use of the objective correlative, his objective style, and his love of irony and understatement.

BETWEEN DREAM AND REALITY

Such Chekhov stories as ''Sleepy'' and ''The Bishop'' make use of another significant modern short story technique: focusing on reality as an ambiguous mixture of the psychic and the external. ''Sleepy'' marks a sort of realistic half-way point between the symbolic use of the hypnogogic state by Poe and its being pushed to surrealistic extremes by Kafka. Chekhov presents a basically realistic situation of the young Varka being literally caught in a hypnogogic state between desirable sleep and undesirable reality. The two realms blend indistinguishably in her mind until the hallucination takes over completely and she strangles the baby so she can sleep as ''soundly as the dead.'' Although the irony of the ending is obvious, it is the hypnotic rhythm of the events and the hallucinatory images that blend dream and reality which makes the story a significant treatment of the short story device of dissolving the rhythm of everyday reality into the purely psychic.

The two modern short story writers who have pushed this technique to extremes are Katherine Anne Porter and Franz Kafka—Porter by using illness and the approach of death to create dream-like realms of psychic reality and Kafka by making use of crisis situations to transform everyday states into nightmarish and surrealistic experiences. In ''Pale Horse, Pale Rider,'' Miranda is caught up in a dual world of dream and delirium made up both of the real world of war and death and the fantasy world of her illness and her love for the young man Adam. Porter takes Chekhov's use of the hallucinatory state and pushes it to ritualistic extremes to embody Miranda's death wish. Similarly, Kafka's ''The Judgement'' begins in a realistic way, until as a result of a crisis confrontation between father and son, it turns into hallucinatory unreality which dramatizes suppressed emotional forces finally bursting forth. What makes this movement from phenomenal reality into the hallucination of dream so different from the early nineteenth-century use of the motif is that the dream-like reality is presented as ''realistically'' and as concretely as external reality itself.

With ''The Bishop,'' Chekhov blurs the lines between fantasy and reality

for a more serious thematic purpose than in the relatively simple "Sleepy."
For here he links it with a theme that forms the center of one of his most
frequently discussed works, "A Dreary Story," a theme which also pre-
occupies the stories of Porter and Kafka, as well as the stories of many
other modern short story writers later on—the conflict between the presentational self and the problematical "real" self; the result is a lack of genuine
communication and sympathy between the central character and others.
The Bishop feels that the whole time he has been a Bishop, "not one person
had spoken to him genuinely, simply, as to a human being. . . . he still felt
that he had missed what was most important, something of which he had
dimly dreamed in the past." (I, 46-47). Caught in the rhythm of his professional reality, the Bishop searches for his real self in reverie and hallucinatory memory. In this story, Chekhov moves closer to the kind of grotesque
distortion of nightmare reality characteristic of Kafka. From the Bishop's
sense of confusion, it is only a relatively small step to Kafka's country
doctor, who in "great perplexity" is caught between external reality and
psychic nightmare.

Katherine Anne Porter, in "The Jilting of Granny Weatherall," intensifies the hallucinatory effect of illness and impending death that we see in
"The Bishop" by centering her story on Granny on her deathbed, hovering
between hallucination and memory and trying to justify her past presentational self. Both the crucial past event of Granny's life and her present
situation are so blended together that it is difficult for the reader to separate
them. Like "The Bishop," the story mingles past and present, but Porter
exceeds Chekhov's use of the technique by presenting seemingly disconnected and irrelevant details of Granny's physical and psychic experience in
such a fragmented way that the reader must tie the various details together
in order to understand the overall pattern of Granny's failure and the cause
of her final jilting.

The best known story of Franz Kafka which presents the theme of the
presentational self within a framework of nightmarish situation and detail is
of course "Metamorphosis." Here Kafka pushes the hallucinatory device
of Chekhov to its utmost extreme by forcing Gregor Samsa to face his real
self in a metaphor that must be taken as reality. The drastic step Kafka
takes is to make the transformation of the psychic into the physical the
precipitating premise which the entire story follows. The only suspension of
disbelief required in the story is that the reader accept the premise that
Gregor Samsa awakes one morning from uneasy dreams to find himself
transformed into a giant dung beetle. Once one accepts this event, the rest
of the story is quite prosaic and realistic. The transformation of Gregor
indicates the objectification of an inner state; the basic tension in the story
that makes the reader not sure whether to laugh or to cry is between the
horrifying yet absurd content and the matter-of-fact realistic style.

IMPRESSIONISM AND ART AS REALITY

In Chekhov's "A Dreary Story," Professor Stepanovitch, like the Bishop, searches for his real self in the face of his impending death. Also like the Bishop, he desires to be loved not for his fame or label, but as an ordinary man. In the climactic moment of realization, similar to that epiphanic moment of Gabriel in Joyce's "The Dead," the professor, striving to know himself, comes to the realization that there is no common bond to connect all his thoughts, feelings, and ideas. "Every feeling and every thought exists apart in me; and in all my criticisms of science, the theatre, literature, my pupils, and in all the pictures my imagination draws, even the most skillful analyst could not find what is called a general idea, or the god of a living man. And if there is not that, then there is nothing" (I, 529). Although this lack of a general idea is often cited as the professor's ultimate negative characteristic as a man, as well as reflective of Chekhov's own most negative characteristic as an artist, such a critical judgment reveals a failure to understand Chekhov's modern point of view and indeed the modern short story. The professor's lack of a general idea ironically is the basis for his one means of salvation, the acceptance of the relativistic and impressionistic view via art which his young ward Katia objectifies. But as Katia tells him, he has no instinct or feeling for art, and his philosophizing about it only reveals he does not understand it.

Chekhov's adoption of such a relativistic and impressionistic point of view is what makes him both a master of the short story and an innovator of its modernity. As Nadine Gordimer has said about short story writers: "theirs is the art of the only thing one can be sure of—the present moment. . . . A discrete moment of truth is aimed at—not *the* moment of truth, because the short story doesn't deal in cumulatives."[12] Peter Stowell has made a strong case for understanding Chekhov's modernism as a result of his impressionistic point of view. The ambiguous and tenuous nature of experience perceived by the impressionist, says Stowell,

drives the author to render perceptually blurred bewilderment, rather than either the subject or the object. What is rendered is the mood, sense, feel, and atmosphere that exists between perceiver and perceived, subject and object. Literary impressionists discovered a new way to depict a new way of seeing and knowing. Literary impressionists discovered modernism."[13]

More recently, Suzanne C. Ferguson has attempted to show that the so-called modern short story is not a discrete genre at all, but rather a manifestation of impressionism. As Ferguson points out, "when all we have in the world is our own experience of it, all received knowledge becomes suspect, and the very nature of knowledge becomes problematic" and we must "confront the possibility that we cannot know anything for certain, that the processes we follow in search for truth may yield only fictions."[14]

Although indeed Ferguson's suggestion may reflect the negative side of the modernist temperament, there is also a positive aspect to such relativism which has been explored by such so-called postmodernist writers as Jorge Borges, John Barth, Robert Coover, and others; that is, that if reality is a fictional construct and the writer wishes to focus on the nature of reality, then he has little choice but to focus on the nature of art and fiction-making itself. If reality is a fiction, an artistic construct, then art perhaps provides the only means to experience reality. Both sides of this modernist predisposition can be seen in such Chekhov stories as, on the one hand, "The House with an Attic" and on the other hand, "Easter Eve" and "The Student."

For Chekhov, art as a means to experience true reality is a complex religious, aesthetic, and sympathetic process. Like the professor in "A Dreary Story," the artist in "The House with an Attic" is too bound by "general ideas," too wedded to philosophizing and rhetoric to truly enter into the human realm of art and participate in its mysterious unity. He says a man should feel superior even to what is beyond his understanding; otherwise he is not a man but a mouse afraid of everything. "Phenomena I don't understand," he tells the young Genia, "I face boldly, and am not overwhelmed by them. I am above them" (I, 545). Unlike Olga in "The Grasshopper" who only knows the external trappings of art, Genia, nicknamed "Misuc," genuinely wishes the artist to initiate her into the domain of the "Eternal and the Beautiful." But it is a realm that the artist knows only through rhetoric.

The central scene in the story is the artist's confrontation with Genia's older sister, Lida, who scorns him for not portraying the privations of the peasants. While she insists that the highest and holiest thing for a civilized being to do is to serve his neighbors, he says the highest vocation of man is spiritual activity—"the perpetual search for truth and the meaning of life." Becoming carried away with his own rhetoric, he insists: "When science and art are real, they aim not at temporary, private ends, but at eternal and universal—they seek for truth and the meaning of life, they seek for God, for the soul" (I, 552). While both Lida and the artist are individually right in their emphases on serving the other and searching for the eternal, neither actually genuinely embodies these ideals, any more than the artist and the doctor embody them in "Aniuta." Their failure is reflected by contrast with Genia whom they both misuse and manipulate for their own ends.

For Chekhov, the only way that the eternal can be achieved is aesthetically through a unification with the human. It is best embodied in his two most mystic stories which deal with the nature of art: "Easter Eve" and "The Student." Both stories focus on the tension between disorder and harmony, between separation resulting from everyday reality and unity achieved by means of story and song. In an in-between time between death and resurrection, in an in-between place on the ferry between darkness and chaos, Ieronim tells his story of Brother Nikolai and his extraordinary gift of writing hymns of praise. Chekhov comes as close here as anywhere in his letters and notes to describing his own aesthetic. As Ieronim says, canticles are quite a different thing from writing histories or sermons; moreover, it is not enough to know well the life of the saint or the conventions that govern the writing of canticles. What matters, he says, is the beauty and sweetness of it.

> Everything must be harmonious, brief and complete. There must be in every line softness, graciousness and tenderness; not one word should be harsh or rough or unsuitable. It must be written so that the worshipper may rejoice at heart and weep, while his mind is stirred and he is thrown into a tremor. (I, 464)

In contrast to the silence of the dark river and the remembered beauty of Nikolai's songs is the chaos and restlessness of the celebration the narrator enters, where everyone is too caught up in the "childishly irresponsible joy, seeking a pretext to break out and vent itself in some movement, even in senseless jostling and shoving" to listen to the songs of Nikolai. The narrator looks for the dead brother but does not regret not seeing him. "God knows, perhaps if I had seen him I should have lost the picture my imagination paints for me now" (I, 468). Indeed, it is the creation of Nikolai in the narrator's imagination that justifies Ieronim's story, just as it is Nikolai's songs that sustain Ieronim. For the key to the eternal for Chekhov is the art work which serves to unify human experience; thus Ieronim sees the face of his brother in the face of everyone.

"The Student" begins with a sense of disorder and lack of harmony. However, it is once again song or story that serves to heal a fractured sense of reality. After the student tells the story of the Last Supper and Peter's denial of Christ, which itself takes up about one third of this very short story, he says he imagines Peter weeping, "The garden was deathly still and very dark, and in the silence there came the sound of muffled sobbing." And with this final imaginative projection, the power of the story affects the two listeners. The student says the fact that they are affected must mean that what happened to Peter has some relation to them, to the present, to the desolate village, to himself, and to all people. The widow wept not because of the way he told the tale, but "because her whole being was deeply affected by what happened in Peter's soul."

Although it may not be the manner of the student's oral telling which affects the two women, it is indeed the story itself. For, although the story does not reveal what is passing through Peter's soul, it compels the reader/ listener to sympathetically identify with Peter in his complex moment of realization. Indeed the revelation of character by means of story presentation of a crucial moment in which the reader must then imaginatively participate is the key to Chekhov's much discussed "objectivity" and yet "sympathetic" presentation. The student thus feels joy at the sense of an unbroken chain running from the past to the present. He feels that "truth and beauty" which had guided life there in the garden had continued without interruption: "always they were the most important influences working on human life and everything on the earth . . . and life suddenly seemed to him enchanting, ravishing, marvelous and full of deep meaning."[15] As in "Easter Eve," here we see the only means by which Chekhov feels that the eternal can be achieved, through the aesthetic experience and sense of unity that story and song create.

Both Sherwood Anderson and James Joyce similarly focus on the significance of the aesthetic experience as being the means both for a religious participation with the "eternal" and a sympathetic participation with the other. For example, Joyce's "The Sisters" focuses on story and art as a religious/aesthetic experience which dominates the collection *The Dubliners*, and Anderson's "Death in The Woods" centers around "story as the only means to know the other. "The Sisters," like both "Easter Eve" and "The Student," emphasizes the religious-like nature of the aesthetic experience which the old priest has communicated to the young boy while he was alive and which he embodies to him now in his death. "Death in the Woods" is particularly like "The Student" in its emphasis on how only story itself can reveal the mysterious nature of human communion.

Like Chekhov, both Anderson and Joyce focus on the central themes of isolation and the need for human sympathy and the moral failure of inaction which dominate the modernist movement in the early twentieth century; both abjure highly plotted stories in favor of seemingly static episodes and "slices" of reality; both depend on unity of feeling to create a sense of "storyness"; and both establish a sense of the seemingly casual out of what is deliberately patterned, creating significance out of the trivial by judicious selection of detail and meaningful ordering of the parts. The result is an objective-ironic style which has characterized the modern short story up to the present day. It is a style that, even as it seems realistic on its surface, in fact emphasizes the radical difference between the routine of everyday reality and the incisive nature of story itself as the only means to know true reality. Contemporary short story writers push this Chekhovian realization to even more aesthetic extremes.

THE CONTEMPORARY SHORT STORY

The contemporary short story writer most influenced by the Chekhovian objective/ironic style is Bernard Malamud, and the Chekhov story that seems most similar to Malamud's stories is "Rothschild's Fiddle," not only because the central conflict involves a Jew, but because of its pathetic/comic ironic tone. Iakov Ivanov's business as a coffinmaker is bad in his village because people die so seldom. His unjustified hatred for the Jewish flautist Rothschild who plays even the merriest tunes sadly, and his feeling of financial loss and ruin align Iakov with all those figures that Malamud's Manischevitz identifies in "The Jewbird" when he says to his wife, "A wonderful thing, Fanny. Believe me, there are Jews everywhere." Chekhov's attempt to capture the sense of Yiddish folktale in "Rothschild's Fiddle" makes the story closer to a parable than most of his other best known stories.

Iakov feels distressed when his wife dies, for he knows that he has never spoken a kind word to her and has shouted at her for his losses. That Iakov has always been concerned with profit and loss rather than his family is also revealed when his wife asks him if he remembers when they had a baby and it died. He cannot remember and tells her she is dreaming. Iakov's epiphanic realization comes after his wife's death when he goes to the riverbank and remembers the child his wife had mentioned. But Chekhov's irony is more complex here than the simple sentimentality that such a realization might have elicited. Even as Iakov becomes lost in the pleasure of the pastoral scene, he wonders why he has never come here before and thinks of ways he could have made money at the riverbank. He laments once again his losses and thinks that if people did not act from envy and anger, as he has with his wife and Rothschild, they could get great "profit" from one another.

When he becomes ill and knows that he is dying, Iakov thinks that one good thing about it is that he will not have to eat and pay taxes. Thus he thinks life is a loss while death is a gain, for since we lie in the grave so long, we may realize immense profits. As he is dying, only Rothschild is there to pity him, and thus Iakov leaves Rothschild his fiddle. As Rothschild later tries to play the tune Iakov played, the result is so sad that everyone who hears it weeps. The new song so delights the town that the merchants and government officials vie with each other to get Rothschild to play for them. Thus, at the end, a profit is realized from Iakov's death.

"Rothschild's Fiddle" is an ironic parable-like story about the common Chekhov theme of loss and the lack of human communion which Malamud typically makes his own. Malamud's short stories are often closer to the oral tradition of parable than they are to the realistic fiction of social reality. However, although one can discern traces of the Yiddish tale in Malamud, one also realizes that his short stories reflect the tight symbolic structure and ironic and distanced point of view that we have come to associate with the short story since Chekhov. Malamud's stories move inevitably toward a conclusion in which complex moral dilemmas are not so much resolved as they are frozen in a symbolic final epiphany or ironic gesture. His characters are always caught in what might be called the demand for sympathy and responsibility. But the moral/aesthetic configuration of his stories is such that the reader is not permitted the luxury of an easy moral judgment.

The fact that Jews, that is, those who are alienated and suffering, are everywhere, which seems so obvious in "Rothschild's Fiddle," is of course a common theme in such Malamud stories as "The Mourners" in which the landlord Gruber, after trying to evict the unwanted and self-centered Kessler, finally pulls a sheet over himself and kneels to the floor to become a mourner with the old man. It is the central dilemma in "The Loan" in which Kobotsky arrives to ask for a loan from his old friend, Lieb the baker. When Lieb's wife Bessie, who has her own history of woes to recite, will not allow the loan, the two old friends can only embrace and part forever as the stench of the corpse-like burned bread lingers in their nostrils. Like "Rothschild's Fiddle," these stories present one sufferer who can understand the suffering of another. The bitter-sweet conclusions of most of Malamud's tales are typical of his Chekhovian refusal to give in to either sentimentality or condescension.

However, perhaps the contemporary short story writer who is closest to Chekhov is Raymond Carver. In Carver's most recent collection of stories, *What We Talk About When We Talk About Love*, language is used so sparingly and the plots are so minimal that the stories seem pallidly drained patterns with no flesh and life in them. The stories are so short and lean that they seem to have plot only as we reconstruct them in our memory. Whatever theme they may have is embodied in the bare outlines of the event and in the spare dialogue of characters who are so overcome by event and so lacking in language that the theme is unsayable. Characters often have no names or only first names and are so briefly described that they seem to have no physical presence at all; certainly they have no distinct identity but rather seem to be shadowy presences trapped in their own inarticulateness.

The charge lodged against Carver is the same one once lodged against Chekhov, that his fiction is dehumanized and therefore cold and unfeeling. In a typical Carver story, "Why Don't You Dance," plot is minimal; event is mysterious; character is negligible. A man puts all his furniture out in his front yard and runs an extension cord out so that things work just as they did when they were inside. A young couple stop by, look at the furniture, try out the bed, have a drink, and the girl dances with the owner. The conversation is functional, devoted primarily toward making purchases in a perfectly banal, garage-sale way. At the conclusion, the young wife tells someone about the event. "She kept talking. She told everyone. There was more to it, and she was trying to get it talked out. After a time, she quit trying." The problem of the story is that the event cannot be talked out; it is completely objectified in the spare description of the event itself. Although there is no exposition in the story, we know that a marriage is over, that the secret life of the house has been externalized on the front lawn, that the owner has made a desperate metaphor of his marriage, that the hopeful young couple play out a mock scenario of that marriage which presages their own, and that the event itself is a parody of events not told, but kept hidden, like the seven-eighths of the iceberg that Hemingway said could be left beneath the surface of prose if the writer knew his subject well enough.

THE WILL TO STYLE

From its beginnings as a separately recognized literary form, the short story has always been more closely associated with lyric poetry than with its overgrown narrative neighbor, the novel. Regardless of whether short fiction has clung to the legendary tale form of its early ancestry, as in Hawthorne, or whether it has moved toward the presentation of the single event, as in Chekhov, the form has always been a "much in little" proposition which conceals more than it reveals and leaves much unsaid. However, there are two basic means by which the short story has pursued its movement away from the linearity of prose toward the spatiality of poetry—either by using the metaphoric and plurasignative language of the poem or by radically limiting its selection of the presented event.

The result has been two completely different textures in short fiction—the former characterized by such writers as Eudora Welty in the forties and fifties and Bernard Malamud in the sixties and seventies whose styles are thick with metaphor and myth, and the latter characterized by such writers as Hemingway in the twenties and thirties and Raymond Carver in the seventies and eighties whose styles are thin to the point of disappearing. This second style, which could be said to have been started by Chekhov, became reaffirmed as the primary mode of the "literary" or "artistic" short story (as opposed to the still-popular tale form) in the twenties by Mansfield, Anderson, and Joyce; and it was later combined with the metaphoric mode by such writers as Faulkner, Katherine Anne Porter, Flannery O'Connor, and others to create a modern short story which still maintains some of the characteristics of the old romance form even as it seems to be a radically realistic depiction of a single crucial episode.

The charge often made against the Chekhovian story—that it is dehumanized and therefore cold and unfeeling—has been made about the short story as a form since Hawthorne was criticized for his "bloodless" parables. However, such a charge ignores the nature of art that has characterized Western culture since the early nineteenth century and which Ortega y Gasset so clearly delineated in *The Dehumanization of Art*. In their nostalgia for the bourgeois security of nineteenth-century realism, critics of the short story forget that the royal road to art, as Ortega delineates is, "the will to style." And to stylize "means to deform reality, to derealize: style involves dehumanization." Given this definition of art, it is easy to see that the short story as a form has always embodied "the will to style."[16] The short story writer realizes that the artist must not confuse reality with idea, that he must inevitably turn his back on alleged reality and, as Ortega insists, "take the ideas for what they are—mere subjective patterns—and make them live as such, lean and angular, but pure and transparent."

The lyricism of the Chekhovian short story lies in this will to style in which reality is derealized and ideas live solely as ideas. Thus Chekhov's stories are more "poetic," that is, more "artistic" than we usually expect fiction to be; they help define the difference between the loose and baggy monstrous novel and the taut, gemlike short story. One final implication of Chekhov's focus on the "will to style" is the inevitable self-consciousness of fiction as fiction. If the term "modernism" suggests, as most critics seem to agree, a reaction against nineteenth-century bourgeois realism, which, a la Chekhov, Joyce, Anderson, and others, manifested itself as a frustration of conventional expectations about the cause-and-effect nature of plot and the "as-if-real" nature of character; then postmodernism pushes this movement even further so that contemporary fiction is less and less about objective reality and more and more about its own creative processes.

The primary effect of this mode of thought on contemporary fiction is that the story has a tendency to loosen its illusion of reality to explore the reality of its illusion. Rather than presenting itself "as if" it were real—a mimetic mirroring of external reality—postmodernist fiction makes its own artistic conventions and devices the subject of the story as well as its theme. The underlying assumption is that the forms of art are explainable by the laws of art; literary language is not a proxy for something else, but rather an object of study itself. The short story as a genre has always been more apt to lay bare its fictionality than the novel, which has traditionally tried to cover it up. Fictional self-consciousness in the short story does not allow the reader to maintain the comfortable cover-up assumption that what is depicted is real; instead the reader is made uncomfortably aware that the only reality is the process of depiction itself—the fiction-making process, the language act.

Although Anton Chekhov could not have anticipated the far-reaching implications of his experimentation with the short story as a seemingly realistic, yet highly stylized, form in the work of John Barth, Donald Barthelme, Robert Coover, and Raymond Carver, it is clear that the contemporary short story, for all of its much complained-of "unreadability," owes a significant debt to the much-criticized "storyless" stories of Chekhov. For it is with Chekhov that the short story was liberated from its adherence to the parabolic exemplum and fiction generally was liberated from the tedium of the realistic novel. With Chekhov, the short story took on a new respectability and began to be seen as the most appropriate narrative form to reflect the modern temperament. There can be no understanding of the short story as a genre without an understanding of Chekhov's contribution to the form. Conrad Aiken's assessment of him in 1921 has yet to be challenged: "Possibly the greatest writer of the short story who has ever lived."[17]

NOTES

1. Early reviews of Chekhov can be found in *Chekhov: The Critical Heritage*, ed. Victor Emeljanow (London: Routledge and Kegan Paul, 1981). See the twelfth essay in this volume by John Tulloch, "Chekhov Abroad: Western Criticism."

2. Conrad Aiken, "Anton Chekhov," 1921; reprinted in *Collected Criticism* (New York: Oxford University Press, 1968), pp. 148-53.

3. D. S. Mirsky, "Chekhov and the English," 1927; reprinted in *Russian Literature and Modern English Fiction*, ed. Donald Davie (University of Chicago Press, 1965), pp. 203-213.

4. Eudora Welty, "The Reading and Writing of Short Stories," 1949; reprinted in *Short Story Theories*, ed. Charles E. May (Athens: Ohio University Press, 1976), pp. 159-177.

5. John Dewey, *Art of Experience* (New York: G. P. Putnam's Sons, 1934), p. 37.

6. Quoted by Gorham Munson, "The Recapture of the Storyable," *The University Review* 10 (Autumn 1943): 37-44.

7. *Stephen Hero*, ed. Theodore Spencer (New York: New Directions, 1944), p. 51.

8. Georg Lukács, *The Theory of the Novel*, trans. Anna Bostock (Cambridge, Mass.: MIT Press, 1971), p. 51.

9. *The Image of Chekhov*, trans. Robert Payne (New York: Alfred A. Knopf, 1976), p. 104. In this edition "Misery" ("Toska") is translated as "Heartache."

10. *Select Tales of Tchehov*, trans. Constance Garnett (London: Chatto and Windus, 1961), I, 16. Further citations from this edition are identified by page and volume in parenthesis in the text.

11. *Death in the Afternoon* (New York: Charles Scribner's Sons, 1931), p. 192.

12. Nadine Gordimer, "The Flash of Fireflies," in *Short Story Theories*, p. 178.

13. Peter Stowell, *Literary Impressionism: James and Chekhov* (Athens: University of Georgia Press, 1980), p. 243.

14. Suzanne C. Ferguson, "Defining the Short Story: Impressionism and Form," *Modern Fiction Studies* 28 (Spring 1982): 13-14.

15. *The Image of Chekhov*, pp. 222-23.

16. *The Dehumanization of Art and Other Writings on Art and Culture* (Garden City, N.Y.: Doubleday Anchor Books, 1956), p. 23.

17. *Collected Criticism*, p. 149.

PART V
Criticism

11

Victor Terras

CHEKHOV AT HOME: RUSSIAN CRITICISM

Like some other major Russian writers, Chekhov entered literature through the back door of journalism, in his case N. A. Leikin's popular satirical journal *Oskolki* (*Fragments*). He had published hundreds of short stories, humoresques, and feuilletons before he received critical attention. Chekhov's first collection of stories to receive serious reviews was *Motley Tales* (1886). The reviews were largely positive, though Chekhov had reason to be angry at those he felt were unfair.[1] Through the 1880s he did not particularly stand out among a galaxy of prose writers, most of whom are today totally forgotten.[2] The honor to have discovered Chekhov belongs to D. V. Grigorovich, who was the first to predict that Chekhov would be a classic one day.[3]

Chekhov made his first thrust to the forefront of Russian literary life with his plays *Ivanov* (1887-1889) and *The Wood Demon* (1889). However, neither play was a popular success, and both were widely rebuffed by the critics, who quite correctly pointed out the very traits that were later hailed as distinctive features of the new Chekhovian theatre: plotlessness, absence of a central hero or heroine, a lack of clearly delineated relations between characters, and a certain fuzziness as regards the play's genre ("comedy," "drama," or "tragedy"). Altogether, critics felt that Chekhov had failed to transform "life" into "drama" and saw his innovations merely as faulty dramatic technique.

While Chekhov's serious dramatic efforts of the late 1880s were failures, some stories of the same period, in which he developed analogous tendencies, "Name-Day" (1888), "The Steppe" (1888), and especially "A Dreary Story" (1889), established him as a major writer. This success was, however, accompanied by considerable controversy. In retrospect, the negative opinions expressed by some prestigious critics can be attributed to the fact that Chekhov's stories, much as his plays, were judged by established standards. There were, of course, the usual politically motivated reactions. Conservative critics, such as Iurii Nikolaev in *Moskovskie vedomosti* (*Moscow News*), December 14, 1889, accused Chekhov of unfounded pessimism and slanderous misrepresentation of the "famous Russian scientist" in "A Dreary Story," in whom they believed they recognized the great surgeon N. I. Pirogov. The populist N. K. Mikhailovskii, in an essay entitled "On Fathers and Children, and on Mr. Chekhov" (1890), charged Chekhov with aimlessness, moral indifference, and a lack of ideals, traits which the critic saw not only as a sign of the times, but also as a personal trait of Chekhov's. Mikhailovskii also speaks of an "unfinished quality" (*nedodelannost'*) of Chekhov's style, as in the nature descriptions in "The Steppe," obviously failing to appreciate Chekhov's impressionistic technique. Views similar to Mikhailovskii's were expressed by other representatives of the progressive Left, such as A. M. Skabichevskii, who used Chekhov's stories as occasions to expound his social ideas.

After Chekhov developed into one of Russia's leading writers in the 1890s, he remained controversial.[4] His relationship with Tolstoi provides some examples. Chekhov and Tolstoi were fond of each other and admired each other's art, but they could also be very critical of each other. Tolstoi disapproved of Chekhov's liberal views, which he sometimes found simply immoral.[5] Characteristically, Tolstoi said of Chekhov's story "The Darling" (1898) that Chekhov had meant to curse his heroine, but that the god of poetry had not allowed him to do this but had ordered him to bless her.[6] On the other hand, Tolstoi recognized the novelty and originality of Chekhov's art, which he dubbed "impressionist."[7] However, Tolstoi disapproved of Chekhov's dramatic style to the end. Chekhov acknowledged that he had been under Tolstoi's influence for several years, with a peak in 1886-1887. In certain instances contemporary critics recognized Tolstoi's manner in Chekhov's stories, particularly in "Name-Day" and in "A Dreary Story."[8] After 1890 Chekhov became disillusioned with Tolstoi's philosophy, and some of his works were written, at least in part, to refute Tolstoi's doctrines of non-resistance to evil, the evils of romantic love, moralist aesthetics, and opposition to progress based on science. "Ward No. 6" (1892) and "The Duel" (1891) are among Chekhov's more explicitly anti-Tolstoian works.[9]

Once they had recognized him as a major writer, Chekhov's contemporaries tended to create their image of him around their own political and philosophical views. This is true of the most famous of them, Maksim Gorkii, whose "Reminiscences of Chekhov" are considered a classic. Gorkii, a professed disciple of Chekhov, was one of the first to recognize Chekhov's full greatness. He saw in him the summit of "critical realism" as well as its end—to Gorkii the Marxist, the next step would be the heroic literature of the Revolution. Gorkii saw in Chekhov not only the atmosphere of "a melancholy day of late autumn,"[10] but also love of life and confidence in a better future, faith in man and in the Russian people. In addition, Gorkii was one of the first to see Chekhov's art as a fusion of uncompromising realism with "inspired and deeply conceived symbolism."[11] However, Gorkii infuses Chekhov's symbols with meanings that accommodate his own world view. Compare his reading of "The Darling" with Tolstoi's: "Here anxiously, like a gray mouse, scurries 'The Darling,' the dear, meek woman who loves so slavishly and who can love so much. You can slap her cheek and she won't even dare to utter a sigh aloud, the meek slave." (Gorkii, *Reminiscences*, pp. 84-85).

Nevertheless, Gorkii's understanding of Chekhov was much more subtle than that of any contemporary, save Tolstoi. V. G. Korolenko, a contemporary who in Chekhov's lifetime could consider himself Chekhov's equal and of whom Chekhov was exceptionally fond,[12] saw, as did others, a change in Chekhov's art, from youthful optimism to a later pessimism, which he tentatively ascribed to Chekhov's illness. A. I. Kuprin, on the other hand, vigorously denied that Chekhov was a pessimist at all.[13] While critics of the progressive Left, such as Mikhailovskii, Skabichevskii, P. B. Struve, V. V. Veresaev, and V. I. Ivanov-Razumnik, criticized Chekhov for his alleged "lack of ideals," but credited him with a profound understanding of the maladies of Russian society, several major critics of the Right harshly condemned him, recognizing in Chekhov's positivism a mortal enemy of their own religious world view.[14]

D. S. Merezhkovskii warned that Chekhov's masterful depictions of Russian everyday life (*byt*) were a dead end: "Chekhovian *byt* is the bare present, without past or future, only a frozen, motionless moment, a dead stop in contemporary Russian life, without any link to world history or world culture."[15] Merezhkovskii suggested that Chekhov's optimistic prophecies had a hollow ring and that the real message that came across from his works was that of the bankruptcy of the Russian intelligentsia and its "progressive" ideology. Merezhkovskii went as far as likening life as shown in Chekhov's last plays, *Three Sisters* and *The Cherry Orchard*, to a condition of nonbeing, or the existence of the living dead in Dostoevskii's story "Bobok." Consistently with her husband's view, Zinaida Hippius (under her critic's pen name Anton Krainii) called Chekhov "the last bard of decomposing trivia."[16]

Lev Shestov was just as resolute in condemning Chekhov. He called him "an overstrained, abnormal person" (*nadorvavshiisia, nenormal'nyi chelovek*) and a "bard of hopelessness" (p. 3) who delighted in presenting people to whom nothing was left but to "throw themselves down on the floor and beat their heads against the floor" (p. 14).[17] Chekhov, said Shestov, was a "necromancer" (*volkhv, kudesnik, zaklinatel'*) with an exceptional fascination for death, decomposition, decay, and hopelessness (pp. 23-24). Besides these extravagant charges, one also finds in Shestov some just observations on Chekhov's poetics, which he perceives as purposely violating literary conventions in order to create a semblance of "ordinary life."

Chekhov's image among wide circles of educated Russians was fixed in articles by the respected academic scholars D. N. Ovsianiko-Kulikovskii (1853-1920) and S. A. Vengerov (1855-1920). Ovsianiko-Kulikovskii saw Chekhov as an artist who with consummate skill selected those traits of life that served the creation of a desired mood, usually somber.[18] Vengerov's article was included in the Brokgauz-Efron Encyclopedia, Vol. 76 (1903), pp. 777-781, and was therefore particularly influential. Vengerov stressed the impressionistic, fragmentary, elliptic nature of Chekhov's art. He also saw Chekhov as the "historian" of the gloomy period of the 1880s when despair and hopelessness gripped the most sensitive elements of Russian society. Furthermore, Vengerov drew attention to Chekhov's dispassionate manner and his refusal to become involved with his heroes. He charged Chekhov with political "indifferentism" and a negative attitude toward the men and women of the 1860s, while conceding that Chekhov was even more negative toward conservative tendencies in Russian life.

When Chekhov resumed his career as a dramatist with *The Seagull* in 1896, the premiere of the play at the St. Petersburg Aleksandra Theatre created a scandal. The initial reviews were also largely negative. But the triumphant success of the play at the Moscow Art Theatre on December 17, 1898 soon led to Chekhov's general recognition as an innovative dramatist. Leading writers, directors, and actors showed great interest in *The Seagull* and *Uncle Vania*, which immediately followed it. Once the Moscow Art Theatre had broken the ice, the general public also appreciated Chekhov's new theatre. One of the signs of the distinctive and innovative quality of Chekhov's theatre was the appearance of a host of parodies which as a rule bore out the very same traits that had been pointed out by theatre critics.

Chekhov's theatre is inseparably linked with the Moscow Art Theatre and its great directors K. S. Stanislavskii and V. I. Nemirovich-Danchenko. The latter had a hand in the transformation of *The Wood Demon* into *Uncle Vania*, and Stanislavskii, often against Chekhov's objections, created the peculiar stage and sound effects that were for a long time characteristic not only of the Moscow Art Theatre stagings of Chekhov's plays but also of Chekhovian theatre at large. Therefore, the writings of Nemirovich-Danchenko and Stanislavskii, as well as the reminiscences and comments of the actors of the Moscow Art Theatre who participated in the creation of the new "Chekhovian" theatre, are an indispensable source in the study of Chekhov's plays.

After the Revolution of 1917, the Marxist critics who now dominated the literary scene found themselves in just as much disagreement on the merits of Chekhov's art as their predecessors. A. V. Lunacharskii, People's Commissar of Public Education and himself a playwright, was very positive about Chekhov, whom he believed to have been "in love with life," while the Bolshevik ideologue P. I. Lebedev-Polianskii found only "hopeless pessimism" in Chekhov.[19] Purists of the "On Guard" group, such as M. S. Olminskii (1863-1933) and G. Lelevich (1901-1945), as well as some members of "Lef," such as O. M. Brik, N. N. Aseev, and S. M. Tretiakov,[20] considered Chekhov too bland ideologically and too much concerned with private instead of social problems to be a proper example for Soviet writers.[21] On the other hand, Chekhov also had some passionate apologists who were also communist activists, among them Iu. M. Libedinskii, E. D. Zozulia, and especially M. E. Koltsov (1898-1942), who found that Chekhov had been "a socially conscious writer of the highest order, a bold and merciless satirist of the epoch preceding ours, whose heroes, albeit in a new guise and often in possession of a trade union card, occupy the backwaters of our restructured country even to this day."[22]

In the early 1920s some voices were heard declaring Chekhov's theatre *passé* and demanding its removal from the Soviet stage. While this never came about, there was some effect on the staging of Chekhov's plays. In 1924 the Leningrad Comedy Theatre (*Teatr Komedii*) staged *The Cherry Orchard* as a satirical comedy, with modest success. Ten years later this experiment was repeated in a more radical way at R. N. Simonov's Studio Theatre. Several scenes were added to demonstrate the degeneracy of the gentry, Ranevskaia was presented carrying on with Iasha, her young servant, Lopakhin was made into a *kulak* stereotype, and so on. This experiment was no success either and was severely criticized by Iu. V. Sobolev, among others.[23] However, these experiments induced the Moscow Art Theatre to introduce some changes in their version of the play (a livelier dialogue, speeded-up tempo). At any rate, Chekhov continued to be the Soviet public's favorite.

V. E. Meierkhold's reworking of three of Chekhov's vaudevilles (*The Anniversary, The Proposal,* and *The Bear*) into a single farce, *33 Fainting Fits* (with each announced by a sign: "Fainting Fit No. 1"), in 1935 may be mentioned as a curiosity. Iurii Sobolev's play *In the Ravine,* based on the story of that title and "The Peasants" (1897), was staged at Moscow Art Theatre 2 in the same year, with indifferent success. Meanwhile, Chekhov's vaudevilles were often reshaped and updated to fit Soviet reality, outright or as parodies.

In the 1920s scholarly study of Chekhov's works began in earnest. The first scholarly edition of Chekhov's *Collected Works* in twelve volumes (1930-1933) was a labor of love. Most of its organizers and collaborators were writers, journalists, critics, and playwrights: Lunacharskii, Koltsov, V. M. Friche, and others. In the late 1920s and early 1930s a beginning was made toward a critical analysis of Chekhov's early works.[24] A. B. Derman (1880-1952), himself a short story writer and novelist, laid the foundation for a structural analysis of Chekhov's prose.[25] Derman's early work is generally critical of Chekhov and sometimes simply negative, mostly on ideological grounds. But Derman, who at that stage was close to the socio-logical school of literary criticism, seriously tried to establish a connection between aesthetic and socio-psychological phenomena, suggesting, for example, that the plotlessness of Chekhov's works depends not only on his peculiar type of talent but also on "that dim and heavy Russian reality whose contemporary and observer he was" (p. 97)

Derman believed he had discovered a certain "disharmony in Chekhov's nature, resting with the fact that, a man of far ranging and strikingly clear intellect, he was also endowed with 'silence of the heart' " (p. 130). Derman also thought that Chekhov was aware of this condition, suffered from it, and projected it into his works, "The Wife" (1892), for example (pp. 209-210). In Derman's opinion, Chekhov's celebrated piece of advice to Lidiia Avilova to remain cold particularly when writing on emotional sub-jects was "not any objective law of creativity, discovered by Chekhov, but rather the elevation of a personal trait, and a rare one at that, to a principle" (pp. 241-242). Besides many such questionable observations, Derman makes many interesting and plausible points regarding Chekhov's imagery, language, and style, all of which he felt were just as innovative as Chekhov's treatment of plot and narrative structure. Derman corrected many of his positions in his later writings. The insights gathered in his posthumous book, *On Chekhov's Craftsmanship*, are presented in the second part of this essay.[26]

While Derman's work concentrated on Chekhov's fiction, S. D. Balu-khatyi's (1892-1945) studies dealt with Chekhov's theatre.[27] Balukhatyi's work is of high quality throughout, combining a thorough knowledge of texts, background material, and stagecraft. His method is sensibly eclectic, combining a structural with a historical and biographical approach, and seeking to find a common denominator for these aspects. For example, Balukhatyi points out that the success of Chekhov's later plays, after the failure of *Ivanov* and *The Wood Demon*, was in part due to the appearance on the Russian stage of Ibsen, Hauptmann, Maeterlinck, and other "modernist" dramatists; thus critics, after 1896, were also able to recognize Chekhov's stagecraft as an expression of a new, idiosyncratic dramaturgic manner (pp. 74, 116). Chekhov, Balukhatyi also notes, took the resounding failure of *The Seagull* as a personal affront, because it was, "in the selection of its thematic material, a public, dramatically stylized confession of its author" (p. 105). Balukhatyi, who explains his findings regarding the structure and movement of Chekhov's plays by numerous diagrams, comes up with these basic traits of Chekhovian drama, each emerging more clearly in each successive play: a minimum of events, as plot is replaced by the course of daily life (*byt*); replacement of thematically focused scenes with the normal course of everyday life; avoidance of "dramatic" situations; absence of a continuous or focused dialogue (the dialogue is often inter-rupted by inconsequential phrases and actions); foundation of the dramatic quality of the play on emotional relations between characters, but unlike conventional drama, never resolving these relations; and use of scenic composition to enhance lyric and emotional effects.

The 1940s and 1950s produced a more or less definitive edition of Chekhov's *Collected Works*, which included his letters.[28] Unfortunately, these were badly bowdlerized, and many cuts were made in them for political and nationalistic considerations. (A twelve-volume 1963-1964 edition restored some of the cut passages.) A variety of biographic material was also published. It was synthesized in *Chekhov as Remembered by His Contemporaries* (Moscow, 1952, 1960) and in Nina Gitovich's *Chronicle of Chekhov's Life and Work* (Moscow, 1955), a compilation of biographical material arranged chronologically, day by day. Furthermore, what may be called a "canonic" interpretation of Chekhov's works gradually emerged from studies by Balukhatyi, Derman, G. A. Bialyi, P. M. Bitsilli, G. B. Berdnikov, V. V. Ermilov, L. P. Gromov, A. P. Chudakov, T. K. Shakh-Azizova, and many others. The secondary literature on Chekhov is huge. Only a cursory outline of the principal insights that seem to be current in Russian Chekhov criticism since the 1940s can be given here.

It is generally agreed that Chekhov was an eminently conscious artist— without, however, having a set "system." Soviet scholars suggest that Chekhov's scientific background and scientific world view were a major factor in his literary work.[29] It is also recognized that Chekhov conceived of his art as "labor" and that he worked according to a preconceived plan; and that he always took an active interest in technique, as evidenced by his frequent advice to younger writers. He was not, however, a writer "from the notebook," but relied on his memory and imagination, which were of the visual rather than aural type.[30] Chekhov's unerring literary judgment is noted by many critics. His advice to Gorkii and others is presented in evidence.

It has been recognized that Chekhov was in a way a synthesizer—and popularizer—of the great literature that preceded him. Peter Bitsilli, in particular, presents evidence of many echoes in Chekhov's works of Gogol, Turgenev, Tolstoi, Nikolai Leskov, Vsevolod Garshin, Nikolai Pomialovskii,and others. But Chekhov also responded to works by relatively minor authors. "The Lady with a Lapdog" (1899) was very likely a polemic response to a story, "Mimochka Taking the Waters," by L. I. Veselitskaia, which appeared in *The Herald of Europe* in 1891 and had met with Tolstoi's approval.[31] Chekhov's dependence on world literature has also been pointed out. Even Chekhov's contemporaries had noticed the resemblance of Chekhov's manner to that of Guy de Maupassant, whom Chekhov admired. The influence of Paul Bourget's novel *Le disciple* (1889) on "A Dreary Story" was also soon noticed.[32] Bitsilli has shown that many of Chekhov's stories are new variations on old themes, "The Kiss" (1887), for instance, with its age-old motif of the wrong man getting kissed. The novelty is that no recognition follows (Bitsilli, p. 126) Shakh-Azizova observes a variety of traits in which Chekhovian drama converges with Western Naturalist and Symbolist drama (Ibsen, Hauptmann, Strindberg, Björnson, Maeterlinck, and others). She demonstrates that in Chekhov many traits of modern drama appear in a consciously pursued and highly refined form.[33]

In the 1920s D. S. Mirsky (who altogether had a low opinion of Chekhov's art and quite wrongly thought that Chekhov was already hopelessly dated) suggested that in Russia Chekhov "was always regarded as a distinctly 'lowbrow' writer."[34] This opinion has been discarded. Derman draws attention to Chekhov's persistent refusal to stoop to the level of an inferior reader. In comparing the two versions (of 1883 and 1886) of the story "The Fat and the Thin One," Derman shows that Chekhov has "readdressed" the story, as it were, from the average reader, who gets what he expects, to the intelligent reader, who is encouraged to think (Derman, 1959, pp. 38-40). Derman also points out that, in spite of Chekhov's assertions to the contrary, the writer followed criticism of his works attentively, that it had a significant effect on his work, and that this was true even of "unfair" reviews, for example, Mikhailovskii's patently unfair review of "The Peasants" (Derman, 1929, pp. 118-119).

Since the 1950s, Soviet criticism has generally adopted the position that Chekhov was an honest realist, whose objectivity, moreover, was in step with the movement of history. Thus, Leonid Gromov says that "the discrepancy between Chekhov's theoretical statements and his creative practice is striking—in spite of his subjective tendency to be a dispassionate observer of the life process, he was a biased judge" (p. 37). Gromov and other Soviet critics refuse to see that Chekhov, especially in his later years, was concerned more with grasping those rare glimpses of beauty that life presented to him than with propagating any social or political ideas. Instead, they look for an implied social message even where Chekhov's concern clearly lies elsewhere. For example, in the story "Lights" (1888), Gromov finds an appeal for sympathy with the plight of educated women and is happy to discover that a contemporary critic, A. M. Skabichevskii, had read the story in this way (p. 166). M. Gushchin finds pointedly anti-capitalist messages in several of Chekhov's stories, but particularly in "Three Years" (1895), which he reads as a rejoinder to P. D. Boborykin's pro-capitalist novel *The Divide*.[35]

In some instances, the Soviet critics' search for *socialité* in Chekhov leads to questionable interpretations. For example, Derman reads the scene in "The Peasants," where Nikolai tries on his frock-coat and blissfully reminisces about the happy days when he was a waiter in Moscow, as meant to convey the bitter irony of the utter degradation of being a waiter perceived as a paradisiac state by this poor wretch (Derman, 1959, p. 41).

Gromov explains the absence of "distinct socio-political convictions" in the hero of "A Dreary Story" by the fact that among the friends of his youth were not only the "revolutionary democrat" Nekrasov, but also the liberal Kavelin—hence the professor's "eclecticism"! (Gromov, p. 181). Extrapolations from Chekhov's works of his historical realization of the futility of populism and other "idealist" movements[36] and of the coming revolution[37] also seem questionable in view of Chekhov's notorious refusal to subscribe to any ideology and the complaints of his politically active contemporaries charging him with "indifferentism."

Since the apolitical quality of much of Chekhov's art can hardly be denied (even so orthodox a critic as V. Ermilov admits it), the tendency in Russian criticism has been to seek Chekhov's "humanism" in ethic concerns. Even before the Revolution, S. N. Bulgakov saw "the question of the moral weakness, of the powerlessness of the good in the soul of the average human being" as the dominant trait of Chekhov's art.[38] Bitsilli suggests that in Chekhov's world man is a monad, an indivisible whole, whose basic movement is directed at overcoming one's empirical "I" (Bitsilli, p. 117). When Derman suggests that "Chekhov's most important legacy is to take one's material not from the surface, where it is immediately visible, but to unearth it from the depths of life," he apparently expresses a similar understanding (Derman, 1959, pp. 94-95).

The novel way in which Chekhov treated human character was observed even by his contemporaries. M. O. Gershenzon, with his usual perceptiveness, observed that, unlike Tolstoi who penetrated to the very core of the human soul, "Chekhov never entered the sealed apparatus of the human soul, but captured with extraordinary precision the most minute manifestations of the chemical process taking place within it."[39] S. A. Vengerov said that Chekhov "always painted in outline and schematically, i.e., giving not the whole man . . . not so much a portrait, as a silhouette."[40] Somewhat later, D. S. Mirsky denied that Chekhov was a creator of characters and suggested that Chekhovian characters were basically "types" and lacked an individualized voice (Mirsky, p. 377). Bitsilli likewise denied that Chekhov was a creator of characters, drawing attention to the allegoric nature of many of Chekhov's most famous stories and types, such as "Gusev" and "The Man in a Case" (Bitsilli, p. 124). In Soviet criticism, Chekhov's peculiar treatment of character is considered a virtue. Derman admires Chekhov's uncanny ability to draw a character with a few strokes of the brush (Derman, 1959, p. 152). Chudakov points out that Chekhov, in contrast to Tolstoi's analytic style, sees his characters as wholes.[41] He also suggests that the novelty of Chekhovian characters lies precisely in the randomness of associations between idea and character (Chudakov, p. 185).

The short story before Chekhov had a highly structured form with conventions which covered every aspect. While Chekhov's early stories largely followed these conventions, his mature stories revolutionized the genre. The fact that Chekhov's stories were somehow "different" was registered even by his contemporaries, but it took critics some time to understand what exactly he was doing differently.

As regards the dichotomy of "continuous" versus "fragmentary" narrative,[42] Derman observes that Chekhov gravitates toward the fragmentary, giving his reader milestones rather than the whole course of events, and in fact manages to create miniature novels by using this technique (Derman, 1959, pp. 79-80, 150-51). This quality of Chekhov's composition was interpreted as "formlessness" and "incompleteness" by some of his contemporaries, such as Mikhailovskii, who in reviewing "The Peasants" charged Chekhov with "hurried writing" and called the story "a mere draft."[43] Modern Russian critics, such as Chudakov, instead speak of the "randomness" of Chekhov's composition which is, of course, a consciously applied and artful literary device (Chudakov, p. 187).

The plotlessness of Chekhov's stories was a gradually developing trait. Derman suggests that Chekhov arrived at it via a transitional form, that of "motionless movement" (*nepodvizhnoe dvizhenie*), such as in the stories "An Avenger" (1887) and "Cold Blood" (1887), and sees "The Steppe" as a turning point in this, as well as in other respects (Derman, 1959, p. 58). Hostile contemporaries interpreted the plotlessness of Chekhov's works as a mirror image of his world view. Shestov (referring to *The Seagull*, but implying that what he said applied to Chekhov's work at large) said that "here, in violation of all literary principles, the basis of action is not a logical development of human passions, not the inevitable connection between the preceding and the following, but naked chance, demonstratively left uncovered" (Shestov, p. 13), and deduced from this that Chekhov's consciousness was lacking any central organizing idea (p. 25).

Soviet critics, who have some difficulty embracing Chekhov's plotlessness, recognize it without putting much emphasis on Chekhov's well-attested rationale for it, namely, that there are no plots in life. Chudakov establishes Chekhov's "new apprehension of the world—one of randomness —the randomness of its depiction, in all its unselected multiplicity" (p. 175), without drawing the obvious inference that such apprehension of the world is diametrically opposed to Soviet ideology.

Chekhov's earlier stories, if they have a plot, tend to have a conventional exposition and finale, and usually an equally conventional surprise point. Derman demonstrates how Chekhov gradually does away with the exposition and reduces plot development (*zaviazka*), but continues to pay attention to the finale (Derman, 1959, p. 80). Following A. G. Gornfeld's article "Chekhov's Finales" (*Krasnaia nov* [*Red Virgin Soil*], 1939, nos. 8-9), Derman describes Chekhov's finales as truncated, ambiguous, open-ended, or problematic, such as when the conclusion of a story leaves the hero deeply in thought about what has been the subject of the story. Pointlessness thus becomes the point.

Chekhov was intensely aware of the importance of "point of view" in the short story.[44] But it was not his forte, as Mirsky pointed out, overstating his case somewhat (p. 377). Chudakov observes a distinct progression from a subjective narrative voice in Chekhov's first period, to an objective manner in the second, and on to a polyphonic interplay of both in the third.[45] Chudakov, Sergei Antonov, and other more recent critics correct earlier views, which missed the fact that, in "The Steppe," for example, some of the descriptions are presented through the eyes of a nine-year-old boy. Chudakov shows, furthermore, that a similar development takes place in Chekhov's treatment of space: the early Chekhov's narrators depict things from their own point of view; in the second period, space is adapted to the hero's—or some other character's—viewpoint; in the third period, space becomes multiple as a direct result of the many-faceted make-up of narrative voice and characters' voices.

The introduction of lyric elements into his stories and plays has been recognized as one of the distinctive traits of Chekhov's art. Bitsilli suggests that "The Steppe" is really a poema, "analogous to Pushkin's 'novel in verse' " (p. 62). Derman produces examples of lyric intermezzi, "which serve the purpose of creating a certain lyric mood" (Derman, 1959, pp. 103-104), and shows how Chekhov smuggles lyric digressions even into the stream-of-consciousness of his characters (pp. 125-126). Bitsilli demonstrates how Chekhov uses the whole arsenal of the lyric poet: metaphor, symbol, emphasis, nuance, hint, loaded syntax, significant detail, and so on. Bitsilli, Derman, and others observe the importance of rhythm in Chekhov's mature prose, drawing attention to such devices as strophic and triadic arrangement of text; repetition, contrast, and variation of imagery; alternating tension and relaxation of mood; rhythmically organized syntax; attention to "le mot juste" and euphonic detail; and ample use of onomatopoeic words.[46]

Many critics, including Bitsilli, Gromov (who cites N. L. Brodskii as a predecessor), Derman, and Antonov, suggest that the composition of Chekhov's stories is musical in its "musical development of 'theme' and 'counter-theme,' framed by 'side themes,' with repetition of images, symbols, epithets, as well as of expressions of motion, sound, and color analogous to repetition of melodic units, tonalities, harmonies, and tempi" (Bitsilli, p. 75). Derman corroborates these observations with quotes from Chekhov's correspondence which suggest that Chekhov himself perceived his work in terms of musical composition (Derman, 1959, pp. 102, 121) and by the authority of musical composers, such as Dimitrii Shostakovich, who recognized "symphonic structure" in Chekhov's story "The Black Monk" (1894) (p. 116).

It was probably Merezhkovskii, in a lecture given in December 1892, who was the first to call Chekhov an impressionist. Subsequently Tolstoi, Lunacharskii, and others used the same term to describe Chekhov's art. What they meant was that Chekhov had abandoned continuity and was concentrating on selected details to enhance certain effects and to create a certain atmosphere. As early as 1903, a critic called Chekhov's manner "pointillist" (*punktirnyi*, from *punktir*, "dotted line").[47]

The consistent use of significant (symbolic) detail was another facet of Chekhov's impressionist technique that was soon noticed. Chekhov himself was fully conscious of this trait. He was grateful to Grigorovich, who "was the only one to have noticed the description of the fresh snow in 'An Attack of Nerves' (1888)."[48] Antonov discusses the "Chekhovian," that is, significant or symbolic detail, giving many examples (p. 160), and so does Derman, who actually develops the notion of landscape as leitmotif in Chekhov (Derman, 1959, pp. 107-113). Chudakov stresses that Chekhov's symbolic objects belong equally to two realms: the real and the symbolic (p. 131).

"Chekhovian mood" (*chekhovskoe nastroenie*) became proverbial in Russia. It meant a mood of futility and gloom, in which some critics also saw the redeeming qualities of beauty,[49] or sympathy and pity.[50] More recently, Soviet critics have tended to minimize these traits, emphasizing instead Chekhov's vigorous satire, bitter indictments of bourgeois society, and optimistic visions of a better future.[51]

The fact that Chekhov was a bold and sometimes radical innovator was more readily recognized by the critics of his plays than by those of his stories, even though it was recognized later that these innovations pointed in the same direction in both genres.[52] Today many Russian critics, Chudakov, for example, do not draw a sharp line between Chekhov's stories and plays when trying to determine the distinctive traits of his art.

Bitsilli probably correctly plots Chekhov's position as a playwright "halfway from 'realism' to 'symbolism' " (p. 85). V. E. Meierkhold, who had played Treplev in the epoch-making performance of *The Seagull* (and also Tuzenbakh in *Three Sisters*), felt that Chekhov was a Symbolist and should be staged as such, but as a director he never contributed anything outstanding to the interpretation of Chekhov's theatre.[53] His montage of three vaudevilles by Chekhov into a single grotesque, *33 Fainting Fits*, in which he sought to dramatize the neurasthenia and general decadence of the bourgeoisie, was neither a public nor a critical success.[54]

It is a well-attested fact that Chekhov was not in full agreement with the Moscow Art Theatre's stagings of his plays. He felt that Nemirovich-Danchenko and Stanislavskii were overdoing their realism and that they were slanting the text too much toward the emotional, overemphasizing the bleakness and hopelessness of life. Chekhov wanted it all to be livelier, more like "real people," yet also without outright imitation of reality instead of art. Bitsilli suggests that there was a reason for such disagreement. Chekhov, says Bitsilli, transferred the characters of his stories to the stage. When put on stage, they inevitably attain a certain independence and their inherent inability to act leads to an actionless play. In a story, the narrator can take care of that problem by giving meaning and even direction to the story. It was for this reason that some contemporary critics felt that Chekhov's plays were suited for reading but not for the stage.[55]

It is understandable, therefore, that some Soviet critics, G. Berdnikov, for example, have sought to find a certain direction and implied message in Chekhov's plays, specifically a message that "life cannot go on this way" and that a change is imminent.[56] Some Soviet directors have applied such an interpretation to their stagings of Chekhov's plays, but not very convincingly.[57]

Balukhatyi and others have described in detail the various ways in which Chekhov the dramatist challenged the conventions of the Russian stage of his day. He did away with the division of characters into "main" and "secondary." He jettisoned the traditional plot and its several prescribed stages (exposition, denouement, and such). Derman shows how there is progressively less "plot" in each successive play (Derman, 1959, pp. 60-61). Chekhov abandoned the *scene* as a structural sub-unit, as the appearance on stage of a new character may or may not introduce a new theme (Balukhatyi, p. 79). Chudakov points out Chekhov's novel technique in the treatment of "things." While pre-Chekhovian drama had "settings" whose material elements were integrated with the text as a whole, in Chekhov's plays elements of the setting ("things") are often independent (Chudakov, pp. 105-111).

Balukhatyi observes that Chekhov does away with dramatic dialogue in a conventional sense, replacing it by a discontinuous text featuring unmotivated interruptions, "double takes," and randomness of thematic elements. The whole system is based on imitation of "everyday discourse, non-systemic as a matter of principle" (Balukhatyi, p. 134). Few scenes may be interpreted as advancing the plot through energetic or expressive discourse (p. 135). The significant pause is, of course, one of Chekhov's trademarks (pp. 97-99). Bitsilli, on the other hand, points out that Chekhov has retained some conventional devices that do not fit the basic naturalism of his plays, such as eavesdropping (in *The Cherry Orchard*) and stereotyped characters (Solenyi in *Three Sisters*). Bitsilli also observes a number of inconsistencies caused by a clash between Chekhov's basic naturalism and his retention of certain conventions of the stage (pp. 85-87).

Balukhatyi defines the principle of Chekhov's dramatic composition as "organizing the material of his *sujet* after the fashion of everyday life" (*bytovym obrazom*) and "creating its dynamic scheme on a lyric basis" (p. 102). External events (*sobytiia*) are replaced by inner experience (*perezhivaniia*). Hence, the play has no real beginning and no real end (pp. 115-116). Development of characters is replaced by gradual revelation of the characteristic movements of their souls (p. 128). Derman suggests that the developments of a Chekhovian play aim at bringing to the surface that which is not immediately visible, for example, the evil role which Serebriakov, a man of no obvious vices, plays in the lives of those around him (Derman, 1959, pp. 94-95).

In summary, Chekhov the dramatist (and short story writer), as seen by more recent Russian critics, is basically a realist, but a realist who was not satisfied merely to register the facts of life, who viewed them critically and who vigorously condemned the society he described. Chekhov's psychology is also seen in these terms. But first and foremost, Soviet critics will generally say that Chekhov was a humanist, a believer in the dignity of humankind and in progressive ideals. However, Soviet critics also point out the innovative dramatic technique and symbolic devices of Chekhov's plays (and short stories). These patterns of interpretation appear, usually in a somewhat overstated and hence not so subtle form, in the many versions of Chekhov's plays and dramatized versions of his stories on the Soviet stage, screen, and television.

NOTES

1. A. Derman, *Tvorcheskii portret Chekhova* (Moscow, 1929), p. 118.

2. Leonid Gromov, *Realizm A. P. Chekhova vtoroi poloviny 80-kh godov* (Rostov-na-Donu, 1958), pp. 78-105.

3. See *Anton Chekhov's Life and Thought: Selected Letters and Commentary*, ed. Simon Karlinsky (Berkeley: University of California Press, 1975), pp. 58-60.

4. "Chekhov was being torn to pieces by all kinds of political and literary factions: he was made out to be a positivist, a socialist, a Marxist, a populist, a decadent, and even a mystic," wrote D. S. Merezhkovskii, *Chekhov i Gor'kii* (St. Petersburg, 1906), p. 50.

5. Tolstoi's diary entry of January 16, 1900: "Read Chekhov's 'Lady with a Lapdog.' This is all Nietzsche. People who have failed to develop a clear worldview separating good and evil. In the past, they were still timid and were searching; now, thinking that they are beyond good and evil, they remain this side of it, i.e., almost like animals." See A. M. Turkov, "Raznoglasiia po 'zhenskomu voprosu'," *Chekhov i Lev Tolstoi* ed. L. D. Opulskaia et al. (Moscow, 1980), p. 266.

6. *Ibid.*, p. 264.

7. See V. A. Kovalev, "Lev Tolstoi o chekhovskikh detaliakh," *Chekhov i Lev Tolstoi* (Moscow, 1980), pp. 144-145.

8. See A. P. Chudakov, " 'Tolstovskii epizod' v poetike Chekhova," *Chekhov i Lev Tolstoi*, pp. 167 and 172.

9. See Derman, *Tvorcheskii portret Chekhova*, pp. 210-214. Other examples have been brought up by later scholars, for example, M. L. Semanova, " 'Kreitserova sanata' L. N. Tolstogo i 'Ariadna' A. P. Chekhova," *Chekhov i Lev Tolstoi*, pp. 225-253.

10. Maxim Gorky, *Reminiscences* (New York: Dover, 1946), p. 84.

11. M. Gor'kii, *Sobranie sochinenii v 30-ti tomakh* (Moscow, 1953), XXIII, 317.

12. Derman, *Tvorcheskii portret Chekhova*, pp. 125-29.

13. See *A. P. Chekhov v vospominaniiakh sovremennikov*, ed. S. N. Golubov et al. (Moscow, 1960), pp. 135-148 (Korolenko) and pp. 539-69 (Kuprin).

14. V. V. Rozanov put it simply: "Chekhov?—Nothing special. What about Chekhov? He observed life and put down what he saw, that's all." (Quoted from E. Spektorskii, *Chekhov* [Belgrade, 1930], p. 3.)

15. D. S. Merezhkovskii, "Chekhov kak bytopisatel' " in *Anton Pavlovich Chekhov. Ego zhizn' i sochineniia: Sbornik kritiko-literaturnykh statei*, ed. V. Pokrovskii (Moscow, 1907), pp. 191-92.

16. Quoted from Spektorskii, *Chekhov*, p. 3.

17. Lev Shestov, "Tvorchestvo iz nichego (A. P. Chekhov)," in his *Nachala i kontsy* (St. Petersburg, 1908), p. 30.

18. D. N. Ovsianiko-Kulikovskii, "Tvorchestvo Chekhova," *Anton Pavlovich Chekhov*, ed. V. Pokrovskii (Moscow, 1907), pp. 77-86.

19. See Derman, *Tvorcheskii portret Chekhova*, p. 326.

20. V. V. Maiakovskii, an ally of Meierkhold, and hence constantly attacking the Moscow Art Theatre, was ambivalent about Chekhov. In his early essay, "Two Chekhovs" (1914), he had praised the master of the simple and proper word, but rejected the "Chekhovian mood." After the Revolution, he seems to have been more negative. See, for example, his "Three Thousand and Three Sisters" (1928).

21. M. Semanova, *Chekhov i sovetskaia literatura* (Moscow and Leningrad, 1966), pp. 182-83.

22. Mikhail Kol'tsov, "Chekhov bez grima," *Pravda* (June 15, 1928).

23. See Semanova, *Chekhov i sovetskaia literatura*, pp. 213-218.

24. L. Myshkovskaia, *Chekhov i iumoristicheskie zhurnaly 80-kh godov* (Moscow, 1929), M. Elizarova, "Chekhovskii rasskaz i gazetnaia khronika," *Literaturnaia ucheba* 9 (1933): 20-35.

25. Derman, *Tvorcheskii portret Chekhova*.

26. A. Derman, *O masterstve Chekhova* (Moscow, 1959).

27. S. Balukhatyi, *Problemy dramaturgicheskogo analiza: Chekhov* (Leningrad, 1927).

28. A. P. Chekhov, *Polnoe sobranie sochinenii i pisem v 20-ti tomakh* (Moscow, 1944-1951).

29. Gromov, *Realizm A. P. Chekhova vtoroi poloviny 80-h godov*, pp. 41-42.

30. Derman, *O masterstve Chekhova*, p. 201.

31. Turkov, "Raznoglasiia po 'zhenskomu voprosu'," p. 267.

32. Gromov, *Realizm A. P. Chekhova vtoroi poloviny 80-h godov*, p. 175.

33. T. K. Shakh-Azizova, *Chekhov i zapadno-evropeiskaia drama ego vremeni* (Moscow, 1966).

34. D. S. Mirsky, *A History of Russian Literature from Its Beginnings to 1900* (New York: Vintage Books, 1958), p. 383.

35. M. Gushchin, *Tovrchestvo A. P. Chekhova: Ocherki* (Kharkov, 1954), p. 142.

36. G. Berdnikov, *A. P. Chekhov: Ideinye is tvorcheskie iskaniia* (Moscow and Leningrad, 1961), pp. 484-488.

37. Gushchin, *A. P. Chekhov*, pp. 168-176.

38. S. N. Bulgakov, "Ideinoe soderzhanie tvorchestva Chekhova," *Anton Pavlovich Chekhov*, ed. V. Pokrovskii (Moscow, 1907), p. 91.

39. M. Gershenzon, "Literaturnoe obozrenie," *Nauchnoe slovo* 3 (1904): 161-162.

40. Chudakov, " 'Tolstovskii epizod' v poetike Chekhova," p. 191.

41. Ibid., p. 175.

42. B. Tomashevskii, *Teoriia literatury: Poetika* (Moscow and Leningrad, 1928), p. 192.

43. See Gushchin, *A. P. Chekhov*, p. 155n.

44. "In order to depict some horse thieves in 700 lines, I must speak and think in their tone and feel as they do" . . . (Letter to A. S. Suvorin, April. 1, 1890, *Polnoe sobranie sochinenii*, XV, 51).

45. While most critics distinguish only two periods in Chekhov's career as a writer, Chudakov sees three: the early Chekhov, 1888-1894, and 1895-1904. See A. P. Chudakov, *Chekhov's Poetics* (Ann Arbor, Mich., 1983), pp. 1-102. Sergei P. Antonov, *Pis'ma o rasskaze* (Moscow, 1964), pp. 136-38, discusses point-of-view in Chekhov in some detail.

46. P. Bitsilli, *Tvorchestvo Chekhova: Opyt stilisticheskogo analiza* (Sofia, 1942), pp. 62-69, makes a detailed analysis of "The Steppe" to illustrate these points.

47. V. P. Albov, "Dva momenta v razvitii tvorchestva Chekhova," *Mir Bozhii* 1 (1903): 89.

48. Chekhov's letter to Suvorin, December 23, 1888, *Polnoe sobranie sochinenii*, XV, 257.

49. Iu. Aikhenval'd, "Osnovnoi kolorit proizvedenii Chekhova," *Anton Pavlovich Chekhov*, ed. V. Pokrovskii, pp. 185-89, sees the Midas touch of a golden sadness as Chekhov's basic trait. Even beauty will appear in a haze of sadness.

50. Spektorskii: "Chekhov is the artist of sympathy" (p. 42). Bitsilli sees "pity" (*zhalost'*) as the dominant trait of Chekhov's art (p. 96).

51. See, for example, Gushchin, *A. P. Chekhov*, pp. 132-133.

52. Chekhov himself was more conscious of himself as a rebel in his role of playwright. See Derman, *Tvorcheskii portret Chekhova*, p. 132.

53. See Bitsilli, *Tvorchestvo Chekhova*, pp. 83-84.

54. See Konstantin Rudnitsky, *Meyerhold the Director*, trans. George Petrov (Ann Arbor, Mich., 1981), pp. 524-528.

55. See Bitsilli, *Tvorchestvo Chekhova*, pp. 87-88.

56. G. Berdnikov, *Chekhov-dramaturg: Traditsii i novatorstvo v dramaturgii Chekhova* (Leningrad and Moscow, 1957), pp. 219-220.

57. See Semanova, *Chekhov i sovetskaia literatura*, pp. 205-28.

BIBLIOGRAPHY

Miscellaneous Works Dealing with Chekhov

Anikst, A. *Teoriia dramy v Rossii ot Pushkina do Chekhova*. Moscow, 1972.

Antonov, Sergei P. *Pis'ma o rasskaze*. Moscow, 1964.

A. P. Chekhov v vospominaniiakh sovremennikov. Eds. N. I. Gitovich, and V. Fedorov, Moscow, 1960.

Chekhov i ego vremia. Ed. L. D. Opulskaia et al., Moscow, 1977.

Chekhov i Lev Tolstoi. Ed. L. D. Opulskaia et al., Moscow, 1980.

Chekhov i teatr. Ed. E. D. Surkov, Moscow, 1961.

Kataev, V. B., ed. *Sputniki Chekhova: Sobranie tekstov, stat'i i kommentarii*. Moscow, 1982.

Lyskov, I. P., ed. *A. P. Chekhov v ponimanii kritiki (Materialy dlia kharakteristiki ego tvorchestva)*. Moscow, 1905.

Pokrovskii, V., ed. *Anton Pavlovich Chekhov. Ego zhizn' i sochineniia: Sbornik istoriko-literaturnykh statei*. Moscow, 1907.

Monographic Works on Chekhov

Balukhatyi, S. *Problemy dramaturgicheskogo analiza: Chekhov*. Leningrad, 1927.

_____. *Chekhov-dramaturg*. Leningrad, 1936.

Berdnikov, G. *Chekhov*. (Zhizn' zamechatel'nykh liudei, 549.) Moscow, 1978.

_____. *Chekhov-dramaturg: Traditsii i novatorstvo v dramaturgii A. P. Chekhova*. 2d rev. ed., Moscow, 1972.

Bialyi, G. *Chekhov i russkii realizm: Ocherki*. Leningrad, 1981.

Bitsilli, P. *Tvorchestvo Chekhova: Opyt stilisticheskogo analiza*. Sofia, 1942.

Bunin, I. A. *O Chekhove*. New York: Izd. im. Chekhova, 1955.

Derman, A. *Tvorcheskii portret Chekhova*. Moscow, 1929.

_____. *O masterstve Chekhova*. Moscow, 1959.

Erenburg, Il'ia. *Perechityvaia Chekhova*. Moscow, 1960.

Gromov, Leonid. *Realizm A. P. Chekhova vtoroi poloviny 80-kh godov*. Rostov-na-Donu, 1958.

_____. *Vtvorcheskoi laboratorii A. P. Chekhova*. Rostov-na-Donu, 1963.

Gurvich, I. *Proza Chekhova: Chelovek i deistvitel'nost'*. Moscow, 1970.

Gushchin, M. *Tvorchestvo A. P. Chekhova*. Kharkov, 1954.

Kataev, V. B. *Proza Chekhova: Problemy interpretatsii*. Moscow, 1979.

Kuznetsova, M. V. *Tvorcheskaia evoliutsiia A. P. Chekhova*. Tomsk, 1978.

Lakshin, V. Ia. *Tolstoi i Chekhov*. Moscow, 1975.

_____. *Iskusstvo psikhologicheskoi dramy Chekhova i Tolstogo (Diadia Vania i Zhivoi trup)*. Moscow, 1958.

Merezhkovskii, D. S. *Chekhov i Gor'kii*. St. Petersburg, 1906.

Papernyi, Z. *Zapisnye knizhki Chekhova*. Moscow, 1976.

_____. *"Vopreki vsem pravilam . . .": P'esy i vodevili Chekhova*. Moscow, 1982.

Polotskaia, E. A. *A. P. Chekhov: Dvizhenie khudozhestvennoi mysli*. Moscow, 1979.

Semanova, M. L. *Chekhov i sovetskaia literatura 1917-1935*. Moscow, 1966.

_____. *Chekhov-khudozhnik*. Moscow, 1976.

Shakh-Azizova, T. K. *Chekhov i zapadno-evropeiskaia drama ego vremeni*. Moscow, 1966.

Shestov, Lev. "Tvorchestvo iz nichego (A. P. Chekhov)," in his *Nachalo i kontsy*. St. Petersburg, 1908, pp. 1-68.

Sobolev, Iu. *Chekhov*. Moscow, 1930, 1934.

Spektorskii, E. *Chekhov*. Belgrade, 1930.

Stanislavskii, K. S. *A. P. Chekhov v Moskovskom Khudozhestvennom Teatre*. Moscow, 1947.

Turkov, A. M. *Chekhov i ego vremia*. Moscow, 1980.

Vengerov, S. "Anton Chekhov: Literaturnyi portret," *Vestnik i biblioteka samoobrazovania*, 7 August 1903. Rpt. in *Entsiklopedicheskii slovar'*. Ed. I. E. Andreevskii. LXXVI (St. Petersburg, 1903), 777-81.

Vorovskii, V. V. "A. P. Chekhov" (1910). In his *Literaturno-kriticheskie stat'i* (Moscow, 1956), pp. 249-53.

Zaitsev, Boris. *Chekhov: Literaturnaia biografiia*. New York, 1954.

12

John Tulloch

CHEKHOV ABROAD: WESTERN CRITICISM

EARLY CRITICISM: THE TRAGEDY OF RUSSIAN LIFE

Chekhov was known to Western critics early—well before his death in 1904.[1] In the first two decades of criticism three features—his Russianness, his naturalism, and his rejection of the well-made story or play—were isolated as signs of his particular authorship.

From the earliest reviews to the most recent criticism, Chekhov has been interpreted as an "artist" in his very resistance to the political. Critics in the 1890s like E. J. Dillon and Abraham Cahan argued that because of censorship nobody was "more completely fettered and crippled than Russian writers" (Dillon, 1891).[2] However, this was a blessing in disguise since it prevented the fatal Russian literary propensity of "sermonizing" (Cahan, 1899).[3] These critics felt that even great Russian writers like Tolstoi and Turgenev were "discoloured" at times by "petty party bias." In contrast, Chekhov was "as free as the March wind" (Dillon), a "man without convictions" or "social ideas" (Cahan) who let Russian life "expose its own wounds," and was thus begrudged by local critics as a "kind of political heathen."

Some Western critics were more explicit about the particular Russian "wounds" that were revealed through Chekhov's work. Christian Brinton (1904)[4] and Maurice Baring (1907)[5] compared Chekhov's time of "indifferentism" and "stagnation" with the period of "heroic" social activity after the Crimean War and the liberation of the serfs, which was represented by such "majestic apostles" as Dostoevskii, Goncharov, Tolstoi and Turgenev.

Some of the key historical events that were crucial to Chekhov's authorship—the disaster of the Crimean War, the period following the emancipation of the serfs (which was in fact a time of expanding professionalism in the *zemstvo* areas, particularly in Chekhov's field of medicine)—were noted by these early critics.[6] But the scope of their analysis was limited to the more visible confrontation between the ruling class on the one hand and the revolutionaries and men of "ideas" on the other. Russia, with its censors and revolutionaries, was "foreign" and somewhat exotic, rather than a place with sociological and historical processes not so dissimilar from those in the critics' own countries. Consequently, rather than placing him in his own socially dynamic context, Western critics only read the negative part of Chekhov's social palette: resistance against the ruling political system which, Brinton argued, he blamed "by subtle inference" for "all this misery and stupidity"; and resistance against the revolutionists who, the *Times Literary Supplement* obituary on Chekhov said, "can explode an occasional bomb but whose promised revolution seems no nearer now than it was thirty years ago."[7]

In this binary perception of a "barren ice-bound empire" futilely opposed by hot-headed revolutionaries, there could be little quarter for hope. Art revealed itself in the interplay of negatives. As Dillon put it in his early review, "Chekhov plainly intimates that life in Russia has but two seasons, like the steppe—winter with its paralysing frost, before nature gives any sign of life or movement, and summer which with its fierce heat eats up everything green, leaving nought but parched drooping grass behind."

If early critics were unable to find a positive social space for Chekhov, they quickly did find him a literary one. This was the "artistic objectivity in which his colleagues are so sadly deficient" (Dillon, 1891), literature "drawn straight from nature" (Briusov, 1904)[8] "devoid of underlying ideas" (Cahan, 1899), painting not preaching, and recording life with "a mocking tenderness" (Brinton, 1904). Chekhov, most critics felt, was the artist of unrelieved pessimism. His humour was applauded, but it was an "irresponsible gaiety" (Long, 1902)[9] which laughed at the futility of human life as "an infinite grinding of the petty against the base." Either Chekhov was an artist of "profound melancholy" (Dillon) or "a mixture of satire and sadness" (Brinton), though for most critics satire was too positive a word for his comedy. Satire, it was argued, implied some alternative position, some glimmer of hope, whereas Chekhov was "wholly objective." He was concerned, Long argued, with a "shameless stripping of the last rags of dignity from the human soul. . . . It is not sufficient for his heroes to be insignificant and insipid—they must know it."

Some critics found Chekhov's comedy less brutal than Long, and spoke of a "kindly humour that illuminates the general gloom" and a "mocking tenderness" over social injustice. But this was seen as part of the same objective principle. He smiled when others wept and cried aloud. "Others told what Russia should be, Chekhov told Russia what it was and is. The one-time physician knew that diagnosis comes before prescription" (Brinton). The *Times Literary Supplement* obituary assessment of Chekhov in fact defined his career in terms of the development of this humour, from the "roaring farce" of his early pieces, through the farce that was "merely the grotesque setting of tragedy" of the second stage, to the hopelessness of his mature writing. Given his "objectivity" as a physician, given also the "unrelieved gloom" of Russian society, and without any understanding of the particular type of doctor Chekhov was, the easiest and most plausible way of defining him was as a naturalist. Maurice Baring argued that Chekhov was an even purer naturalist than those in the West, like Ibsen and Shaw. This was because Russian literature had "never done but one thing—to depict life as clearly as it saw it and as simply as it could." Baring argued that because Russian writers encountered reality "in the very air that they breathe," there had never been need for a naturalist school in Russia. The convention of the well-made story "never has existed in Russia" and so did not have to be opposed. While the naturalists of Norway, France, Germany, and England are "bent on proving a thesis," in Russia the play and the novel "has been a looking-glass for the use of the public." Chekhov's discovery, said Baring, was "that real life, as we see it every day, can be made just as interesting on the stage as the catastrophes or the difficulties which are more or less exceptional, but which are chosen by dramatists as their material because they are dramatic."[10]

Chekhov's pessimistic naturalism was defined in its differences from that of the West, and these differences were seen as causally Russian. This in turn explained Chekhov's characteristic literary innovations.

Baring's description of the intimate Chekhovian revelation ("glimpses . . . of a thousand nothings") and impressionistic literary structure was defined in contrast to the Scribian convention of the well-made play. Chekhov plays were "real" because the "trivial incidents of every day" seeped out of them "by a word, a phrase, a gesture, the humming of a tune, or the smelling of a flower," and not "by any pressure of an outside and artificial machinery, never owing to the necessity of a situation, the demands of a plot, or the exigencies of a problem."[11]

This sense of Chekhov as an innovator of the tiny details of life normally hidden by the conventions of Western writers was common in the early period. In particular, this was tied in to his "lack of a unifying idea." The refusal to preach (equated with not having any social and political position) supposedly allowed Chekhov to see more clearly what his more passionate colleagues were blind to. Chekhov was a "literary miniaturist" (Dillon), refusing generalisation for a "mosaic of colours" (Long). His was the art of "fleeting impression" and "kaleidoscopic quality," a literature revealing the "evanescent flinders of life" and the "fleeting trifles of reality" in an "absolutely storyless" structure (Cahan). His "striking want of incident" and "usual avoidance of anything approaching a worked-up denouement" (Keeton, 1904)[12] or "startling events" (Baring) allowed "vital glimpses of nature and character" (Brinton) as we might perceive them ourselves in real life. This, St. John Hankin wrote in 1907, "is a picture of life" which, without "old-fashioned . . . surprises and coincidences," went beyond description to reveal people's souls.[13]

Yet despite the occasional notion of a search for a reality beyond the surface of appearances, Chekhov, it was thought, never found anything other than futility. As the *Times Literary Supplement* review put it, "he observed life and, looking beneath the surface, found that there were riddles which he could not answer . . . Life . . . was futile." Baring was one of the few in this period to sense hope. "The atmosphere of Chekhov's plays is laden with gloom, but it is a darkness of the last hour before the dawn begins. His note is . . . of invincible trust in the coming day." Baring was unable to say why there might be hope in Chekhov's world view, and others dismissed Chekhov as neurotically constructing a "nightmare society" out of touch with the "mind of the world, as modern civilisation has made it . . . even in Russia" (Bates, 1903).[14]

A dominant "foreign" interpretation of Chekhov had been established. Bates's "neurotic" and Long's "universal" Chekhov were at this stage arguing against the grain. And they, too, were convinced of his unrelenting pessimism. The feature of most Chekhov criticism in this period was its empiricism. The Chekhov surface of appearances was taken to be equivalent to his world view—and to his art. In most cases critics created a causal chain of explanation, beginning with an undynamic and stagnant concept of Russian history, and working through a naturalistic notion of Chekhov's unmediating fidelity to this social futility. Consequently, his genius was found, not in the larger spaces appropriate to social change, but in the diagnosis of the "objective" physician viewing the hopeless depravity of Russian reality, and allowing it to seep out through the interstices of minor characterisation.

THE MIDDLE PERIOD: THE DIVINE COMEDY OF ART

Few in those early years considered Chekhov's as a constructed art. One who did was the playwright St. John Hankin:

The truth is Chekhov's plays—and indeed all plays of whatsoever school which are effective in the theatre—are and must be "constructed," and this applies to the modern naturalistic playwright just as much to his conventional predecessors. His methods of construction are different from theirs but "construct" he must.

As an artist himself, Hankin was reacting to the "formless" Chekhov. A similar view was put by the novelist Arnold Bennett in 1909.[15] "The basis of convention remains, but as the art develops it finds more and more subtle methods fitting life to convention. . . . Chekhov . . . seems to have achieved absolute realism. . . . But . . . beneath the outward simplicity of his work is concealed the most wondrous artifice, the artifice that is embedded in nearly all great art.'' Bennett still thought of Chekhov as a great naturalist. But the emphasis now was on artistic convention and the special creativity which revealed reality.

Hankin's and Bennett's concerns as artists to emphasize the conventionality of great art were early signs of an alternative to the early empiricist tradition, which was to achieve considerable force in the 1920s, especially among writers. This was that ''reality'' in literature was constructed through the conventions of art. An important result was a subtle shift from the pessimistically ''naturalist'' Chekhov of the early empiricist criticism (though this persisted in some areas, particularly in popular newspaper criticism) to either (1) the view that social reality is hidden below the surface of events and requires the consciousness of the great artist to reveal it, or (2) the view that all is convention, that there is no reality at all beyond the artist's perception. The first of these alternatives is an idealist form of realism, the second is a conventionalism which, already lurking in Hankin and Bennett, was to become important in later criticism (as in H. Peter Stowell's *Literary Impressionism: James and Chekhov*). In contrast to either of these (but hardly developed at this time) is the sociologically realist position which, as Terry Lovell puts it, develops ''models of real structures and processes which lie at a 'deeper' level of reality'' than the surface of appearances.[16] For critics in this period, a ''deeper'' level of reality was not social, but revealed (or even constructed) in the consciousness of the artist.

So, for instance, the playwright and critic George Calderon wrote in 1912 that it was a mark of the great artist in Chekhov that he was more ''expressly conscious'' than ordinary people ''of the fact that our experience and our impulses are very little private to ourselves, almost always shared with a group of other people.''[17] But the ''underlying order'' thus revealed was not the Russian social system. The individual artistry of Chekhov related group emotions to the ''private life of feelings and opinions . . . lived far down beneath the surface, in the innermost recesses of the soul,'' and in so doing mingled tragedy (the individual suffering, seen at close hand) with comedy (the more orderly ''Life seen from a distance''). Chekhov relished ''the incongruity between the actual disorder of the world and the underlying order. . . . His plays are tragedies with the texture of comedy.'' Chekhov the empiricist scientist viewed without passion or rancour the disordered surface of life, but Chekhov the conventionalist artist smiled, with a little irony and compassion, at the comedy of the human illusion of reality. In Leonard Woolf's words, there was as well as ''detachment . . . a tiny tremor of the conjuror's hand.''[18]

Emphasis on the ''construction,'' ''artifice,'' and ''conventionality'' of the creative representation of reality leads imperceptibly in Chekhov criticism to the notion of subjective artistic truth. Since our access to reality is through the creativity of the artist's vision, the aesthetic quality of that subjective view rather than the socially systematic relations of the world becomes our only guarantee of wisdom. Conventionalism proper, as Lovell

has pointed out, only departs from this subjectivism in locating creativity "not in each individual, but in the collectivity," and it was an important
feature of Western Chekhov criticism in the 1920s that the "Art" collectivity grew in coherence as more and more novelists, playwrights, and
serious critics rejected the notion of Chekhov as a formless, feckless, and
"foreign" recorder of nature.[19] This was an artist's construction of Chekhovian realism—a world made more real than the surface of events
available to the mundane observer.

The novelist Margaret Jameson perhaps stated the position the most
clearly in 1920.

The drama of Chekhov is the only modern realism that has attempted a vision of
reality. For reality is not a matter of facts: it is a matter of artistic conception. In the
strictest sense of the term, art creates life. Life is an artist's vision of it. . . . It needs
the supreme creative activity that makes order in the disorder confronting the
untutored vision of life.[20]

Similarly, Edmund Wilson spoke of *The Cherry Orchard* as going beyond
merely conveying the impression of life with the aim of producing "not
merely something real, but something beautiful—something valid as art."[21]

"Valid art" was seen as something outside the prosaic history and sociology
of the time. For Wilson *The Cherry Orchard* is not only "a whole complex of
social relations presented with the most convincing exactitude."[22] Arnold
Bennett, Zola, and Dreiser had achieved this kind of exactitude in a "dreary"
naturalism of the proletariat and middle class. But in Chekhov social exactitude was elevated to the beauty of the universal. "The beauty . . . the charm
which hangs about the Russian gentry even in decay is somehow put upon the
stage in such a way that their futility is never dreary, but moving, their ineptitude touched with the tragedy of all human failure."[23]

For the idealist critic it was consciousness that moulded reality, not social
"exactitude" which moulded consciousness. This was so even where, as in
Virginia Woolf's case, the cultural nature of Chekhov interpretation was
recognised. For instance, in 1920 Woolf criticised "all the comforts and all
the decencies of English upper-class life" which disfigured a production of
The Cherry Orchard.[24] Shaw, of course, felt that Chekhov's plays "fitted
all the country houses of Europe. . . . The same nice people, the same utter
futility."[25] But for Woolf the clash of different cultures disturbed an
individual imaginary experience which she had entered with "relief and
abandonment." "I had, on my imaginary stage, tried to give effect to my
sense that the human soul is free from all trappings and crossed incessantly
by thoughts and emotions which wing their way from here, from there,
from the furthest horizons."[26]

In Woolf's imagination there are, it seems, as many realities as there are
thoughts about reality, while for Margaret Jameson the only final reality is
Art itself, and she gently chides Chekhov for losing his confidence in this

truth. Like Wilson, Jameson favourably contrasts Chekhov with dramatists of social "manners." Tolstoi, Gorkii, and Shaw are lesser artists because whereas they "sought the meaning in an ideal of life that a social revolution might accomplish," Chekhov "reached deeper, to question the value of life, to criticise its forms."[27] For Jameson, actual historical conditions ("a phase of reality") are relatively trivial. Only the form of life, universal and beautiful, is worthy of the best artist's art.

So Jameson complains of Tolstoi's and Gorkii's preoccupation with the "maundering peasants and cursing outcasts"[28] of Russian hovels, in contrast to Chekhov who chose "distinctive" characters—people from the "educated classes" with "artistic capacity or imaginative charm." The failure of this sensitive class to "lift the misery of the people by their own efforts" is itself lifted to art by Chekhov. "Above the waste of fine lives and brave effort is the sense of a triumphant activity that creates new forms in destroying old. The artist dies, but life and art, the spirit of life, change and are recreated without end."[29] According to Jameson, Chekhov's weakness was that, recognising "the inevitable failure, the decay of life," he sometimes retreated into hopelessness. But his greater achievement was in knowing "that life itself is perpetual discontent, with no peace attainable" and "that the creative activity constantly changing must shatter the old forms of art to find expression for the new spirit."[30]

Life, change, "protest," historical movement are all, in this analysis, limited to art—and art becomes, in effect, the only authentic reality. The search for social change, which Chekhov believed in so firmly, becomes no more than the struggle for new forms—a displacement that Chekhov himself dismissed in *The Seagull.*

By 1925 this artist's view had achieved a high-culture orthodoxy, apparent in *The Times'* review of *The Seagull. "The Seagull* with its . . . futile failures and still more futile successes" generated "exaltation" rather than depression, because "one feels the gratification of having gained not a new but a deeper vision of life, and entry into the more recondite secrets of the human heart."[31]

This theme of Chekhov's art raising the wretchedness of social life to the triumphant secrets of the heart, the soul, or the spirit became conventional in the 1920s, alleviating the naturalistic pessimism of the earlier reading. So, for instance, R. A. Parker, writing in 1923, argued that Chekhov did not aim primarily "to reproduce Russian life. . . . He was a realist only in the sense that every true artist is a realist—since he sought to crystallize and to give form to the inner spiritual realities of life. He never aimed at mere superficial or external representation."[32]

The new critical coding allowed, as *The Times* noted, a strategic rescue, plucking optimism out of pessimism, the spiritual out of the material, and eternal "Art" out of the brute facticity of history. John Middleton Murry was typical.

He is like a man who contemplates a perfect work of art; but the work of creation has been his, and has consisted in the gradual adjustment of his vision until he could see the frustration of human destinies and the arbitrary infliction of pain as processes no less inevitable, natural, and beautiful than the flowering of a plant."[33]

For Murry, Chekhov's aesthetic was in advance of other modern writers (who asked whether life "was just or good") because it was more classical, reconciling "the greatest diversity of content with the greatest possible unity of aesthetic expression."[34] Chekhov's first full-length monographer, William Gerhardie, was another in the 1920s who placed Chekhov as distinctively modern by contrasting him with those who "reported life not as it was really lived, but as they thought it *should* be lived."[35] For Gerhardie, Chekhov's distinction was in combining the romance of "illusions and dreams," the stream of "private, self-conscious perception," and "life as it is" naturalism in a multi-layered generic structure. "It is the wanton incompatibility of the reality of life with our romantic, smoother private visions of what life ought to be . . . which has seized him, and because he saw beauty in it, has made him a creative artist." In Gerhardie's view the "balance" of the three generic elements which "gives his work a life-like touch" lay in Chekhov's recognition of the "elusiveness of life," life as it was, yet the defiant expectation also, "in spite of reality, that life ought to be more: we sense a kind of absolute beauty which is more like a song or a poem— 'romantic'—and this is the comic-pathos of our falling short of it."[36]

Although there were differences in the positions of these writers (as between Gerhardie's generic "balance" and Murry's classical aesthetic, for example), nearly all of them worked within the same broader paradigm, which emphasised poetic beauty as against social tragedy, relishing a Chekhovian ambivalence that captured reality in aestheticist terms and at the same time valuing the universal at the expense of the historical. S. Hoare, writing in 1923, is one of many critics symptomatic of this now dominant trend, when he contrasted writers with an "attitude to life" (Flaubert, Conrad, Hardy) with the Chekhovian "quality of beauty inherent in all life." Hoare works away from the messy exploitations of human history to the permanence of aesthetic order where beauty, "suddenly plucked from out of the flux of life," has been "made somehow radiantly immobile. . . . This is the nature of Chekhov's art, to reveal a universal quality by giving to his subject its greatest particularity."[37]

The Chekhovian genre of comic-pathos is established in this continuous flux. For Hoare, each work is an arrest of movement, pinpointing in its texture the recurring quality of life. "Quality" and "texture" are aesthetic terms, establishing their meaning in relation to what they are not. They are *not* "pattern," understood by Hoare as a social term inseparably related to an "attitude" to life.

Social pattern, in a realist analysis, requires a different kind of search, looking for historical order behind the flux of daily appearances. In the 1930s, a few attempts were made at a realist analysis of Chekhov, but none of them became the familiar currency of Chekhov criticism in the years that followed. In 1932 G. Z. Patrick pointed out that "truth" for Chekhov was the activity of science, and "beauty" the "beauty of the coming life" which was

entirely bound up with his dream of universal higher education. . . . Persistently and tirelessly he spoke of the common masses as living "worse than cattle"; and he proceeded to point out that such a state of things in Russia was due to the lack of individual freedom and the restrictions for the lower classes in educational opportunities.[38]

In 1936 Herbert Howarth placed Patrick's perception on a more sociological basis, by relating Chekhov to the upwardly mobile Russian middle class. Not foreseeing the Revolution, Chekhov "expects the new middleman (Lopakhin, the successful merchant) to seize the power." However, "Chekhov does not believe that this rule will be satisfactory. . . . He believes that man must be equipped with more than business ability to be fit for social life; and this recognition represents a negative demand for education." As Howarth rightly points out, education for Chekhov involves "the discovery of theoretical truth in order that it may be applied to practice. . . . In *Uncle Vanya* Astrov personifies this attitude. He is a medical man and a planter of forests."[39]

Patrick's and Howarth's approaches to the Chekhov text were unsophisticated. But this is not sufficient reason to explain their disappearance from the Chekhov critical agenda.[40] It was their realist epistemology which was—and to some extent has remained—unacceptable. To see grounds for this, in terms of Chekhov criticism, we will look briefly at the 1920s when the "Art" discourse was establishing itself by absorbing other critical challenges.[41]

In 1912 the *Times Literary Supplement* had argued that Western audiences might be impatient with a drama "in which the characters let circumstance ride over them" and in which there was "no exercise of the dynamics of drama as we understand it in Western Europe. . . . Crude, barbaric, and false as our English drama is, it is all reared on the assumption that men and women . . . are at least great enough to fight their fate to the end. It exalts passion, ambition and the power of the will."[42]

With Russia a potential ally in the First World War, a number of critics found "pussyfooters" like Konstantine in *The Seagull* a feebly dangerous example to contemporary youth. H. de Fuller commented in 1916 that "the only answer that a normal American can make to this sort of thing is that, if the boy had had the advantage of athletic sport, he would doubtless have worked off most of the vague feelings which he mistook for the stirrings of genius."[43] The same year a *New York Tribune* critic wrote that "Theodore

Roosevelt would undoubtedly be intensely annoyed by *The Seagull*," but fortunately the "Russia of the day's cablegrams is so far from the Russia of *The Seagull* that it is doubtful if the play will continue to be nationally true when the war is over."[44] Similarly, in 1917 the British critic Hamilton Fyfe argued that "Chekhov plays . . . leave behind a misleading impression of the Russian character, and this it is important to erase. . . . During the war the Russian nature has developed, become firmer, grown towards Western energy and away from Eastern do-nothing fatalism."[45]

After the war, serious critics like James Agate made fun of these "Horseback Hall" views, for which there are "few wounds that a ride to hounds will not heal."[46] But by then the Russian Revolution had given a new meaning to the "man of will" so desired of Russia during the war. In 1920 Francis Hackett considered the "hopelessness" and "lack of ideals" in Chekhov from an altered perspective, contrasting his characters favourably with the "men unduly purposeful" of war and revolution. "Who wants to hope for oneself or anyone else, if hope has no better basis than that which the public actions of 1914-1920 disclose? Our generation now knows . . . that humanity works on a tiny margin of decency and that a few mistakes here and there must mean that decency is to be sacrificed and the barbarian put into control." Now the man unduly purposeful who was "riding the world from one Holy War to another" devalued the very notion of "exalted hopes."[47] And critics like M. P. Willcocks[48] and Ralph Wright[49] found Chekhov's "little things of beauty"—"the scent of wood smoke," Andrei's "many happy solitary hours playing the violin"—more to their taste than Shaw's view of "the dawn of a new age from the vantage point of a windy mountain top."

Far from being "foreign," Chekhov was now seen as relevant to English country life, Irish country life, and even Main Street U.S.A. Shaw's "waste product" view of the Treplevs and Ranevskaias was frequently contrasted with Chekhov's sense of the "frail beauty of their uselessness."[50] Chekhov was the intellectuals' artist, finding, S. P. Sherman wrote in 1925, "sympathetic and intelligent friends among disenchanted writers of the post-war period."[51] The critique of Chekhov for a "cult of inefficiency" was, Sherman insisted, a partisan's argument, a shallow put-down by those who put passions and war before culture.

A. Werth, writing in 1925, was easily able to give contemporary identity to the two kinds of "mechanically" successful men to whom he said Chekhov was most averse: the Lopakhin-type businessman and the Soviet-style official who lived "according to programmes, theories and strict principles." Against these, Chekhov sided with "all the artists for art's sake, all the idealists who strive not so much after an ideal but . . . for the sake of striving."[52] On the one side of these "artists for art's sake" there were, St. John Ervine complained, the philistine "shop-keeper syndicates" which controlled the theatres, and on the other side socialists and government soup-kitchens.[53]

On the one hand, as Brooks Atkinson wrote in the *New York Times* of the Wall Street Crash,

after a period in which the vitality of the country has been dissipated in speculation and . . . the only leadership in the theatre comes from shrewdly operated business offices—Chekhov is writing of things we know. . . . During Chekhov's time the stagnating force was political. With us . . . a cheerful surrender of art to business.[54]

On the other hand, there was the Soviet example where, as one Western critic commented in 1938, "one trembles to think what would have happened to those sisters if their ambition to return to Moscow had been achieved. They would probably have ended up as three corpses in the Moskva River."[55]

An aestheticist criticism was being written which opposed men unduly purposeful in both Russia and the Western world. There was, of course, resistance to this dominant view. During the Second World War Burton Rascoe returned to the critical spirit of the First by saying that far from being at the bottom of the Moskva River, the three sisters were alive, well, and working in the trenches; and that compared with these contemporary Russian women and their American counterparts working in the factories, Chekhov's sisters "seem to be three completely uninteresting females whose aspirations are trivial and whose fate is unimportant."[56] But in the milieu of the interwar years, the Chekhov of infrangible beauty elevated above social turmoil was attractive to many.

The translation of Chekhov's letters and notebooks into English during the 1920s might have been expected to pose a more systematic challenge to aestheticist criticism, since they revealed a "positive" Chekhov who, Edward Garnett wrote in 1921, "fused the detached, impartial attitude of the modern scientist with a deep humanism . . . By 'clear knowledge'—that was Chekhov's hope for men, a hope which, in this era of Europe's violence and lying, shines afar off like a star."[57]

During this same period, the increasingly "comic" Chekhov was readily absorbed into the aestheticist reading. It was comedy, as we have seen, which supposedly provided Chekhov with the artistic "distance" from which to survey the plain of human melancholia. But Chekhov the "scientific reformer" was harder to absorb. Robert Lynd said in 1920 that the accusation that Chekhov had "nothing to give his fellows but a philosophy of hopelessness . . . takes one's breath away. . . . He was active in service as a philanthropist. . . He was equally generous as author, doctor and reformer."[58] Other critics noted Chekhov's work for public health, common-school education, and penal reform.

Yet Chekhov the "social reformer"' had little effect on textual interpretation. Middleton Murry denied the textual validity of Chekhov's non-literary comments altogether, saying it was a crime to publish his notebooks and thus strengthen "a deplorable tendency that is already much too prevalent among those who meddle with letters . . . to approach an author by the backstairs."[59] In more sophisticated cases, the "reforming" Chekhov was contained by a critical discourse that constructed both "science" and "art" in a very particular way. Science, like art, was separated from its contact with the social and historical, becoming eternally and universally "objective." Consequently, science had nothing to do with ideas of social reform. As M. P. Willcocks put it (making Chekhov sound like Tuzenbakh), Chekhov as scientist plumbed "the depths of the atomic world," finding there "mysterious life" and without any theories "as to the whence and whither of this ocean of life." This "objectivity" (applied to *people* as well as tides) was then contrasted with the "dream of an unfulfilled promise of Heaven," the revolutionary promise which "is the secret of Europe's dominion of fear today."[60]

In a more specific reading, as in the *Times Literary Supplement* review of the Koteliansky and Woolf *Notebooks*, this scientific objectivity was tied down still further. Chekhov became a "Behaviourist in fiction," and his reformist comments were dismissed as themselves unscientific: "Remember this and you will not take his philosophy or his bleeding heart too seriously."[61]

Thus interpreted, Chekhov's science became the bedrock for a very particular construction of "art." If, on the one hand, with the ruthless objectivity of the scientist, Chekhov revealed humankind's animal failings, on the other hand as an artist he avoided the "glass cage . . . of detachment."[62] His, we recall, was not the detachment of a man "really bored with common people and contemptuous of the common lot," but rather that of the humane artist elevated, as Willcocks put it, "above the clouds," laughing and weeping with scorn and compassion at the endless round of the human comedy. "Although," Atkinson wrote, "Chekhov was a physician, he developed it more artfully than scientifically."[63] The combination of the empiricist scientist, and conventionalist (or at the least, idealist) artist had created the necessary criticial space for the "ambivalence" readings of the most recent period.

CONTEMPORARY CRITICISM: THE TENSION OF AMBIGUITY

Chekhov never wholly adopted naturalism, nor did he ever relinquish it. . . . The mood of indecision was Chekhov's prevailing mood. . . . Wisdom compelled withdrawal and indifference; but there was something greater than wisdom that impelled one to action—life itself, the vital principle. . . . It was in this tension, impossible to resolve, that Chekhov found the dynamic principle of his art. (Maurice Valency)[64]

For all Chekhov's undoubted pessimism over the human condition he is not an adherent of a theory of implacable determinism. . . . Man creates meaning, he gives embodiment to his "history," his destiny. His first step, everywhere, must be to recognize his fate in himself. (R. L. Jackson)[65]

The artist tended to oust the scientist in his make-up, but the central body of his work (roughly between 1888 and 1895) forces us to reconcile the two. . . . Chekhov came to accept without revulsion, the animal in man as had new trends in psychology, in which he was so interested. . . . His morality has an existentialist provisionality about it. He clearly believed human life to be an anomaly in a dead cosmos. . . . Chekhov admires the human being who can make the most of his latencies. (Donald Rayfield)[66]

Chekhov is painfully aware throughout his works of human limitations and the fact of death. Such things weigh heavily with him, as do poverty and grief, because in his view there is no restitution for them. Often, too, Chekhov expresses the pain of grief or the finality of death against a background of indifference in the natural world. . . . Yet, if this seems a denial of life's values and energies, it should also be remembered that the same sense of human beings themselves having to determine whatever life is about is behind Chekhov's hope in human purposiveness and progress. The balances emerging from this are precarious. (Beverley Hahn)[67]

There is the possibility that what familiarity with the scientific method gave him was a heightened sense of the absurd; specialised training in the rational and logical processes of scientific work may have sharpened his awareness of the irrational in life. (Karl Kramer)[68]

A radical reading of life . . . is the "reduction" to essentials . . . of living experience; the refusal to be distracted by the "natural surface appearance". It is the consistency of art rather than the consistency of representation. . . . The naturalists, however, insisted on representation, and accepted the limits of normal expression. . . . The elaboration of substitute devices (like symbols) is an attempt to escape from the limitations which in the interest of naturalism have been voluntarily self-imposed. . . . But to take the play beyond naturalism, to make it something more than an entertaining, but limited collection of human sketches, this unexamined experience would have to be faced and understood. . . . Chekhov only refines the form, he does not overcome it. (Raymond Williams)[69]

These quotations, taken from some of the more significant criticism of the last 30 years, emphasise an ambivalence in Chekhov which is the source of artistic "tension." All of them take his "naturalism" (or associated scientific view) as the pole of the artistic tension that he reacts against. All of them (with the exception of Williams) understand naturalism as a world view (rather than as critical epistemology), a "scientific" limitation on humanity which Chekhov's "art," "classical humanism," "existentialism," "absurdism," "modernism" works to liberate—but always in a dialectic of closure and openness, as a continuing tension.

The point here is that the tension of empiricism and conventionalism ("naturalism" and "art") which constituted the authorship of Chekhov in the earlier criticism generated the discursive space for nearly all Western interpretation after the war. New critical positions—such as existentialism and absurdism—could easily be accommodated while never in fact going outside that space. The common feature of these readings is their rejection of realism as a critical position, and their neglect of historical specificity, by which is meant any sense of the particular combination of naturalism with human purpose and scientific compassion which marked *this* writer in this society at this time—the fact, for instance, that Chekhov was part of a particular social movement in the *zemstvo* areas after the Crimean War, and with the particular Social Darwinist belief that by changing the environment one might change people and reform society.

Instead, scientific naturalism and artistic individualism have been drawn on as though they were global historical paradigms, displacing "naive" concepts of progress with a sense of comic absurdity, and leaving as the positive space for art, not the arena of social practise and change Chekhov believed in, but life discovered individually and in the interstices, as resistance to existential *angst*. And so, when Trofimov makes his well-known speech about "workers . . . fed abominably, forced to sleep without proper beds . . . with bed bugs, filthy smells, and a permeating damp," critics can easily recognise the revolutionary rhetoric and disdain Soviet interpretation that takes Trofimov to represent the positive Chekhov. But they are unable to recognise that the words are based closely on those of Chekhov's friend and fellow *zemstvo* doctor, P. I. Kurkin, in contrasting recent factory conditions with the contemporary ones where "everywhere have been constructed vast, clean and dry barracks with proper floors and camp bed covered with straw"—reforms that Chekhov knew about, approved of, and were the result of research by his own university teacher, Erisman.[70] When Chekhov says that the people he most admires are the evolutionist scientists G. A. Zakharin, F. F. Erisman, and A. O. Ostroumov it means something, for his texts as well as his life.[71] It locates Trofimov's rhetoric, for example, in terms of a particular reformist perspective. But in the Chekhov criticism described here the artistic response of resistance replaces the social one, forging a tension of ambiguity out of the certainty of natural indifference and social meaninglessness.

Chekhov criticism in the West has proliferated since 1945, but hardly any of it has moved outside the empiricist and conventionalist paradigm described in this essay. Since there is little space to take this far, this section concludes with a brief look at three interpretations of Chekhov that have been particularly significant in recent years: David Magarshack's *The Real Chekhov*, J. L. Styan's *Chekhov in Performance*, and H. Peter Stowell's *Literary Impressionism*.

Potentially Magarshack opens the way for a socio-historical analysis in *The Real Chekhov*, since he argues that the "true" Chekhov will only emerge through an understanding of his personal and social background, and that the gloomy "mood" interpretations of later Chekhov productions owed a lot to the influence in the West of Stanislavskii and his perception (as dispossessed property owner) of social change in Russia. Yet, Magarshack avoids anything beyond an empiricist analysis of Chekhov's "back-

ground'' in terms of his spoken "intentions.'' His concerns are not in fact
social context but comedy and tragedy. Chekhov's plays are comedies when
he says they are. They have become tragedies in performance because of
Stansilavskii and "inadequate translations.''

Comedy, Magarshack says, resides in the playwright allowing the audience
always to be "ahead of the character on the stage,'' so that it can laugh at
the interaction of silly individuals, each so bound up with great ideas that he
or she can never begin to understand the reality behind the delusions of
others. The final scene between Konstantine and Nina in *The Seagull* "is a
good example of the incongruities that typify a classical comedy situation,''
except that in Chekhov there is never a happy ending.[72] The audience now
shares the artistic elevation from which to smile at human folly.

Magarshack's emphasis on the classical comedy situation and the Chekhovian mark of authorship (the transition from classical to indirect action
comedy) in fact draws attention away from Chekhov's own social values.
For Magarshack "real" change is of the personal kind—Nina's way out of
"the maze of dreams and images . . . back to reality,'' and Sonia's "faith
and courage alone that will rebuild the ruins.'' Accordingly, any belief that
"sweeping away the old order" will bring decent change is "facile
optimism.''[73] To be "realistic" (as against "comic") is to understand that
there are no movements for social change which are better than banal, and
Chekhov's "artistry" is in bringing the audience pleasure in that fact ahead
of the characters.

If Magarshack's *The Real Chekhov* works to elevate the author/critic
relationship as a process of true "reading" (the work as the author
intended), J. L. Styan's *Chekhov in Performance* is as clearly designed to
promote *theatre* as the "real" Chekhov. Indeed, the book aspires to
scholarship *via* a "stage sense." For Styan, true objectivity inheres in the
theatre—in "good" drama—and Chekhov's theatrical development (as
part of naturalist theatre's fight against "declamatory acting") "is also the
story of his progress toward objectivity in his beliefs and art." By claiming
Chekhov's "objectivity" for the theatre, Styan converts it into the familiar
impersonality and lack of commitment. An objective view of the world is
the "delighted objectivity an audience feels when all its senses are in play.''[74]

Despite Styan's reference to Brecht, this is Brecht stripped of his commitment to a theatre of social change. Alienation is a matter of the "objectively
amusing," and (a familiar view) Chekhov's novel mode of symphonic
acting elaborates the general "comedy of self deceit" in which the tragedy
of innocent life crushed by human experience and indifference is artistically
elevated so that the "comedy of the little pains of human pride and vanity"
may be "re-experienced exquisitely" by an audience.[75]

Social history, it seems, is at best cyclical, as we voyeuristically reexperi-
ence the inevitble tragedies of youth and so become mature. There is no new
social order available, since Chekhov would never be "so naive" as to

believe that "in any conceivable new society people would not, then as now, be insensitive or over-sensitive, turn cynical or destructive, fail to realise themselves or to exercise their gifts, suffer unrequited love or make bad marriages."[76] And so, having abstracted the matter of social change to the imponderable level of human nature, and at the same time reduced it to the level of requited love and good marriages, Styan is able to move on to *The Cherry Orchard*, where the feudal social order itself justifies the "exquisite balance of art."

For Magarshack Chekhovian comedy lies in our mature recognition of the disparity between reality and human illusion. For Styan his comedy is exquisitely balanced between farce which precludes and tragedy which demands compassion for human weakness. This structure of "comi-tragic ambivalence" is also crucial to audience participation. "Ambivalence is the source of all that is truly participatory in comedy. . . . He divides us against ourselves and splits our attention in order to arouse us. . . . We must neither condemn nor condone." Soviet audiences may find rousing polemics in Trofimov, and Western audiences may weep for the owners of the cherry orchard. "But if production allows either the heroics of prophecy or the melodrama of dispossession, then all of Chekhov's care for balance is set at nought and the fabric of the play torn apart."[77]

H. Peter Stowell takes Styan's starting assumption of the "many faced ambivalence" of the human personality much further in *Literary Impressionism: James and Chekhov* to construct a ruthlessly convention-alist reading. Rejecting evidence that Chekhov's works were fundamentally influenced by "the determinism of Darwin, and the methodology of Claude Bernard" (which he ascribes only to Zola), Stowell defines Chekhov's as "a world where characters must learn to change and adapt to a changing environment." This is not, however, Chekhov's evolutionist sense of changing the environment to change society, but a phenomenological subjectivism derived from modernism. Chekhov people "become painfully aware of the subjective limitations of knowledge. They perceive ambiguous surfaces that only reveal more surfaces, as they come to realise that appearances are the only reality." Truth then becomes "a matter of interpretation, differing always for a different interpreter."[78]

Chekhov's poetic/dramatic form ("literary impressionism") eliminates the omniscient author, causal narrative structure, and motivated character-isation. As the text deconstructs itself, Styan's sense of the nice balance of juxtaposed impressions has become dynamic, a matter of endless transition. In this drama of shifting instants of perception and "flashes of frozen time," Chekhov's famous pauses operate, for Stowell, rather like the blank footage in some modernist films—to provoke audience involvement, and as a challenge to the narrative's linearity. But whereas in post-Brechtian films such challenges to the syntagmatic flow of the narrative act as a radical space for critical rational thought, here "artistic" ambivalence and relativity of perception is the goal.

"Beginning with impressionism," Stowell argues, "unknowability rather than knowability becomes a major concern of literature."[79] Ambivalence for Stowell is recognising that "one surface is as real as any other," that all is relative and not therefore properly subject to the "hopelessly ephemeral dream" of social change. In Stowell's analysis, as for so many critics before him, in the Chekhov text "the naturalistic comes in conflict with the poetic, inertia struggles against purposeless activity."[80] Stowell's terms are more systematically conventionalist, but his description of the Chekhovian character as caught in the transitional moment between "romantic desire for a transcendental glimpse into the 'Truth' of human consciousness" and "realisation that there is no 'Truth'," returns us in the 1980s essentially to the paradigm of the 1920s.

A REALIST POSTSCRIPT

Raymond Williams's Chekhovian ambiguity is of quite a different order from these others. Again, he regrets Chekhov's naturalism—but here as a mode of analysis and representation which cannot expose the causal nature of the social structure. To distinguish, as Williams does, between the "natural surface appearance" and the "underlying" behind it—in contrast to Stowell's "The impressionist takes the world of appearances as reality, rather than struggling with the phantom issue of appearance versus reality"—is to assert the need for a realist theory which, as Williams's writing developed, distinguished between "naturalism as a doctrine of character formed by environment" and "realism which . . . insisted on the dynamic quality of all 'environments,' and on the possibility of intervention to change them."[81]

Williams's analytical position as a Marxist may have prevented him from seeing the relevance of his own understanding of realism to Chekhov, who was a reformist, not a revolutionary. At any rate, the most plausible recent realist account, which has applied Williams's distinction between naturalism and realism to Chekhov, has come from his Cambridge colleague, Peter Holland, who argues that "Even if we accept Meierkhold's picture of Chekhov as a dramatist who disdained naturalism in its fullest sense, that does not contradict a Chekhov whose aim is to make society clear, to analyse society directly."[82]

Holland speaks with approval of recent English productions of *Three Sisters* and *The Cherry Orchard* by Edward Bond and Trevor Griffiths which established "Chekhov as social critic, rather than romantic dreamer." Griffiths had argued that *The Cherry Orchard*'s "specific historicity and precise sociological imagination had been bleached of all meanings beyond those required to convey the necessary 'natural' sense that the fine will always be undermined by the crude and that the 'human condition' can for all essential purposes be equated with 'the plight of the middle classes'."[83]

This was a writer's critique of the "Englishness" of Chekhov productions which was very different from Virginia Woolf's in the 1920s, and Holland extends it by arguing against the supposed arbitrariness of Chekhov's symbols and signifiers. "As a sign the storm need not be arbitrary at all; Vania chooses to make it so. . . . Vania's illusions are rejected and under-cut by the reality of the storm."[84]

Magarshack's incongruity between fact and illusion, Jackson's "man *creates* meaning," even Stowell's "inertia struggling against purposeless activity" can all be accommodated by Holland's analysis. But in this realist account of a realist author, the tension between nature and ideal is made a matter of social responsibility. It is a reality that can be changed.

Astrov's great dreams of reafforestation combine the beauty of the tree and the reality of planting. He can see the woods for what they are, a source of timber, and at the same time as an example of continuity and grandeur. If Lopakhin is not capable of setting his ideals so high, both are visionaries who see no point in visions unless they can be carried out. Both respond directly to the reality of society and social change.[85]

It is Holland's relating of "visions" to the actual possibility of social change, rather than to the comedy of the human round, which marks the crucial difference between his analysis and nearly all described in this chapter. Here "ambiguity" is a social space prior to being an artistic one. Ambiguity is certainly important in Chekhov. But it is an ambiguity with very precise social and historical dimensions. As suggested in *Chekhov: A Structuralist Study*, it was the ambiguity of a reformer in an autocracy that needed to modernise scientifically but culturally stay the same; it was the ambiguity of a doctor who believed in the vision of his medical peers but not his literary ones, and felt his own writing held back accordingly; it was the ambiguity of a planter of trees who, like Astrov, saw the way to a better social and natural environment, but felt crushed by the scope of oppression around him.

These are the "ambiguities and complexities of personal and social life" which, as Janet Woolf notes,[86] mark the construction of authorship, and they flow through to the text as a polyphony of voices. But in a realist text like Chekhov's, shifting discourses are always converted to "knowledge" in the end. As Jan van der Eng has pointed out in his analysis of ambiguous narrative relations in Chekhov, textual fragments which, at the first time of reading (in earlier narrative chains), seem "out of place," are retrospec-tively read as the real underlying the narrative surface of events, part of a "hierarchically superior" chain of meaning that "begins to run through the whole story, supplements deficient information, sets forth new implications and reveals the main thematic issue of the story."[87] And that thematic issue, generally, as well as in the case of "The Lady with a Lapdog" which van der Eng analyses, is not eternal beauty but social self-knowledge. Perhaps it is time that critics took those well-known words of Chekhov seriously: "All I wanted to say honestly to people: 'Have a look at yourselves and see how bad and dreary your lives are!' The important thing is that people should realise that, for when they do, they will most certainly create another and better life for themselves."[88]

As Thomas Mann said in 1955, without an understanding of the "desire for a better reality" in Chekhov, detailed critical considerations of his language and form are misplaced because they are inseparably related.

For Chekhov was a doctor . . . by passionate conviction. . . . he believed science to be one of the forces making for progress, the great antagonist of scandalous conditions, since it enlightens the heads and the hearts of men. . . . What interests me . . . is the recognition of the connection between Chekhov's gradual mastery of form and his increasing sensitiveness to the moral evils of his age. . . . For the thing that broke through was directly connected with the form and the language . . . from the desire for a better reality . . . imaged in the language."[89]

For too long Western critics have pinpointed the value-laden assumptions of Soviet interpretation of Chekhov without equally questioning their own epistemologies. Despite the huge proliferation of criticism, these have remained remarkably uniform in their construction of Chekhov in the space between empiricism and conventionalism. For this reason this article avoids that familiar itinerary from "gloomy" (Toumanova et al.) to "positive" (Magarshack) Chekhov, rounded off by some throwaway comments about more "radical" or "feminist" interpretations since the late 1960s.[90] One recent critic,[91] for instance, places Virginia Llewellyn Smith's *Anton Chekhov and the Lady with the Dog* within a "feminist" development in criticism, whereas it seems that her thesis that "Chekhov's ambivalent attitude to love" reveals itself in the "dissociation from facts and retreat into a dream world" is better understood (as Ronald Hingley indicates in his introduction) within the "irony of life" interpretation which has been dominant since the 1920s.[92] It is clearly not the case that Chekhov's concern is with "the impossibility of man, of women . . . attaining any sort of effective rapport with another human being" (Hingley), although the personal sexual problems which Smith tries to describe may well have been operating in the context of Chekhov's specifically social concerns.[93] *That* ambiguity—in the construction of Chekhov's authorship between codes of language, personal biography (as sexed being and artist), socially reforming values, and so forth, would be a valuable focus of analysis. But so far there has been no Sartre in Chekhov criticism.

NOTES

1. In this chapter my reference to "Western critics" is almost entirely to British/ American criticism. European criticism emerges from such a different tradition as to need a separate study in itself.

2. E. J. Dillon, "Recent Russian Literature" *Review of Reviews* 4 (July-December 1891): 79-83.

3. A. Cahan, "The Younger Russian Writers," *Forum* 28 (September 1899): 119-128.

4. C. Brinton, "Anton Chekhov," *Critic* 45 (October 1904): 318-320.

5. M. Baring, *New Quarterly* 1 (1907-1908): 405-429.

6. See J. Tulloch, *Chekhov: A Structuralist Study* (London: Macmillan, 1980), ch. 3.

7. *Times Literary Supplement "Anton Chekhov,"* (July 22, 1904): 229.

8. V. Briusov, *Athenaeum* (September 3, 1904): 312-314.

9. R. Long, *Fortnightly Review* 72 (July-December 1902): 103-118.

10. Baring, op. cit.

11. *Ibid.*

12. A. Keeton, "Anton Chekhov" *Academy and Literature* (January 9, 1904): 40.

13. St. John Hankin, *Academy* 72 (June 15, 1907): 585.

14. A. Bates, *Russian Drama* (London: Short and Stanley, 1903), p. 18.

15. A. Bennett, *New Age* (March 18, 1909): 423.

16. T. Lovell, *Pictures of Reality* (London: British Film Institute, 1980), p. 18. Lovell's distinction as epistemologies between empiricism, conventionalism, and realism (and, within realism, between idealist and materialist realism) is crucial to the argument of this chapter. Following Lovell I will call this sociological realism "realism."

17. G. Calderon, Introduction to his translation of *Two Plays by Tchekof, The Seagull and The Cherry Orchard.* (London: G. Richards, 1912).

18. L. Woolf, *New Statesman* (August 11, 1917): 446-448.

19. Lovell, *Pictures of Reality*, p. 12.

20. M. Jameson, *Modern Drama in Europe* (London: W. Collins, 1920).

21. E. Wilson, "The Moscow Art Theatre," *Dial* 74 (January 1923): 319.

22. *Ibid.*

23. *Ibid.*

24. V. Woolf, "The Cherry Orchard," *New Statesman* (July 24, 1920): 446.

25. B. Shaw, *Collected Plays with Their Prefaces* (London: Bodley Head, 1972), p. 13.

26. Woolf, op. cit.

27. Jameson, op. cit.

28. *Ibid.*

29. *Ibid.*

30. *Ibid.*

31. *The Times* (October 20, 1925): 12.

32. R. Parker, *Independent* 110 (February 17, 1923): 140.

33. J. M. Murry, "Thoughts on Chekhov," in *Aspects of Literature* (London: Collins, 1920).

34. *Ibid.*

35. W. Gerhardie, "The Secret of Chekhov's Literary Power," *Forum* 70 (November 1923): 2144-2148.

36. *Ibid.*

37. S. Hoare, "Anton Chekhov," *Golden Hind* 2 (October 1923): 9-14.

38. G. Z. Patrick, "Chekhov's Positive Vision," *Slavonic Review* 10 (April 1932): 658-668.

39. H. Howarth, "Chekhov on Work," *Adelphia* 12 (August 1936): 309-311.

40. To the extent that, until writing this chapter in 1984, I had never heard of Howarth, despite extensive coverage of secondary sources on Chekhov when writing my own analysis.

41. To consider the wider implications of the development of this idealist and anti-historical criticism within the literary institution, see T. Eagleton, *Literary Theory* (Oxford: Basil Blackwell, 1983), ch. 1.

42. *Times Literary Supplement* (February 1, 1912): 45.

43. H. de Fuller, "*The Seagull,*"*Nation* (June 1, 1916): 45.

44. *New York Tribune, "The Seagull"* (May 24, 1916): 11.

45. H. Fyfe, *English Review* 24 (May 1917): 408-414.

46. J. Agate, "*Uncle Vanya,*" *Saturday Review* 132 (December 21, 1921): 658.

47. F. Hackett, *New Republic* (April 21, 1920): 254.

48. M. P. Willcocks, *English Review* 34 (March 1922): 207-216.

49. R. Wright, *Everyman* 15 (March 20, 1920): 513-514.

50. G. Sutton, *Bookman* 61 (December 1921): 169.

51. S. P. Sherman, "Chekhov's, Chekhovians, Chekhovism," *New York Herald Tribune Books* 6 (November 5, 1925): 1.

52. A. Werth, *Slavonic Review* 3 (March 1925): 622-641.

53. St. John Ervine, *Observer* (July 18, 1920): 11.

54. B. Atkinson, *New York Times* (June 2, 1929): Pt. 8, p. 1.

55. P.T., "*The Three Sisters,*"*New English Weekly* (February 10, 1938): 354-355.

56. B. Rascoe, "*The Three Sisters,*" *New York World-Telegram* (December 22, 1942).

57. E. Garnett, "The Modernity of Chekhov," *Quarterly Review* 236 (October 1921): 257-269.

58. R. Lynd, "Chekhov's Letters to His Friend," *Nation* (February 28, 1920): 742.

59. J. M. Murry, *Nation and Athenaeum* (June 4, 1921): 365.

60. M. P. Willcocks, *English Review* 34 (March 1922): 207-216.

61. *Times Literary Supplement "The Notes of Anton Chekhov,"* (April 21, 1921): 257.

62. F. Hackett, *New Republic* (April 21, 1920): 254.

63. B. Atkinson, *New York Times* (November 18, 1928): Pt. 9, p. 1. This and most of the references from early Chekhov criticism are from the very useful collection, V. Emeljanov, ed., *Chekhov: The Critical Heritage* (London: Routledge, 1981).

64. M. Valency, *The Breaking String: The Plays of Anton Chekhov* (New York: Oxford University Press, 1966), pp. 80, 125.

65. R. L. Jackson, "*The Seagull*: The Empty Well, the Dry Lake, and the Cold Cave," in *Chekhov: A Collection of Critical Essays* (Englewood Cliffs, N.J.: Prentice-Hall, 1967), pp. 106, 107, 111.

66. D. Rayfield, *Chekhov: The Evolution of His Art* (London: P. Elek, 1975), pp. 12, 299.

67. B. Hahn, *Chekhov: A Study of the Major Stories and Plays* (London: Cambridge University Press, 1977), pp. 7, 312, 318.

68. K. Kramer, *The Chameleon and the Dream: The Image of Reality in Chekhov's Stories* (The Hague: Mouton, 1970), p. 318.

69. R. Williams, *Drama from Ibsen to Eliot* (New York: Penguin, 1964), pp. 24, 145-146, 151.

70. See Tulloch, *Chekhov*, ch. 1.

71. *Ibid.*, chs. 3-7.

72. David Magarshack, *The Real Chekhov: An Introduction to Chekhov's Last Plays* (London: Allen and Unwin, 1972), p. 69.

73. *Ibid.*

74. J. L. Styan, *Chekhov in Performance* (Cambridge: Cambirdge University Press, 1971), p. 3.

75. *Ibid.*

76. *Ibid.*, p. 236.

77. *Ibid.*, pp. 247-248, 245-246.

78. H. Peter Stowell, *Literary Impressionism: James and Chekhov* (Athens: University of Georgia Press, 1980), p. 243.

79. *Ibid.*, p. 23.

80. *Ibid.*, p. 159.

81. R. Williams, "Realism, Naturalism and Their Alternatives," *Cine-Tracts* 1, 3 (1977-1978): 5.

82. P. Holland, "Chekhov and the Resistant Symbol," *Themes in Drama; IV: Drama and Symbolism* (Cambridge and New York: Cambridge University Press, 1982), p. 237.

83. *Ibid.*

84. *Ibid.*, p. 233.

85. *Ibid.*, p. 239.

86. J. Wolff, *The Social Production of Art* (London: Macmillan, 1981), p. 136.

87. J. van der Eng, "On Descriptive Narrative Poetics," in J. van der Eng, J. Meijer, and H. Schmid, *On the Theory of Descriptive Poetics: Anton P. Chekhov as Story-Teller and Playwright* (Lisse: de Ridder Press, 1978), p. 91.

88. Cited in David Magarshack, *Chekhov the Dramatist* (New York: Hill and Wang, 1960).

89. T. Mann, "Anton Chekhov: An Essay," *The Listener*, March 3, 1955, pp. 371, 373. Mann's analytical interest in Chekhov's "desire for a better reality . . . imaged in the language" has been taken furthest in the work of Peter Holland; also see T. Winner, *Chekhov and His Prose* (New York: Holt, Rinehart and Winston, 1966), and for discussion of Winner and Barthes, see Tulloch, *Chekhov*, ch. 2.

90. In any case, this is not accurate, since criticism rejected the "gloomy" Chekhov by at least the 1920s.

91. N. Moravcevich, "Women in Chekhov's Plays," in J.-P. Barricelli, *Chekhov's Great Plays: A Critical Anthology* (New York: New York University Press, 1981), pp. 201-202.

92. V. L. Smith, *Anton Chekhov and the Lady with the Dog* (London: Oxford University Press, 1973), p. 219.

93. *Ibid.*, p. ix. For an alternative view on the relationship between men and women in Chekhov, see Tulloch, *Chekhov*, ch. 7.

PART VI

Chekhov's Works in Performance

13

Laurence Senelick

CHEKHOV ON STAGE

For better or worse, Chekhov's major plays were written at a time when the stage director was becoming a dominant factor in the modern theatre. The technical innovations of the modern stage, including electric lighting and veristic scenery in imitation of "real life," called for a single vision to unify the whole. Coincidentally, Chekhov's plays are not traditional star vehicles, but require strong and coordinated ensemble playing, best achieved under the experienced baton of a single "conductor." Much of what occurs in them occurs under and between the lines, so that virtuoso solo performing is insufficient to achieve the desired result. Therefore, the stage history of Chekhov's drama is a chronicle less of great performances in individual roles than of the successes and failures of directors and acting companies in realizing his plays.[1]

Chekhov's early plays were produced quickly partly because there was a paucity of good Russian drama in the 1880s, partly because he had a strong reputation as a writer of comic fiction, and partly because the government monopoly on theatres was canceled in 1882. The subsequent proliferation of private theatres and theatrical clubs attracted a new, more intellectual public, already familiar with Chekhov's writing. By September 1889, he had three plays running simultaneously in Moscow: *The Proposal* at Goreva's Theatre, *The Bear* at Abramova's, and *Ivanov* at Korsh's. This last play had been written for Korsh in 1887 and had been staged with loving care, although, except for V. H. Davydov in the lead and Glama-Meshcherskaia as Anna, the cast was weak. Nor were audiences properly preconditioned for this drama of a "superfluous man."

Some expected to see a merry farce in the style of Chekhov's stories of the time . . . others expected something new and more original from him—and were not disappointed. The success seemed spotty: some hissed, others, the majority, applauded loudly and called for the author, but, by and large, *Ivanov* was not understood.[2]

The last act in particular was disliked, and the play was withdrawn after three performances. This experience introduced Chekhov to the exquisite anguish of having a play produced.

When a revised version of *Ivanov* appeared at the State Alexandra Theatre in St. Petersburg in 1889, it was greeted with an ovation. But Chekhov remained dissatisfied: he wished to see a more energetic player than Davydov in the lead, and he approved only of Shepetova as Anna because she seemed to suffer and live on stage. Chekhov grew increasingly aware that his plays required a new conscientiousness in the actors, a willingness to jettison convention; the Alexandra company had complained at an early practice-session that they had no punchy exit-lines or strong curtains.[3]

The Wood Demon failed abysmally at Abramova's in 1889, and the first production of *The Seagull* at the Alexandra on October 17, 1896, has come down in theatrical legend as an unqualified disaster, although this is an exaggeration. The cast was a strong one, including Davydov as Sorin, the popular comedian Konstantin Varlamov (who had already played Lebedev in *Ivanov* and Chubukov in *The Proposal*) as Shamraev, the handsome *jeune premier* Roman Apollonskii as Treplev, and the brilliant young actress Vera Kommissarzhevskaia (who had cut her teeth on Sasha in 1889) as Nina. There was only a week's worth of rehearsal, with Chekhov in attendance, frequently prompting the actors and correcting the director Evtikhii Karpov. Like most sensitive playwrights, Chekhov was dismayed by the wasted rehearsal time, the actors' inability to avoid cliché and their stunting of his brain-children, but by the last rehearsal his expectations had risen.

These expectations were dashed on opening night, for the audience had come with expectations of its own. Looking for farce comedy, they laughed, booed, and whistled at whatever struck them as funny, from Nina's first-act soliloquy to the dead seagull to the actors' ad-libs when they forgot their lines. Chekhov fled the theatre, vowing never again to write for the stage. Nevertheless, the following performances, played to more thoughtful audiences, showed the actors more secure. Before *The Seagull* left the repertory in early November, it had become an esteemed play, with Kommissarzhevskaia's performance acclaimed as luminous. It was successfully revived in Kiev, Taganrog, and other provincial cities, providing Chekhov with handsome royalties.[4]

It was left to the newly founded Moscow Art Theatre (MAT) to discover a viable style for Chekhov, when it revived *The Seagull* in 1898 as the ultimate production of its shaky first season.[5] Vladimir Nemirovich-

Danchenko, an admirer of the play, forced it on his reluctant colleague Konstantin Stanislavskii, who at first found it incomprehensible and unsympathetic. He retired to his country estate to compose a directorial score (*partitura*) which he sent to Moscow where Danchenko rehearsed it with the actors, who included young Vsevolod Meierkhold as Treplev, Olga Knipper as Arkadina, and A. L. Vishnevskii, a boyhood friend of Chekhov's, as Dorn. Stanislavskii was to assume the role of Trigorin.

Stanislavskii's fundamental approach to staging *The Seagull* differed little from his direction of an historical play like A. K. Tolstoi's *Tsar Fedor Ioannavich*. He sought in contemporary Russian life the same picturesque groupings, the same telling mannerisms, the same pregnant pauses that had enthralled audiences with his archaeological reconstruction of seventeenth-century Muscovy. Rather than inquiring into Chekhov's deeper meaning, Stanislavskii viewed the play in terms of romantic melodrama: Nina was an innocent ruined by that "scoundrelly Lovelace" Trigorin, and Treplev was a misunderstood Byronic genius. Nor, at this stage of his development, did he seek to elicit performances from the actors organically. Their every move, thought, and intonation were prescribed by his score and learned by rote.

The opening night was a triumph, confirming the theatre's success; henceforth a seagull would be the MAT's trademark. But Chekhov was less than ecstatic. He thought that Stanislavskii misinterpreted Trigorin by making him too elegant and formal. He detested Roksanova's Nina. Whatever his misgivings, the middle-class professional audiences took to it precisely because, for the first time, "the way we live now" was subjected to the same careful reproduction that had hitherto been lavished only on the past. Instead of seeing a collection of more or less interesting performances, the spectators beheld their own tics and heard their own speech patterns scrupulously copied.

Taking advantage of the outdoor settings of the early acts and the dimly lit interior of the last act, Stanislavskii laid on climatic and atmospheric effects to create mood (*nastroenie*). The method worked so well with *The Seagull* that it became standard operating procedure at the MAT in treating Chekhov's later plays and, indeed, those of almost any author.

Contrary to popular belief, Chekhov was not so won over by the MAT approach that he bequeathed it his plays as his acknowledged interpreter. His recension of *The Wood Demon*, now called *Uncle Vania*, was first submitted to the Malyi Theatre, but its Board requested that the unflattering references to Professor Serebriakov be toned down. Chekhov withdrew the play and handed it over to Danchenko. With Stanislavskii as Astrov, his wife Lilina as Sonia, and Knipper as Elena, its success was decent but nothing out of the ordinary.

Chekhov's growing attachment to Olga Knipper and the MAT's solicitation of a play written specifically for it eventuated in *Three Sisters*, a drama whose large cast and elaborate situations are directly linked to Chekhov's awareness of who would be playing what. He did insist on a military expert to make sure the actors would not caricature the officers they enacted. The sense of real life created was so vivid that in time prospective ticket-buyers would propose "paying a call on the Prozorovs," rather than going to see a play. This aspect of homely familiarity was attacked by some as indicative of the play's triviality; but these hostile critics were misled by the MAT's sedulous reproduction of surface detail and its emotionally fraught silences. It did not pursue any meaning beyond the illustration of wasted provincial lives.[6]

As director and actor, Stanislavskii tended to side with specific characters, something Chekhov himself avoided. Just as *The Seagull* had been seen as an unequal competition between the Wunderkind Treplev and the hack Trigorin, so the MAT's *Three Sisters* identified with the longings of Masha, Olga, and Irina, while it scorned Natasha's philistinism and vulgarity. In the process, it ignored the character flaws that undercut the sisters themselves and wallowed in despair.

A more extreme form of this partisanship showed up in the production of *The Cherry Orchard* (1904). Lopakhin is arguably the closest thing to a protagonist in Chekhov's intent, for he stressed the businessman's delicacy of spirit beneath his boorish exterior; Chekhov meant the part for Stanislavskii, himself the scion of a mercantile family. But Stanislavskii cast himself as the indolent *barin* Gaev and consequently shifted the emphasis to make the plight of the dispossessed gentry the focus of sympathy and concern. Chekhov had likewise intended the role of the governess Charlotta to be taken by his now-wife Knipper; but she was cast as Ranevskaia, thus giving the part more centrality than Chekhov planned. Stanislavskii also insisted that the original ending of Act Two, an enigmatic scene between Charlotta and the old retainer Firs, was too downbeat to conclude an act. It was at his instigation that it finished with a quasi-love scene between Trofimov and Ania. Such directorial choices, later enhanced by the nostalgic retrospective of post-revolutionary emigrés, turned *The Cherry Orchard* into an elegy for a nest of gentry demolished by coarse "progress," instead of a more even-handed treatment of the subject.

Chekhov was willing to allow favorite actors like Ivan Moskvin (as Epikhodov) to keep their ad-libs, but he was distressed by what he considered a reduction of his characters to cry-babies by Stanislavskii's slow pacing of the play and by his addiction to atmospheric sound effects and overly naturalistic detail. Still, the influence of the MAT productions was overwhelming. As a tyro director, Meierkhold staged carbon-copies of them in the provinces, and he was only one of many. Chekhov became so equated with wistful *grisaille* and refined neurosis even before his death that an hilarious production of *The Anniversary* at the Alexandra in 1903 was condemned as unseemly and un-Chekhovian by some critics.

MAT tours to Germany and later to France and the United States ushered in Chekhov's plays in so polished and persuasive a format that most directors were content to create facsimiles of these originals. This led to a certain flatness and standardization in the staging of Chekhov and promoted an image of him as the subfusc bard of "twilight Russia." The sluggish rhythms, deliberate underplaying, and mournful cadences in these epigonic productions were not counterbalanced, as they were at the MAT, by consummate acting, comic touches, and intimacy with the subject matter. In Germany, in particular, gloom and doom became the keynote, and kept Chekhov from winning popularity there. It is noteworthy that the greatest German director of the period, Max Reinhardt, staged only *The Bear* (Kleines Theatre, Berlin, 1905).

With the Revolution Chekhov went out of fashion in Russia. As the leftist poet Vladimir Maiakovskii commented in the prologue to his agit-prop play *Mystery-Bouffe*, you go to the theatre, and "You look and see—/Auntie Manyas/and Uncle Vanyas,/flopping on divans. /But neither uncles nor aunties/Interest us,/Uncle and aunties we can get at home." Whatever the virtues of Chekhov's plays, they were dismissed as irrelevant to the Soviet era, for in the 1920s to be pessimistic and not "actively progressive" was *démodé*. The MAT refurbished *Uncle Vania* in 1927 and *The Cherry Orchard* in 1929, but was attacked nonetheless, by Gorkii among others, for playing them as dramas, not comedies. The first attempt to stage *The Cherry Orchard* as the farce its author had called it was made by N. I. Sobolshchikov-Samarin in Nizhnyi-Novgorod in 1929. *The Cherry Orchard* was the only Chekhov play to be revived in the 1930s, with Lopakhin spotlighted as a man necessary to Russian advancement, a forerunner of the Five-Year-Plans.

Significantly, the two greatest directors of the Bolshevik era were interested in Chekhov's farces, not his full-length plays. In 1920, Evgenii Vakhtangov prepared an evening of one-acts, *The Wedding, The Anniversary*, and a dramatization of the short story "Thieves" at the MAT Third Studio. He began work on *The Wedding* with the question, "How are we to portray Chekhov's characters, are we to defend them or condemn them?" In effect, he used music to accomplish both aims. At the play's start, the characters were clearly grotesques caught up in a manic quadrille; at the end, their backs to the audience, they listened to a *triste* quadrille as their dreams of a general, that is, of a more beautiful life, evaporated, and they returned to sordid reality. Each of the actors singled out the most squalid features of his character: the father-in-law was an opportunistic Babbitt, hiding behind the mask of a good fellow; the bridegroom was a tedious malcontent; the bride showed more interest in food than in her new husband. Only the "General" contributed warmth and charm, and when he rushed out crying "Chelove-e-ek! Chelove-e-ek!" (both "Man!" and "Waiter!"), the audience was so shattered it could not applaud. Michael

Chekhov, the writer's nephew, who had guffawed throughout could, at the final curtain, whisper only "What a horror! What a horror!"

Vakhtangov's advice to the actors rehearsing *The Anniversary* was to play not comedy but vaudeville, not Chekhov but Antosha Chekhonte. By cluttering the stage and reducing its space, he rendered the action caricatural and eccentric, forcing the players into unexpected and bizarre behavior. So successful were these one-acts that they were revived at studios, concerts, and troop shows well into the Second World War, setting an accepted style for Chekhov's farces.[7]

Meierkhold did not turn to Chekhov until 1935, the seventy-fifth anniversary of the writer's birth, when he presented three farces, *The Anniversary*, *The Bear*, and *The Proposal*, under the collective title *33 Fainting Fits*, computed by Meierkhold to be the number of fainting-fits that occur in the plays. He announced to his cast that these, accompanied by music, would constitute the leitmotiv of the performance to create a sequence of *jeux de théâtre*. To the world at large, he proclaimed more portentously and less candidly that the swoons exemplified the neurasthenic legacy of the pre-revolutionary intelligentsia. This kind of double-talk was not uncommon among artists under Stalin. Meierkhold lumbered the vaudevilles with innumerable props, detailed pantomime, and elaborate physical gags: on occasion they proved richly funny, but for the most part they clogged the action and overburdened the plays with directorial ingenuity.[8]

Abroad, Chekhov has never earned full citizenship on the French stage to the degree that Gogol, Tolstoi, or even dramatizations of Dostoevskii have. Perhaps this is due to the French tradition of acting which relies more on external technique than on inner intensity, or simply to a temperamental incompatibility.

Not surprisingly, then, the first staging of Chekhov in France was prompted by a Russian, Georges Pitoëff, whose *Uncle Vania*, played in Russian in Lausanne and Geneva, came to the Salle Privée in Paris in October 1915. Despite empty houses, he revived it in French in 1921, when Lucien Descaves wrote, "It is of an undeniable anguish and beauty."[9] Installed at the Théâtre des Champs-Elysées, Pitoëff's *Seagull* lacked the money and manpower to copy the MAT. Few Parisians cared for the play's "desperate romanticism," although Ludmilla was praised for her Nina. For several years, Pitoëff, who worshipped Chekhov, refrained from producing him, but in 1928 he mounted a *Three Sisters*. "Chekhov," he said, "compels us to love a society composed of insignificant creatures, representatives of the vast majority. But these creatures, precursors of the great upheavals, contain germs of faith, ardor, genius and resignation;" however contemptible they are, an "inner fire devours them."[10] The critics were alert to the magic of the staging, which made a virtue of necessity by using only cloth, a few sticks of furniture, and the orchestration of beautiful voices to produce its effects. But audiences stayed away in droves.

Pitoëff's only full-fledged success with Chekhov came in the year of his death, 1938, with a revival of *The Seagull*: "every moment snatches from the spectators gasps of surprise and astonishment" at the truth revealed.[11] It ran for months when audiences, poised on the brink of war, made earnest efforts to appreciate the meaning of Chekhov's characters. In the 1960s Pitoëff's son Sacha carried on the good work with *Uncle Vania* and *Ivanov*, in which he starred.

It was fortunate that the first British production of Chekhov, *The Seagull* at the Glasgow Repertory Theatre (November 1908), was translated and staged by the knowledgeable George Calderon, who declared that "a play of Tchekhof is a reverie, not a concatenation of events."[12] He strove for transitions from group moods into individual reactions, to achieve something close to Stanislavskii's "through-line" or "super-objective" *avant la lettre*, despite the inability of British actors to maintain an inner life when not speaking lines. Calderon was also aware that Chekhov's plays were not crude naturalism, and the Scottish reviewers were quick to pick up on what they called the play's "Ibsenite symbolism," its "odd and elusive symbolism." "The impression of overwhelming humanity owed much to the fine all round acting . . . for the ensemble was so perfect that it would almost seem invidious to select individual names."[13]

The "onlie begettor" of Chekhov in London was George Bernard Shaw who characterized the Stage Society *Cherry Orchard* (1911) as "the most important [production] in England since that of *A Doll's House*" (*The World*, June 6, 1911). But the Stage Society, primed for social messages and drama of reform, was bemused by the self-involvement of the characters; audiences and critics alike failed to understand the play, which it regarded as meaningful only to Russians. Matters were made worse by Kenelm Foss's draggy direction and the miscasting of an inexperienced young amateur as Ranevskaia. The public interpreted the play in the light of traditional well-made drama and thus took Lopakhin to be a brutish villain, the Gaev family to be charming victims, and, in one case, Epikhodov to be the "raisonneur." The Adelphi Play Society's *Seagull* (Little Theatre, 1912) and the Stage Society's *Uncle Vania* (Aldwych, 1914) were equally inept and poorly received; it was not until after World War I that the British were prepared to appreciate Chekhov.

The mood of embittered disillusionment that swept over English society in the wake of the Great War's futile devastation suddenly made the yearnings and fecklessness of Chekhov's people seem relevant. In the 1920s, J. Middleton Murry, Katherine Mansfield, S. S. Koteliansky, and others proselytized for Chekhov as a literary paragon: his plays were seized on as reflections of contemporary malaise. Another agent in popularizing Chekhov was the emigré director Theodore Komisarjevsky (Fedor Kommissarzhevskii), who launched a series of Chekhovian productions far better integrated and skillfully mounted than had been seen before: *Ivanov* (Duke of York's, 1925), *Three Sisters* (Barnes, 1926, with John Gielgud as Tuzenbakh); *The Cherry Orchard* (Barnes, 1926, Charles Laughton as Epikhodov); *Uncle Vania* (Barnes, 1926); *Three Sisters* (Fortune, 1929); and *The Seagull* (New, 1936, with Gielgud as Trigorin, Edith Evans as Arkadina, and Peggy Ashcroft as Nina).

Komisarjevsky had no qualms about cutting the plays and interpreting them to emphasize the more mawkish facets of the relationships. Gielgud relates of the 1926 *Three Sisters*:

The play was dressed in 1880's costumes, and Tusenbach, shorn of the lines about his ugliness, was played (by Komisarjevsky's express direction) as a romantic juvenile. . . . When I questioned him about the "ugly" lines being cut, he shrugged his expressive shoulders and said, "My dear boy, the English public always demand a love interest."[14]

This promoted in the public's mind an image of Chekhov as pastel-colored, moonstruck, and, as a character in *Private Lives* says of white elephants, "very, very sweet." Still, for the actors, Gielgud recalled, "playing Chekhov in the twenties and thirties was to us like discovering a new form.[15]

The only English productions before World War II that rivaled Komisarjevsky's in quality were Tyrone Guthrie's *Cherry Orchard* at the Old Vic (1933), remarkable for Charles Laughton as Lopakhin and his wife Elsa Lanchester as Charlotta; and a *Three Sisters* at the Queen's Theatre (1938) directed by Michel St.-Denis, a nephew of Jacques Copeau and founder of the Compagnie des Quinze. Recollected by many as one of the best examples of teamwork ever seen on the London stage, it revelled in a superb cast that ranged from Michael Redgrave as Tuzenbakh to Alec Guinness as Fedotik. Given eight weeks to rehearse, instead of the usual four, the cast had been able to grow into their roles to a remarkable degree. For the first time, English audiences were seeing an indigenous company approximate the MAT.[16]

It also instilled life into what had become a cliché of Chekhovian production, the languorous maundering of trivial people. Ivor Brown, after the Old Vic's *Three Sisters* of 1935, had been reminded of "those sororal duos and trios who croon their heartbreak into microphones."[17] The reviewer of Komisarjevsky's *Seagull* (1936) for *The New English Weekly* had asserted that "no producer who still interprets Chekhov yearningly and in slow motion is going to get any praise from me"; he lambasted the staging as "beyond description soulful and an invisible hassock for the reverential is supplied to every seat."[18] Clearly, a fresh approach was called for.

Chekhov was a stranger to American stages (except for a dim 1916 *Seagull*, put on by the Washington Square Players in New York) when the Moscow Art Theatre arrived on its tours of 1923-1924. Its repertory included *Three Sisters*, *The Cherry Orchard*, *Uncle Vania*, and *Ivanov*, in many cases with the actors who had originally created the roles. Even though these revivals of decades-old productions in no way represented the MAT's current researches, and even though Stanislavskii came out of acting retirement only in order to swell the box-office receipts, the Chekhovian performances were a revelation to American playgoers. Most of the actors and sensation-seekers who attended knew no Russian, but they were struck by the ensemble playing and the extra dimension that Chekhov took on when transferred from the page to the stage so thoroughly.

The earliest results of this confrontation could be seen at the Civic Repertory Theatre, directed by Eva Le Gallienne, an actress of broad culture and taste: *Three Sisters* (1926), *The Cherry Orchard* (1928 and 1933, with Alla Nazimova as Ranevskaia), and *The Seagull* (1929). Le Gallienne's ambitions usually outstripped her capabilities, for although she tried to emulate the MAT's stage pictures and deliberate rhythms, her casts were mediocre and her achievements more admirable for good intentions than for exciting productions. Even so, through her efforts, audiences began to develop a taste for Chekhov. The shrewd producer Jed Harris must have considered his box-office when he mounted a well-received *Uncle Vania* with the Broadway star Osgood Perkins as Astrov and the Hollywood celebrity Lillian Gish as Elena (Cort Theatre, New York, 1930).

Harris's was the virgin attempt to acclimate Chekhov to Broadway by titivating him with popular actors. In 1938, Alfred Lunt and Lynn Fontanne impersonated Trigorin and Arkadina in Stark Young's new, spare translation of *The Seagull* (Shubert Theatre, New York) surrounded by a remarkable, if disparate, group of players, including Sydney Greenstreet as Sorin, Uta Hagen as Nina, and Margaret Webster as Masha. The chief critical complaint was that the production was too glamorous and bright in hue; it told the story neatly enough, but sophisticated playgoers missed the half-tones and plangency they had come to expect of the Chekhovian ethos. Even less well received, though popular with the average matinee lady, was *Three Sisters* staged by Guthrie McClintic (Ethel Barrymore Theatre, New York, 1942); once again, the cast was composed of luminaries of the American stage and screen: Katharine Cornell (Masha), Judith Anderson (Olga), Ruth Gordon (Natasha), Dennis King (Vershinin), and Edmund Gwenn (Chebutykin), who came of differing backgrounds and acted in differing styles. McClintic claimed that he was not trying to recreate a Russian ambience, but for all that he seemed to subscribe to the view that Chekhov's play is a dreary tragedy, peopled by three wonderful women and a she-monster. Stark Young was compelled to remark that "Chekhov in performance in English nearly always suffers from what seems to be some sort of notion we have that thinking is slow, that when you are, as it were, philosophizing you must go slow."[19]

Italy came late to Chekhov with an *Uncle Vania* (*Zio Giovanni*) played by the Palmarini-Campa-Capodgalio Company in Florence in 1922; an important *Cherry Orchard* was directed by visiting Nemirovich-Danchenko in Italian with a "big-nosed and black-eyed" troupe headed by the emigrée actress Tatiana Pavlova in Milan (1933). Danchenko had often differed with Stanislavskii over the interpretation of Chekhov, and in Italy he wrote:

I decided to try to do what I always thought about this play and the way Chekhov thought of it. I always found that Olga Knipper, for all her charm, simplicity and affecting qualities, does not play it right, but quite wrongly in fact. She sort of over-loads it with high drama. Chekhov told me "Ranevskaia has a wasp-waist," which was his laconic way of defining her unusual flippancy and extreme frivolity. Which led me, with my director's flair, to think such a change of form would lend the whole performance great lightness, grace, a tone of comedy. . . . From her first line, the audience took Pavlova to be a fascinating, tender, moving but impossibly frivolous person. And, without exaggerating, each of her lines prompted a sympathetic laugh. The whole play began to glow with comic quality, but when Ranevskaia wept, the audience wept with her.[20]

Danchenko, who also wanted Chekhov to be filmed in Hollywood by Lewis Milestone, returned to Russia with the idea of revitalizing *Three Sisters*, whose characters he saw not as futile and trivial but as splendid and beautiful because of the fineness of their minds. He defined the play as a "longing for life," to be performed in a style of "virile strength."[21] The original production had sought to depict stifling provinciality; Danchenko added fresh air and flowers. Everything from uniforms to dressing-gowns was made beautiful; everything debasing or cold was eliminated. Instead of Lilina's insinuatingly sweet and inescapable Natasha, A. Georgievskaia made her crassly vulgar and raucous, a striking contrast to the sisters' musi-cality. The final hymn to the future was performed without Chebutykin's ironical counterpoint. Michel St.-Denis, who saw this "optimistic" revision in 1940, remarked:

It was a production of a very high standard, but it was Chekhov simplified both in style and meaning. The simplification of the out-of-door set for the last act was welcome but lacked unity. The play had been speeded up in tempo. . . . The poetic values had been damaged in favour of a more optimistic, more clearly constructive meaning. Nostalgic melancholy, even despair, had given way to positive declarations.[22]

Despite this attempt to bring Chekhov in line with Soviet positivism, he underwent another eclipse in the USSR during the Great Patriotic War. The next important innovations arrived with two productions of *The Seagull* in 1944. Aleksandr Tairov, director of the Kamernyi Theatre, who had come under increasing attack for his "formalism" and "aestheticism," tried an optimistic outlook that attested to man's capability to overcome all obstacles through belief in his own potential. This was an admirably sound Marxist line to take, and Nina, played by Alisa Koonen, was consequently set up on a pedestal. If the production followed Danchenko ideologically, formally it was like a concert reading. Sets, costumes, and make-up were eliminated to reveal "Chekhov the poet, akin to Pushkin and Shakespeare."²³ There were only a few armchairs, a garden bench, and a white piano on which the stuffed seagull stood.

Iurii Zavadskii took a different tack. He emphasized the claustrophobia and penury of the environment (only Dorn was elegantly dressed) and focused on Arkadina and Trigorin as the sole characters who believed in themselves. M. Astangov presented the most fiery Treplev so far seen in Russia, a clumsy overgrown lout, continually out of step with life. Zavadskii later staged the first production of *The Wood Demon* (Mossovet Theatre, 1960) in an attempt to explore the background of Chekhov's *oeuvre*. The title character (Nikolai Mordvinov) was meant to be heroic, but his distance from the others, who ate continuously throughout the play, rendered him ludicrous.²⁴

The first major breakthrough in staging Chekhov in Russia came with Georgii Tovstonogov's *Three Sisters* (Bolshoi Dramatic Theatre, Leningrad, 1965). He found a way to bring out the play's contemporaneity, without discarding the MAT traditions, by locating the sisters within an enormous stage setting full of open spaces. (Actually, the first attempt to do away with the traditional box-set in a Chekhov production had come five years earlier, when Joseph Svoboda used projected, impressionistic images for Otmar Krejča's *Seagull* at the Prague Narodni Divadlo.) His designer, S. Iunovich, kept to a black-grey-white palette and provided stage islands that jutted out into the audience to create a theatrical equivalent of the "close-up" for a public raised on movies. The tone of the production was epic, emphasizing the wind of history blowing through the characters' lives. As act followed act, it became harder to breathe, hopes were shattered by the passage of time. Only Natasha was aided by time, which opened up perspectives to her: children, love affairs, new rooms.²⁵

Anatolii Efros, something of an adult *terrible*, caused considerable controversy with his *Seagull* (Lenin-Komsomol Theatre, Moscow, 1966) and *Three Sisters* (Malaia Bronnaia Theatre, Moscow, 1967). Noted for their sharpness, wit, and stridency, they were deemed brilliant by some, crude and vulgar by others. *The Seagull* presented two characteristically Efrosian themes: uncompromised youth having to come to terms with grown-up life (a popular topic in the postwar plays of Viktor Rozov and Eduard Radzinskii), and the incompatibility of talent with fakery. Treplev, made the nexus of the play, was active, restless, and childlike in V. Smirnitskii's rendition; his Act One milieu was not a forest, but simple, clean, unpainted planks from which his stage was constructed. The other characters, having lost the meaning of their existence, were hostile to one another in a nasty, unambiguous way. Nina (O. Iakovleva) was seen as a direct antithesis to Treplev: pragmatic, single-mindedly ambitious, and aggressive.

Efros's *Three Sisters* was the play as it might be viewed by Treplev, performed stormily without half-tones or shading: every petty grievance exploded into a loud quarrel or scandal. Motivation was in terms of sex: Natasha had sexual needs which frigid Andrei could not meet, so she was justified in taking a lover; Irina was a capricious *demi-vierge*, Masha a coarse predator, and Olga repressed and repressive. Within an art nouveau frame, the play moved from ironic farce to lachrymose drama, but, since the characters did not change from act to act, the hysterics of the finale seemed oddly unmotivated.

Boris Livanov experimented with the Hamlet elements in *The Seagull* at the MAT in 1969, using an *art nouveau* setting by Enar Stenberg and dressing Treplev in a white blouse and black cloak, reminiscent of the melancholy Dane. O. Srizhenov played the youth as a tragic hero, constantly declaiming his monologues; his Symbolist play was taken seriously. Arkadina was costumed as gorgeously as the Queen of Denmark, and Nina and Masha were transmuted into emblems of heavenly love and earthly love, respectively. Useful as this may have been in analyzing Treplev, it left the rest of the play nowhere.

Oleg Efremov's *Seagull* at the Sovremennik in 1970 was meant as a counterblast to Livanov, by putting the emphasis on everyday life and by inserting variants from Chekhov's drafts to show the characters living or wishing to live by art alone. In place of Chekhov's "several tons of love," no one loved anyone, except for Polina who carried her hopeless torch for Dorn. Art was the crux: this confused motivations in several cases. The most sensational piece of business came during Trigorin's exposition of his literary life to Nina: the two of them spent it digging up the flowerbed for worms to use as bait.

The irrepressible Efros returned to Chekhov with an iconoclastic *Cherry Orchard* in 1975, when he was guest director at the Taganka, Moscow. The set by Valerii Levental suggested a graveyard, hemmed in by billowing window-curtains and family portraits. The play began and ended with a framing device in which the characters sang a gay song mournfully: this single-mindedly bleak approach must have had appeal, for Galina Volchek imitated it when she staged the same play at the Sovremennik the following year. Efros saw both Lopakhin and Trofimov as suitors for Ranevskaia sharing similar aims. Vladimir Vysotskii, the popular *chansonnier*, with his shoulder-length hair and proneness to hysterics, made a deviant Lopakhin; Alla Demidova was more in the mainstream, her Ranevskaia a neurotic lady of fashion.[26]

These experiments took on meaning in the light of the MAT tradition. Critics and spectators could savor the divagations from standard interpretations. Outside of Russia after the war, Chekhov productions either doggedly trudged in the footsteps of Stanislavskii or experimented in ways that were wildly eccentric. One of these was Orazio Costa Giovangigli's *The*

Cherry Orchard (Teatro Quirino, Rome, 1946), which acknowledged Stanislavskii while trying to bring out the play's universality through the décor. The settings by the director's brother Tullio were reminiscent of the surrealistic canvasses of Giorgio de Chirico and Salvador Dali—ghostly, poignant, and packed with symbols. Costa speculated that in future he would dispense with realism altogether, to bring the play closer to electronic music.[27] But Italy settled down to more staid versions, like the sensitive and pastel *Cherry Orchard* of the Brechtian Giorgio Strehler (Piccolo Teatro de Milano, 1955), and Luchino Visconti's MAT clones, *Three Sisters* (1953) and *The Seagull* (1955, both Teatro Eliseo, Rome).

Aside from such fugitive productions as St.-Denis's *Seagull* at the Theatre Hebértot in 1954, Paris neglected Chekhov until the important staging of *The Cherry Orchard* by the Compagnie Barrault-Renaud, also in 1954. Jean-Louis Barrault realized that the brisk French actor, accustomed to playing his text, had to slow down if he was to realize the action between the lines. "Therefore, *The Cherry Orchard, in French*, unfolds *for Frenchmen*, with a French slowness and not with a Russian slowness that would be meaningful only for Russians." Barrault held the play to be a parable, infused with lyric realism, and went more for mood than for naturalistic detail.[28]

Americans less delicately tried to naturalize Chekhov by equating his society with their own. The Provincetown Playhouse transmogrified *Platonov* into *Fireworks on the James* in 1940, and, more memorably, Joshua Logan wrote and directed *The Wisteria Trees* (Martin Beck, New York, 1950) which moved the locale of *The Cherry Orchard* to a post-bellum Southern plantation, with the servants black ex-slaves, Lopakhin an enriched sharecropper, and Ranevskaia played by Helen Hayes in her coyest, most dewy-eyed fashion.

Paradoxically, most American playwrights of the time were steeped in Chekhov and wrote what they thought to be a kind of poetic realism that matched his. He had a direct influence on Clifford Odets and Irwin Shaw before the war; during the 1950s, Robert Anderson, William Inge, Arthur Miller, Paddy Chayefsky, and others gave evidence of the power of example. Miller confessed, "I fairly worshipped Chekhov at an early time in my life . . . the depth of feeling in his work, its truthfulness and the rigor with which he hewed to the inner reality of his people are treasured qualities to me."[29] But the actors and directors who were capable of brilliantly interpreting the works of these men found their technique and training inadequate to cope with the master himself. Then too, the commercialism of the American stage with its brief rehearsal period and its short-lived acting companies militated against the density of texture that a Chekhov production requires.

The American theatre's deficiencies surfaced most obviously in the much-heralded *Three Sisters*, directed in 1963 by Lee Strasberg for the Actor's

Studio of New York, the Mecca of Method. Working on a version of the play prepared by the poet Randall Jarrell, and with a galaxy of Studio alumni such as Kim Stanley (Masha), Geraldine Page (Olga), Shirley Knight (Irina), Kevin McCarthy (Vershinin), and Luther Adler, veteran of the Group Theater (Chebutykin), Strasberg, a self-proclaimed disciple of Stanislavskii, proved to be pedestrian director who gave line-readings and relied on run-throughs. The consequent performances were uncoordinated, wanting in pace, detail, and continuity, "a formless, uninflected evening by the samovar."[30] The critics were kinder to Tyrone Guthrie's *Three Sisters* at the new Minneapolis Repertory Theatre, one of the first professional Chekhov productions to be played in the round.

By the late 1960s, the bankruptcy of traditional modes of Chekhovian staging had become evident and coincided with the anti-establishment ferment of theatrical collectives, Grotowskianism, and the drug culture. An interesting *Seagull* by André Gregory and the Manhattan Project (Publick Theatre, New York, 1974) improvised the lines in an unspecified time period, in three settings by Ming Cho Lee that forced the audience to move into new positions from act to act. The discoveries made about the text opened avenues to a fresh consideration of Chekhov, even though the acting was rather raw. Less radical than it seemed at first was the all-black *Cherry Orchard* at the Publick (1973), directed by Michael Schultz: the interpretation was respectful and dull, with a Ranevskaia who melded with the Lady of the Camellias. The only novelties were to have the landowners lighter skinned than the servants and the tramp in Act II address Firs in an African dialect, as if the lower orders shared a private *patois*.

Broadway continued to manhandle Chekhov in its inimitable fashion. The immensely popular *farceur* Neil Simon concocted a patchwork called *The Good Doctor* (1973), a farrago of sketches drawn from Chekhov's stories and plays. Intended as an homage, it (to quote the more facetious reviewers) "Simonized" the Russian and denatured both writers: Chekhov became caricatural and slapstick, Simon pallid and tentative, with sentimentality substituted for pathos. It was more Sholem Aleichem's world than Chekhov's. At the Circle in the Square that year, Mike Nichols directed a flashy *Uncle Vania*, another cluster of media personalities loosely held in colloidal suspension. George C. Scott and Nicol Williamson were mismatched as Astrov and Vania, and Julie Christie hopelessly out of her depth as Elena. The play sold out to audiences that had never heard of Chekhov but longed to see movie stars in the flesh.

Undoubtedly the most portentous and discussed Chekhov production in the United States between 1960 and 1980 was the work of a Rumanian director, Andrei Serban, who staged *The Cherry Orchard* in 1977 (Vivian Beaumont Theatre, New York). The cast combined experienced actors like Irene Worth (Ranevskaia) with vital young talent, such as Raul Julia (Lopakhin) and Meryl Streep (Duniasha). The tableaux were set against a luminous cyclorama, to create a panoramic rather than intimate effect, as of a peopled landscape. Serban filled the stage with visual metaphors: a cage-like ballroom, a plough dragged across a field by peasants; at the end, a cherry branch placed by a child in front of an enormous factory. "All this is meant to elicit emotion rather than give information," Serban explained.[31] The acting was electric but eclectic, ranging from Worth's sensitive and subtle gestures to Streep's athletic pratfalls. The visual images were irreproachable, but meaning was lost in farcical business and abrupt mood changes. It has been suggested that Serban was anxious to exorcise the demon of Stanislavskii that bedevilled his Eastern European background. His subsequent productions have seemed less impressive: *The Seagull* (1980) was a step back toward tradition, and *Three Sisters* (American Repertory Theatre, Cambridge, Massachusetts, 1983) made a concerted effort to present the characters as an obnoxious and monotonous kindergarten of spoiled brats.[32] In 1983, his *Uncle Vania* at La Mama, New York, was notable primarily for a cavernous set by Santo Loquasto, 50 feet by 20, which kept the characters continually isolated from one another. Although the cast was headed by Joseph Chaikin, the acting was motley and undistinguished, punctuated by such jarring moments as Vania sitting on the professor's lap and the professor lecherously pawing Elena. The critical consensus that Serban had a stunning visual sense but was incapable of producing a well-acted, coherent reading of Chekhov seemed confirmed.

Serban's *Vania* had begun with Sonia speaking her final "aria" to the strains of *I Puritani* emerging from the morning-glory horn of an old Victrola. A similar inversion was offered by another Rumanian, the director Lucian Pintilie, for his *Seagull* at the Guthrie Theatre, Minneapolis (1984). The play opened with the final moments from Act Four, before returning to the first act: this circular structure was enhanced by Radu Boruzescu's set of giant mylar screens that threw back reflections of the narcissistic characters. The central visual metaphor was Treplev's platform stage, always on view, its back to the audience, suggesting a motif of life as performance.

In England, productions of Chekhov well into the 1970s relied more on strong individual performances than on directorial concepts. Laurence Olivier had played Astrov in a well-liked *Uncle Vania* at the New Theatre in 1945, with Ralph Richardson in the title part; Olivier returned to the role in 1962 at the Chichester Festival, this time teamed with Michael Redgrave. The most original aspect of the production was its employment of a single set in the round for all the acts. This made sense economically and technically, but played hob with Chekhov's symbolic progress from exterior to interior.[33] Chichester was also the scene of Jonathan Miller's nosological *Seagull* of 1974; as a physician, Miller shared Chekhov's clinical acumen, which found expression in the well-observed symptoms of the characters. Treplev's Oedipal complex was anatomized to a fare-thee-well, aided by

Irene Worth's crooning a nursery song as she bandaged his head; in the last act, Sorin (George Howe) exhibited the effects of his stroke in his thickened speech. Ingenious details of behavior stripped the characters bare, and the counterbalances between their selves and their attitudes to life were exposed with measured clarity. Another Chichester production, Patrick Garland's *Cherry Orchard*, was over-weighted by the Ranevskaia of Claire Bloom, so luxuriant in emotion that the audience had spent its sympathies by the time the second act ended. As in Efros's *Orchard*, it was clear that Lopakhin (Emrys James) was wooing Varia solely because he was in love with her foster-mother.

The Cherry Orchard adapted by Trevor Griffiths, a playwright of social-ist leanings (Nottingham, 1977), invested all its positive significance in Lopakhin as it dwelt on the social inequities among the characters. Jonathan Miller returned to Chekhov with an austere and authoritarian *Three Sisters* (Cambridge Theatre, 1976) that undercut the usual romantic sympathy audiences have for the threesome. In each of these cases there was a conscious effort to work against the *idées reçus* of Chekhov and to acclimate him to our times by thwarting the popular image.

Meanwhile, *The Seagull* had been tamed by other performing arts. Thomas Pasatiri's opera, which had its premiere at the Houston Grand Opera in 1974 and was later revived at the Kennedy Center, Washington, D.C., in 1978, was acclaimed for its aspirations; however, the exigencies of the musical form reduced the play to a bald series of love triangles. The same reductive process could be observed in Mariia Plisetskaia's ballet of *The Seagull*, based on a scenario by P. Shchedrin and V. Levental, which put Nina and Treplev at the center of the action (Bolshoi Theatre, Moscow, 1980). Choreographically, Nina was so identified with the bird that roman-ticism was unavoidable. Chekhov's tons of love were increased a hundred-fold, and matters were not helped by three interludes that represented the announcement, failure, and criticism of the first production of *The Seagull* at the Alexandra, on a drop-curtain.[34]

Another endeavor to translate Chekhov's concerns into a more accessible medium was Thomas Kilroy's transference of *The Seagull* to *fin-de-siècle* Ireland (Royal Court Theatre, London, 1981). For many British playgoers, it made the social and economic context more readily comprehensible and brought the characters more clearly into focus. It also pointed up the jokes: when Anna Massey as Isobel Desmond (the Arkadina figure) responded to her son's play by exclaiming, "Good Lord, it's one of those Celtic things," it brought down the house.

Most recently, leading directors who have hitherto neglected Chekhov have been turning to him both as a control against which to test their experiments and as a classic who provides inexhaustible material for their explorations. The willfully avant-garde Taganka Theatre in Moscow was attacked more virulently than usual by establishment critics for its first

Chekhovian venture, *Three Sisters*. The director Iurii Liubimov began the drama by sliding open a wall of the theatre to reveal a military band and the Moscow street outside the building; when closed, the wall's mirrored surface reflected the audience. This opening statement more than hinted that the sisters' plight was a contemporary one with existential overtones. The characters, isolated from one another, wandered desolately about until they banged into the sheet-metal stage walls engraved with iconic figures.

Peter Brook, possibly the most prestigious director on the world scene, embarked on his first Chekhov, *The Cherry Orchard* (Bouffes du Nord, Paris, 1981) as "a theatrical movement purely played. . . . From the start I wanted to avoid sentimentality, a false Chekhovian manner that is not in the text. This is not gloomy, romantic, long and slow. It's a comic play about real life." Played in French with an international cast that included Brook's wife Natasha Parry as Ranevskaia, Niels Arestrup as Lopakhin, and Michel Piccoli as Gaev, and with the accessories stripped to a carpet, a few cushions, and some straight-backed chairs to prevent the essentials from being lost in a welter of set-pieces, *The Cherry Orchard* was wrought into a poem about "life and death and transition and change." "While playing the specifics," Brook stated, "we also try to play the myth—the secret play."[35] Many modern directors have tried to bring out the comedy; Brook was one of the few to do so without descending to farce, and one of the few to create a true ensemble.

In this survey of the past century of Chekhov on stage, a pattern of change stands out. The MAT perfected a presentation that was seamless, each moment filled to suggest life ticking by inexorably. Attempts to reproduce this effect elsewhere usually fell short because the premises and capacities of the actors were too various. Currently, the directorial strategy is to extract a given aspect and lend it inordinate attention, individual moments standing out from the whole, as in a series of variety turns. But the desiderata for a strong and lucid production still emerge from the ruck of second-rate efforts. One needs an insightful and imaginative director, aware of tradition but not cowed by it, who knows the text *à fond* but can regard it afresh; a company of sensitive actors who have worked together long enough to form a community intuitive to one another's rhythms; and an audience ready to shed its prejudices and preconceptions, and to respond with alert discrimination to every tremor of the play's pulse. It is a rare combination but not an impossible one.

NOTES

1. There is no single work on the stage history of Chekhov's plays. Copious bibliographies can be found in I. F. Masanov, *Chekhoviana, Vypusk I. Sistematicheskii ukazatel' literatury o Chekhove i ego tvorchestve* (Moscow, 1929), pp. 45-58, 93; E. A. Polotskaia, *Anton Pavlovich Chekhov. Rekomendatel'nyi ukazatel' literatury*

{Moscow, 1955); S. D. Balukhatyi and N. V. Petrov, *Dramaturgiia Chekhova: k postanovke p'esy "Vishnevyi sad" v Khar'kovskom teatre russkoi dramy* (Khar'kov, 1935); and B. I. Aleksandrov, *A. P. Chekhov Seminarii*. 2d ed. (Moscow-Leningrad, 1964), pp. 108-110, 114-116, 150-156, 169-172, 174-178, 181-183. The Chekhov jubilee volume of *Literaturnoe nasledstvo* (Moscow, 1960) contained essays surveying Chekhov's impact in France (Sophie Lafitte), Czechoslovakia (Sh. Sh. Bogatyrev), the United States (Thomas G. Winner), and England (M. A. Shereshevskaia). See also the first part of *Chekhovskie chteniia v Ialte: Chekhov i teatr* (Moscow, 1976).

2. M. P. Chekhov, *Vokrug Chekhova: Vstrechi i vpechatleniia* (Moscow, 1980), pp. 186-187.

3. Letter of N. A. Leikin to Chekhov, February 23, 1889, in A. P. Chekhov, *Polnoe sobranie sochinenii i pisem v 30-ti tomakh. Sochineniia* (Moscow, 1978), XII, 343.

4. Eugene Bristow, "Let's Hear It for the Losers; or Chekhov, Komissar-zhevskaya, and *The Sea Gull* at Petersburg in 1896," *Theatre History Studies* 2 (1982): 1-14; and Clara Hollois, "Chekhov's Reaction to Two Interpretations of Nina," *Theatre Survey* 24 (May/November 1983): 117-126.

5. The literature on the Moscow Art Theatre is voluminous. In addition to its founders' memoirs—K. S. Stanislavskii, *My Life in Art*, trans. J. J. Robbins (New York: Little, Brown, 1924) and Vl. I. Nemirovich-Danchenko, *My Life in the Russian Theatre*, trans. J. Cournos (London: Geoffrey Bles, 1937)—the reader is referred to Marianna Stroeva, *Chekhov i Khudozhestvennyi teatr* (Moscow, 1955); Marianna Stroeva, *Rezhisserskie iskaniia Stanislavskogo 1898-1917* (Moscow, 1973); N. Efros, *Moskovskii Khudozhestvennyi teatr 1898-1923* (Moscow-St. Petersburg, 1924); Michael Heim, "Chekhov and the Moscow Art Theatre," in *Chekhov's Great Plays*, ed. J.-P. Barricelli (New York: New York University Press, 1981): pp. 133-143; and S. D. Balukhaty, *The Seagull Produced by Stanislavsky*, trans. D. Magarshack (London: Dennis Dobson, 1952).

6. M. N. Stroyeva, "*The Three Sisters* at the MAT," *Tulane Drama Review* 9, 1 (Fall 1964): 42-56.

7. Ruben Simonov, *S Vakhtangovym* (Moscow, 1959), pp. 5-64; Boris Zakhava, *Sovremenniki* (Moscow, 1969), pp. 269-273.

8. K. Rudnitskii, *Rezhisser Meierkhol'd* (Moscow, 1969), pp. 474-481 (available in a bad translation as *Meyerhold the Director* [Ann Arbor, Mich.: Ardis, 1982]); Edward Braun, *The Theatre of Meyerhold: Revolution on the Modern Stage* (London: Eyre Methuen, 1979), pp. 259-261. A fascinating account of the rehearsals is given by Norris Houghton, *Moscow Rehearsals* (New York: Harcourt, Brace, 1936), pp. 99-101, 108-117.

9. Clement Borgal, *Metteurs en scène* (Paris: Fernore, 1963), p. 176. See also L. I. Gitelman, *Russkaia Klassika Na frantsuzkoi stsene* (Leningrad, 1978), pp. 95-133.

10. Borgal, p. 189. A description of its effect on susceptible spectators is given by Jean Nepveu, "Message de Tchekhov," *Cahiers de la Compagnie Jean-Louis Barrault-Madeleine Renaud* (Paris: Julliard, 1954): VI, 74-77.

11. Jean-Richard Bloch, quoted in Borgal, *Mettreurs en scène*, p. 196.

12. George Calderon, "The Russian Stage," *Quarterly Review* (July 1912): 28.

13. "Ibsenite symbolism," *Glasgow University Magazine* (November 10, 1909);

"odd and elusive," "The impression of overwhelming humanity . . . ," *Glasgow Herald* (November 3, 1909), quoted in Jan McDonald, "Production of Chekhov's Plays in Britain before 1914," *Theatre Notebook* 34, 1 (1980); 25-36. Excerpts from the reviews of major productions of Chekhov in England and the United States can be found in *Chekhov: The Critical Heritage*, ed. Victor Emeljanow (London: Routledge and Kegan Paul, 1981), which includes the cast lists in an appendix. Two dissertations have been devoted to the subject: Robert E. Tracy, "The Flight of the Seagull: Chekhov on the English Stage" (Harvard University, 1959), and Zev Raviv, "The Productions of Chekhov's Plays on the American Professional Stage" (Yale University, 1964).

14. John Gielgud, *Stage Directions* (New York: Capricorn Books, 1966), p. 87. See also Victor Emeljanow, "Komisarjevsky Directs Chekhov in London,"*Theatre Notebook* 37, 2 (1983): 66-76.

15. Gielgud, p. 95.

16. St.-Denis later did a *Cherry Orchard* at the Aldwych in 1961 with Gielgud as Gaev, Peggy Ashcroft as Ranevskaia, and Dorothy Tutin as Varia. See the interviews in *Great Acting*, ed. Hal Burton (New York: Hill and Wang, 1967), pp. 93, 107-109, 141-142.

17. *Observer* (November 17, 1935): 17.

18. *New English Weekly* (June 18, 1936): 194-195.

19. *New Republic* (December 28, 1942): 858.

20. Letter to S. L. Bertonson, February 6, 1933, in K. Arenskii, *Pis'ma v Khollivud. Po materialam arkhiva S. L. Bertonsona* (Monterey, Calif.: K. Arensburger, 1968), pp. 189-90.

21. *Vl. I. Nemirovich-Danchenko vedet repetitsiiu "Tri Sestry" A. P. Chekhova v postanovke MKhAT 1940 goda* (Moscow, 1965), pp. 149, 159, 189. Excerpts in English appear in "Danchenko Directs: Notes on *Three Sisters*," *Theatre Arts Monthly* (October 1943).

22. Michel St.-Denis, *Theatre, the Rediscovery of Style* (New York: Theatre Arts Books, 1960), p. 53.

23. A. Ia. Tairov, *O teatre* (Moscow, 1970), pp. 394-399.

24. See Babochkin's comment in *World Theatre* 9, 2 (Summer 1960): 115-161. The best survey of post-revolutionary Chekhov productions in the Soviet Union is K. Rudnitskii, *Spectakli raznykh let* (Moscow, 1974), pp. 67-185.

25. Georgii Tovstonogov, "Chekhov's *Three Sisters*," *The Drama Review* 13, 2 (Winter 1968): 146-155. A detailed analysis of Otmar Krejča's *Three Sisters* and *Seagull* can be found in *Voies de la création théâtrale IX* (Paris: Eds. du centre national de la recherche scientifique, 1982).

26. Spencer Golub and Maria Szewcow, "The Theatre of Anatolij Efros," *Theatre Quarterly* 7, 26 (Summer 1977): 18-47.

27. *World Theatre* 9, 2 (Summer 1960): 124-125.

28. J. L. Barrault, "Pourquoi *La Cerisaie?*", *Cahiers de la Compagnie Madeleine Renaud-Jean-Louis Barrault* VI (Paris: Julliard, 1954): 87-97.

29. Private letter to the author, May 6, 1981.

30. Gordon Rogoff, "Fire and Ice: Lee Strasberg," *Tulane Drama Review* (Winter 1964): 152-153.

31. "Serban Defends His 'Cherry Orchard,' " *New York Times* (March 13, 1977).

32. A fuller and more favorable description of the production is given by Jerrold A.

Phillips, "Serban's *Three Sisters*," in *Newsnotes on Soviet and East European Drama and Theatre* 3, 2 (June 1983): 10-13. See also Laurence Shyer, "Andrei Serban Directs Chekhov: *The Seagull* in New York and Japan," *Theater* (New Haven) (Fall/Winter 1981): 56-65.

33. The problem raised by this production is discussed in Michel St.-Denis, "Chekhov and the Modern Stage," *Drama Survey* 3 (Spring-Summer 1963): 77-83. A useful survey of Chekhov in London between 1945 and 1956 can be found in Andrey Williamson, *Theatre of Two Decades* (New York: Macmillan, 1951), pp. 204-207, and *Contemporary Theatre 1953-1956* (New York: Macmillan, 1956), pp. 147-149.

34. S. Davlekamova, "Ozhidanie," *Teatr* 4 (April 1981): 21-30.

35. Mel Gussow, "Peter Brooks Returns to Chekhov's Vision," *New York Times* (August 19, 1981).

NOTEWORTHY STAGE PRODUCTIONS

Chaika (The Seagull) Alexandra Theatre, St. Petersburg, October 17, 1896
Director: E. P. Karpov
With: A. M. Diuzhikova (Arkadina), R. B. Apollonskii (Treplev), V. N. Davydov (Sorin), V. F. Kommissarzhevskaia (Nina), K. A. Varlamov (Shamraev), A. I. Abarinova (Polina), M. M. Chitau (Masha), N. F. Sazonov (Trigorin), M. I. Pisarev (Dorn).

Chaika (The Seagull) Moscow Art Theatre, December 17, 1898 (in rep. until 1905)
Directors: K. S. Stanislavskii, V. I. Nemirovich-Danchenko
Designer: V. A. Simov
With: O. L. Knipper (Arkadina), K. S. Stanislavskii (Trigorin), V. V. Luzhskii (Sorin), V. E. Meierkhold (Treplev), M. L. Roksanova (Nina), M. G. Savitskaia (Masha), E. M. Raevskaia (Polina), A. L. Vishnevskii (Dorn), I. A. Tikhomirov (Medvedenko), A. R. Artem (Shamraev).

Diadia Vania (Uncle Vania) Moscow Art Theatre, October 26, 1899 (in rep. until 1928)
Directors: K. S. Stanislavskii, V. I. Nemirovich-Danchenko
Designer: V. A. Simov
With: K. S. Stanislavskii (Astrov), A. L. Vishnevskii (Vania), O. L. Knipper (Elena), M. P. Lilina (Sonia), V. V. Luzhskii (Serebriakov), A. R. Artem (Telegin).

Tri Sestry (Three Sisters) Moscow Art Theatre, January 31, 1901 (rep. until 1923)
Directors: K. S. Stanislavskii, V. I. Nemirovich-Danchenko, V. V. Luzhskii
Designer: V. A. Simov
With: O. L. Knipper (Masha), M. P. Lilina (Natasha), N. N. Litovskaia (Irina), M. G. Savitskaia (Olga), K. S. Stanislavskii (Vershinin), V. I. Kachalov (Tuzenbakh), A. R. Artem (Chebutykin), A. L. Vishnevskii (Kulygin), L. M. Leonidov (Solenyi), A. N. Lavrentev (Fedotik), I. M. Moskvin (Rode), M. A. Samarova (Anfisa), V. V. Luzhskii (Andrei).

Vishnevyi sad (The Cherry Orchard) Moscow Art Theatre, January 17, 1904 (in rep. until 1950)

Directors: K. S. Stanislavskii, V. I. Nemirovich-Danchenko
Designer: V. A. Simov
With: O. L. Knipper (Ranevskaia), K. S. Stanislavskii (Gaev), M. P. Lilina (Ania),
V. I. Kachalov (Trofimov), L. M. Leonidov (Lopakhin), I. M. Moskvin
(Epikhodov), A. R. Artem (Firs), M. G. Savitskaia (Varia), E. P. Muratova
(Charlotta), N. G. Aleksandrov (Iasha), S. V. Khaliutina (Duniasha), V. F.
Gribunin (Simeonov-Pishchik).

Ivanov Moscow Art Theatre, October 19, 1904 (in rep. until 1924)
Director: V. I. Nemirovich-Danchenko
Designer: V. A. Simov
With: V. I. Kachalov (Ivanov), O. L. Knipper (Anna), K. S. Stanislavskii (Shabel-
skii), V. V. Luzhskii (Lebedev), L. M. Leonidov (Borkin), I. M. Moskvin
(Lvov), O. V. Baklanova (Sasha).

The Seagull Royalty Theatre, Glasgow, November 2, 1909
Director: George Calderon
With: Mary Jerrold (Arkadina), Campbell Gullan (Trigorin), Irene Clark (Nina),
Milton Rosmer (Treplev), Lola Duncan (Masha), Laurence Hanray (Sorin),
M. R. Morand (Dorn).

Chekhovskii vecher (*Chekhov Evening; The Wedding: The Anniversary; Thieves*)
Third Studio of the Moscow Art Theatre, November 15, 1921
Director: Evgenii Vakhtangov
Designer: I. Rabinovich
With: B. V. Shchukin (Zhigalov in *The Wedding*, Merik in *Thieves*); T. M.
Shchukina-Shukhmina (Bride's mother); I. M. Kudriavtsev (Aplombov);
I. M. Tolchanov (Niunin in *the Wedding*, Kalashnikov in *Thieves*), E.
Liaudanskaia (Zmeiukina), N. I. Gorchakov (Best Man), I. Lobashkov (Iat),
B. Zakhava (Mozgovoi), O. Basov (Revunov-Karaulov), R. Simonov (Dymba),
B. M. Korolev (Shipuchin), M. F. Nekrasova (Merchutkina), E. G. Alekseeva
and N. P. Risunova (Liubka), V. V. Balikhin (Army Doctor).

The Seagull Little Theatre, London, October 19, 1925
Director and Designer: Theodore Komisarjevsky
With: Miriam Lewes (Arkadina), Randolph McLeod (Trigorin), Valerie Taylor
(Nina), John Gielgud (Treplev), Margaret Swallow (Masha), Alexander
Sarner (Dorn), Hubert Harben (Sorin), James Whale (Medvedenko), Ine
Cameron (Polina).

Three Sisters 14th Street Theatre, New York, October 26, 1926
Director: Eva Le Gallienne
Designer: G. E. Calthrop
With: Beatrice Terrie (Olga), Eva Le Gallienne (Masha), Rose Hobart (Irina), Alan
Birmingham (Andrei), Beatrice de Neergaard (Natasha), Ego Brecher
(Vershinin), Sayre Crawley (Chebutykin), Paul Leyssac (Kulygin), Harold
Mouton (Tuzenbakh), Sidney Machet (Solenyi).

The Cherry Orchard 14th Street Theatre, New York, October 14, 1928
Director: Eva Le Gallienne

230   A Chekhov Companion

Designer: Aline Bernstein
With: Alla Nazimova (Ranevskaia), Donald Cameron (Lopakhin), Eva Le Gallienne
(Varia), Paul Leyssac (Gaev), Beatrice de Neergaard (Duniasha), John
Eldridge (Epikhodov), Josephine Hutchinson (Ania), Sayre Crawley (Firs),
Leona Roberts (Charlotta), Walter Beck (Simeonov-Pishchik), Harold Moul-
ton (Trofimov).

Les Trois soeurs (*Three Sisters*) Theatre des Arts, Paris, February 3, 1929
Director and Designer: Georges Pitoëff
With: Liudmila Pitoëff (Irina), Mariia Germanova (Olga), Marie Calph (Masha),
Georges Pitoëff (Tuzenbakh), Paulette Pax (Natasha).

Uncle Vania Cort Theatre, New York, April 15, 1930
Director: Jed Harris
Designer: Jo Mielziner
With: Walter Connolly (Vania), Joanna Roos (Sonia), Osgood Perkins (Astrov),
Eugene Powers (Serebriakov), Lillian Gish (Elena), Eduardo Cianelli
(Telegin), Kate Mayhew (Marina).

The Cherry Orchard Old Vic, London, October 9, 1933
Director: Tyrone Guthrie
Designers: Frederick Crooke and Sophia Harris
With: Athene Seyler (Ranevskaia), Charles Laughton (Lopakhin), Flora Robson
(Varia), Leon Quartermaine (Gaev), Barbara Wilcox (Duniasha), Marius
Goring (Epikhodov), Ursula Jeans (Ania), Morland Graham (Firs), Elsa Lan-
chester (Charlotta), Roger Livesey (Simeonov-Pishchik), Dennis Arundell
(Trofimov), James Mason (Iasha).

33 Obmoroka (*33 Fainting Fits: The Proposal, The Bear, The Anniversary*) Meierkhold
Theatre, Moscow, January 25, 1935
Director: V. E. Meierkhold
Designer: V. Shestakov
With: V. Gromov (Chubukov), I. Ilinskii (Lomov), E. Loginova (Natalia), Z. Raikh
(Popova), N. Bogoliubov (Smirnov), N. Serebrianikova (Merchutkina),
M. Chikul (Shipuchin), A. Kelberer (Khirin).

The Seagull New Theatre, London, May 20, 1936
Director and Designer: Theodore Komisarjevsky
With: Edith Evans (Arkadina), John Gielgud (Trigorin), Peggy Ashcroft (Nina),
Stephen Haggard (Treplev), Martita Hunt (Masha), Leon Quartermaine
(Dorn), Frederick Lloyd (Sorin), Ivor Bernard (Medvedenko), Clare Harris
(Polina).

Three Sisters Queen's Theatre, London, January 28, 1938
Director: Michel St.-Denis
Designer: Motley
With: Peggy Ashcroft (Irina), Gwen Ffrangcon-Davies (Olga), Carol Goodner
(Masha), Angela Baddeley (Natasha), George Devine (Andrei), John Gielgud
(Vershinin), Frederick Lloyd (Chebutykin), Leon Quartermaine (Kulygin),
Michael Redgrave (Tuzenbakh), Glen Byam Shaw (Solenyi), Alec Guinness
(Fedotik).

The Seagull Shubert Theatre, New York, March 28, 1938
Director: Robert Milton
Designer: Robert Edmond Jones
With: Lynn Fontanne (Arkadina), Alfred Lunt (Trigorin), Uta Hagen (Nina),
Richard Whorf (Treplev), Margaret Webster (Masha), John Barclay (Dorn),
Sydney Greenstreet (Sorin), O. Z. Whitehead (Medvedenko), Edith King
(Polina).

La Mouette (*The Seagull*) Theatre des Mathurins, Paris, January 17, 1939
Director and Designer: Georges Pitoëff
With: Liudmilla Pitoëff (Nina), Georges Pitoëff (Trigorin), Mariia Germanova
(Arkadina).

Tri Sestry (*Three Sisters*) Moscow Art Theatre, April 24, 1940
Directors: V. I. Nemirovich-Danchenko, N. N. Litovtseva, I. M. Raevskii
Designer: V. V. Dmitriev
With: A. O. Stepanova (Irina), K. N. Elanskaia (Olga), A. K. Tarasova (Masha),
N. K. Svobodin (Tuzenbakh), A. N. Gribov (Chebutykin), A. Georgievskaia
(Natasha), M. P. Bolduman (Vershinin), B. N. Livanov (Solenyi), N. I.
Dorokhin (Fedotik), V. A. Orlov (Kulygin).

The Three Sisters Barrymore Theatre, New York, December 21, 1942
Director: Guthrie McClintic
Designer: Motley
With: Judith Anderson (Olga), Katherine Cornell (Masha), Gertrude Musgrove
(Irina), Eric Dressler (Andrei), Ruth Gordon (Natasha), Dennis King
(Vershinin), Edmund Gwenn (Chebutykin), Tom Powers (Kulygin), Alex-
ander Knox (Tuzenbakh), McKay Morris (Solenyi), Kirk Douglas (Orderly).

Uncle Vania New Theatre, London (Old Vic Company), January 16, 1945
Director: John Burrell
Designer: Tanya Moiseiwitsch
With: Ralph Richardson (Vania), Joyce Redman (Sonia), Laurence Olivier (Astrov),
Harcourt Williams (Serebriakov), Margaret Leighton (Elena), George Relph
(Telegin), Sybil Thorndike (Marina).

La Cerisaie (*The Cherry Orchard*) Théâtre de Marigny, Paris, Oct. 7, 1954
Director: Jean-Louis Barrault
Designer: Wakhevitch
With: Madeleine Renaud (Ranevskaia), Pierre Bertin (Gaev), Jean Dessailly
(Lopakhin), Simone Valère (Varia), Jean-Louis Barrault (Trofimov), Marie-
Hélène Daste (Charlotta), André Brunot (Firs), Jean Servier (Simeonov-
Pishchik), Jean Gillard (Epikhodov), Natalie Nerval (Duniasha), Jean-Pierre
Granval (Iasha), F. Goléa (Ania).

Uncle Vania Chichester Festival Theatre, July 1962
Director: Laurence Olivier
Designers: Sean Kenny and Beatrice Dawson
With: Sybil Thorndike (Marina), Laurence Olivier (Astrov), Michael Redgrave
(Vania), Max Adrian (Serebriakov), Lewis Casson (Telegin), Joan Plowright

(Sonia), Rosemary Harris (Elena), Fay Compton (Mariia Vasilevna), Robert Lang (Efim).

Tri Sestry (*Three Sisters*) Gorkii Theatre, Leningrad, January 1965
Director: G. Tovstonogov
Designer: S. Iunovich
With: I. Kopelian (Vershinin), Z. Sharko (Olga), E. Popova (Irina), T. Doronina (Masha), S. Iurskii (Tuzenbakh), K. Lavrov (Solenyi), N. Trofimov (Chebutykin), L. Makarova (Natasha), O. Basilashvili (Andrei).

Ivanov Phoenix Theatre, London, September 30, 1965
Director: John Gielgud
Designer: Rouben Ter-Arutunian
With: John Gielgud (Ivanov), Yvonne Mitchell (Anna), Edward Atienza (Shabel-skii), Roland Culver (Lebedev), Angela Baddeley (Ziuziushka), Claire Bloom (Sasha), Richard Pasco (Lvov), Helen Christie (Babakina), Ronald Radd (Borkin).

Chaika (*The Seagull*) Lenin Komsomol Theatre, Moscow, 1966
Director: Anatolii Efros
Designers: V. Lalevich and N. Sosunov
With: A. Dmitrieva (Masha), L. Durov (Medvedenko), A. Pelevina (Dorn), V. Solovev (Shamraev), V. Smirnitskii (Treplev), E. Fadeeva (Arkadina), O. Iakovleva (Nina), A. Shirvindt (Trigorin).

Vishnevyi Sad (*The Cherry Orchard*) Taganka Theatre, Moscow, 1975
Director: Anatolii Efros
Designer: Valerii Levental
With: A. Demidova (Ranevskaia), V. Sternberg (Gaev), V. Vysotskii (Lopakhin), V. Zolotukhin (Trofimov), N. Tsub (Ania), T. Zukova (Varia), F. Antipov (Simeonov-Pishchik), M. Politsemaiko (Charlotta), R. Dzabrailov (Epikhodov), T. Sidorenko (Duniasha), G. Roninson (Firs), V. Suliakovskii (Iasha), V. Korolev (Passer-by).

The Cherry Orchard Vivian Beaumont Theatre, New York, February 17, 1977
Director: Andrei Serban
Designer: Santo Loquasto
With: Raul Julia (Lopakhin), Meryl Streep (Duniasha), Max Wright (Epikhodov), Marybeth Hurt (Ania), Irene Worth (Ranevskaia), Priscilla Smith (Varia), George Voskovec (Gaev), Elizabeth Franz (Charlotta), C. K. Alexander (Simeonov-Pishchik), Ben Masters (Iasha), Dwight Marfield (Firs), Michael Cristofer (Trofimov).

La Cerisaie (*The Cherry Orchard*) Les Bouffes du Nord, Paris, May 1981
Director: Peter Brook
Designer: Chloe Obolenskii
With: Natasha Parry (Ranevskaia), Niels Arestrup (Lopakhin), Michel Piccoli (Gav), Robert Murzeau (Firs), Maurice Benichou (Trofimov), Irina Brook (Ania).

14

H. Peter Stowell

CHEKHOV INTO FILM

Chekhov has fared extremely well on the silver screen. A surprising number of films have been based on his prose and plays. According to Jay Leyda's partial filmography, at least five silent and seven sound films were produced in Russia and the Soviet Union between 1911 and 1971.[1] And there have been more recent productions, as well as those films made in the United States, England, and France.[2] It is not difficult to see why Chekhov has been so popular among filmmakers. On the most obvious level, short stories and plays approximate the running times of both feature length and short films. It is almost an adage among filmmakers that short stories are the best source for films because they provide a manageable narrative framework and characters who are not too fully developed. The incident of the short story becomes the springboard out of which filmmakers can create their own work without being obligated to render the overabundance of detail that characterizes the novel. Chekhov is even more helpful, for his modernist style is short on description and metaphor and long on rendition and metonymy. This means that most occurrences in his prose can be translated almost wholesale because they are not based solely on linguistic tropes. Chekhov's realism dovetails with what Siegfried Kracauer considers the essence of film, its gravitation toward the recording and revealing of physical reality.[3] Chekhov's stress on mood, atmosphere, and setting is what plays to the strengths of cinema. His method of characterization suggests psychological interiorization through action and dialogue rather than psychological description, and this too is easily transposed onto film. Finally, Chekhov's approach to point of view which usually floats between first and third person seems compatible with a mechanically recording camera that can by its placement swing between subjectivity and objectivity. It may be an overstatement to say that Chekhov's stories were written to be filmed, but it is not stretching the point to say that Chekhov's stories are wonderfully filmable.

Short films adapted from Chekhov stories constitute a subgenre that can be divided into Chekhov's early anecdotal stories and one-act farces and those stories of his middle and more mature period. Short films have suffered the same fate as short stories and one-act plays; rarely are they taken as seriously as longer works. Yet there are some short films that quite accurately capture the flavor and essence of Chekhov's art. In the 1940s and 1950s a number of young Soviet filmmakers used Chekhov's short works as springboards into careers as feature film directors.[4] Without having to deal with the logistics of a full-length narrative they could demonstrate control over technique, nuance, and tone. They could try their hand at comedy that was both broad enough not to require great maturity, yet delicate enough to show their intelligence.

The history of the short film is strewn with the kind of shaggy dog stories that are the essential ingredients of "The Wallet," "The Boarding House," "Revenge," and "A Work of Art." Since the basis of these tales is narrative rather than linguistic, they translate onto the screen quite easily. Of these four stories, "The Boarding House" is the most shaggy doggedly humorous and is filmed with a light, breezy touch. But it is the least Chekhovian of the early stories. It does not have the endless steppe imagery of "The Wallet," the zero ending and dissipated denouement of "Revenge,"[5] or the comic parodying of artistic taste in "A Work of Art." In these stories Chekhov had not reached literary maturity, so the filmed adaptations tend to fare extremely well by comparison. The essence of Chekhov's early work was narrative rather than linguistic.

Three short stories form a neat children's trilogy: "The Fugitive," "Sleepy," and "Volodia." They constitute a chronological progression from childhood through adolescence. Each film develops a different technique for presenting point of view. Chekhov himself used his "children's stories" as experiments in perceptual point of view, whereby the confusing swirl of the outside world could be rendered realistically.

"The Fugitive" is an episodic tale of a seven-year-old boy who must stay overnight at a hospital for treatment of his infected arm. One would have expected this story to be filmed traditionally and objectively. It is to Maurice Fasquel's credit that he saw Chekhov's real intention and filmed "The Fugitive" as an exercise in point of view. Fasquel, like the great Japanese director Yasujiro Ozu, has understood the subtle value of lowered camera placement. According to traditional cinema coding, the camera is placed at the height of a standing adult's chest. But Ozu lowered his camera to the level of a kneeling or sitting adult's chest. Since this is the usual physical position of the older generation, Ozu was able to visually establish and reinforce the cultural gap between the Easternized older people and the Westernized youth. In "The Fugitive" Fasquel has subtly brought his camera down to the chest-high perspective of his young protagonist. This shift in camera placement imperceptibly draws the viewer into identifying with the boy's physical and psychological point of view.

"Sleepy" is one of Chekhov's great stories; it transcends the mere appellation of "children's story." "Sleepy" has greater potential for filmed adaptation than any other Chekhov story. It is a highly imagistic story with a surrealistic use of spatial and temporal shifts, and its transitions between dream and reality are based on sensory associations. The one filmed version of "Sleepy" (entitled "Desire to Sleep"), again directed by Maurice Fasquel, is a short, trenchant, interesting film. Unlike the other Chekhov films, "Desire to Sleep" boldly changes a central element of the story. Instead of Varka dreaming of people trudging down the road and falling in the mud, the filmmaker has Varka dream of a beautiful couch in an empty palatial room. This dream is more explicit as a means of wish-fulfillment than Chekhov's carefully worked out infant/death image structure. The dream of falling in the mud only yields fruition in Chekhov's highly complex fugue structure because it equates sleep with death. The filmmaker has understood that fusion between sleep and death, too. For instance, in an extremely effective transitional device the filmmaker has fused in a match cut the bundle of her dead father's clothes with the bundling that wraps the baby. In Varka's fantasy her mother comes toward her (and the camera) with her father's clothes, then in a quick match cut the mistress of Varka's reality hands her the bundled-up child. The infant and death have been fused through the dream and the reality. The dream of the couch has reinforced her desperate desire for sleep more directly than the story. For the filmmaker, two desires drive Varka—sleep and release from oppression. The couch and the rich setting express those needs.

The film's changes were also made to more visually and surreally contrast the setting of the dream with that of her dark, oppressive existence in the cottage. The contrasts between the mise-en-scènes of dreams and reality are effective: bright, almost overexposed fill lighting versus dark key lighting; huge empty space versus closed, filled space; rich surroundings versus poor ones; the enormous presence of a place to sleep versus the total absence of a place to sleep.

The final film of Fasquel's "children's trilogy" is a quite faithful rendition of Chekhov's 1887 story "Volodia." The difficult tasks of this film are to render Chekhov's descriptions of Volodia's thoughts and Chekhov's clinical description of the suicide. The first problem was solved by a voice-over narrator who describes Volodia's feelings and by an actor's actions and expressions.

Chekhov's realism turns on the reader at the end of this story, which until its conclusion has seemed to be no more than a series of normal adolescent crises. Not only does Volodia surprisingly shoot himself, but Chekhov has him viewing the act with a careful, curious detachment. It is here that the film loses Chekhov's impact by refusing to show anything of the suicide itself. Instead, in a tried and true cinema technique of the time, the camera leaves Volodia handling the gun and cuts to a gentleman entering the hallway. It tracks down the corridor until it stops at the door to Volodia's room. The shot is heard. Then the narrator says, "They would find his face among the bottles and glasses." He continues narrating the last five lines of Chekhov's prose. But what the filmmaker has left out is what provides the chill in Chekhov's tale: "Volodia put the barrel in his mouth again, gripping with his teeth, then squeezed something with his finger. A shot rang out. Something struck Volodia with fearful force at the back of his head and he fell across the table." This is the kind of realistic description that made Chekhov the precursor to Hemingway, but the film fails to find a correlative for this daring look at death.

At this point we shift from the short films to the major feature films. The most well known of these are *The Grasshopper* (1955) and *The Lady with the Dog* (1960).[6] Both were international successes filmed by recognized directors. They are the best filmed representatives of Chekhov's major prose work. Rarely have films of a writer's important works been so carefully rendered as to achieve a balance between literary fidelity and filmic integrity.

Geoffrey Wagner in his critical work, *The Novel and the Cinema*, believes there are three basic modes of adaptation: transposition, commentary, and analogy.[7] By Wagner's standards, *The Grasshopper* and *The Lady with the Dog* are clearly transpositions, since both are limited to rendering the essential narrative structure, action, and characters of the original literary work. The short story offers the filmmaker a greater potential for both fidelity and freedom.

These two stories are a filmmaker's dream because Chekhov's effects are gained at the expense of descriptive language, that notoriously troublesome aspect of literary adaptation, and because they fall into a category that V. V. Golubkov calls Chekhov's lyrico-dramatic stories. There are three characteristics of this category: (1) dramatic conflicts between a person's search for happiness, freedom, and truth and society's traditional beliefs and prejudices; (2) a penetrating lyricism that colors the characters, giving the stories moods of light melancholy and a dream of what is beautiful; (3) and, finally, a complexity of structure and intonation.[8] These are qualities which when viewed more generally (that is, as dramatic conflict, creation of mood and intonation, and complexity of narrative structure) suit and even play to the strengths of cinema.

The dramatic conflict that Golubkov speaks of in Chekhov's best stories is thoroughly exploited by Samson Samsonov in *The Grasshopper*. The conflict centers on unpretentious goodness represented by Dymov versus pompous fatuousness represented by Olga and Riabovskii. Samsonov's most effective transpositional device is to surround the representatives of each side of the conflict with a metonymic mise-en-scène. To this end Samsonov radically alters Chekhov's beginning in favor of a context that expresses the values of the hero. Rather than Chekhov's wedding scene, Samsonov removes Dymov from Olga's milieu, the soirée, and shows the dedicated doctor walking home with his good friend Korostelev. In Chekhov's story Korostelev does not appear until almost the midpoint. Samsonov, on the other hand, wants to show the conflict immediately so as to heighten the initial dramatic impact.

The opening scene of the film is doubly important, for it displays the lyricism associated with Dymov. It is a soft spring evening, so blossoms are featured prominently in the foreground in the first shot. The camera follows the quiet intimacy of these two old friends. (Korostelev, by the way, is cast and costumed so as to fit into the line of filmed Anton Chekhov look-alikes, the others appearing in *The Fugitive* and *A Work of Art*. This device on the part of film directors is to give the viewer a positive response to the character, that is, Chekhov as "the good doctor.").

This opening scene stands in sharp contrast to what Dymov next encounters. At Olga's soirée there is no connection to nature—the bright lights glare, and the human relationships are shallow. Dymov is a stranger in his own home; the film makes this clear. Since Olga is at home in this environment, the conflict has been effectively dramatized and the values asserted. Furthermore, Dymov enters unnoticed and unrecognized, whereas Riabovskii enters in a grand manner. Riabovskii belongs at the soirée and Dymov does not; hence, the conflict between these two men is immediately apparent.

Golubkov believes that Chekhov's lyrico-dramatic stories have complex intonations that include dreams of a better life, dramatic intensity, humor, and satire. Has Samsonov been able to capture the complex tonalities of Chekhov's mature story? At the very heart of Chekhov's vision is the sense that some characters have a good life and don't know it or want more, that some have a materially good life but a spiritually bad one, that some deserve a good life but don't appear to achieve it, that those who don't deserve it appear to have it, and that virtually all of them seem to dream of a far distant good life that has eluded them. Chekhov never actually visualizes the good life.

It can only be imagined by the reader based on each character's sense of loss. The temptation for a filmmaker would be to actually show the dreams (as Olivier did with Irina in *Three Sisters*). Samsonov wisely follows Chekhov's method of indirection, transposing only the language Chekhov's characters use to describe their vision of the good life. By not producing the visual images of such a life, Samsonov retains the same ironic tone that infuses Chekhov's text.

Samsonov develops a more powerful dramatic intensity through individual scenes, whereas Chekhov relies on a more uniform tension. One example is the scene when Olga returns to Dymov after her Volga fling with

Riabovskii. The setting is darkened and the acting resonant. Samsonov has Olga return through the empty, dark drawing room, that setting associated with her triumphant soirées. In the lonely distance of the brightly lit dining room Dymov sits alone eating and reading. This imagery in advance of the actual encounter between them (which does not exist in the Chekhov story) is what deepens the dramatic intensity of the scene.

The Lady with the Dog is the finest film adaptation of Chekhov's prose because without sacrificing cinematic integrity it captures the essence of his bittersweet mood, complex dramatic structure, and nuances of characterization. Joseph Heifitz chose to emphasize mood over narrative in the film's opening, establishing the placid and languid mundaneness of this summer retreat. The first shot marks Heifitz as a Chekhovian kindred spirit: an unromantic view of a lazy, debris-spotted sea against an unattractive pebble beach on which goats are scavenging. This shot isn't "about" anything, so by normal standards it seems to be a pointless indulgence. But its mundane lyricism establishes that perfect Chekhovian ironic touch.

From that shot Heifitz switches to the inside of an empty café where a few bored, hot characters amble in to continue their gossiping. Then Gurov enters (though there is little to identify him as the protagonist). He sits alone reading the paper as languid, repetitive music plays over this scene. Then through the window, in the distance, the lady with the dog is sighted by the other men. Gurov does not share their avid curiosity, looking up only to catch a glimpse of her, then returning to his paper before she passes. It is a brilliant scene because it objectifies and distances Anna. It places in ironic perspective their later "passion." The Chekhovian mood has been achieved —and carefully so—in just a few shots, and all of them are the filmmaker's alone; none of this occurs in the story.

Most of the filmed versions of Chekhov's stories have remained faithful to his narratives. Chekhov painstakingly constructed them so that each element has a function in the patterns of similarity and difference, repetition and variation. The basic structures of both story and film in *The Lady with the Dog* are similar, but there are interesting differences. For instance, their segmenting follows different patterns. The story has eleven scenes while the film has fourteen, and although both are divided into four broader sections, Heifitz has redistributed them, thus altering the narrative's rhythm and progression.

As can be seen from Table 1, Chekhov has chosen to develop a short introduction and finale (I and IV) with longer middle sections, whereas the film progresses with ever-shortened sequences so that the tension increasingly tightens. Even more important is the way in which each segment of the film either repeats or varies the scenes of the first sequence (indicated in the table by capital letters in parentheses). This opening section has a clear progression of different scenes (A through F) ending with a parting. Each subsequent sequence ends with some form of parting (F). The midsection

Table 1
Narrative Structure

Story	Film
I	**I**
1. Introduction: Gurov (A)	Introduction: Gurov sees Anna (A)
2. Gurov picks up Anna (B)	Gurov picks up Anna (B)
II	
3. Consummation of affair (C)	Consummation of affair (C)
4.	Anna's guilt; Gurov's boredom (D)
5. Trip to Oreanda (D)	Trip to Oreanda (E)
6. Continuing affair; station goodbye (C-E)	Continuing affair; station goodbye (F)
III	**II**
7. Moscow; winter (A)	Moscow; winter (A)
8.	Wife's soirée; Gurov remembers Anna (G)
9.	Search for Anna after seeing dog (A-B)
10. Need to talk of empty life (A)	Need to talk of empty life (A)
11. Christmas: leaves for Anna's; searches for Anna (E)	Christmas: leaves for Anna's (F)
	III
12. At the theatre (B)	Searches for Anna; at theatre (B-C)
IV	
13. Continued affair (C)	Continued affair (D-F)
	IV
14. Finale: parting? (C-E)	Finale: parting? (D-F)

(Part II) replays some scenes from Part I (A, B, F) and develops one new scene (G). Part III begins to mix the scenic currents together so that the structure becomes more complex and tinged by paradox.

One can begin to see the cyclical nature of the work through this structural arrangement. The major motif, parting, is repeated in four scenes. Three other motifs also play a major role: "A," Gurov's empty life alone; "B," Gurov's quest for a relationship; and "D," the boredom-excitement of their continuing affair. The film ends, then, on the paradoxical fusion of parting and continuance, which is just what Chekhov intended.

While the film has basically adhered to the story's structure, Heifitz has made structure a more explicit concern in his film. This is often necessary in a medium that does not allow for reflection during the viewing experience. Heifitz has correctly compensated for the different medium while remaining faithful to the original story. One can ask no more of an adaptation.

In 1972 Abram Room, the celebrated director of the 1926 classic, *Bed and Sofa*, directed an early story of Chekhov's, "Belated Flowers." This is a curious mixture of talents and modes. At the age of seventy-eight and near the end of his life, Room was an unabashed romantic; Chekhov at twenty-two had not yet found his gentle, ironic voice. Room treats the story of Princess Marusia Priklonskii's death as a bittersweet tragedy; Chekov was too young and temperamentally unsuited to create a full-scale tragedy. Neither the story nor the film is entirely successful. Chekhov developed a tragic superstructure, but his realism, his young cynicism, his satiric portrayals, and his ultimate sense of irony do not mesh successfully. Room at least has a unified version and so sees this story as a romantic tragedy: the aristocratic flower, who is crushed by her poverty and sensitivity, finds love at the last moment of her life.

Room's signature for the film's tone is Hector Berlioz's romantic "Symphonie Fantastique," which he uses quite experimentally. The film opens showing the orchestra playing the piece, then after the narrative has begun, the orchestra will suddenly reemerge to introduce a character or set the tone. This is a rather startling technique, given Room's traditional direction throughout the narrative sequences; yet the infusion of Room's romantic spirit pervades the film, giving it an understated beauty in both visual and human terms.

The difference between Chekhov's and Room's vision of this story is conveyed in their handling of the conclusion. From the moment Princess Marusia wins the doctor's heart to the time she dies three days later in the south of France takes Chekhov exactly one page to describe. This is typical of Chekhov's understated, terse, and anticlimactic method. Room, on the other hand, lavishes time on this late-blooming romance. He has extended the train trip, complete with Marusia's recognition of her epiphany of happiness; he has invented the doctor's attempt to save her life with world-renowned specialists; and he has her die in the doctor's arms at a ball.

Most filmmakers with Room's romantic temperament would be seduced into closing the film on the high tragic note of her death. Room, however, remained faithful to Chekhov's ironic ending. The doctor returns to his greedy practice, keeping Marusia's spendthrift brother, Egorushka, around as his only reminder of her: "The doctor took him [Egorushka] into his home and dotes upon him. Egorushka's chin reminds him of Marusia's chin, and because of this he allows Egorushka to squander his five ruble notes. Egorushka is perfectly contented." These are the last lines of Chekhov's story, and they are spoken by a narrator in Room's film. Chekhov's spirit has not been completely removed from this film.

Few, however, upon seeing Emil Loteanu's lushly beautiful film, *The Shooting Party* (1977), would imagine it to be based on a Chekhov work. Much of the problem lies with Chekhov. This was his youthful attempt at a novel, and, as is generally true of his longer early works, he tries to do too much. If "Belated Flowers" is at least partially Chekhov's parody of romanticism that engendered a romantic film, then *The Shooting Party* is a parody of crime fiction (an inherently anti-realistic genre) which has again fostered a romantic film. But this time there is almost no hint of any Chekhovian mood or irony. Again this is partially Chekhov's doing, since his novel is long on parody and short on irony. And the ironies that are present are of a narrative sort, the "twists of fate" variety.

This is the only instance where the film is far superior to the Chekhov work. Chekhov's muddled, plodding, and convoluted novel has been replaced by a stylish modern film that represents the kind of work the Soviets consistently produced for export in the 1970s. These films are (1) wonderfully crafted, beautifully shot, and modernistically constructed; (2) chosen and shot so as to show off the allure of the Russian landscape and folk tradition; and (3) carefully selected to refer to a decadent, pre-revolutionary aristocratic or bourgeois setting. On the surface, then, it is easy to see why Chekhov remains so popular among Soviet filmmakers. Without any rhetoric or blatant propagandizing Chekhov provides filmmakers with situation after situation that inherently critiques pre-revolutionary society, while still keeping both feet planted firmly in the Russian soil. *The Shooting Party* is one of the best examples of this strategy.

The issues involved in adapting a play to film are often quite different from those of the literature-into-film process.[9] At first glance it might appear that the play and the film are closely allied. For instance, the concept of mise-en-scène which is so important to film signification is, of course, a theatrical term. Those elements covered by this term—setting, lighting, costuming, and actors' behavior and movement—are shared by the cinema and the theatre. Both are considered performing arts. Each renders thought into dialogue or action; neither easily absorbs descriptive language from a narrative or authorial source, and both rely on direct sound. Finally, the narrative structuring and segmenting of films have often been based on theatrical conventions—hence the term *screenplay*, or in earlier times, the *photoplay*.

Why is it, then, that films adapted from plays have fared so poorly? One clue may be that the close bonds between the two arts actually imprison and doom most filmed versions. Shackled to the play with little idea of how to break loose and become a film, these filmed plays rarely have an identity or integrity of their own. Plays and films have three basic elements in common: mise-en-scène, sound, and narrativity. Film adds to its arsenal editing and cinematographic properties (framing, camera angles and distances, lenses, film stock, and so forth). Theatre exploits the intimacy of human contact and the tension of live performances. It is not surprising, then, that the breach between these two arts is most often caused by those qualities they do not share, driving filmmakers to rely on the common denominators of mise-en-scène, sound, and narrative structure.

There is, of course, no prescriptive or programmatic formula for adaptation, and the films based on Chekhov's plays graphically make this point. For instance, the two best films, Andrei Konchalovskii's *Uncle Vania* (1972) and Laurence Olivier's 1970 version of *Three Sisters*, could not be more different. The adaptations of Chekhov's plays form a continuum that ranges from the unabashedly theatrical version of *Three Sisters* by the Actors Studio to the intensely filmic *Uncle Vania*:

Three Sisters, Paul Bogart, 1966

Three Sisters, Laurence Olivier, 1970

The Seagull, Juli Karasik, 1971

The Seagull, Sidney Lumet, 1968

Three Sisters, Samson Samsonov, 1964

Uncle Vania, Andrei Konchalovskii, 1972

Bogart's version of the *Three Sisters* was originally videotaped as no more than a record of the Actors Studio production. Bogart, who had no film directing experience at the time, chose, as most theatrical directors do, to retain virtually every line from the play. His directional style is based on the premise that establishing shots should be used during pauses and medium close-ups during dialogue.

Laurence Olivier, though a product of the theatre, had proven himelf an inventive film director before he tackled the *Three Sisters*. Unlike his *Hamlet* which is a militantly filmic production, Olivier chose to accept and confront the theatrical conventions in the *Three Sisters*. And, unlike *Hamlet*, he kept the play's text intact. Olivier saw *Hamlet* as a play of action that could suit the cinema's predilection for prowling camera movement and location shifts. *Three Sisters*, however, is a play of inaction, which Oliver exploited by playing up the theatrically stylized mise-en-scène. This also gave fuller expression to Chekhov's ensemble technique which stresses human interaction. So while the camera followed *Hamlet* closely, in *Three Sisters* it is pulled back and remains stationary. Yet, at the same time, Olivier has utilized editing and camera placement so as to take advantage of the cinema's potential without violating Chekhov's theatricality.

Although Olivier has mounted theatrical sets and placed his actors and actresses in theatrical positions, he has, almost subversively, taken the camera into account. For instance, he suggests character isolation through series of one-shots, a traditional film technique. But he accentuates their separation by placing the first character on the left-hand side of the screen and then placing the second character in the next shot on the right-hand side of the screen. In the final scene Chebutykin whispers the news of the Baron's death to Olga. They are in the foreground while Irina, to whom this is most important, is in the deep background. But suddenly Olivier cuts to a reverse angle. This immediately rivets our attention on the now fore-grounded Irina. This shot also balances the theatricality of poses against the naturalism of reverse angle perspective. Then, for the final speeches by the sisters, Olivier returns to the theatrical conventions and compositions.

Juli Karasik, in his version of *The Seagull*, chose an approach different from Olivier's. He has cut the text radically, streamlining it into a more plotted narrative by eliminating all "talky" irrelevancies. He preferred a naturalistic mise-en-scène enhanced by a wide-screen aspect ratio. At the same time, he presses close-ups, medium close-ups, and incredibly long takes on the viewer, so that his film becomes the most oppressively static of all the Chekhov adaptations.

Karasik's directorial choices, radical and irreverent as they may be, lead to a certain coherence. He has dropped any pretense of comedy, thereby unifying the tone but running counter to Chekhov's intentions. He has directed the actors and actresses to play even the most wrenching scenes in a more subdued manner, and so he avoids the trap of melodrama, too common in Chekhov productions.

Sidney Lumet chose still another approach for his version of *The Seagull*. He retained the entire text; then opened the play up to a surprising freedom of action. Much of the film is shot outdoors with great emphasis on the physical beauty of the location, while inside the camera is forever moving. Lumet is clearly trying to make a film out of a play. Yet all the interior shots are based on theatrical compositions. Lumet has opened up the play consid-erably. The first five minutes of the film are completely without dialogue as the camera follows Nina riding her horse toward Sorin's estate, then Arkadina and Trigorin getting out of bed, and finally Masha and Medve-denko strolling in the tall grass together. The effect is to give us a pastoral sense of space.

The settings of the two *Seagull* productions are very different. Lumet's version conveys the opulence and beauty of a huge estate, while Karasik's turns Lumet's estate into a rustic cramped dacha. Lumet in the beginning of Act Two turns the croquet game into a luxurious impressionistic painting of wealthy indolence while Karasik dispenses with croquet altogether in favor of a small front yard gathering with field hands working in the background. One could say that these are, in fact, consistent ideological signifiers. The

Soviet version shows the once-wealthy bourgeoisie in reduced circumstances, but still unaware that their lazy, petty life is secured by those workers shown in the background.

It is Lumet's ending, however, that truly reveals his misguided intentions. During the lotto game Masha's role as the caller of numbers has been abstracted to the point that the viewer has no sense of her function in the game. She becomes purely a symbol of absurdity and meaninglessness. Karasik, on the other hand, found the balance between functional and symbolic action. We understand Masha's purpose in the game. And Karasik has cut each of the player's lines to one staccato utterance apiece, giving the scene a ritualized quality. This has the effect of ritualizing the penultimate moment rather than the conclusion—something that Chekhov felt strongly about. Lumet, who has attempted to remain slavishly faithful to the text, destroys its integrity in the conclusion by showing Konstantin floating dead in the lake. He has forced the connection between Konstantin and the seagull, and overly dramatized the death of both. When Dorn silently and solemnly returns, the camera pans and holds on each character's face so that they can register the dramatically appropriate response. Then the camera rises above the darkened room. "The End." This is a far cry from Chekhov's intention of having Dorn return as though nothing had happened, unable to face the rest of the group. He sings a bit, mentions an article he has read, then, taking the unlikely Trigorin aside, says, "The fact is, Konstantin Gavrilovich has shot himself."

Samson Samsonov's *Three Sisters* has a more theatrical mise-en-scène than Lumet's *Seagull*, but compensates with a more freely moving camera.[10] Samsonov, too, opens up the beginning and ending of the play (the traditional trick of filmmakers) by having the camera glide through the birch grove, track rapidly along the fence that separates them from the town but is also visible to them, and moves up and down the pathway that seems to signify escape. He opens the film on a flashforward of the tragic sisters all dressed in black. Then with the sound of the military band and a long dissolve, Samsonov follows the vital, youthful Irina, dressed now in white, as she anticipates the coming of the adored officers. Beyond these militantly cinematic devices, this film suffers from overacting and statically composed shots. Samsonov is the only director who was willing to edit the text of the *Three Sisters*. The film is an odd mélange of contradictory approaches.

Only Konchalovskii's *Uncle Vania* is truly a film. Like Olivier, and unlike any of the other directors, Konchalovskii clearly thought out the relationship of form to content and made a firm commitment to a style. Far too often film directors make the arbitrary decision that the essence of film is (1) the moving camera, (2) the naturalistic use of outdoor locations, the so-called opening-up of a filmed play, and (3) the excising of "irrelevant" and "talky" dialogue. All the camera movement in the world will not in itself make a play look and feel like a film. Konchalovskii realized that editing, framing, and composition are more purely filmic and that it was possible to film a play emphasizing these elements rather than the traditional common denominators. He also knew that you do not wrench a play out of its locale just to "open-it-up." His *Uncle Vania* never leaves the house, yet it has no sense of theatrical setting. Much of this is accomplished through editing, that great forgotten art of filmed plays.

Editing allows for movement and tension within confined spaces. In this way Konchalovskii retains the integrity of Chekhov's space, while diminishing the stasis of long takes. Through editing he is able to use labyrinthine space as a metaphor for a major theme in the play. In Act III Serebriakov says, "I don't care for this house. It's a labyrinth, that's what it is. Twenty-six enormous rooms, everyone scatters off in different directions, and you can never find a single person." More so than in any theatrical setting, film is able to capture this labyrinth. On film it is possible to show the maze of rooms and to disorient the viewer spatially. Chekhov could only suggest through language the spatial dislocation that becomes the metaphor for interpersonal and psychological dislocation.

Konchalovskii has edited the original text quite severely, but rather than simply leave those excised passages on the cutting room floor, as all the other directors did, he found ways to represent them visually. Often the language in an emotionally charged scene is cut in favor of rendering the emotion through acting, setting, and lighting. Rather than cut the "irrelevancies," which Chekhov thought were relevant irrelevancies, or the "talkiness" of characters whose very essence depends on us seeing them ramble on at length, Konchalovskii judiciously reduced the roles of the secondary characters.

The dominant elements of Konchalovskii's style center on color, lighting, composition, framing, and editing. The color scheme of this film is powerfully experimental. Each act has been divided into an eerily monochromatic pale magenta segment (suggesting the old sepia tone photographs and movies) and a full color segment. The monochromatic tone conveys the sense of a washed-out loneliness, emptiness, and sameness, while the color segments reinvest these people's lives with vitality. Chekhov felt this ambivalence with respect to his characters, and so Konchalovskii has discovered an extremely effective cinematic correlative for transposing that ambivalence.

The monochromatic beginning and ending of the film frame the entrance and departure of Serebriakov and his beautiful wife, Elena. They are the catalysts of the play, the ones who excite the passions of the other characters. And since they arrive after the opening monochromatic segment and leave before the final one, Konchalovskii has visually reinforced the notion that their monotonous days far outnumber their vital, passionate ones.

Uncle Vania has not been framed or composed in a theatrical manner. Instead, characters are often half out of the frame, or only a hand, for instance, is shown in the frame. There is a strong suggestion of off-screen space. And the camera placement thoroughly destroys any sense of the proscenium arch. Space becomes fluid and fragmented. The entire sphere of space is used rather than just the three-dimensionality of a frontal or diagonal perspective. The untheatrical compositions of this film also mark it as unusual. Characters are often half-hidden by objects or are extremely fore- or backgrounded. And no composition is static because the angles are always changing, the lighting breaks across the characters in new ways, and different objects form new compositional relationships with the characters. The camera prowls; characters move in front of the camera. The camera tries to remain unobtrusive in theatrically filmed plays, but here it becomes a force, a new character, along with the heightened interest in objects that this film takes. Photographs, clocks, maps, mirrors, and barometers, as well as doors, doorways, and hallways, all begin to take on lives of their own.

Konchalovskii's lighting techniques further distinguish this film from most filmed plays, which usually do no more than adjust their fill lighting for the time of day or night, being careful to keep their characters in full view. *Uncle Vania* is lit so as to suggest all the hidden, repressed facets of these people's lives. They are dramatically sculpted by the complex and imaginative contours of light and dark. And they are bound far more intimately to the objects of their world by the way Konchalovskii has composed the shots.

Most theatrical editing is no more than functional, with traditional cuts to people for speech, reaction, or establishment of spatial orientation. *Uncle Vania*, however, has a variety of complex editing patterns: extreme close-ups followed by extreme deep focus shots; long takes followed by short takes; many reverse angle shots to force the emphasis on three-dimensional space; and poetic dissolves that convey the elusiveness of time.

Konchalovskii has vigorously applied the techniques of his medium to the meanings of this play. Through color, framing, composition, lighting, and editing he has communicated the ideas of isolation between people, the labyrinth of the house, the half-hidden qualities of these people's lives, and their sameness and individuality. Not all of these notions have been conveyed solely through technique, because the acting is without question the most moving, least theatrical, and most naturalistic of all the filmed plays. Finally, Konchalovskii has suggested timelessness through costuming. By dressing his characters in clothes that would be appropriate for both the late nineteenth century and today he has given the play contemporaneity. This is a brilliant film and a brilliant rendering of Chekhov. It sparkles with cinematic vitality and human emotion without sacrificing the essence of Chekhov's vision.

For students of Chekhov the final question that must be asked of these filmed versions of his stories and plays is, have they as a whole captured his particular atmosphere and vision? Have these films, in other words, remained faithful to their original sources? Chekhov is probably the most successfully filmed major author. That is, a considerable body of his work has been filmed, the filmmakers' primary goal has been to express the essence of the original literary works, and the expression has resulted in films that have integrity as films. If there is one common denominator to all these films, it is that they took the transposition of Chekhov's themes, narratives, and atmosphere to be their first responsibility. One can always argue with each film's interpretation of these elements, but no filmmaker has used the original solely for the purposes of commentary or analogy. So, from the standpoint of those primarily interested in Chekhov, one could say that the collective goal of filmed fidelity to Chekhov's works has been achieved. The films, then, stand in a direct relationship to Chekhov's works and can be viewed as modern extensions and interpretations of them in a different medium.

From the perspective of a student of cinema, however, none of the filmed adaptations has achieved the status of a film classic, a landmark in the history of cinema. There is a sense that the truly great films must at some point distance themselves from their original literary sources so that the visions and styles become, in the balance, those of the filmmakers. Those that come closest to achieving this transcendence are Heifitz's *The Lady with the Dog* and Konchalovskii's *Uncle Vania*. What is remarkable is that so many of these adaptations have, in fact, been filmed with integrity for the medium. The consistency of this phenomenon attests to the inherent filmability of—in particular—Chekhov's stories. Chekhov and cinema have a symbiosis that augurs well for future adaptations.

NOTES

1. Jay Leyda, *Kino: A History of the Russian and Soviet Film* (New York: Collier Books, 1973), pp. 414-465.

2. My contribution to this volume is not an exhaustive study of every extant film, but instead limits the survey to those films available for rental by U.S. 16 mm. distributors. These films represent the most highly regarded adaptations and are, of course, accessible to those wishing to use them in film, language, or literature classes. My guiding principle within this limited format has been to concentrate on those films that do both Chekhov and the film medium justice.

3. Siegfried Kracauer, *Theory of Film* (New York: Oxford University Press, 1960), p. 28.

4. Leyda, p. 346.

5. Thomas Winner, *Chekhov and His Prose* (New York: Holt, Rinehart and Winston, 1966), p. 10.

6. The English title of the story on which this film is based is rendered elsewhere in this collection as "The Lady with a Lapdog."

7. Geoffrey Wagner, *The Novel and the Cinema* (Cranbury, N.J.: Associated University Presses, 1975), pp. 219-233.

8. V. V. Golubkov, "Cexov's Lyrico-Dramatic Stories," in *Anton Cexov as a Master of Story Writing*, eds. Leo Hulanicki and David Savignac (The Hague: Mouton, 1976), pp. 136-137.

9. The three most valuable sources for insight and information on the theatre-into-film process are: Sergei Eisenstein, "Through Theater to Cinema," in *Film Form* (New York: Harcourt, Brace, and World, 1949), pp. 3-17; Andre Bazin, "Theater and Cinema," in *What Is Cinema?*, trans. Hugh Gray (Berkeley: University of California Press, 1967), pp. 76-124; and Roger Manvell, *Theater and Film* (Cranbury, N.J.: Associated Presses, 1979).

10. Manvell, "Three Sisters," in *Theater and Film*, pp. 93-105. A description of cinema techniques in Samsonov's film.

ANNOTATED SELECTIVE FILMOGRAPHY

1944

Iubilei (The Anniversary)
Prod.: Mosfilm
Dir.: Vladimir Petrov
Photo.: Vladimir Iakovlev
Stilted and theatrical, but somewhat amusing.
16 mm. dist.: Films Inc.

Svad'ba (The Wedding)
Prod.: Tbilisi Studios
Dir.: Isidor Annenskii
Photo.: Iuri Ekelchik
Vibrant, well acted, and interestingly filmed. Extends Chekhov's one-act play.
16 mm. dist.: Films Inc.

1953

The Boor
Prod.: Dynamic Films Inc.
Dir.: Nathan Zucker
With: Monty Woolley
A Monty Woolley vehicle. Explicitly theatrical. Good vaudeville, which Chekhov intended it to be.
16 mm. dist.: Films Inc.

1955

Poprygun'ia (The Grasshopper)
Prod.: Mosfilm
Dir.: Samson Samsonov
Photo: F. Dobronravov and V. Monakhov
With: Sergei Bondarchuk, Ludmila Tselikovskaia, Vladimir Druzhnikov
A faithful and successful version of a well-known story.
16 mm. dist.: Films Inc.

1959

Khudozhestvo (*A Work of Art*)
Prod.: Mosfilm
Dir.: M. Kovalev
Photo.: U. Maslennikov
Very faithful short film, well executed.
16 mm. dist.: Films Inc.

1960

Dama s sobachkoi (*The Lady with the Dog*)
Prod.: Lenfilm
Dir.: Joseph Heifitz
Photo.: Andrei Moskvin, Dmitri Meskhièv
With: Iia Savvina, Aleksei Batalov
One of the very best adaptations, faithful and cinematic. Praised by Ingmar Bergman.
16 mm. dist.: Films Inc.

1964

Tri sestry (*Three Sisters*)
Prod: Mosfilm
Dir: Samson Samsonov
Photo.: F. Dobronravov
With: Liubov Sokolva, Margarita Volodina, Tatiana Malchenko, Lev Ivanov
Overly dramatic, but both cinematic and theatrical. Excised text.
16 mm. dist.: Corinth Films

1966

Three Sisters
Prod.: Ely Landau-Actors Studio Inc.
Dir.: Paul Bogart
Photo.: Ed Henning
With: Sandy Dennis, Geraldine Page, Kim Stanley, Shelley Winters, Luther Adler,
      James Olson, Kevin McCarthy
Completely theatrical production, strangely acted. Complete text.
16 mm. dist.: Kit Parker Films

1968

The Seagull
Prod.: Warner Bros.
Dir.: Sidney Lumet
Photo.: Gerry Fisher
With: James Mason, Simone Signoret, Vanessa Redgrave, David Warner
Beautifully filmed but overblown production. Complete text.
16 mm. dist.: Kit Parker Films

1970

Three Sisters
Prod.: Ely Landau Organization Inc.
Dir.: Laurence Olivier
Photo.: Geoffrey Unsworth
With: Jeanne Watts, Joan Plowright, Louise Purnell, Derek Jacobi, Laurence
    Olivier, Alan Bates, Sheila Reid
Perfect balance between film and theatre with fine controlled performances. Com-
    plete text.
16 mm. dist.: Films Inc.

1971

Chaika (The Seagull)
Prod.: Mosfilm
Dir.: Juli Karasik
Photo.: Mikhail Suslov
With: Alla Demidova, Vladimir Chetverifov, Liudmila Savelèva
Realistically filmed, controlled performances. Excised text.
16 mm. dist.: Corinth Films

1972

Diadia Vania (Uncle Vania)
Prod.: Mosfilm
Dir.: Andrei Konchalovskii
Photo.: Georgi Rerberg, Evgenii Guslinskii
With: Innokentii Smoktunovskii, Sergei Bondurchuk, Vladimir Zeldin, Irina Kup-
    chenko, Irina Miroshchnichenko
A brilliant film and a brilliant adaptation of the play. Extremely well acted. Excised
    text.
16 mm. dist.: Corinth Films

Tzvety zapozdalye (Belated flowers)
Prod.: Mosfilm
Dir.: Abram Room
Photo.: Leonid Krainenkov
With: Olga Zhizneva, Irina Laurentèva, Aleksandr Lazarev
Interesting film of an early Chekhov story. Quite faithful to story line but romantic
    in spirit.
16 mm. dist.: Corinth Films

1977

Drama na okhote (The Shooting Party)
Prod.: Mosfilm
Dir.: Emil Loteanu

Photo.: Anatoli Petritskii, Vladimir Nakhabtsev
With: Galina Beliaèva, Oleg Iankovskii, Kiril Lavrov
Lushly filmed version of early Chekhov novel. Modern in technique.
16 mm. dist.: Corinth Films

Dates Unknown

None of these films has original credits, so it is impossible to fix dates to
any of them, much less country of origin. All have been directed by
Maurice Fasquel, but the settings look authentically Russian. None of
the films appears in the Library of Congress Catalog of Copyright
Entries: Motion Pictures. The look and feel of the films would seem to
place their production in the late 1950s or early 1960s. All are narrated
by John Gielgud, but it seems that these narrations have been added for
English-speaking audiences. All are available either individually or
together from Films Inc. under the heading "A Chekhov Treasury."
They range from fourteen to twenty-seven minutes each and are inexpensive to rent. The quality of the films is quite high, and there has been
a real effort to remain faithful to the spirit, if not the details, of
Chekhov's stories.

Desire to Sleep
Volodia
Rothschild's Violin
The Boarding House
Revenge
The Wallet
The Fugitive

PART VII

Chekhov As Correspondent and Social Observer

15

Thomas Eekman

CHEKHOV AS CORRESPONDENT

Tear this letter to pieces. In general make a habit of tearing up letters.

(Chekhov to his brother Alexander, April 26, 1888)[1]

An unusually prolific correspondent, Chekhov left an epistolary legacy noteworthy for its vastness and its characteristic, often humorous tone. The total number of letters he composed during his brief lifetime remains unknown. However, the latest edition of his *Complete Works and Letters* contains some 4,400 letters (including telegrams, short notes, and post-scripts to other people's letters). These, compiled from a 29-year span, amount to over 150 preserved letters per year, almost one every other day of his entire life from the age of 15. And it is known that a large number of letters was lost.[2]

Chekhov singularly disliked the idea of his letters being published.[3] He did not write them with the knowledge or the intent that they would be printed and read.[4] Still, Chekhov's popularity and the charm of his letters stimulated wide interest in them. Aside from the appearance of single letters in various publications, the first collection in book form came out five years after his death.[5] Following a modest selection published in 1910, Mariia Pavlovna Chekhova, his sister, brought out a six-volume edition (1912-1916) containing 2,000 letters.[6] At least four other collections ensued (including Chekhov's correspondence with his wife Olga Knipper) before volumes XIII through XX of his *Complete Works* appeared in 1948-1951, containing some 4,200 letters. In the new 30-volume edition of his *Complete Works and Letters* (1974-1982), the letters and annotations to them occupy no less than 12 volumes.

Of the letters he received, Chekhov himself carefully and systematically preserved about 10,000, of which approximately 7,000 are kept in Russian archives, mainly in the Lenin Library in Moscow.[7] Relatively few (those of his wife, his sister, his brother Alexander, and of several other writers) have been published. A serious gap in the collection results from the absence of the letters of his most important and prolific correspondent, Aleksei Sergeevich Suvorin, the main editor and owner of the St. Petersburg daily newspaper *Novoe vremia* (*New Times*). The letters were either lost or, more probably, destroyed by Suvorin himself.

Clearly imposing by virtue of their abundance, Chekhov's letters are remarkable for the slightly bantering, facetious, light, and lively spirit that pervades a majority of them. Chekhov's sense of humor, his endeavor to amuse people or to convey his own good spirits to them, is visible in many of his letters, from the earliest to the last. His humor ranged over a wide spectrum, from beneficience to cutting sarcasm, depending on the addressee.

A large part of his correspondence consists, understandably, of more or less formal and business letters, messages to persons he did not know intimately. Among these letters, only a few have a special significance for the reader of our time. For example, fourteen letters to Grigorii Rossolimo, Chekhov's fellow student in medical school, have been preserved. The Rossolimo correspondence is of no particular interest, with the exception of a letter dated October 11, 1899, in which Chekhov speaks about the influence of medical science on his literary activities.

Also significant is the letter of April 10, 1890, to Vukol Lavrov, a co-editor of the moderately liberal monthly *Russkaia mysl'* (*Russian Thought*). In this letter Chekhov reacted vehemently for being qualified in the March issue of the journal as a priest of "unprincipled writing." The letter of 1890 is often cited, because in it Chekhov expressed ideas about the press, the role of the *literateur*, and his own place as a "modest writer."

More valuable are the long series of letters to those few people with whom Chekhov was really close. Among them are friends and "brothers-in-arms," like Aleksei Pleshcheev (62 letters to him are extant), who, especially in the years 1888-1890, often was Chekhov's first critic as the literary collaborator of the *Severnyi vestnik* (*Northern Messenger*); or Ivan Leont'ev, who wrote prose under the pseudonym "Shcheglov" in the 1880s but later turned to drama, and with whom Chekhov exchanged views on literature (67 letters). Much more frequent is the correspondence with Nikolai Leikin (168 letters, but many more must have existed). Leikin was a humorist, an unusually prolific but completely forgotten writer—the author of thousands of short stories and scenes, and of many novels, plays, and so on—and, most important for Chekhov, the editor of the weekly magazine *Oskolki* (*Fragments*), in which he printed a large number of Chekhov's stories in the years 1883-1887. The business element dominates their correspondence, but Chekhov often expressed to his employer and friend more personal opinions and ideas. In 1887 Chekhov's collaboration with Leikin came to an end; in a letter to Suvorin (November 3, 1888), Chekhov called Leikin "a bourgeois to the marrow."

In comparison, Chekhov's relationship with Aleksei Suvorin was much closer, longer, more meaningful and productive than his relationship with Leikin. Suvorin, a writer and journalist, was twenty-six years older than Chekhov but, nevertheless, remained his most intimate and revered friend from December 1885, when the two met during Chekhov's first visit to St. Petersburg, until the mid 1890s, when the friendship with Suvorin and his family "petered out." Over a sixteen-year period, Chekhov wrote Suvorin at least 333 letters (this is the number of letters preserved, there may have been more). Many of these letters are among the most interesting ones he ever wrote.

The only persons to whom Chekhov wrote more letters than to Suvorin were Olga Knipper, who was his wife (and "grass widow") during the last three years of his life, and his sister Mariia Pavlovna. Many of the letters to his sister (for example, from his trips to Europe and Sakhalin, or from Yalta) were also addressed to the entire family (that is, his parents and his younger brothers, when they still lived with their parents). Chekhov always remained close to his nearest relatives; when he was away from home, or when they were, he would write regularly.

Instead of saying a few words about Chekhov's correspondence with each of a great number of persons, the focus here is on just two correspondents— his brother Alexander and his friend Lidiia Mizinova— representing his relations with his family and his circle of friends, respectively.

Alexander Chekhov, Chekhov's eldest brother, was his first addressee. In a postscript to a letter by his other elder brother, Nikolai, Chekhov wished Alexander "optimum et maximum." Chekhov was only fifteen at the time but liked to exhibit his knowledge of Latin, just as he showed off his German in the next preserved letter, written some eight months afterward to the same Alexander. The beginning of this letter, written around February 20, 1883, may serve as an example of the tone in his letters to his brother:

My benign brother Alexander Pavlovich! First of all I congratulate you and your better half with the successful parturition and acquisition, and the city of Taganrog with a fresh little citizeness. May the newborn baby (cross yourself!) live for many years, brimming over (cross yourself!) with physical and moral beauty, with riches and a golden voice, and with loquaciousness; and may she, when the time comes, hook a gallant husband (cross yourself, idiot!), after first having seduced all Taganrog high school boys and driven them to despair!!!

They regularly exchanged letters until April 1904, two months before Chekhov's death, when he wrote two last letters to his eldest brother. With no other close relative, except his sister, did Chekhov have such an extensive

and lively correspondence. Of his letters to Alexander, 198 have been preserved and published, while the Lenin Library has in its possession 381
(including 3 telegrams and a few short notes) from Alexander to his
brother.[8]

Many of these letters are of a purely business character; some contain
pieces of medical advice.[9] The missives to Alexander often have gibing
and teasing epithets such as *Gusev* (Mr. Goose) and its many variations, or
"Not the Real Chekhov"; with no other addressee did Chekhov use so
many of them. Unrelentingly comical, the nicknames Chekhov devised for
his brother depended on Alexander's business and familial activities: "My
customs service brother," "Catcher of smugglers, of people, of the
universe, my customs brother, finest of all people, Alexander Pavlych,"
"My photographic and philoprogenitive brother," "My firefighting
brother" (Alexander had published a *History of Fire Fighting* and, in 1892,
became the editor of a new magazine, *The Fireman*), "Your Widowership"
(after the death of Alexander's first wife), "Mr. A. Grayhaired" (a pseudonym under which Alexander published), "Pseudo-dramatist, whom my
laurels prevent from sleeping." The name Sasha, the hypocoristic form of
Alexander, also appears in many variants: Sashechka, Sash(sh)ichka, and
so on.

No less comical are the epithets that evince a critical attitude, mockery, or
disapproval on the part of Chekhov toward his brother. Although some
letters demonstrate an obvious underlying affection, unkindness and insen-
sitivity to Alexander found their way into Chekhov's epistolary demeanor.
In his introduction to *Letters of Anton Chekhov*, Simon Karlinsky speaks
of "the vituperative, painfully humorous letters to Chekhov's older brother
Alexander" which were not included in that collection.[10] Chekhov
addresses his brother with terms like "My Frivolous and Ridiculous Brother
Alexander," *Filiniuga* (a Chekhov neologism), *malen'kaia pol'za* (the nick-
name given to the hero of Chekhov's story "My Life," Misail Poloznev),
"Big night owl, small use, bribe taker, blackmailer, all the filthy things my
mind can think of," *Nichtozhestvo* (Nonentity), "Pen bandit and press
swindler."

Some of the appellations refer to the lower-middle-class milieu from
which the Chekhovs emerged: "Proletarian! Indigent brother! Honest
toiler, exploited by the rich!," and *Taganrogskii meshchanin* (Taganrog
philistine). Some also suggest a mocking attitude toward their father, a conservative, parochial, severe, and ultra-religious person. "My illegitimately
living and illegitimately perishing brother" refers to Alexander's first wife,
who had been married before and thus, according to church regulations,
could not be married to him. "Our two-faced free-thinking brother"
alludes to Alexander's turning away from Orthodox Christian beliefs and
customs, thus incurring their father's resentment.

Alexander, at whom these mildly offensive names were hurled, was born five years before Anton. He studied physics in Moscow but never utilized his skills. He tried his hand at short story writing and managed to place his younger brother in the Moscow light-caliber weekly press. After marrying and fathering three children, Alexander held jobs in the customs offices of Taganrog and other towns in order to provide for the family. Later, with Chekhov's help, he received a modest but permanent position in the editorial offices of *New Times*, where he stayed from 1886 until his death in 1913.

A journalist and fiction writer, Alexander wrote approximately 30 short stories, novellas, and novels and at least one play that was staged. Although he was never recognized as a writer, he seems, nonetheless, to have possessed some talent and an encyclopedic knowledge. His main obstacle was vodka, for which Chekhov, who liked to drink too, but in moderation, chided him: *Da i na kakoi leshii pit'?* (And why the hell should you drink? October 13, 1888).[11] He certainly lacked Chekhov's energy, his ambition to produce works of artistic value, and his literary genius. He stayed with *New Times* even when Chekhov became completely disgusted with it in the 1890s.

Preferring Alexander's letters to his fiction, Chekhov rarely had words of praise for new works by his brother. In March 1883, Chekhov wrote to the editor of *Oskolki* (*Fragments*), N. A. Leikin: "I'm sending you a short piece, 'The Pipe' by Agafopod Edinitsyn, a Moscow scribbler." Leikin did not publish the story written under Alexander's pseudonym but inquired about the author, as can be deduced from Chekhov's letter of April 1883. Chekhov described his brother as one

who has worked for Moscow magazines for the last few years. He has written a lot, and one time with success: he could live by his pen. He was a humorist, but then he ventured into lyricism, phantasmagoria and, it seems, he got lost as an author. He would like to abandon lyricism now, but it's too late, he got stuck in it. His letters are replete with humor, you can't think of anything funnier; but as soon as he writes something for a magazine it's all wrong, he starts to stumble. If he were a little bit younger, an excellent worker [for a magazine] could have been made out of him. He is not a bad humorous writer.

Alexander not only had a comical bent, but he also liked obscene remarks and stories, which explains the series of ellipses in Soviet editions of his letters. As a judge of Chekhov's humor, Alexander wrote in November 1877 that "your anecdotes will be taken. Today, I'll post two of your jokes to *Budil'nik* (*Alarm Clock*): 'Which sex uses the most make-up' and 'God Granted' (children). The rest is weak. Send some more short and witty texts. The long ones are pale."[12] On October 14, 1878, Alexander reviewed, in detail, Chekhov's lost play *Fatherlessness* and gave him some professional advice.

In 1882, from Taganrog, Alexander proferred advice on a different matter. A series of drawings by Nikolai with texts by Chekhov, called "The Wedding Season," appeared in the popular weekly *Zritel'* (*The Spectator*). Various figures in the drawings bore a strong caricatural resemblance to certain acquaintances of the Chekhovs in Taganrog. The persons in question saw the magazine, recognized themselves, and became deeply offended. "This caricature is regarded," Alexander wrote to his brothers, "as an expression of the blackest ingratitude here." Chekhov accepted Alexander's advice to stay away and postponed visiting his home town for five years, until 1887.

Chekhov, however, was not without his share of advice for Alexander after a disagreement at the end of 1888. In his letter of January 1889, Chekhov condemns Alexander's

horrible, absolutely impossible behavior toward Natalia Aleksandrovna [Alexander's second wife] and the cook. Please forgive me, but to treat women, whoever they are, in such a way is unworthy of a decent and loving man. Which heavenly or earthly power gave you the right to make slaves out of them? . . . Please remember that despotism and lies have destroyed your mother's young years. Despotism and lies have mutilated our childhood. . . . I interceded as well as I could and my conscience is clear. Be magnanimous and consider the disagreement finished.

Soon the correspondence and mutual visits resumed.

Still, a discordant note remained a part of their relationship. Alexander was conscious of his failure as a writer and of being dwarfed by his brother's success. In a letter for his brother's birthday, Janary 14-16, 1887, Alexander admits that he is now

some impersonal, nameless appendage. I am the brother of Chekhov. . . . Always and everywhere I am introduced or recommended as such. My individuality is gone. Menelaos was the queen's husband; and I am Anton's brother. And you can't eradicate that impersonal state. If I committed a crime, they would pity you. . . . If I did a heroic deed, they would say, "do you know who did that? The brother of that famous . . . etc." I should try to do myself in! However, that wouldn't help either. Things would be even worse: I would turn into the deceased *brother* of the great writer. . . . No, it's still better to live and to be healthy, to hell with it! . . . I can't do anything about it, because you are immortal.

And two weeks later (January 29, 1887):

A curious role fell to my share. In literary circles people introduce themselves enthusiastically to me, thinking that I'm Anton, and in artistic circles thinking I'm Nikolai. First, they shake my hand forcefully, but later, when they have found out they were wrong, they hardly extend two fingers to me.

Although he was generally accepted by Suvorin and other literary-journalistic figures, Alexander defined his position in St. Petersburg and the Russian world of letters as peripheral, "at the edge." Agreeing with Alexander that the *New Times* staff was of little account, Chekhov wrote:

It's a pity that you ceased rubbing shoulders with the *New Times* people. It is true, they are Zulus, but smart Zulus, from whom you can learn a lot. . . . You are indispensable for *New Times*. . . . A counterbalancing party is necessary, a party of young, fresh and independent people. . . . I believe that if there were two or three new people on the editorial board who would loudly call nonsense, nonsense, Mr. Elpe would not dare to try to annihilate Darwin nor Burenin to peck at Nadson. At each meeting with Suvorin, I speak frankly, and I think such openness is useful. "I don't like . . . " is already sufficient to manifest your independence. (Sepember 7-8, 1887)

As Chekhov gradually moved away from the *New Times* and, in a way, from Suvorin too, Alexander's position became precarious. In his letter of March 31, 1893, Alexander told his brother about quarrels that had taken place within the editorial board.

I am still holding out, but I, too, have been obliquely given to understand that, after your letter to the old man, not one Chekhov can be tolerated on the editorial board. And I certainly believe that's true. The Dauphin [nickname of Suvorin's oldest son] is crossing out things in my articles and notes and taking them to pieces, just terrible. Nor does he want to print my stories. I don't know the contents of your letter to the old man, but I know its consequences. . . . Sooner or later, when I am not smart enough to leave by myself, they will ask me to go.

It is not clear to which letter his brother is referring.[13] Chekhov wrote him back on April 4:

I was planning to write to Suvorin, but didn't write a single line, so the letter of mine that upset the Dauphin and his brother so much is sheer invention. But once these discussions take place, let it be: the old building has started to crack and must tumble down. I feel sorry for the old man, he has written me a remorseful letter. I shall probably not have to break definitively with him. As far as the editors and Dauphins are concerned, I don't care at all for any kind of relations with them. In recent years, I have grown indifferent and feel that my *anima* is so free of the worries of the vain world that I really couldn't care less about what is being said and thought on the editorial staff. Besides, in my opinion, I am divided by 7375 versts from Zhitel [the pseudonym of one of the regular collaborators of *New Times*] & Co. As journalists they are simply repulsive to me, as I have told you more than once.

On September 4, 1893, Chekhov wrote: "Keep aloof from those sons-of-bitches and don't praise them. It's a vile pack." And on February 5, 1899:

The *New Times* makes a terrible impression. It's not a newspaper, it's a circus, it's a pack of hungry jackals that bite each other in the tails, the devil knows what it is. . . . In the Zola affair, *New Times* has simply behaved despicably. The old man and I exchanged letters on that subject (in a very moderate tone), and then we both fell silent. I don't want to write and I don't want his letters. (From Nice, February 23, 1898: cf. also the letter of July 30, 1898)[14]

In the early years, Chekhov was a rival of his brother in the field of humorous literature, jokingly boasting of his success. But even in his earliest years, 1882-1883, Chekhov advised Alexander on his literary work: "Frivolous and ridiculous brother! Why would you translate when there is time to write original pieces?" (November 19 or before, 1882). "The translation is not always good. It is all right, but from you I expect something better" (December 25, 1882-January 1-2, 1883). His long letter of February 20, 1883 is full of advice:

You are not born a subjective scribbler. . . . That's not inborn, but acquired. . . . And to dispose of that acquired subjectivity is as easy as pie. . . . All you have to do is to be a little more honest: leave yourself out of the picture everywhere, don't push yourself forward as a hero of your novel, part with yourself even if only for a half hour.

You have one story in which a young couple is kissing, whispering and talking nonsense. . . . Not one sensible word, nothing but *complacence*! And you didn't write with the reader in mind. You wrote it because *you* like that idle talk. Why don't you describe the dinner, how and what they were eating, what kind of cook there was, what a vulgar person your hero is, satisfied with his lazy happiness, how your heroine is faring, how ridiculous she is in her love for this smug, overfed goose with the napkin around his neck. . . . Everybody likes to see well-fed, satisfied people, that is true, but in order to portray them it is not sufficient to mention what they said and how often they kissed. Something else is necessary too: you have to get rid of the personal impression which honeymoon happiness makes on anybody who isn't embittered. Subjectivity is a horrible thing! If for no other reason, it's bad because it betrays the poor author from head to feet. I bet all priests' daughters and scribes' wives who read your works are in love with you, and if you were a German, you would drink free beer in all *Bierhallen* with German waitresses. If you could free yourself of that subjectivity, that muddle, a most useful artist might grow out of you. You have such a knack of laughing, of pestering and ridiculing people—you have such a smooth style, you have experienced such a lot and seen all too much. . . . Ah, such good material gets lost.

In his next letter of April 17 or 18, 1883, Chekhov abandons the moralizing tone, but he suggests to his brother that they cooperate in a research project combining his newly acquired knowledge as a medical student with Alexander's interest in human character. "Don't you want to work in science? I am occupying myself now, and will continue to do that, with one little question: the women's question."

Then he specifies the theme of the project: "The history of sexual authority" ["of authority in sexual relationships" would be more appropriate]. He expounds his ideas on the subject with the conclusion that "*homo* is the one who has the authority: the man (husband) stands higher. She (the woman) can be a good doctor, a good lawyer, etc., but when it comes to *creativity*, she is a goose. A perfect organism creates, but women have not yet created anything. George Sand is no Newton, no Shakespeare. She is not a thinker."

The fourth-year student Chekhov expounded ideas which he considered new and his own, but which were clearly part of, or a result of, a way of thinking quite widespread among scientists and the intelligentsia in Russia at that time. It was a grandiose plan encompassing zoology, anthropology, history, and the history of knowledge. However, Alexander apparently did not take up the idea. He probably never wrote a word about it, and Chekhov, in his letter of May 13, 1883, admitted that he "somehow during the holidays, having had a drop too much, wrote about a project dealing with sexual authority. . . . It can be done, but first we have to publish it as a small brochure." That was the end of the project.

Except for just one letter from 1884, there is a gap in their correspondence between 1883 and 1886. In the meantime, Chekhov had arranged for his brother's employment with *New Times*. He chastised him for the stories in which Alexander depicted oppressed lower civil servants (January 4, 1886). That theme, according to Chekhov, was totally out of date. He forgot that he himself very recently had portrayed characters from this category.[15] He warned Alexander in the same letter: "All of Piter [the popular name for St. Petersburg] follows the work of the Chekhov brothers." He gave him some more advice and finished with: "Don't be mad at me for the moralizing."

The letter of May 10 of the same year, one of the most often quoted letters to Alexander, contains a sort of credo of the young writer, who reports that "with the five stories printed in *New Times*, I have caused a tumult in Piter." He offers Alexander some advice regarding the story "The City of the Future," which the latter planned to write. It would be a work of art, Chekhov told him, "only on these conditions: 1. no politico-economico-social verbal effusions, 2. objectivity throughout, 3. truth in the description of characters and objects, 4. extreme brevity, 5. audacity and originality; eschew cliches, 6. warmheartedness." A paragraph on nature description follows: "You will evoke a moonlit night by writing that on the mill dam a glass fragment of a broken bottle flashed like a bright little star, and that the black shadow of a dog or a wolf rolled along like a ball."

One of the next preserved letters, dated January 8, 1887, is the first one in which Chekhov urgently asks Alexander to go to the *New Times* office (and this time also to the *St. Petersburg Gazette* office) to receive Chekhov's honoraria and send them to him. As a contributor to *New Times*, Chekhov often had business with the editorial and administrative offices, and he made ample use of Alexander's services. To a certain extent he was entitled to do so because he was the breadwinner of the Chekhov family in Moscow, providing for their parents, sister, and younger brother. In the epistles dated January 20-25 and 26, 1887, Chekhov continues to give his brother orders. "Remember and realize: your admittedly larcenous nature notwithstanding, I'm entrusting big sums to you!"

In the following letters the orders continue. Frequently, they are given in a facetious tone. Typical of this epistolary manner is a sentence from the letter of February 22, 1887: "Don't touch my works with your dirty fingers. Remember your nothingness and don't forget that you're an ex-customs man. It is your destiny to take bribes, and not to stick your nose into the Temple of Fame. For the rest, I forgive you."

In the letter of March 19, 1887, he instructs Alexander to be the "master's eye" for the collection of his stories *New Times* was going to print: "For this labor I will allow you to call yourself on your visiting cards 'the famous writer's brother'. . . . In general, do everything you find useful and harmless for my pocket and my fame." This, in tandem with Alexander's complaint that he was nothing more than his brother's brother, suggests that Chekhov was not always as psychologically insightful and compassionate as we are used to viewing him. At times he seems to have been more understanding with his fictional characters than with his own brother. It is all humorous and ironic but at the same time somehow dry, pungent, and unfeeling.[16]

Chekhov's letter of August 2-5, 1887, begins in a different mood: "Who could suppose that out of a rotter such a genius would grow? Your latest story, "In the Lighthouse," is great and wonderful. Probably you stole it from some great writer. . . . An intelligent word after thirty stupid years!"

After these begrudged laudatory lines, he returns to criticism:

The beginning would not be trite if it were put somewhere in the middle of the story and broken up. Also, Olia is good for nothing, like all your female characters. You definitely don't know women! My dear fellow, you cannot eternally stick to one female type! Where and when (I don't speak of your high school years) have you seen such Olias? Doesn't it make more sense and show more talent if you, next to such wonderful characters as the Tatar and the daddy, put a nice, living woman (not a doll), a real character? . . . In none of your stories is there a woman who is human, they are all some sort of hopping blancmanges that talk with the tongue of spoiled cabaret *ingenues*. . . . My regards to your famiy, but not to you. You are not a genius and there is nothing that we have in common.[17]

He continued to dictate to his brother in a condescendingly bantering way. In 1888, when he was awarded the Pushkin Prize for literature by the Imperial Academy of Sciences, he wrote to Alexander (November 16):

The letter of attorney I am sending to you opens the following rosy perspectives to you: 1. You go to the Academy of Sciences and there you receive 500 laurels. In the Academy, you request in my name that you be made an Academician. [The second request has to do with the staging of Chekhov's plays.] I am laying all these pleasant obligations upon you not so much out of the desire to afford you pleasure, but out of respect for your parents.

During the first years of Chekhov's life in Melikhovo, some of the pride and satisfaction he felt at possessing an estate, at being a landowner, was manifested in letters to his brother. The remarks are in the same abrasive but humorous spirit:

Unworthy brother! Remember that you owe me numerous benefits and that you are, after all, only a poor relative who has to respect me, as I possess my own estate and horses. With you it's nothing but misery and penury. Besides, you have a weakness for alcoholic beverages. Better yourself! . . . Pitying you, your brother, landowner, and useful member of society, A. Chekhov. (April 15, 1894)

This feigned condescension is to be found in most letters of the 1890s. "I received the book" (Alexander had sent him his collection of *Christmas Stories*, December 30, 1894), "and your intention to compete with me on the book market I find quite insolent. Nobody is going to buy your book because everybody knows that you are a person of immoral behavior and always drunk." And on May 11, 1899:

We have visits of aristocratic guests, for example, the Malkiels. Tea is being served, as in the better houses, with little napkins. You would no doubt be removed from the table, as stinking is not permitted. . . . Write more often, don't be embarrassed. I wanted to send you my old pants, but I changed my mind: I am afraid it will make you think too much of yourself. . . . Tuus frater bonus Antonius.

Another aspect of their correspondence was the expression of intimate feelings and concerns which Chekhov revealed only to Alexander. An example is the long letter Chekhov wrote after the premiere of his first produced play, *Ivanov* (November 20, 1887; see also the letter of November 24, signed "Yours, Schiller Shakespearovich Goethe"); he shared with his brother the feelings and trepidations of the young playwright who has made his debut. In Alexander's letter of August 18, 1888, he asked Chekhov's advice about proposing to a common acquaintance. Chekhov, in response, pointed out that a marriage should be built on love (August 28). Chekhov also wrote his brother at moments of depression. In the letter of March 16, 1893, from Melikhovo, he writes:

I am overcome by a physical and mental flabbiness, as if I had overslept myself. A dismal situation. I don't feel any pain, but I constantly feel like lying down on my bed or on a couch. I'm reading a lot, but sluggishly, without appetite. In my heart it's like in an empty sour milk jar. Partly I explain this mood by the weather (five degrees below zero), partly by old age, partly by the indefiniteness of goals in my existence.

The next letter is similar in its report of Chekhov's ill health and his right to "call myself an invalid" because of the impairment of his lungs, hemoptysis. His family in Melikhovo was not aware of his illness or his stay in a clinic: Chekhov wrote about it to Alexander only. During the last five or six years of Chekhov's life, however, their correspondence was less frequent and less intimate.

Aside from Olga Knipper, the woman to whom Chekhov wrote most frequently was Lidiia Stakhevna (Lika) Mizinova. Ten years her elder, Chekhov cared for her a great deal, as evidenced by over 60 letters to her that have been preserved. Approximately the same number of letters to Elena Mikhailovna Shavrova are extant, but she was a writer, with whom Chekhov corresponded on a more professional level. Although at times confidential, his letters to her are for the most part formally polite and serious.

It was different with Lika.[18] In the very first letter to her that has been preserved and published (January 11, 1891), he calls her "Ah, Likisha, Likisha!" Yet, he always addresses her with the polite form *Vy* up to the last preserved letter of January 29, 1900.[19] Then their correspondence comes to an end because their ways and interests parted. Lika had had an affair with Chekhov's friend, Ignatii Potapenko, which culminated in the birth of a child in Switzerland in October 1894. This, however, did not impede their mutual correspondence. Not only are there no references to this episode in her life, but also Chekhov keeps writing her in the same tone.

In his letters to Lika he constantly expresses the probably very sincere wish to see her. He liked to chat with her, to talk about common friends and acquaintances, about everyday events in his life, but his true feelings toward her remained hidden under a neutral tone or teasing attitude. This attitude was, as Ernest J. Simmons wrote, "a curious combination of seriousness and elaborate raillery, as though he wished to discourage an affection which he suspected but yet was afraid did not exist."[20]

Again the epithets at the head of his letters as well as the signatures are indicative of the general tone: "Duma scribe" (since Mizinova served for some time in the Moscow City Council of the Duma), "Golden, mother-of-pearl and lisle-thread Lika," "Dear Melita" (one of the characters in Franz Grillparzer's play *Sappho*, which was then staged in Moscow). Among other endearing terms, the most frequent and simple was "Milaia Lik(usi)a." His letter of June 12, 1891, he signed with a pierced heart. In one letter he is "Pet'ka," in the next one "The Marshall of Bow-wowbility," in a third he pretends it is written by his sister (June-July 1891).

Examples of cruel humor, humor at the expense of the addressee, are also to be found in some of the letters to Lika. Typical is this sentence in the letter of March 29, 1892:

What kind of tortures do we have to devise for you if you don't come to us? I'll pour boiling water over you and tear a piece of beef out of your back with white hot pliers. . . . Write me at least two lines, Melita. Don't relegate us to premature oblivion. Pretend at least that you still remember us. Deceive us, Lika. Deception is better than indifference.

On April 22, 1893, he writes: "I wish that during that exams [in the school where she was teaching] the inspector would pull at your braids, which you don't have. . . . Entirely yours, you understand: entirely." The postscript teasingly alludes to a child they supposedly had: "Our child is all right."

When his new friend of *Russian Thought*, Golcev, had seen him after visiting Lika in Moscow, Chekhov wrote to her (July 23, 1893): "He also said your facial expression is intelligent; but he did not say a word about your beauty. Evidently, you are not beautiful—which is, of course, very, very vexing for me as an interested party."

In a similar vein, he writes on September 18, 1897: "I am thinking of you and of the reason why you like to talk and write so much about lopsided people [*krivobokie*). After some thought, I concluded that it must be because, in all probability, something is wrong with your own sides." He then teases her in several letters about her lopsidedness (*krivobokost'*). He also likes to allude to her having other admirers and lovers. In particular, he hints at the painter Levitan, whom she seems to have liked very much, as well as Potapenko. The sexual element in a broad sense—expressions of love, longing for the other, intimacies, teasing with erotic overtones—is stronger in his letters to Lika than to any other addressee. In spite of Simon Karlinsky's contention that Mizinova was no more than a "rather casual friend," there can be no doubt that their relationship was more intimate, notably in the years 1891-1893 or 1894.[21]

In his letter of March 27, 1892, he writes: "Lika, it is freezing hard outside and in my heart. . . . Alas, I am already an old young man; my love has no sun and does not produce spring either for myself or for the bird I love. Lika, it is not you I love so ardently. In you I love the sufferings of the past and my lost youth." The last sentence is a quotation from Lermontov, but the other quoted sentences from this letter could, if taken seriously, point to a tragic "impotence of the heart," so common in Turgenev's and Chekhov's works. However, on December 2 of the same year, he writes:

Dear Lika! Misha [his youngest brother] is in a hurry to leave for Moscow, to go to the tax collector's office. If that tax collector's office is a brunette in a red blouse, then give her my regards, as she will come to you for dinner today. Lika, it'll soon be summer! I wish you all the best, but don't be in the dumps and come here as soon as you can; I miss my tax collector's office.

The "brunette" refers to Countess Mamuna, who was at that time Misha's fiancée. By putting Mamuna and Mizinova on a par, he alludes to a similar position for Lika.

As soon as their relationship seemed to take a somewhat more serious turn, he would mockingly retreat. In the letter of March 29, 1892, he complains: "There is no way of secluding oneself. And more importantly, there is no Melita and no hope that I'll see her today or tomorrow. . . . Yours from top to toe, with all my heart and soul, until the last breath, to the point of self-oblivion, of turning crazy, of frenzy. Antoine Tiekoff (pronunciation of Prince Urusov)."

As is so often the case, one doesn't know how serious, how deeply felt and meant such statements were, where the impression received from one sentence is taken away or contradicted by the next. The retreat, the fear of being tied down to someone, is present in the letter of June 28, 1892:

Noble, decent Lika! As soon as you wrote me that my letters don't commit to anything, I felt greatly relieved, and now I'm writing you a long letter without any fear that some aunt of yours, reading these lines, will marry me to such a monster as you are. I, for my part, also hurry to reassure you that, in my eyes, your letters have only the significance of fragrant flowers, but not of documents; tell Baron Stackelberg, your cousin, and the dragoon officers that I shall not stand in their way. We Chekhovs, unlike they, the Ballases [Lika had an admirer by that name], don't keep young girls from living. That's our principle. So you are free.

Cantaloupe, I know: having reached mature age, you stopped loving me. But send me three thousand rubles out of gratitude for the past happiness. . . . There's a big crocodile within you, Lika, and I am actually doing the right thing when I heed common sense, and not my heart, into which you have sunk your teeth. Away, away from me! Or no, Lika, whatever comes of it, allow my head to turn giddy from your perfume and help me to draw the lasso tighter which you have already thrown around my neck. . . .

With abject deference I kiss your powder box and I envy your old shoes that see you everyday. Write me about your successes. Be well and don't forget me, who is vanquished by you. The King of Media.

Various feelings and thoughts are expressed in this letter. Lika had complained that he wrote letters without unreservedly opening his heart, which was probably true of his behavior in their personal contact as well. He fears total surrender to her, that there are other competitors for her love, and that she does not love him. He is torn between a personal bond, the need to have the lasso drawn tighter, and the urge to be free of Lika.

Thus Chekhov, so keen on contact with people in general and young women in particular, was unwilling, or unable, or intuitively averse to surrender and unite with Lika, or for that matter with any other partner. He must have awakened false expectations in several women, and certainly in Lidiia Mizinova. When his interest in her time and again came to naught, she accused him of egoism. He complained that she had "fished out of a dictionary of foreign words the word 'egoism' and treats me to it in every letter" (September 1, 1893). A year later, he wrote ominously: "I have an almost uninterrupted cough. Obviously, I have let my health slip just as much as I did you."

When she pressed him, he assumed a defensive attitude. In October 1896, he writes: "You write that our hour of bliss will come in 310 days. I am very glad, but can't we postpone that bliss another two-three years? I am so afraid. . . . I am coming in early November and will put up at your place—on the condition that you will not permit yourself liberties.'' Even more reticent is the next letter (November 11-13, 1896). He comes to Moscow but apparently does not visit her. He mentions the possibility of her coming to the restaurant of his hotel, but "after the supper I go down to my room and go to bed, happy to be finally alone." He will leave Moscow "abstaining from everything superfluous and not allowing anybody liberties, not even on persistent demands." Finally, in his last preserved letter to her, he tells her: "In your letters, as in real life, you are a most interesting woman" (January 23, 1900). At this point, Lika was certainly no more to Chekhov than a very interesting woman. He was strongly involved in his relationship with Olga Knipper.

The two series of letters, reflecting the life-long relationship with his oldest brother and approximately ten years of contact with Lidiia Mizinova, two persons who meant a great deal to him and who had a certain significance for his work, show how Chekhov, a man disinclined to bare his soul, managed to hide behind jokes and raillery at the cost of those near to him, a sort of aggressive self-defense. His early writing shows a "bacchanalia of gaiety," and the letters of those years "glow with hilarity."[22] Countless authors have "marveled at this astonishing attitude towards people, . . . his tenderness and affection."[23] But it only deepens our understanding of Chekhov when we realize and admit that this glow may sometimes cover an emotional coldness, this tenderness may alternate with an unkind prickliness. Chekhov has been rightfully characterized as "the dramatist of the emotional side of man's nature."[24] In his plays, but also in his prose, he probes into the emotional life of his heroes. But he felt no need (or was lacking in courage) to share his own more delicate sentiments and sympathies with others.

That is one discovery to which the reading of his letters leads. One reason why these letters are so valuable and have been collected, published, reissued, and translated is that they are a true companion to Chekhov's works, a mirror of his life and times, his thinking, and his relationships with other people. Though unintentionally so, they are fascinating literature in their own right. Just as some writers would not be complete without their diaries, autobiographies, auto-comments, or the annotations and reminiscences of others, Chekhov would be incomplete without the collection of thousands of letters that reveal him as an accomplished correspondent and allow glimpses into his inner self.

NOTES

1. A. P. Chekhov, *Polnoe sobranie sochinenii i pisem v 30-ti tomakh. Pis'ma* (Moscow, 1974-1983), II, 259. All subsequent citations of Chekhov's letters are from this edition and are identified by addressee and date.

2. Stated by I. S. Ezhov in his Introduction to *Pis'ma A. P. Chekhovu ego brata Aleksandra Chekhova* (Moscow, 1939), p. 22. N. I. Gitovich confirms in her Introduction to Chekhov's letters, *Polnoe sobranie sochinenii i pisem. Pis'ma*, I, 305, that "an enormous amount of Chekhov's letters remain unknown." In Volume I of this edition alone, 242 letters are mentioned that are known from references to have existed but that did not survive—among them 30 to Alexander (not counting numerous letters addressed to the whole family). His youngest brother, Mikhail Chekhov, stated: "Anton wrote us frequently from Taganrog and his letters were full of humor and consolation. They got lost in the innermost recesses of Moscow apartments." See *Vokrug Chekhova, vstrechi i vpechatleniia* (Moscow, 1964), p. 78.

3. On February 5, 1900, he wrote to A. Prugavin, who wanted to publish some of his letters in connection with his help to victims of the famine: "Forgive me, but I am against your publishing them . . . this would tie my hands in the future: whenever I would write letters, I would not be free anymore, for it would seem to me that I am writing for the press."

4. In a letter of June 21, 1887, to Alexander Chekhov, he writes jokingly in a postscript: "You may print this letter in fifty years in the *Russian Antiquities*."

5. Only 325 letters were included in this volume collected by B. N. Bochkarev, *Pis'ma A. P. Chekhova* (Moscow, 1909).

6. *Sobranie pisem A. P. Chekhova*, ed. V. Brender (Moscow, 1910, I); and *Pis'ma A. P. Chekhova*. Mariia Chekhova herself was the publisher of Volumes I-III, and Knigoizdatel'stvo pisatelei v Moskve of Volumes IV-VI and of the second printing of I-III.

7. See N. I. Gitovich, "Sud'ba epistoliarnogo naslediia Chekhova," *Polnoe sobranie sochinenii i pisem. Pis'ma*, I, 305, n. 1. See also Avrahm Yarmolinsky, ed., *Letters of Anton Chekhov* (New York: Viking Press, 1973), p. XIV.

8. Ezhov, Introduction to *Pis'ma A. P. Chekhova*, p. 22. Alexander was not Chekhov's most frequent addressee; his sister Mariia was, with 436 letters in the *Collected Works and Letters* (1974), followed by Olga Knipper (413 letters) and A. S. Suvorin (337 letters). Of Chekhov's letters to N. A. Leikin, 168 have been published.

9. Sometimes they were serious, sometimes jocular, for example, when he wrote (September 22-23, 1895): "From the description of your illness I conclude that you have an abominable syphilis plus a gigantic fistule in your anus, that developed because of an uninterrupted stream of gas."

10. *Letters of Anton Chekhov*, trans. Michael H. Heim and Simon Karlinsky (New York: Harper & Row, 1973), p. X.

11. Alcohol, however, was not Alexander's worst enemy during his entire life, as is claimed by I. S. Ezhov in his Introduction to *Pis'ma Chekhovu*, p. 22. In Alexander's letter of November 3, 1899, it turns out that he was an honorary member of the "Alcohol Society" for "his endeavor to build clinics and to obtain islands for colonies." He had made a trip to the Aland Islands (Finland) to investigate possibilities of setting up colonies for alcoholics in 1897; in that year he also published a brochure entitled *Alcoholism and the Possible Fight Against It*.

12. All citations of Alexander Chekhov's letters in this essay are from *Pis'ma A. P. Chekhovu ego brata Aleksandra Chekhova*.

13. Possibly it was the letter of February 24, cited below, in which Chekhov writes about Aleksei Alekseevich Suvorin and points to his responsibility and independence

as a journalist. He had been attacked, to Suvorin's dismay, but "they attack not your son, but A. A. Suvorin, a journalist."

14. In his letter of February 23, 1887, to Alexander, Chekhov also mentions the anger of the students and the reading public at Suvorin and *New Times*. But he does not clearly take sides. He also mentions that "many intellectuals" plan to send Suvorin a letter expressing their thanks for his publishing activity.

15. There are many examples: "Reading," "A Liberal," or "Whist" from 1884, "The Crow," "Small Fry," or "Exclamation Mark" from 1885.

16. See Chekhov's letter of October 21, 1887: "Carry out my charges without frowning. You will be lavishly rewarded: a future historian will mention you in my biography: 'He had a brother Aleksei, who carried out his orders, by which he contributed considerably to the development of Anton's talent.' "

17. However, to Alexander's story "Otreshennye i uvolennye" of 1895, Chekhov reacted rather positively: "it is very clever and well done. . . . You are making progress and I begin to recognize you as a fifth grade student" (January 19, 1895).

18. For details about Mizinova and her relationship with Chekhov, see Ernest J. Simmons, *Chekhov: A Biography* (Chicago: Chicago University Press, 1962).

19. Except in a short letter of June-July 1891, from Bogimovo, where he pretends the letter is from someone else.

20. Simmons, *Chekhov: A Biography*, p. 243.

21. *Letters of Anton Chekhov*, p. 189.

22. Kornei Chukovskii, *O Chekhove* (Moscow, 1967), pp. 12, 13.

23. *Ibid.*, p. 34.

24. Harvey Pitcher, *The Chekhov Play: A New Interpretation* (London: Chatto and Windus, 1973), pp. 12, 214.

16

Joseph L. Conrad

CHEKHOV AS SOCIAL OBSERVER: *THE ISLAND OF SAKHALIN*

> *I am not going for observations or impressions . . .*
> *(Letter to I. L. Leontev [Shcheglov], March 22,1890)*
>
> *I saw everything*: therefore, the problem is now not *what* I saw, but *how*
> I saw it.
> (Letter to Aleksei Suvorin, September 11, 1890)

In his letter to Leontev, written one month before departing on April 21, 1890, to inspect the penal colonies on Sakhalin, Anton Chekhov denied that his primary purpose was to collect observations or be stimulated by new impressions. He wrote, rather, that he wanted "simply to live a half-year differently" from the way he had lived up to that time.[1] Chekhov's motivation and preparation for the trip were much discussed by his contemporaries (sister, brother, friends, et al.) and have been treated in considerable detail by historians of literature, officials of the Tsarist and Soviet Russian governments, and by many others.[2] The introduction and notes to *Ostrov Sakhalin: Iz putevykh zapisok* (*The Island of Sakhalin: Travel Notes*) in the recent, definitive edition of Chekhov's works and letters bring together the essential information found in many earlier publications and as yet unpublished archival materials.[3] It is not the purpose of this essay to review the history of Chekhov's trip or the serial publication of the major portions of his commentaries in the journal *Russkaia mysl'* (*Russian Thought*), but rather to examine his assessment of the life and lives he found there.[4] As he wrote, it is not so much *what* he saw as *how* he saw it.[5]

The material Chekhov gathered during his three-month (July 11 —October 13, 1890) inspection of the penal colonies is impressive. In that short period he studied all aspects of the daily lives of the colonies' administrators, exiled settlers, and almost 6,000 convicts and their warders.[6] His stated purpose was to assemble statistical data. Using prison records, church documents, and personal interviews, he meticulously compiled information about each resident of the island until he had completed some 10,000 census cards, most of which are now kept in Soviet archives.[7] Those cards give the names.[8] age and place of birth, religious faith, time in the colony, primary occupation, marital status, eligibility for and receipt of financial support from the state, and details of the subject's illness (almost all convicts and exiles suffered from some disease, with diptheria, fevers, pneumonia, scurvy, syphilis, tuberculosis, and typhus at times reaching almost epidemic status).[9] But these details, collected so diligently, are of less significance than Chekhov's observations about the routine lives of those condemned to Sakhalin. He described their occupations (farming, forced labor in the mines, working as servants for administrators, and so on); conditions in the prisons and methods of punishment; schools and medical facilities; relations between the sexes, love affairs, weddings, births and funerals, and even children's games.

Of course, in bringing so much information about this distant island to readers in European Russia, Chekhov did not suppress his literary talent. Alongside the abundant statistical data, he depicted the climate and landscape in passages stylistically reminiscent of his better short stories. And now and then he introduced dramatized scenes consisting of dialogue between himself and those he interviewed. (In fact, the text reads like the commentary of an informed tour guide and, given the reader's involuntary responses to Chekhov's observations, almost becomes a dialogue in itself.) His comparisons between conditions on Sakhalin and those of European Russia emphasize the considerable differences in weather and village life. And his generalized picture, his focus on the common aspects of life rather than on the unusual, succeeds in presenting the penal colony as something from "the time of slave markets"[10] and, as he later termed it in a letter to Suvorin, "hell itself."[11]

Which statistics were of interest to Chekhov as he traveled through the island? In each settlement he noted the number of houses, households, the ratio of men to women, and the amount of land tilled. For example, he described the village of Korsakovskoe, not far from the main administrative center Aleksandrovsk, as having a population of 272, of whom 153 were male and 119 female, and comprising 58 households. He commented on the general prosperity by noting that Korsakovskoe was little different from a thriving Aleksandrovsk suburb: "Eight households have two buildings; there is one bathhouse for every nine households. Forty-five have horses, and forty-nine have cows. Many have two horses and three to four cows each" (77/108). By contrast, Krasnyi Iar had 51 households, but only 90 inhabitants, of whom the men outnumbered the women two to one. Since there was insufficient arable land to support the population, the villagers had been unable to plant enough potatoes, and all received a food ration. Chekhov's judgment was: "I do not know who selected the Krasnyi Iar site, but it is evident that it was entrusted to incompetent people who had never been in a village, and most important, had never thought about an agricultural colony" (88/119).

If living conditions in the rural villages were bad, the situation in the mining town of Due, founded in 1857, was much worse. Due had 291 inhabitants, of whom 167 were male and 124 female. Chekhov described the pervasive poverty, where crowded living quarters found people of all ages, related or not, living in one room. The town itself was surrounded by desolate mountains on one side and the constant roar of the sea on the other, and the weather was habitually dreary. But what struck him most were the moans from the settlement overseer's office and the omnipresent sound of leg-irons and chains. The effect of all these details at first dulls the reader's senses. Yet soon one begins to see the enormity of the wasted human potential, the degradation of any residual values the exiles and convicts may have brought to the colonies.

But the statistical data are ultimately uninteresting, and Chekhov's purpose was to encourage interest and, hopefully, changes in the penal system. To enable the reader to visualize life there, he describes Korsakovskoe in such terms as to make it seem similar to a normal Russian village: it is Sunday, after lunch, the weather is warm, the men are sleeping in the shade, the women getting together for gossip, the children playing in the street. The dogs appear to be well fed, and there are flowers in the gardens. And when the old tramp (*brodiaga*) employed to tend the cattle brings the herd to town, "the air is filled with summer sounds: the lowing of the cattle, the striking of the whip, the shouts of women and children chasing the calves, the dull sound of bare feet and hooves on the dusty, manure-filled path—and when it started smelling like milk, the illusion was complete" (77/109).

This landscape, like many in his short stories, develops a mood of comfort: it depicts a warm Sunday afternoon when everyone is content, even the dogs have plenty to eat. Here Chekhov has employed all the senses: sight, sound, smell, the tactile sensation of warmth, and the indirect suggestion of taste (the reference to lunch, and the well-fed dogs).[12] The scene is one of homey, Russian village life. But this is only a momentary impression, and the reader soon recalls Chekhov's earlier commentary on the lives led inside the huts, a description that is considerably less poetic:

Judging by the furnishings, this is not an *izba*, not a room, but rather a cell for solitary confinement. Where there are women and children, no matter what else, it is similar to normal housekeeping and peasant life, but still, even there the absence of something important is felt: there is no grandfather or grandmother, no old icons or inherited furniture; it seems that the household lacks a past, has no traditions. There is no icon corner, or else it is very barren and dim, without an icon lamp or any decorations; there are no traditional customs. . . . There is no cat, you do not hear the cricket on winter evenings; but the main thing is that there is no feeling of the homeland (*rodina*). (37/73)

There his description of the spiritual barrenness is in direct contrast to the portrayal of apparent comfort on a warm Sunday afternoon in Korsakovskoe.

The passage just cited represents Chekhov's summarization of the physical appearance and the furnishings of many huts and, of course, the pervasive feeling of a lack of those things that had come to be associated with Russian village life: a grandparent lying on the stove, the icon in its corner, and the continuity of folk traditions. Somewhat later, another description of the typical living conditions inside such a hut reinforces the reader's impression of spiritual emptiness and squalor. Assuming the men are occupied with penal labor, Chekhov asks: What do the adult women do when the weather is bad and the uninterrupted clanging of chains can be heard outside? He informs us:

In a given hut consisting more often than not of one room, you will find the convict's family, and with it a soldier's family, two or three convict boarders or guests, and in the same room adolescents, two or three cradles in the corners, and chickens and a dog. Garbage is strewn outside the hut and there are puddles made from tossed-out dishwater. There is nothing to do, nothing to eat, the people are tired of talking and cursing, and it is boring to go outside. How monotonously depressing everything is, and filthy too, and what misery! (*kakaia toska!*))

He then introduces a mini-scene to dramatize the situation more vividly:

The convict husband comes home from work in the evening. He wants to eat and sleep, but his wife begins to weep and wail: "You have ruined us, damn you. My life is lost, the children are lost!" And the soldier lying on the stove grumbles: "Well, she's begun to howl." Everyone is almost asleep, the children have cried their fill and are long since calmed down, but the wife cannot sleep; She is thinking and listening to the roar of the sea. Now she is miserable (*uzh ee muchaet toska*) for she pities her husband; she is ashamed that she could not keep from reproaching him. But it is the same story over again on the next day. (100/129)

Reading these passages, we recognize Chekhov the writer using his special skills to make the lower depths of Sakhalin come alive. The outdoor village scene is a landscape pregnant with what later critics would term the "Chekhovian mood" (*nastroenie*). But the reader quickly recognizes that all is not what it seems, that the physical squalor and its lack of cultural traditions lead these poor souls to an all-consuming spiritual depression that is echoed by the eternal roar of the sea outside.[13] The unfortunate woman in this particular scene suddenly feels pity for her husband's misery and is filled with self-reproach—yet Chekhov's closing statement that all this will be repeated raises an individual episode to the level of omnipresent despair. Passages such as these are very different from the seemingly dispassionate reporting of statistics found in much of *The Island*. Describing yet another village, Chekhov assesses the situation with the comment: "The poverty is truly scandalous" (119/147).

Conditions within the prisons were even more depressing, and Chekhov's descriptions of them take their toll on the reader. But in one, that of Rykovskoe, he was surprised by the sense of order, cleanliness, and discipline that prevailed: "there was such cleanliness (*chistota*) that it could satisfy the most rigid sanitary inspection, and it was apparent that this neatness (*opriatnost'*) was always maintained here no matter who visited" (134/159). As a model prison, it could be cited as an example of the government's concern for the convicts housed there. But Chekhov soon saw the guiding force behind the external order: the warden who "unfortunately had a strong passion for the birch rod. . . . His constant concern for people and at the same time for the rod, his ecstasy over corporal punishment, his brutality if you will, constitute an entirely incongruous and inexplicable combination" (134-135/160). Thus, what he saw, that is, order, cleanliness, and apparent discipline, is immediately tempered by his insight into the terrible reality of the warden's sadism, the almost incomprehensible coexistence of good and evil.

Chekhov witnessed punishment by the rod in Due, and noted the anticipatory fear and excruciating pain of the prisoner. He described the cursory examination by the German doctor to determine how many lashes could be "safely" administered; the indifferent scribe, warden, and doctor writing their official reports; the methodological strokes delivered by a muscular executioner to priestlike enumeration of the blows announced by the overseer; and, finally, the eager plea of an army medic to watch the flogging. His conclusion: "It is not only the prisoners who are coarsened and brutalized by corporal punishment, but those, too, who punish and witness the flogging. Educated persons are no exception" (332/338). Of course, the general state of conditions in the prisons was not entirely unknown to the Russian reading public, but Chekhov added a new dimension to their understanding not only of the extent of the systematic debasement of those condemned to Sakhalin, but also of the corruption of the persons responsible for the exiles and convicts.

One of Chekhov's major purposes in *The Island of Sakhalin* was to expose the inhuman treatment of women and children living there, and he devoted considerable space to this problem.[14] Once in the colonies, he had found that females were considered little more than purchasable property.[15] One of the factors contributing to such attitudes, which prevailed throughout the island, was overcrowded conditions. In Due he found one dwelling inhabited by 27 families composed of Russian and Tatar convicts, their legal wives or mistresses, and many children, including adolescent females. He wrote: "From such barbaric conditions, where girls fifteen to sixteen years old are forced to sleep alongside convicts, the reader may judge how much disrespect and contempt surround these women and children who voluntarily followed their husbands and fathers, and how little they are valued here" (101-102/131).

Official census figures had suggested a ratio of 53 women for every 100 men in the colonies. Yet Chekhov's calculations showed a far greater imbalance; he found the ratio to be approximately one woman for four men. While not considered equal in any civilized sense, women were prized as mates and housekeepers. Legal marriage was possible, but cohabitation was just as common, and, far from being opposed, such arrangements were officially encouraged. Chekhov noted: "Illegal, or as they call it here, free cohabitation has no opponents among the administration or the clergy. On the contrary, it is promoted and sanctioned. There are settlements where you will not find even one legal marriage. Such couples set up housekeeping on the same basis as legal ones. They bear children for the colony" (35/71-72).

In the early years of the penal colonies (1860-1875), arriving females had been seen as new candidates for brothels, both within the prisons and in the settlements. However, by 1890 the distribution of women was determined by power relationships within the colonies. The arrival of a boatload of females, no matter whether they were convicted prostitutes, counterfeiters, arsonists, or even murderesses, or women freely joining their convict husbands, made the then current debates in European Russia about the "woman question" seem irrelevant.[16] All incoming women were assigned by officials in Aleksandrovsk to one of the three major administrative districts of the island: the youngest and prettiest were retained in the Aleksandrovsk district, the oldest and infirm were sent to the southernmost, and those falling between these categories were assigned to the eastern district. In the south, the regional director and the settlement inspector personally made the distribution according to whether or not a settler was "worthy of getting a woman" (234; *dostoin poluchit' babu*; 249).

Chekhov once observed the arrival of women in Aleksandrovsk. Tired and afraid of the unknown they faced, they were herded into a large barracks room to spend the night before being seen by the men who had applied for "a woman." His description of the men who came for the morning viewing is one of the most moving passages in the book:

Their appearance is somehow special, indeed they look like bridegrooms. . . . When they all get to the post, they are permitted to enter the barracks and are left there with the women. The first quarter hour is spent in unavoidable tribute to embarrassment and a feeling of awkwardness. The grooms wander among the cots, silently and sternly looking over the women who sit with their eyes lowered. Each makes his choice; without any sour facial expressions or sneers, but quite seriously, "humanely" (*po-chelovechestvu*) taking into account homeliness, age, and criminal appearance. He takes a good look and tries to guess by her face which one will be a good housekeeper. Now a youngish or even an older one strikes his fancy; he sits down next to her and begins a spirited conversation. She asks if he has a samovar, a horse, a two-year-old calf, what kind of roof his house has, whether of planks or straw. He answers that he has a samovar, a horse, a calf, and that his house has a wooden roof. Only after the housekeeping examination, when both feel that a deal has been concluded, does she dare to ask: "But you won't hurt me in any way, will you?" (235; *A obizhat' vy menia ne budete?* 249)

Chekhov adds that after the interview the man takes his officially provided concubine home on a wagon rented perhaps with his last kopeck. Once there, she starts the samovar, and the neighbors remark enviously that "so-and-so's already got a woman."[17]

That passage represents Chekhov's literary talent at its best. Another observer might have written simply: "The men come in the morning, look the women over, ask a few questions, and when an agreement is reached, take them home." Instead, Chekhov begins with an allusion to normally happy momentous occasions (weddings) by likening the men to bridegrooms and describing the care they have taken in dressing, and then notes everyone's very human, embarrassed silence; he describes in gently ironic terms the selection process (accomplished "*humanely*") with its "spirited" conversation about basic problems of survival (food, shelter, animals, and so on), and once all that has been settled, he records the woman's touching question: "*A obizhat' vy menia ne budete?*"

The shortage of women was so great that almost no females were excluded as candidates for distribution. Chekhov writes that many women of 50 or more were concubines of much younger exiles and overseers alike, and that it was often the case that both mother and daughter came to Sakhalin and were given over as housekeepers. He saw several young girls, even prepubertal ones, living with older men. He also noted that women of almost any age became pregnant, even those who would otherwise have been thought to have been beyond normal child-bearing years.

But a woman was valued for reasons other than housekeeping and increasing the population of the colonies. Even as a mistress or concubine, she was entitled to a daily ration of food, and this might be the only source of nourishment for the man with whom she lived. In addition to this often essential contribution, a woman could bring money for the household. Bored and lonely, she might resume, or turn to, prostitution, an activity which her mate sometimes encouraged. In this case, Chekhov noted, the man would take over responsibility for the samovar and other household duties, and he would suffer in silence when the woman chided him for deficiencies in their lives. Chekhov pointed out that this situation was in considerable contrast to the widespread practice of wife-beating which could be found everywhere in the colonies.

According to Chekhov's calculations some 40 percent of the women on Sakhalin were not convicts or exiles, but had followed their husbands for love, out of a religious conviction that only God could separate man and wife, or because of the stigma of being a convict's wife and the resulting taunts from her fellow villagers. Nor were the women all Russian. He saw Tatar, Jewish, Gypsy, Polish, and German women among those who had followed their men to the distant prison colony. Having left their homes knowing that life would not be easy, they were nevertheless shocked to find the poverty, hunger, and despair that awaited them. But Chekhov saw that they, too, soon became resigned to their situation and turned to prostitution; some even involved their own fourteen- and fifteen-year-old daughters by arranging marriage or cohabitation for them.

While the number of legally married couples was somewhat larger than that of common-law cohabitation (860 versus 782 households, respectively), Chekhov found that a legal marriage was generally viewed as a luxury, not a necessity. Curious about local wedding customs, he discovered that the ceremony and attending festivities could sometimes be happy and noisy as in the case of Ukrainian weddings in the Tymovskoe region, or even in the capital Aleksandrovsk, where printed invitations like those in Moscow were often sent. But on the whole, he witnessed weddings which he described as modest and sadly dull (253; *skromno i skuchno*; 266). In a short passage he writes of one wedding ceremony, attended by both legally free and convict women, waiting impatiently for it to begin:

Now someone whispered excitedly "They're coming!" The members of the choir began to clear their throats. A wave of people came through the door, someone shouted sternly, and the couple entered: he, a convict typesetter about twenty-five, in a frock coat and starched collar turned at the corners, wearing a white tie, and she, a female convict three or four years younger, in a blue dress with white lace and a flower in her hair. . . . The groom's party, typesetters, were also wearing white ties. Father Egor stepped from behind the altar, leafed through a little book at the lectern: "Our Lord be praised!" he proclaimed, and the ceremony began. When the priest asked God to wed them in glory and honor, and placed the wreaths on their heads, the women's faces had an expression of tenderness and joy, and it seemed it was forgotten that the wedding was taking place in a prison church in penal exile, far, far away from their homeland. . . . But when the church was empty after the ceremony, and smelled of candles which the watchman hastened to put out, there was a feeling of sadness. They went out to the front. Rain. There was a crowd in the dark around the doors, and two carriages: the newly-weds in one, the other empty. "Father, come here," the voices resounded, and tens of hands stretched out to Father Egor from the darkness as if to take hold (*skhvatit'*) of him. "Come, favor us!" Father was seated in the carriage and driven to the newly-weds'. (293/304)

Here Chekhov is not merely reporting a wedding. Using his special talent as a writer, he makes it come alive in three distinct stages. First, there is the attention-getting, introductory "Now" (*Vot*), the hushed excitement of the women, and the choir's posturing. The scene is then enlivened by the entering wave of the wedding party and the stern command for quiet, the emotion in the women's faces. And after this happy mood has been established, Chekhov reminds us that all this is far away, in exile. In the second stage, which is concerned with the ceremony (*venchanie*) itself, the priest's exalted, Biblical language elevates the occasion to one of solemn ritual. But the rituals are soon over and the atmosphere is noticeably changed. The third stage of this event is marked by the smell of hastily extinguished candles, the darkness of the empty church, and the rain outside which combine to create a melancholy mood. These latter details, and Chekhov's description of the beggars pleading for blessings and alms from the departing priest, portray a scene that very effectively contrasts with the momentary feeling of warmth and happiness associated with the wedding. All this is provided with the same skill and feeling of his best fiction.

As a doctor, Chekhov was intrigued by the relatively high birthrate in the colonies.[18] One reason for the women's extraordinary fertility was often given as the weather (which he describes as normally dark, rainy, and cold). Yet even older women who had been childless in Russia found themselves bearing children. He introduced birth statistics for the preceding year (1889) which showed that there was only a slightly higher percentage of babies born per capita there than in European Russia. But he discounted this as a deceptive comparison, for there were relatively fewer women on Sakhalin than on the mainland. Thus, he wrote, their fertility was indeed "significantly higher than in Russia overall." And he offered an explanation for this higher birthrate:

The hunger, their longing for the motherland, the inclination to vice, and imprisonment—the whole sum of unfavorable conditions in exile do not deprive them of their reproductive capacity. . . . The cause of increased female fertility and the high birthrate is, first of all, the emptiness of the exiles' life, the forced staying at home for men and women because of lack of outside industry and earnings, and the monotonous nature of life, for which the satisfaction of sexual instincts is often the only possible recreation, and second, the fact that the majority of the women here are of reproductive age. (254/267)

Just as elsewhere in *The Island*, here the actual situation, that is, what he saw, is given an interpretive explanation. And after commenting that there might be other, less immediate causes for this phenomenon, he continues by making a suggestion often heard after devastating wars:

Perhaps one could look at the high birthrate as a means given by nature to the population for their struggle with harmful, destructive influences and above all with such enemies of the natural order as the small number of inhabitants and the scarcity of women. The greater the danger threatening the population, the more babies are born, and in this sense the reason for the high birthrate may be the unfavorable conditions. (255/268)

This example and many others demonstrate that the pattern of observation which Chekhov developed for his study of life on Sakhalin is consistent: first, the reader is offered statistical data and other relevant facts; then Chekhov's comments suggest that the situation may be otherwise; and finally, he provides his own educated interpretation for the given situation.

Despite the priests' encouragement to "Be fruitful, go forth and multiply" at the end of the wedding ceremony, children born on Sakhalin were received with less than joyous acclamations. Far from being considered a blessing, a new baby was often unwelcome. Chekhov writes that few lullabies were sung and that malevolent laments (*zloveshchie prichityvaniia*) were frequent. Parents would complain that there was nothing to feed the baby and that it would be better if God took the child back. When a baby cried, a parent would often scream: "Shut up, I wish you'd die!" (257; *Zamolchi, chtob ty izdokh!*; 270). Yet in Chekhov's view, the children were the

most useful, most needed and most pleasant people on Sakhalin . . . and even the exiles understand this and value them highly. They bring an element of purity, gentleness and happiness into the coarsened, morally decrepit Sakhalin family. . . . The presence of children gives moral support to the exiles, and . . . often children are the only things that bind the exiled men and women to life, save them from despair, from final degradation. (257/270)

Chekhov's assessment of the lives of young children was not entirely positive, however, for he observed that their innocence was short-lived. He noted that they were indifferent to the sight and sounds of men in chains, and that their activities often involved games reflecting already routine situations. He tells of "Soldiers and Convicts," a game in which a child would bark commands to other playmates considered prisoners, and "Vagrant," where one child was hunted down by playmate-soldiers. Moreover, he found, words such as birch rod, whip, execution, irons and chains, and even concubine were common among the younger children. And he could not help seeing that the longer they lived, the more pale and thin they became, and that child mortality from starvation was a frequent occurrence. The problem was of such magnitude that he criticized official classifications of children as "poorest" or "disabled" for purposes of food distribution, and he firmly recommended that all the hungry should be helped.[19]

If weddings and the birth of a child were little cause for happiness, funerals were considered an end to misery accepted indifferently by adults and with little understanding by children. Chekhov attended a depressing funeral of a mother of two, during which he noticed that the ritual singing of laments was unusually brief (it lasted only two or three minutes). Summoning up his talent for literary landscapes, he first describes the cemetery on a cliff above the "quiet sea, shining in the sun." He tells of the "little crosses, one like the other, all silently marking the convict graves, and two other, larger ones, for the explorer Mitsul' and a supervisor, Selivanov, killed by a convict.'' In a mood of philosophical reflection, he continues:

Mitsul' will still be remembered a while, but all those lying under the little crosses, the ones who were broken, who tried to escape, who clanged with their chains, no one need remember them. Perhaps only somewhere on the Russian steppes around a bonfire, or in a forest, an old trailboss (*staryi obozchik*) will start to tell a tale, out of boredom and loneliness, of how somebody in their village turned to crime; his listener, glancing at the darkness, will shudder and a night bird will cry out—that's all the wake they'll have.

Following this passage, which echoes his beautiful stories "Happiness" (1887) and "The Steppe"(1888), Chekhov goes on:

The newly dug grave was partially filled with water. The convict-pallbearers, puffing, with their faces perspiring, loudly talking about something wholly unrelated to the funeral, finally brought the casket and set it down next to the grave. The casket was wooden, hastily nailed together, and unpainted. "Well?" said one. The quickly raised casket splashed into the water. Chunks of clay crashed down on its lid; the casket shuddered, the water splashed, but the convicts, working with their shovels, continued to talk about something else. . . . The deceased woman's boarder was complaining: "Now where am I going to put the kids? Just try to take care of them! I went to the supervisor, asked him to give me a woman—he won't do it!" (294-95/305-6)

Chekhov was struck by the fact that the funeral procession included the deceased's eldest son, a child of three or four, and he concluded this funeral scene with a literary *tour de force* reminiscent of the endings of several short stories which leave the reader stunned by the unexpected outcome:[20] Chekhov writes that when asked where his mother was, the little boy replied "They buried her!" (*Za-akopali!*) and burst into laughter with a gesture toward the grave (295; *makhnul rukoi*; 306).

In this episode, Chekhov has painted a vivid picture of the final event in human life. He has reintroduced the leitmotif of the sea and philosophical reflection on one's own relative insignificance (and simultaneously reminded his readers of that fact and of his own minor masterpiece, "Happiness," and the longer, but equally enchanting "The Steppe"). The contrast of such an unceremonious event to funerals in European Russia made a lasting impression on Chekhov, and, one can readily imagine, his description of the scene must have greatly affected the contemporary reader.[21]

In sum, Chekhov's monograph on Sakhalin is both similar to and yet very different from his better known stories and plays. Because of his desire to impress the reader with the enormous waste of human potential he found there, the statistical data citing numbers of men and women, births, households and animals, and so forth, sometimes create an effect akin to that of dry, official reporting, a quality unassociated with his artistic works. But the data only initiate discussion of the desperate circumstances of the convicts' and settlers' existence. By shedding light on the hapless fate of women and children in the colonies he reveals a social awareness not entirely common in his time. Here he is concerned not only with the European Russian peasantry, as were many political activists, but with even poorer unfortunates whose very lives were being threatened by the policies of the Tsarist government.

There are still other differences: Chekhov openly records the prevailing attitudes, for example, those held by men toward women and children, administrative neglect of the inhabitants, and everyone's indifference to death. Such attitudes would have been suggested indirectly in his prose fiction or shown by behavior in his plays. Likewise, his straightforward criticisms of governmental policies, specific individuals, and the administration of the colonies as a whole, together with his clearly stated recommendations for changes needed to rectify that "hell itself," are far different in style and temperament from what we are accustomed to finding in Chekhov's literary works.

And yet there are notable similarities between *The Island* and his more famous literary productions. The compassion and skill he applies to dramatize those distant, forgotten lives are felt throughout. The miniature scenes such as the selection of "a woman," the wedding, life inside a typical hut, and the funeral are complete with descriptive adjectives and adverbs, many of which have openly subjective (both positive and negative) tones. And the landscapes, while not as dominant as in many of his short stories, establish a mood of cold, grey monotony and despair which is appropriate to Chekhov's purpose. Thus, *The Island of Sakhalin* emerges as an evocative, highly sympathetic statement for just and humane treatment not only of the male convicts and settlers, but of the women and children as well. In this work, Chekhov's literary skills, his observant understanding, and his own "talent for humanity"[22] combine to present an eloquent appraisal of the unfortunate human condition of all residents of the island.[23]

NOTES

The initial stimulus for this study grew out of research supported by the International Research and Exchanges Board (Moscow, 1974) and by the University of Kansas (Sabbatical Leave, Spring 1976). Writing of the final manuscript was aided by University of Kansas General Research Fund grant No. 3320-XO-0038 (July 1982). An abbreviated version was read at the Second International Chekhov Conference, held at Tufts University, April 1-2, 1983.

1. A. P. Chekhov, *Polnoe sobranie sochinenii i pisem v 30-ti tomakh. Pis'ma* (Moscow, 1976), IV, 45. All citations from the Russian original will be from this

edition and abbreviated as *Sochineniia* (Works) or *Pis'ma* (Letters)). The English text can be found in *Letters of Anton Chekhov*, trans. Michael H. Heim and Simon Karlinsky (New York: Harper & Row, 1973; hereafter abbreviated as *Letters*), pp. 162-164.

2. Chekhov's trip and its position in his development as a writer concerned with social issues are treated by G. Berdnikov, in *A. P. Chekhov: Ideinye i tvorcheskie iskaniia*, 2d ed. (Leningrad, 1970), pp. 261-321. Useful introductions to this topic in English have been written by Ernest J. Simmons in *Chekhov: A Biography* (Boston: Little, Brown and Co., 1962), Kenneth J. Atchity, "Chekhov's Infernal Island" (*Research Studies*, 1968, Washington University Press, pp. 335-340), and by Ronald Hingley, *A New Life of Anton Chekhov* (New York: Alfred A. Knopf, 1976).

3. M. L. Semanova's introductory essay and almost line-by-line commentaries to the text (*Sochineniia*, XIV-XV, 742-886) provide a wealth of sources for those interested in pursuing the subject in greater detail. By contrast, the recent English edition translated by Luba and Michael Terpak, Anton Chekhov, *The Island. A Journey to Sakhalin* (New York: Washington Square Press, 1967), hereafter abbreviated as *Sakhalin*, offers almost no commentary, and the translation itself is often inaccurate. Therefore, all passages cited in English have been revised and corrected according to the original. Nevertheless, corresponding page numbers of the Terpak translation will be included in parentheses for those who do not read Russian, with the English page number followed by the Russian, for example, (77/108).

4. Three installments appeared in 1893 and five in 1894, and a revised, expanded version of the entire work was first published as a special issue of *Russian Thought* in 1895.

5. *Pis'ma*, IV, 133. *Letters*, p. 171.

6. Chekhov cites a census of January 1, 1890, listing 5,905 convicts (*Sochineniia*, XIV-XV, 229) of both sexes. Once the sentence had been served, return to the mainland was forbidden, and the convicts were forced to live on Sakhalin as settlers. Chekhov devotes an entire chapter (XXII) to the problems of attempted escape, punishment, and the settlers' overwhelming desire to return to European Russia.

7. According to the notes (*Sochineniia*, XIV-XV, 754), 7,600 cards are held in Moscow's Lenin Library and 222 in the Central State Archives for Literature and Art (TsGALI).

8. At the outset of his census-taking activity, Chekhov's natural curiosity was aroused by the very names of the convicts. He noticed, for example, the unusual frequency of first names such as Karl and Napoleon. But it was the surnames which struck his fancy:

By some strange chance there are many persons called Bogdanov (God-given) and Bespalov (Missing fingers). There are many curious surnames, Shkandyba (Limper), Zheludok (Stomach), Bezbozhnii (Godless) and Zevak (Yawner). . . . The most common name among the vagrants is Ivan, and the most common surname is Nepomniashchii (Don't-remember). Here are some of the vagrants' names: Mustafa Nepomniashchii, . . . Vasilii Bezotechestva (Basil the Countryless), Iakov Besprozvaniia (Jacob the Nameless), . . . Chelovek Neizvestnogo Zvaniia (Man with Unknown Name). (*Sochineniia*, XIV-XV, 68-69; *Sakhalin*, p. 30)

9. At several places in the text Chekhov mentions diseases suffered by the inhabitants of Sakhalin, and he devotes the whole of Chapter XXIII to such problems and the medical facilities available to treat them.

10. The term *rabovladel'cheskaia epokha* is found only in Chekhov's early manuscripts and does not appear in the final text; see *Sochineniia*, XIV-XV, 593.

11. December 9, 1890; *tselyi ad*; *Pis'ma*, IV, 139; *Letters*, p. 173. And he added: "The poverty, ignorance and pettiness are enough to drive you to despair."

Within the text Chekhov often comments on the observations of earlier visitors to the penal colonies, and he is critical of those who described the prison conditions in less than accurate terms. Here is a representative example:

Some writers saw the round dance (*khorovod*) in Rykovskoe and heard the sounds of the accordion and boisterous songs. But I neither saw nor heard anything of the sort, and I cannot imagine girls dancing the *Khorovod* near the prison. Even if I were to hear a boisterous song, beside the sounds of chains and the guards' shouting, I would consider it a bad sign, for a kind and merciful person would not start singing near a prison. The peasants and settlers and their wives and children are oppressed by the prison regime. The prison situation, . . with its extraordinary strict regulations and unavoidable administrative surveillance, keeps them in constant tension and fear. . . . Escapees, prison usurers and thieves abuse them. The executioner frightens them as he walks down the street. Guards debauch their wives and daughters, but most of all, the prison continually reminds them of their past and of who and where they are. (223/241-242)

12. For an analysis of Chekhov's techniques for nature description, see my "Anton Chekhov's Literary Landscapes," in *Chekhov's Art of Writing. A Collection of Critical Essays*, ed. P. Debreczeny and T. Eekman (Columbus, Ohio: Slavica Publishers, 1977), pp. 82-99.

13. Chekhov introduced the constant roar of the sea in this passage (and elsewhere in *The Island*) as well as in the short stories "Lights" (1888) and "The Lady with the Lapdog" (1899) as a leitmotif suggesting something like the medieval maxim *memento mori*. Here it also contrasts the woman's psychological state with the earlier, appealing scene of Sunday afternoon contentment.

14. Chekhov had noticed the unusual nature of Russian Far East morality even before crossing the Tatar Strait. He writes:

Chivalrous behavior toward women has been developed almost to a cult and yet, at the same time it is not considered reprehensible to let a friend have your wife for money. Or an even better example: on the one hand there is an absence of class prejudice—people treat exiles as equals—but on the other, it is not a sin to shoot down a Chinaman in the forest like a dog. (3/43)

15. Early in his writing career Chekhov had described the plight of lower class Moscow women who were treated as possessions; see especially the stories "Aniuta" and "The Chorus Girl," both written in 1886. For discussion of Chekhov's concern for such women and other, better educated but equally unfortunate females, see Toby W. Clyman, "Chekhov's Victimized Women," in the *Russian Language Journal* 28, 100 (Spring 1974): 26-31.

16. A thorough exposition of the "woman question" in Russia and the Soviet Union can be found in: Richard Stites, *The Women's Liberation Movement in Russia: Feminism, Nihilism, and Bolshevism, 1860-1930* (Princeton, N.J.: Princeton University Press, 1978).

17. Chekhov noted that the male populace scarcely thought of women as human beings, and he quotes a petition presented to one of the local administrators: "We must humbly ask your Excellency to let us have cows for milk in the above-named place and females for housekeeping" (236/251). And he adds: "Human dignity, the

femininity and modesty of a female convict are never taken into consideration. It is as if it were understood that all this were burned out of her by her disgrace or that she had lost it as she went from prison to prison or convict way stations" (237/251).

18. For a stimulating commentary on the influence of Chekhov's medical trainng (and of one of his mentors in particular) on his literary manner of observation, see V. B. Kataev, "O roli shkoly G. A. Zakhar'ina v tvorchestve Chekhova," *Filologicheskie nauki* 6, 11 (1968): 104-107, and *Proza Chekhova: problemy interpretatsii* (Moscow, 1979), especially ch. 2, pp. 87-140.

19. In a footnote he suggested that charitable organizations in Russia should contribute to the feeding of children without worrying about fraud, and he warned: "It is better to be deceived than to deceive oneself" (262/273).

20. For discussion of this technique, see Thomas Winner, *Chekhov and His Prose* (New York: Holt, Rinehart and Winston, 1966), and my "Unresolved Tension in Chekhov's Stories, 1886-1888," *The Slavic and East European Journal* 16 (Spring 1972): 55-64.

21. Chekhov had written of this incident in a letter to A. F. Koni (January 26, 1891; *Pis'ma*, IV, 168; *Letters*, pp. 179-180), but a comparison of the two descriptions reveals the earlier version as matter-of-fact reporting, while the passage in *The Island of Sakhalin* is worthy of his better stories. For an assessment of the effect of Chekhov's monograph on Russian society's views concerning prison management, see Koni's memoir, "Vospominaniia o Chekhove," in A. F. Koni, *Sobranie sochinenii v 8-i tomakh* (Moscow, 1969), VII, 375-391.

22. The narrator in Chekhov's "An Attack of Nerves" (1888) uses this expression to characterize the (Vsevolod) Garshin-like hero, Vasil'ev, who, as a student of law and jurisprudence is disturbed by Moscow's open prostitution and complacent disregard for the women involved. For an analysis of the story, see my "Chekhov's 'An Attack of Nerves,' " *The Slavic and East European Journal* 13, 4 (Winter 1969): 429-443.

23. Chekhov returned to European Russia on December 5, 1890. The experience of having lived somewhat more than "half a year differently" was to have a profound effect on his subsequent literary work. For recent and perceptive treatments of the ties between that experience and his prose fiction, see V. B. Kataev, "Avtor v *Ostrove Sakhaline* i v rasskaze 'Gusev' " in *V tvorcheskoi laboratorii Chekhova* (Moscow, 1974), pp. 232-252, and E. A. Polotskaia, "Posle Sakhalina," in *Chekhov i ego vremia* (Moscow, 1977), pp. 117-137.

PART VIII

Translation

17

Lauren G. Leighton

CHEKHOV IN ENGLISH

Probably no other Russian writer has been as widely translated in English as Chekhov. By widely is meant profusely—by many translators over a significant period of time, in diverse selections by chronology, length, form, type, or theme, and in numerous editions revised by both translator and editors, in accordance with the differing norms of British and American English usage. D. S. Mirsky has said that Chekhov is an easy writer to translate, and this is true if we do not forget that he is an extraordinarily nuanced stylist. Chekhov is otherwise a straightforward writer whose techniques are evident because they are used so consistently throughout his oeuvre. Because he is easy to translate, there are remarkably few differences in choice of syntax and lexicon among his translators. Because his style is so subtle, these few variations can be telling.

English-language translations of Chekhov's works provide the opportunity not only to assess the competence of his translators, but also to trace the history of the art of translation in this century as far as Russian literature is concerned. Theory of translation is well developed in world letters. More has been written about the theory and practice of translation in the past quarter century than in the two millennia before.[1] But with regard to the history of translation—the development of principles and methods— George Steiner was correct when he remarked that "in the history and theory of literature translation has not been a subject of the first importance. It has figured marginally, if at all."[2] In Soviet letters, on the other hand, detailed stylistic histories of translation have been written for several literatures, and Iu. D. Levin has written excellent studies of the evolution of principles of translation.[3] Soviet translators and theorists of translation have established a solid scholarly basis for a history of Soviet translation, and this base is firmly grounded in tested methods of analyzing style and a stable critical terminology.

It is useful to assess the quality of translations of Chekhov's stories and plays in a historical perspective—the evolution of principles, methods, and aesthetics in terms of language and style. How have we treated Chekhov in our world, and how has the art of translation developed in the course of the best part of a century of experience in translating Chekhov? Translations of the stories can be traced from the pioneer work of R. E. C. Long, Mrs. Constance Garnett, and S. S. Koteliansky (with J. M. Murry or Gilbert Cannan) from the early century into the 1930s to Avrahm Yarmolinsky, David Magarshack, Robert Payne, and Ann Dunnigan in the 1950s and 1960s to the recent work of Ronald Hingley and Patrick Miles and Harvey Pitcher. Analyses can concentrate on passages chosen to represent problems of Chekhov's style as a whole and on similarly representative indicators of specific problems of lexicon, syntax, and intonation. Translations of the plays, which have been analyzed before, can be examined for their diction and performance by measuring the most popular texts of Tyrone Guthrie and Leonid Kipnis, Avrahm Yarmolinsky, David Magarshack, Ann Dunnigan, Stark Young, and Ronald Hingley against the older texts. (Separate bibliographies of stories and plays, are appended to this article.) The main questions of historical perspective are: the temporariness of a translation in relation to the enduring quality of its original; the contemporaneity of translation—the condition that each generation translates for itself anew in accord with changing tastes; choice and decision in the process of translation; the development of principles and methods through the process of improving translation on the models of predecessors. Texts will be measured against what Marilyn Rose has called the autonomy spectrum— the gradations of translation types from the free translation or variation at one pole to the still not happily defined, yet vastly preferred, faithful or artistic translation at the median point to the almost universally despised literalist (or precise or scientific or linguistic) method at the opposite pole.[4]

Modern translators know well the historical problems of contemporaneity and temporariness, changes of taste, and the need for each generation to translate for itself anew. Chekhov's style does not seem outdated in Russian because his stories are read in his time and place. His style may very well seem dated because short story techniques have become far more sophisticated (not least thanks to his example) and style tastes have changed. But not *out*dated. When we read Chekhov's stories in the translations of Long or Koteliansky, on the other hand, his style seems definitely outdated to us. These translations do not satisfy us; they even offend us. This is not a question of competence. It is a matter of changing tastes and the condition that where Russians consciously or unconsciously suspend their time judgment of Chekhov himself, readers of translations are accustomed to make severe judgments out of time, in their own time. Even a cursory reading of Long's translations yields the strongly marked British lexical choices of his time. In *The Kiss, and Other Stories* Chekhov's landowners in "The Kiss" become "local country gentlemen" who are served "biscuits" by "footmen," while his army officers are obliged to wear "mufti" and exclaim "I like his cheek!" Long's version of "Women" features "country gentlemen" again, servants who address their masters as "your honour," and peasants who drop in at the local "drink-shop." The same outdated and out-of-place lexicon is obtrusive in Koteliansky and Murry's *The Bet, and Other Stories*. A character in "The Bet" loses his "last farthing," and in "A Dreary Story" we find such British realia as "navvy," "knight," and " 'satis' " (a student's grade). British expressions like "Fire away!" "high-class," and "a nice lot" abound in this translation. Similarly, in Koteliansky's *Tchekhov's Plays and Stories* we find, in "My Life," British realia like "porridge" for *kasha* and "foreman," expressions like "By Jove!" and "queer fish," and silly Anglicized names like "Mr. Cheeky Snout," "Radish," and "Little Profit." Early translators are generally wise about transliterating such realia as *khalat*, *shtchi*, and *kvas*, but they also use the device to cover up uncertain knowledge of Russian culture. Long transcribes *unosni* and *unosniye* for the military technical term "forerider," and Koteliansky and Murry seem not to know that *sossoulki* are ice delicacies. Realia are like anachronisms—it is no more advisable to put English porridge into Russia than it is to put an automobile in the eighteenth century. Experience has banned nationalization—Americanization, Russification—from modern translation aesthetics.

We can see how unobligingly time deals with translations and at the same time begin to appreciate the process of improvement in the art of translation by examining two older versions of a difficult passage in Chekhov, the colloquial speech of old Semën in "In Exile," the first in Koteliansky and Cannan's *The House with the Mezzanine, and Other Stories*, the second in Long's *The Black Monk, and Other Stories*:

"You will get used to it," said Brains with a laugh. "You are young yet and foolish; the milk is hardly dry on your lips, and in your folly you imagine that there is no one unhappier than you. . . ."

"You'll get used to it," said Wiseacre, grinning. "You're young and foolish now—your mother's milk is still wet on your lips, only youth and folly could make you imagine there's no one more miserable than you."

Old Semën's speech is not illiterate, but it is markedly substandard. He says *privyknesh', moloko na gubakh ne obsokhlo, kazhetsia tebe po gluposti*. Long's conveyance of this colloquial standard is better than Koteliansky and Cannan's, at least to the extent that he uses contractions, and his change of the word "laugh" to "grinning" helps him to avoid (almost) the cloying tone of older-man's-advice that ruins Semën's character in Koteliansky and Cannan's misinterpretation. His tone is mean; he does not sympathize with the young Tatar in these and other nagging admonitions. Both translations convey the saying "the milk's not dry on your lips yet" literally, and both are too literary in choice of lexicon: "youth and folly," "imagine," "you will get used to it," and especially the too graceful "you are young yet and foolish."

Ronald Hingley's modern version of the same passage in *The Oxford Chekhov* is superior:

'You'll settle down,' said Foxy with a laugh. 'You're young and stupid yet, you ain't dry behind the ears, like; and you're daft enough to think, you're the unluckiest man on earth.'

Here Semën's speech, and thus his character, have been caught more deftly, and Hingley is also more imaginative. He has replaced the Russian saying with, "you ain't dry behind the ears, like," and has even heightened the original a bit by adding the telling colloquialism "like." *Privyknesh'* has been changed to "you'll settle down." Hingley can be criticized for being too colloquial. "Daft" is too British, and in other passages he obliges Semën to say "that's all daft, mate," "I ain't just another yokel, mate," "I ain't a bumpkin, like," and "it ain't just us stupid peasants that comes a cropper." Viktor Khinkis has warned translators not to go too far in conveying colloquial speech. There has to be a balance between lexical equivalents—neither too weak nor too strongly marked.[5] Hingley is rather more brave than successful here. But he recognizes colloquial speech when he sees it—something that was beyond the competence of Long, Koteliansky, and Cannan. His version can be usefully compared to Ann Dunnigan's modern version in *Selected Stories*, where she refused to reproduce colloquial speech, but at least conveyed Semën's character:

"You'll get used to it!" said Preacher with a laugh. "You're still young and foolish—the milk's hardly dry on your lips—and in your foolishness you think there's no one more unfortunate than you."

Dunnigan has avoided the too literary words that mar the older translations; her vocabulary is appropriately simple. "The milk's hardly dry on your lips," "in your foolishness you think"—these phrases indicate that Semën is jeering at the young Tatar. Dunnigan has erred in the direction of blandscript, as Hingley has erred in favor of colloquiality, but both modern translations are satisfying, as the older versions are not.

Mrs. Garnett has often been cited as an example of an outdated translator, but the fact is that her work has survived extraordinarily well. Her versions are still used by such modern editors as Ralph E. Matlaw, Magarshack, Yarmolinsky, David Greene, and Edmund Wilson (Wilson did not acknowledge his use of her texts). No matter how persistently some modern critics try to dismiss her work as hopelessly "Victorian," she remains an icon—her thirteen-volume collection of stories has just been republished in a new paperback format. An examination of the texts of her first and her subsequently improved translations shows very few changes: the edited texts in Matlaw, Magarshack, Greene, and those noted as "newly improved" by her son David Garnett are almost the same. Perhaps we have been conditioned to "hear" Russian writers in Mrs. Garnett's popular translations, so that we are too receptive to her style, but analysis indicates that her work is superior to that of her contemporaries and that she developed principles of translation far ahead of others. It would undoubtedly be possible to compile a large list of slips from her vast oeuvre, but a search through *The Lady with the Dog, and Other Stories* yields only such examples as "he had been so schooled by bitter experience" in "The Lady with the Dog" and "have a peep at it" in "A Doctor's Visit," while *The Schoolmaster, and Other Stories* offers only "a bit of pie" and "your honour" in "The Schoolmaster" and "how queer it is, really" and "flunkey" in "Enemies." Mrs. Garnett was aware of the dangers of tying a foreign work too closely to one's own time and place, and she clearly made an effort to avoid strongly marked idioms and to be sensible about realia.

A feature that distinguishes old and new translations of Chekhov is that the old swing too far in the direction of either literalism or free translation, often inappropriately, without a strong instinct for when to be more accurate, when to be more imaginative, while the new stay close to the original and know when to be literal or free. This is also true of use of translation devices—modern translators are more adept at using embellishment, compensation, substitution, rephrasing, equivalency, reconstitution. Compare, for example, Mrs. Garnett's version of the seduction scene in "The Lady with the Dog" in her *Select Tales of Tchehov* (the improved 1961 text) with Robert Payne's version of the same scene in *The Image of Chekhov*:

But in this case there was still the *diffidence*, the *angularity* of inexperienced youth, an *awkward feeling* and there was a sense of *consternation* as though someone had suddenly knocked at the door. The attitude of Anna Sergeyevna—"the lady with the dog"—to what had happened was *somehow peculiar*, *very grave*, as though it were her fall—so it seemed, and it was *strange* and *inappropriate*. Her face *drooped and faded*, and on both sides of it her long hair hung down *mournfully*. She mused in a *dejected* attitude like "the woman who was a sinner in an old-fashioned picture."

But here was all the *shyness* and *awkwardness* of inexperienced youth: a feeling of *embarrassment*, as though someone had suddenly knocked on the door. Anna Sergeyevna, "the lady with the pet dog," accepted what had happened in her own special way, *gravely* and *seriously*, as though she had accomplished her own downfall, an attitude which he found *odd* and *disconcerting*. Her features *faded and drooped* away and on both sides of her face the long hair hung *mournfully* down, while she sat musing *disconsolately* like an adulteress in an antique painting.

Mrs. Garnett's version is slightly Victorian—the telling embellishment " 'the woman who was a sinner' " for simply *greshnitsa*. Payne's version is a bit libertarian—his invention of such syntax as "in her own special way" and his outright concoction "as though she had accomplished her own downfall," which in the original is simply "as if it were her own downfall." The Garnett version is more accurate—she retains the key word "angularity" where Payne replaces it with "awkwardness" (and thereby co-opts *nelovkoe chuvstvo*, "awkward feeling," and had to omit it). Mrs. Garnett's word "consternation" for *rassteriannost'* is closer than Payne's "embarrassment," which is too weak for what Anna Sergeyevna feels, while his "disconcerting" is too strong for *nekstati*, which she has caught with "inappropriate." Mrs. Garnett errs by elaborating *zdes'* into "in this case," while Payne recreates the specificity of the scene—the seduction has just occurred *here* in this late afternoon Yalta hotel room. The translators hit on the identical equivalents "faded," "drooped," and "mournfully," but Payne's reversal to create the phrase "faded and drooped away" provides a more graceful phonetic and rhythmic pattern. Payne's choices of "shyness" for *nesmelost'* and "disconsolately" for *unylaia* are better than Mrs. Garnett's "diffidence" and "dejected." Payne has erred by attributing the sense of Anna Sergeyevna's "strange and inappropriate" attitude to Gurov—Chekhov and Mrs. Garnett have it as a vague feeling in the atmosphere of the room. Payne's phraseology is more imaginative and graceful than Mrs. Garnett's, but he takes liberties to please modern readers.

The translators have used the same devices and techniques. Both have embellished (Payne has even invented), compensated, rephrased, substituted. We can argue with a few choices, but both have caught the most important feature of the scene: Chekhov's words progress carefully—with physiological precision—from shy and angular and awkward to strange or odd to mournfully and disconsolately. We can see how well both translators have served Chekhov by comparing their work to Koteliansky's failed version in *Tchekhov's Plays and Stories*:

But here there was the *shyness* and *awkwardness* of inexperienced youth, a feeling of *constraint*, an impression of *perplexity* and *wonder*, as though someone had suddenly knocked on the door. Anna Sergeyevna, "the lady with the dog," took what had happened *somehow seriously, with a particular gravity*, as though thinking that this was her downfall and very *strange* and *improper*. Her features seemed to *sink and wither*, and on either side of her face the long hair hung *mournfully* down; she sat *crestfallen* and *musing, exactly like a woman taken in sin in some old picture*.

"Perplexity and wonder" are not what Anna Sergeyevna feels; "improper" is not what Chekhov intended—Koteliansky has introduced a moral judgment that is alien to Chekhov; the words "sink and wither" are too raw for the Chekhov mood; "a woman taken in sin" is another moralistic concoction. The translator wanders from being overly free to overly literal, and his use of compensation, substitution, and rephrasing is inept. He has not freed himself from the spell of the original Russian—he retains the Russian grammatical construction "but here *there* was" (*bylo*) in the opening line.

Language and taste change; translations lose their vitality. It ought to be true also that art improves, that translators learn from their predecessors' mistakes. Old translations of Chekhov are characteristically both too accurate, to the point of literalism, and too free, to the point of sloppy paraphrase. Long's version of the opening in "Sleepy," in *The Black Monk, and Other Stories*, provides an example of unstable control:

In front of the ikon burns a green lamp; across the room from wall to wall stretches a cord on which hang baby-clothes and a great pair of black trousers. On the ceiling above the lamp shines a great green spot, and the baby-clothes and trousers cast long shadows on the stove, on the cradle, on Varka. . . . When the lamp flickers, the spot and shadows move as if from a draught. It is stifling. There is a smell of soup and boots.

The translation verges on literalism. Long has preserved the original syntax too precisely: "a cord on which hang" (*na kotoroi*), "there is a smell" (*pakhnet*), "shines a great green spot." He has slurred Chekhov's delicate phrasing. Chekhov does not say "across the room from wall to wall"; he says "across the entire room, from one corner to another." Chekhov does not say "on the ceiling above the lamp shines a great green spot"; he says "the icon-lamp throws a large patch of green onto the ceiling." Paraphrase has led to both error and unclear image. Long's syntax is markedly Russian. His version lacks Chekhovian clarity; it is vague and stilted. We can appreciate this by comparing his version with that of Patrick Miles and Harvey Pitcher in *Chekhov: The Early Stories, 1883-1888*:

In front of the icon burns a small green lamp; across the entire room, from one corner to another, stretches a cord with baby-clothes and a pair of big black trousers hanging on it. The icon-lamp throws a large patch of green onto the ceiling, and the baby-clothes and trousers cast long shadows on the stove, the cradle, and Varka. . . . When the lamp begins to flicker, the green patch and the shadows come to life and are set in motion, as if a wind were blowing them. It is stuffy. The room smells of cabbage-soup and bootmaker's wares.

Miles and Pitcher's version is accurate without being literal, imaginative without being pretentious. It is not tied to Chekhov's syntax: the phrase "hanging on it" has been shifted to the end of the sentence, "the room smells of cabbage-soup and bootmaker's wares" is natural to English, more specific to what Chekhov is describing. Miles and Pitcher are more sensitive to the nuances of Chekhov's style: where Long has the shadows cast "on the stove, on the cradle, on Varka," repeating the preposition in a way that makes all three equal, they have "on the stove, the cradle, *and* Varka," thereby moving from the less important and inanimate stove and cradle to the animate and very important Varka, whose perceptions are the basis of the description. The modern version has caught the tone not only of pathos—pity for the tortured Varka trying to stay awake—but also the sinister hint at the story's ending in the telling image "the shadows come to life." The same traces of development in the art of translation can be seen by comparing their versions to Mrs. Garnett's in the text edited for the Norton Critical Edition by Ralph E. Matlaw. Mrs. Garnett reproduces the Russian syntax too literally, as in the repeated Russian construction "there is a string stretched," "there is a big patch of green," "there is a smell." "A little green lamp" sounds too cute for the diminutive *lampadka*, where Miles and Pitcher's "small green lamp" sounds more like Chekhov. Mrs. Garnett has retained the "on which" construction, and she has embellished the concluding line: "There is a smell of cabbage-soup and of the inside of a boot-shop." Miles and Pitcher's version also compares well to other modern texts. Payne, for example, seriously erred by changing Chekhov's present-tense description into the past tense: "A green lamp was burning in front of the icon," "there was a suffocating smell of soup and old boot leather." Many of Chekhov's descriptions, including this one, are written like stage directions: "In front of the icon burns a small green lamp." The tense of his descriptions is almost always important.

Tastes change, and modern perceptions of translation must be kept in a historical perspective. It is not Long's fault that change of English diction makes one of his phrases sound like "that's a great green spot (you have there on your ceiling)." Moreover, in many instances failings occur without regard for time and our hope that the art improves. This shows up especially when Chekhov's stylistic devices are central. We know that Chekhov's techniques are used so consistently as to be compelling. Certain colors are linked with certain moods, objects serve the same functions, shadows and lights set a specific scene. To read Chekhov is to be conditioned—our moods change at his will. Chekhov's translators are conditioned too. None is so obtuse as to miss a color, its shade, its texture. They seldom miss Chekhov's clouds, scissors, ashtrays, lamps, icons, chandeliers, or their impressionistic functions. Chekhov controls his translators as no writer seems ever to have done so. There are no dull literalist or arrogant revisionist translators of Chekhov. He allows his translators to err, even to be inept, for the Chekhov mood will always have its way in the end. There are limits to Chekhov's tolerance, however. When they misuse his devices, he catches them out.

In "A Boring Story," when the professor-narrator follows his aged wife up the stairs to comfort his neurotic daughter, he is aware of the bright spots from the candle dancing over the dark staircase, the trembling of their long shadows, the tangle of his feet in his long dressing-gown. His breath catches and he imagines someone is pursuing him, preparing to seize him from behind. And he thinks: "*Seichas umru zdes', na etoi lestnitse,—dumaiu ia.——Seichas . . .*" This is what he thinks, this is all he thinks. There is no invitation to variation or substitution or strengthening here. The words are simple: now, here, on this staircase. But in *The Bet, and Other Stories* Koteliansky and Murry have given it as " 'I shall die here on the staircase, this second,' I think, 'this second.' " In *Select Tales of Tchehov* Mrs. Garnett has conveyed it as " 'I shall die on the spot, here on the staircase,' I thought. 'On the spot.' " In *Lady with Lapdog, and Other Stories* David Magarshack has it as " 'Any moment now I shall die here on the stairs. . . . Now! Now!' " In *The Oxford Chekhov* Ronald Hingley has " 'I shall die here and now on these stairs,' I think, 'Now———' " Some translators have foregrounded "I shall die," although it is important that the key word does not appear first. The simple words "here" and "now" have been almost obsessively changed to "this second," "on the spot," "any moment now," or exaggerated into "Now! Now!" The broken syntax has been smoothed, as in Magarshack's "Any moment I shall die here and now on these stairs" and Hingley's "I shall die here and now on these stairs." Each translator, anxious to catch the drama of the scene, has strengthened a thought whose effect is lodged in Chekhovian understatement.

Nevertheless, the art of translation has improved, and there are clear indications in Chekhov translations that translators try to learn from their predecessors. Avrahm Yarmolinsky and David Magarshack edited Mrs. Garnett's translations for collections before translating anew for themselves. Ronald Hingley studied all existing translations as part of his preparation of *The Oxford Chekhov*; his work on both original and translated texts is authoritative. Miles and Pitcher examined both Mrs. Garnett and Hingley for their selection of the early stories. Chekhov's modern translators seem clearly to have learned from the pioneers, they have resolved problems of realia, colloquial speech, the spell of the original language, and unstable gradation. They seem to know that translation is an art of approximation and imperfection, and they seem to be especially aware of the importance of choice and decision. We can see this by trying to measure choice and decision in the most readily available collections: Ann Dunnigan's *Selected Stories*, Robert Payne's *The Image of Chekhov*, Ronald Hingley's *The Oxford Chekhov*, and Patrick Miles and Harvey Pitcher's *Chekhov: The Early Stories: 1883-1888*.

It is possible to establish gradations here. Ann Dunnigan is a careful, cautious translator; Hingley's concern is for accurate texts without stinting imagination; Payne is an enthusiastic propagandizer of Chekhov who does not hesitate to invent; Miles and Pitcher are conscious modernizers who nevertheless respect Chekhov's rights. These are faithful translators who can be run on a scale from Dunnigan, the most conservative, to Hingley, the textologist, to Payne, who heightens but is not quite a modernizer, to Miles and Pitcher, who do not depart as fancifully from the original as Payne but whose texts are clearly aimed at modern readers. Useful here is a comparison of Payne's heightened version of "The Student" with Hingley's greater concern for textual fidelity. Where Payne has "the earth herself was in agony" for Chekhov's *samoi prirode zhutko*, Hingley has "striking dread in Nature herself." Where Hingley has simply "he felt famished" for *muchitel'no khotelos' est'*, Payne has "the student was ferociously hungry." For Chekhov's description of the old widow Vasilisia, *vysokaia pukhlaia starukha*, which Hingley has faithfully as "a tall, plump old woman," Payne has the too strong "huge bloated old woman." Where Hingley has "blushed," for simply *pokrasnelo*, Payne has "flushed scarlet." Hingley sticks to "delicately" for *delikatno*, but Payne varies it as "refinement." Where Hingley has "truth and beauty," Payne has elaborated Chekhov's syntax into "the same truth and the same beauty." As can be seen, Hingley makes a conscious effort to find the most faithful equivalent, while Payne does not hesitate to reword or rephrase Chekhov. Hingley's version is not devoid of heightening and embellishment—he turns *vysokii smysl*, which Payne has faithfully as "deep meaning," into "exalted significance." But he has "tall" and "plump," where Payne has "huge" and "bloated," "blushed" instead of "scarlet," "dread" instead of the too strong "agony." Hingley is an authority on Chekhov's texts, and this shows in a few places where Payne has misunderstood Chekhov. The wind does not blow "unreasonably," as Payne has it; it is an "unwelcome" wind (*nekstati*), as Hingley has it both accurately and imaginatively. Payne has made the younger widow Lukeria drop the spoons and look "fixedly in the direction of the student," where Hingley, without elaboration, has her simply and correctly "put down the spoons" and "stare at the student." Payne seems not to have realized that when Vasilisia welcomes the student to the campfire, she does not simply wish him the good fortune to become rich; she alludes to the peasant superstition that he who startles someone in the darkness will some day become rich.

Payne is an eager champion of Chekhov, and he cannot always resist helping Chekhov along in English. Yet he does not arrogantly "improve" Chekhov. His enthusiasm often works in Chekhov's favor, never for his own vanity. Hingley, on the other hand, wants to offer a reliable Chekhov. His concern is for text; he is accurate but inventive too. We can see two other decidedly different approaches to Chekhov by comparing Ann Dunnigan's version of "The Kiss" with Miles and Pitcher's version. Both are modern translations, but where Miles and Pitcher are clearly modernizers—their syntactic and lexical choices suggest they are concerned with audience—Dunnigan has chosen her diction with Chekhov, not the reader, as her orientation. She reproduces Chekhov's sentences very closely, for example. When the self-conscious Ryabovich stands watching the dancers at the Von Rabbek estate, Dunnigan conveys one key sentence this way: "He was enormously delighted to see a man, in plain sight of everyone, take by the waist a girl with whom he was not acquainted and offer his shoulder for her hand, but he could in no way imagine himself in the position of such a man.'' The syntax here is good English, not Russian, but the pattern of the original is followed closely—each clause is in the same sequence as the original, each word in each clause is in the same order. Miles and Pitcher, on the other hand, move deliberately away from the original syntax to create a more graceful, less austere, and at the same time more efficient sentence for the English reader: ''To see a man take a strange girl by the waist in front of everyone and invite her to put her hand on his shoulder appealed to him enormously, but to imagine himself in that man's position was quite beyond him.'' Syntactic parallelism is operative here: ''To see a man take . . . but to imagine himself. . . .'' The participial construction ''a girl with whom'' has been replaced by a simple adjective: ''take a strange girl by the waist.'' Chekhov's straightforward ''offer his shoulder for her hand'' has been embellished into ''invite her to put her hand on his shoulder.''

The instinct of all three translators is sound. Both versions have faithfully repeated Ryabovich's favorite adverb and adjective ''enormous,'' ''enormously,'' as in the sentence just cited and in such exclamations as '' 'I like your house enormously!' '' The lexical choices of the two translations are remarkably similar. But throughout the texts it is evident that Miles and Pitcher prefer to vary, and even to invent and embellish with an eye to modern appeal, where Dunnigan remains close to Chekhov. Where she has ''he no longer envied them, but felt sadly moved,'' they have ''he no longer experienced envy, only a feeling of wistful admiration.'' Where she has the more accurate ''beautifully disciplined family,'' they have ''superbly disciplined family,'' an exaggeration. When Lobytko promises to find beer in the middle of the night ''and you can call me a scoundrel if I don't!'' as Dunnigan carefully has it, Miles and Pitcher add an embellishment, ''Call me a scoundrel if I come back empty-handed!'' Where Dunnigan has the direct but too strong ''probably a psychotic of some sort'' for the Russian word *psikh*, they have varied it and caught the actual colloquial meaning with ''must have been some kind of case.'' For the story's closing sentence Dunnigan has, ''For an instant joy flamed in his breast, but he immediately stifled it and went to bed, and in his wrath with his fate, as though wishing to spite it, did not go to the general's.'' The same sentence in Miles and Pitcher's version reads, ''For a brief moment a feeling of joy blazed up in Ryabovich, but he immediately extinguished it, got into bed, and in defiance of his fate, as if wanting to spite it, did not go to the general's.'' Dunnigan is accurate and business-like. ''For an instant,'' ''stifled it,'' ''in his wrath with his fate''—these choices are close to the original in both letter and spirit. But Miles and Pitcher have heightened the phrases: ''for a brief moment,'' ''extinguished it,'' ''in defiance of his fate.'' Dunnigan has retained the original ''joy flamed in his breast''; Miles and Pitcher have eliminated the dated word ''breast'' and made the feeling specific to

Ryabovich. Dunnigan's version is consistently oriented to Chekhov; Miles and Pitcher have the modern reader in mind. Her version is not imaginative enough; theirs is overly inventive. Her faithful recreations of Chekhov are a bit stilted, rather too plain; their versions read better in English and have greater literary appeal, but they have taken liberties with Chekhov to achieve their modernizing aim.

Seen in historical perspective, English translations of Chekhov's stories are not strongly differentiated by method. Chekhov has enjoyed the attention of distinctly faithful translators of his stories. His translators' failings are of competence and of state of the art, not of a desire to reinterpret or improve him. Modesty is apparent here—to the degree that Chekhov seems successfully to have exerted control over his translators, so also his personal and literary modesty seems to have affected them. It is not simply that Chekhov is easy to translate; it is that his integrity is contagious and his style invites honesty. Among the pioneer translators Long and Koteliansky have failed because they are grammatical slaves without strong literary talent, while Mrs. Garnett is more competent, more skillful, and more enduring. Among the modern translators Dunnigan and Hingley are text-oriented, while Payne, Miles, and Pitcher are reader-oriented. The differences between the generations and among the translators are evident; the most decided difference is that modern translators are clearly superior and have a more sophisticated mastery of the art. They know when to be more literal, when to be more free; they do not confuse accuracy with fidelity.

The problems of translating Chekhov's plays are the same as those of translating his stories, with an added difficult dimension. Plays are performance; translators of plays have to deal not only with style, but also with diction. In a review article "On Translating Chekhov" Eugene K. Bristow has warned: "Theatre, at best, is a synthesis of art and craft. Most of its instruments—actors, director, language, audience—are . . . highly imperfect." The problem here is one of the relations between translation and adaptation. "Translation is the literal rendition that is handed to the producer; adaptation is the final result after the script has been subjected to rewriting, rehearsal, and out-of-town production." Even more, just as the director must interpret, reinterpret, adapt a play in its performance, so also must the translator adapt the translation of a play—to time and place, to audience, to director and actor expectations, to the diction dimension, and, in the case of Chekhov's plays, to "the exact balance of sound, sense, and feeling." It is not enough for the translator of Chekhov's plays to be faithful; the element of performance demands that he be an interpreter, even an adapter. Or rather, what constitutes a faithful translation of a play must be redefined to take performance—diction—into account. There is danger here. Too often translators use the difficulties of translation to justify personal shortcomings—the translator evades difficulties by resorting to paraphrase instead of attending to professional and imaginative solutions of problems of style and language. Think how much greater the danger is when the translator of a play takes the necessity of adapting to a new language and then to a new stage for license to arrogantly reinterpret or cover up. When Bristow says that "as the director may freely convert . . . the point of the script into his theatrical milieu, so may the translator freely transform . . . the point of the original into his own language," he does well to stipulate that this transformation must be comprehended in the "mathematical sense," that is, with regard for the demands of ultimate fidelity to the demands of language, style, and meaning. Adaptation does not mean license for arbitrary reinterpretation; it means, as Bristow insists, a concern for that additional dimension of performance—praxis as well as lexis, action as well as meaning.[6]

English-language translations of Chekhov's plays have not fared as well as his stories. Indicative here is Kornei Chukovsky's well-known demonstration that Miss Marian Fell's pioneer translations have not even done justice to the initial demands of style and meaning, let alone stage diction. In *A High Art* Chukovsky devotes much of one chapter to her failings, which include not only poor conveyances, but also serious misunderstanding and mistranslation of simple matters of language and cultural-historical milieu. Batiushkov is taken for *batiushka* and thereby becomes a priest, Dobroliubov for St. Francis of Assisi (*dobroliubets!*), and General Jomini for Germany. *Gnoi* is confused with *genii*; names, dates, currencies, and numbers are mixed up; characters are given wrong lines that often miss the point. Even discounting Miss Fell's errors, which can be corrected even though there are so many, in the end she has ruined Chekhov's style without even getting so far as problems of performance. In Chukovsky's view, it is "deplorable that she imputes to Chekhov an insipid, colorless, stingy style by excising from his works . . . every vivid, colorful sentence, every vital intonation."[7]

Older translations also suffer from failings of diction. Bristow finds that Mrs. Garnett often misses humor and meaning based on "threads of folk song, folklore, poems, and literary allusions," and his readings of her translations of the plays lead him to second the harsher retrospective assessments of her work. He finds in addition that, while Stark Young's translations have withstood many tests of performance and reading through time, his phrasings are perceptibly of his time and his reproductions of syntax create "a bastard idiom alien to Chekhov's point." He also observes that David Magarshack's experiments with the English of Chekhov's time sometimes introduce "lengthy, scarcely actable 'translationese.' " Bristow's examination of nine translations from 1912 to the present shows that all but one transformed Chekhov's folk saying "with a pig's snout in a row of bakers' stalls" into silk purses and sow's ears, bun shops and pastry shops, jackdaws and peacocks, bulls in China shops, while only Hingley preserved the significant point of the proverb.[8]

Among modern translators of Chekhov's plays, Bristow finds that Ann Dunnigan's translations are too literal and that only Tyrone Guthrie's translations done with Leonid Kipnis and Ronald Hingley's Oxford translations serve performance and diction sufficiently well to be recommended. His assessment is that Stark Young's older translations are still "serviceable," Guthrie's are "worthy," and Hingley's are "reputable experiments." Guthrie sometimes omits, where Hingley does not. Both translators have taken a radical but responsible approach; each "naturalizes the plays and avoids the usual lumpish style." Guthrie does a better job of balancing "sound, sense, and feeling with Chekhov's point"; his mutilations are rare, his overstatements are theatrically effective, and his interpretations are faithful to Chekhov's "vitality, movement, and gesture." Hingley has departed even further from the traditional approach to Chekhov's plays. He reduces the possible ways of rendering character names from over 30 to 4, and he uses "a subtle variety of stylistic devices to convey character relationships, linguistic misunderstandings, and national folklore, song, and verse." His images are inventive but demand a new production style; his diction (his "phrases and rhythmical patterns") is "inherently British" and thus not suited to the American stage.[9]

Modern theorists of translation often speak nowadays of reader-directed and text-directed translations. Translators must decide whether to bring the original author to the reader or oblige the reader to come to the author. Modernizing translators of Chekhov's stories and plays adhere to the former approach, and faithful translators to the latter. An extreme reader-oriented translation is one that "corrects" or "improves" an original to make sure it sells. An extreme text-oriented translation is notable for its dull accuracy and lifeless quality. "Without modesty, translation will traduce," George Steiner has said, "where modesty is constant, it can, sometimes against its own intent of deference, transfigure."[10] Chekhov has generally been treated well in the English-speaking world: his translators have been modest and faithful. Within these parameters, however, there are crucial differences of quality, competence, and approach. Historically, tastes have changed, so that none of the pioneer translations of Chekhov's stories except Mrs. Garnett's has survived. Even in her case it is disappointing that her editors have not moved more forcefully to bring her texts up to date; even more, her greatest value to modern translation is as a reliable model for new translators to consult. This is also true of the translators of the middle period. Nothing is taken away from Magarshack and Yarmolinsky by suggesting that their translations must be updated or they will be superseded. As for the most recent translations, we have clear differences in taste and preference. Dunnigan and Hingley are text-directed translators whose versions are true, accurate, and reliable; Payne, Miles, and Pitcher are reader-directed translators whose liberties are kept honest by modesty. Nevertheless, Hingley's translations, supported as they are by his professional textological work, are clearly superior to all others, old and new, in the former category; Miles and Pitcher's translations are clearly best for the popular reader of good literature. As for Chekhov's plays, Bristow has demonstrated that Guthrie's and Hingley's translations are superior to all others for performance and for innovational approach. Guthrie's versions seem certain to appeal to an American audience, and Hingley's to British theatre-goers. Translations of the plays have not worn well with time—the added diction dimension makes stage works too vulnerable to changing tastes and limitations of competence.

NOTES

1. L. G. Kelly, *The True Interpreter: A History of Translation Theory and Practice in the West* (New York: St. Martin's, 1979); George Steiner, *After Babel: Aspects of Language and Translation* (New York and London: Oxford University Press, 1975); Eugene A. Nida, *Towards a Science of Translating* (Leiden: E. J. Brill, 1964); Jiri Levy, *Iskusstvo perevoda* (Moscow, 1974); Andre Lefevere, *Translating Poetry: Seven Strategies and a Blueprint* (Assen and Amsterdam: Van Gorcum, 1975); Georges Mounin, *Les problemes theoriques de la traduction* (Paris: Gallimard, 1963); Marilyn Gaddis Rose, ed., *Translation Spectrum: Essays in Theory and Practice* (Albany, N.Y.: State University of New York Press, 1975).
2. Steiner, p. 269.
3. *The Art of Translation: Kornei Chukovsky's "A High Art,"* trans. and ed. Lauren G. Leighton (Knoxville, Tenn.: University of Tennessee Press, 1984); A. V. Fedorov, *Osnovy obshchei teorii perevoda*, 4th ed. rev. and enl. (Moscow, 1983); V. M. Rossel's, *Estafeta slova* (Moscow, 1972); O. L. Kundzich, *Slovo i obraz* (Moscow, 1973); G. R. Gachechiladze, *Vvedenie v teoriiu khudozhestvennogo perevoda* (Tiflis, 1970); Iu. D. Levin, "Ob istoricheskoi evoliutsii printsipov perevoda," in *Mezhdunarodnye sviazi russkoi literatury* (Moscow-Leningrad, 1963); "Ob istorizme v podkhode k istorii perevoda," in *Masterstvo perevoda 1962* (Moscow, 1963).
4. Rose, pp. 32-34.
5. Viktor Khinkis, "O pol'ze sorazmernosti i soobraznosti," in *Masterstvo perevoda 1964* (Moscow, 1965), pp. 132-134.
6. Eugene K. Bristow, "On Translating Chekhov," *Quarterly Journal of Speech* 52 (October 1966): 290-294.
7. Leighton, pp. 13-17.
8. Bristow, pp. 292-293.
9. *Ibid.*, pp. 293-294.
10. Steiner, p. 216.

CHEKHOV'S WORKS IN ENGLISH: SELECTIVE COLLECTIONS AND EDITIONS

Chekhov's works have been published so profusely as to make an attempt at a systematic, complete bibliography meaningless. This bibliography includes only the most important collections and lists only the

most important editions of particular collections. Neither is it possible
to list the contents of every collection. Collections have been assembled
with a wide variety of criteria, and not even Mrs. Garnett's thirteen-
volume or Hingley's nine-volume collections pretend to more than a
sampling of Chekhov's stories—528 are extant for the early period
alone. Chekhov never assembled a complete collection of his writings;
not even the definitive Soviet edition of his works has fully sorted out
problems of dating, canonical texts, and variants. Stories and plays are
listed separately. All entries are by name of translator. Prompt books
and scripts of the plays are not included. Only first date of publication is
given, except for revised subsequent editions or reprints.

Stories

Chamot, A. E. *The Grasshopper, and Other Stories.* London: Stanley Paul, 1926;
    Philadelphia: David McKay, 1926.
_____. *The Shooting Party.* London: Stanley Paul, 1926.
_____. *Short Stories.* London: Commodore, 1946.
Chertok, I. C., and Jean Gardner. *Late-Blooming Flowers, and Other Stories.* New
    York/Toronto/London: McGraw-Hill, 1964.
Coulson, Jessie. *Selected Stories.* London, 1963.
Dunnigan, Ann. *Selected Stories.* New York: Signet, 1960.
_____. *Ward Six, and Other Stories.* New York: Signet, 1965.
Fell, Marian. *Russian Silhouettes: More Stories of Russian Life.* London: Duck-
    worth, 1915; Scribner's Sons, 1915.
_____. *Stories of Russian Life.* London: Duckworth, 1914; New York: Scribner's
    Sons, 1914.
Fen, Elisaveta. *Short Stories.* London: Folio Society, 1974.
FitzLyon, April, and Kyril Zinovieff. *The Woman in the Case, and Other Stories.*
    London: Spearman-Calder, 1953.
Garnett, Constance. *The Bishop, and Other Stories.* London: Chatto and Windus,
    1919; New York: Macmillan, 1919.
_____. *The Chorus Girl, and Other Stories.* London: Chatto and Windus, 1920;
    New York: Macmillan, 1920.
_____. *The Cook's Wedding, and Other Stories.* London: Chatto and Windus,
    1922; New York: Macmillan, 1922.
_____. *The Darling, and Other Stories.* London: Chatto and Windus, 1918; New
    York: Macmillan, 1916.
_____. *The Duel, and Other Stories.* London: Chatto and Windus, 1916; New
    York: Macmillan, 1916; New York: Willey Book, 1916.
_____. *Great Stories*, ed. David M. Greene. New York: Dell, 1959.
_____. *The Horse-Stealers, and Other Stories.* New York: Willey Book, 1921.
_____. *The Lady with the Dog, and Other Stories.* London: Chatto and Windus,
    1917; New York: Macmillan, 1917.
_____. *Love, and Other Stories.* Chatto and Windus, 1922; New York: Macmillan,
    1923.

_____. *The Party, and Other Stories*. London: Chatto and Windus, 1917; New York: Macmillan, 1917; New York: Willey Book, 1917.

_____. *The Schoolmaster, and Other Stories*. London: Chatto and Windus, 1920; New York: Macmillan, 1921.

_____. *The Schoolmistress, and Other Stories*. London: Chatto and Windus, 1920; New York: Macmillan, 1921.

_____. *Select Tales of Tchehov*, 13 vols. London: Chatto and Windus, 1916, 1927; New York: Barnes and Noble, n.d.; Toronto: Clarke, Irwin, 1949, 1954, 1961.

_____. *Short Stories*. New York: Book League of America, 1928.

_____. *The Tales of Anton Chekhov*, 13 vols. New York: Ecco Press, 1983.

_____. *The Wife, and Other Stories*. London: Chatto and Windus, 1918; New York: Macmillan, 1918.

_____. *The Witch, and Other Stories*. London: Chatto and Windus, 1918.

Goldberg, Isaac, and Henry T. Schnittkind. *Nine Humorous Tales*. Boston: Stratford Co., 1918.

Gottlieb, Nora. *Early Stories*. London: Bodley Head, 1960.

Hinchliffe, Arnold. *The Sinner from Toledo, and Other Stories*. Rutherford/Madison/Teaneck, N.J.: Fairleigh Dickinson University Press, 1972.

Hingley, Ronald. *The Oxford Chekhov*, 9 vols. Oxford/New York/Toronto/Melbourne: Oxford University Press, 1965-1980.

_____. *Seven Stories*. London/Oxford/New York: Oxford University Press, 1974.

Jones, Frances H. *St. Peter's Day, and Other Stories*. New York: Capricorn, 1959.

Kaye, Adeline Lister. *The Steppe, and Other Stories*. London: W. Heinman, 1915; New York: Frederick A. Stokes, 1915.

Koteliansky, S. S. *Tchekoff's Plays and Stories*. London: J. M. Dent, 1937, rprt. 1946.

Koteliansky, S. S., and Gilbert Cannan. *The House with the Mezzanine, and Other Stories*. New York: Scribner's Sons, 1917.

_____. *My Life, and Other Stories*. London: C. W. Daniel, 1920; New York: Books for Libraries, 1920, rprt. 1971.

Koteliansky, S. S., and J. M. Murry. *The Bet, and Other Stories*. Dublin/London: Maunsel, 1915; Boston: J. W. Luce, 1915.

Litvinov, Ivy. *Short Novels and Stories*. Moscow: Progress, n.d.

Long, R.E.C. *The Black Monk, and Other Stories*. London: Duckworth, 1903.

_____. *The Kiss, and Other Stories*. London: Duckworth, 1908; New York: Scribner's Sons, 1912.

Magarshack, David. *Lady with Lapdog, and Other Stories*, Harmondsworth-Middlesex: Penguin, 1964.

Makanowitsky, Barbara. *Seven Short Novels*. New York, 1963.

Matlaw, Ralph E., ed. *Anton Chekhov's Short Stories: Texts of the Stories. Background. Criticism.* A Norton Critical Edition. New York: Norton, 1979.

Miles, Patrick, and Harvey Pitcher. *Chekhov: The Early Stories, 1883-1888*. London: John Murray, 1982; New York: Macmillan, 1983.

Morton, Miriam. *Shadows and Lights*. Garden City, N.Y.: Doubleday, 1968.

Muchnic, Helen. *The Short Stories of Anton Chekhov*. Avon, Conn.: Cardavon, 1973.

Payne, Robert. *The Image of Chekhov: Forty Stories*. New York: Knopf, 1963.
Pitcher, Harvey, with James Forsyth. *Chuckle with Chekhov: A Selection of Comic Stories*. Cromer: Swallow House Books, 1975.
Rickey, George W. *The Beggar, and Other Stories*. Emmaus, Pa.: The Story Classics, 1949.
_____. *Rothschild's Fiddle, and Other Stories*. New York: Boni and Liveright, 1917.
Schimanskaya, E. R. *My Life*. London, 1943.
Segal, Louis. *The Album, and Five Other Tales*. London: British Russian Gazette and Trade Outlook, 1933; London: Pitman, 1944.
Smith, Ursula. *The Thief, and Other Tales*. New York: Vantage, 1964.
Wilson, Edmund, trans. and ed. *Peasants, and Other Stories*. Garden City, N.Y.: Doubleday Anchor, 1956.
Yarmolinsky, Avrahm. *The Unknown Chekhov: Stories and Other Writings*. London, 1959.
Yarmolinsky, Avrahm, ed. *The Portable Chekhov*. New York: Viking, 1947; 2d ed., 1968.

Plays

Ashmore, Basil. *Don Juan (in the Russian Manner)*. London: P. Nevil, 1952.
Baukhage, Hilmar. *The Boor*. New York: S. French, 1915.
Baukhage, Hilmar, and Barrett H. Clark. *A Marriage Proposal*. New York: S. French, 1914.
Bentley, Eric, and Theodore Hoffman. *The Brute, and Other Farces*. New York: Grove Press, 1958.
Bristow, Eugene K. *Anton Chekhov's Plays*. Norton Critical Edition. New York: Norton, 1977.
Butler, Hubert. *The Cherry Orchard*. Boston: Baker International Play Bureau, 1934.
Calderon, George. *Two Plays by Tchekhof*. London: G. Richards, 1912; London: Cape, 1928.
Caylor, Rose. *Uncle Vanya*. New York: Covici, Friede, 1930.
Cournos, John. *That Worthless Fellow Platonov*. New York: Dutton, 1920.
Covan, Jenny. *The Cherry Orchard*. New York: Brentano's, 1922.
_____. *The Moscow Art Theatre Series of Russian Plays*. New York: Brentano's, 1922.
_____. *Uncle Vanya*. New York: Brentano's, 1922.
Dunnigan, Ann. *The Major Plays*. New York: Signet, 1964.
Fell, Marian. *Five Famous Plays*. London: Duckworth, 1939.
_____. *Ivanoff*. New York: Brentano's, 1923.
_____. *Plays by Anton Tchekoff*. New York: Scribner's Sons, 1912-1916; London: Duckworth, 1913.
_____. *Six Famous Plays*. London: Duckworth, 1949.
Fen, Elisaveta. *Plays*. Baltimore: Penguin, 1954.
_____. *Three Plays*. Baltimore: Penguin, 1951.
Garnett, Constance. *The Cherry Orchard, and Other Plays*. London: Chatto and Windus, 1923; New York: Seltzer, 1924.
_____. *Plays*. London: Chatto and Windus, 1925-1928.

_____. *Plays*. New York: Modern Library, 1930.

_____. *The Three Sisters, and Other Plays*. London: Chatto and Windus, 1923.

Guthrie, Tyrone, and Leonid Kipnis. *The Cherry Orchard*. Minnesota Drama Editions. Minneapolis: University of Minnesota Press, 1965.

_____. *The Three Sisters*. The Avon Theater Library. New York: Avon, 1965.

_____. *Uncle Vanya*. Minnesota Drama Editions. Minneapolis: University of Minnesota Press, 1969.

Hingley, Ronald. *The Oxford Chekhov*, 9 vols. Oxford/New York/Toronto/Melbourne: Oxford University Press, 1965-1980.

House, Roy Temple. *A Bear*. New York: Moods, 1909.

Iliffe, David. *The Seagull*. London: S. French, 1953.

Jarrel, Randall. *The Three Sisters*. New York: Macmillan, 1969.

Koteliansky, S. S. *Tchekoff's Plays and Stories*. London: J. M. Dent, 1937, rprt. 1946.

_____. *Three Plays*. Harmondsworth: Penguin, 1940.

_____. *The Wood Demon*. New York and London: Macmillan, 1926.

Magarshack, David. *Four Plays*. New York: Hill and Wang, 1969.

_____. *Platonov*. New York: Hill and Wang, 1964.

_____. *The Seagull*. London: D. Dobson, 1952.

Mandell, M. S. *The Cherry Garden*. New Haven, Conn.: Yale Courant, 1908.

Nicolaeff, Ariadne, and John Gielgud. *Ivanov*. New York: Theatre Arts Books, 1966.

Nine Plays by Anton Chekhov. New York: Caxton House, 1946.

Plays. New York: Hartsdale House, 1935.

Senelick, Laurence. *The Cherry Orchard*. Arlington Heights, Ill.: AHM, 1977.

_____. *The Cherry Orchard and The Seagull*. Arlington Heights, Ill.: AHM, 1977.

Szogy, Alex. *Ten Early Plays*. New York: Bantam, 1965.

West, Julius. *Five Famous Plays*. London: Duckworth, 1939.

_____. *Four Short Plays*. London: Duckworth, 1915, rprt. 1950.

_____. *Plays by Anton Tchekoff*. London: Duckworth, 1916; New York: Scribner's Sons, 1916.

_____. *The Seagull*. London: Hendersons, 1915.

Yarmolinsky, Avrahm, ed. *The Cherry Orchard*. The Avon Theater Library. New York: Avon, 1965.

The Portable Chekhov. A. Yarmolinsky, ed. New York: Viking, 1947; 2d ed., 1968.

Young, Stark. *Best Plays*. New York: Modern Library, 1956.

_____. *The Cherry Orchard*. New York: S. French, 1947.

_____. *The Seagull*. London and New York: Scribner's Sons, 1939.

_____. *Three Sisters*. New York and Los Angeles: S. French, 1941.

Leonard Polakiewicz

SELECTED BIBLIOGRAPHY

IN ENGLISH

The English bibliography is based largely on the *Modern Language Association International Bibliography of Books and Articles, Arts and Humanities Citation Index*, and *East European Languages and Literatures: A Subject of Names Index to Authors in English Language Journals, 1900-1977* by Garth M. Terry. The critical works on Chekhov in English included here are mostly those published since 1960. For pre-1960 critical works on Chekhov, the reader is advised to consult the A. Heifetz and R. Yachnin bibliographies (see below). To enable the reader to locate more easily a source in a given area of interest, this bibliography is divided into several sections and sub-sections.

Abbreviations of Journals

AL	*RE: Artes Liberales*
ALitASH	*Acta Litteraria Academiae Scientatum Hungaricae*
AUnivST	*Acta Universitatis Stockholmiensis*, Stockholm Slavic Studies No. 2
CLAJ	*College Language Association Journal*
CompD	*Comparative Drama*
ContempR	*Contemporary Review*
CR	*Critical Review*
CSP	*Canadian Slavonic Papers*
DramR	*Drama Review*
DS	*Drama Survey*
DubR	*Dublin Review*
EP	*Essays in Poetics*
EthJ	*Educational Theatre Journal*
HudR	*Hudson Review*

ISE	Ibadan Studies in English
JAMA	Journal of the American Medical Association
JRS	Journal of Russian Studies
LonM	London Magazine
MD	Modern Drama
MFS	Modern Fiction Studies
MLR	Modern Language Review
RBPH	Revue Belge de Philologie et d'Histoire
RLJ	Russian Language Journal
RLT	Russian Literature Triquarterly
RusL	Russian Literature
RusR	Russian Review
SEEJ	Slavic and East European Journal
SEER	Slavonic & East European Review
SEES	Slavic and East European Studies
SlavR	Slavic Review
SovL	Soviet Literature
SR	Sewanee Review
SSF	Studies in Short Fiction
ThQ	Theatre Quarterly
TN	Theatre Notebook
TQ	Texas Quarterly
UlbanR	Ulbandus Review: A Journal of Slavic Languages and Literatures

Bibliographies

For a bibliography of selective collections and editions of Chekhov's stories and plays in English, see Chapter 17.

"Bibliographical Index of the Complete Works of Anton Chekhov." In David Magarshack, *Chekhov: A Life*; 1953 rpt. Westport, Conn.: Greenwood Press, 1970, pp. 393-423.

Heifetz, Anna. *Bibliography of Chekhov's Works Translated into English and Published in America.* New York: New York Public Library, 1929.

_____. *Chekhov in English: A Bibliography of Works by and About Him.* New York: New York Public Library, 1949.

Yachnin, Rissa. *The Chekhov Centennial Chekhov in English: A Selective List of Works by and About Him, 1949-1960.* New York: New York Public Library, 1960.

Primary Literature

Letters

Letters of Anton Chekhov. Selected and ed. A. Yarmolinsky. New York: Viking Press, 1973.

Letters of Anton Chekhov. Trans. by Michael H. Heim in collaboration with Simon Karlinsky. Selection, Commentary, and Introduction by Simon Karlinsky. New York: Harper & Row, 1973.

The Letters of Anton Pavlovich Tchehov to Olga Leonardovna Knipper. Trans. and ed. Constance Garnett. New York: Benjamin Blom, 1966.

Letters on the Short Story, the Drama and Other Literary Topics by Anton Chekhov. Selected and ed. Louis S. Friedland. 2d. ed., rpt. New York: Dover Publications, 1966.

The Life and Letters of Anton Tchekhov. Trans. and ed. S. S. Koteliansky and Philip Tomlinson. 2d. ed., 1925; rpt. New York: Benjamin Blom, 1965.

The Selected Letters of Anton Chekhov. Ed. and Introd. L. Hellman. Trans. S. K. Lederer. London: Hamish Hamilton, 1955.

Secondary Literature

Biographies

Chukovsky, Kornei. *Chekhov the Man*. Trans. P. Rose. London: Hutchinson and Co., 1945.

Hingley, Ronald. *Chekhov: A Biographical and Critical Study*. London: George Allen and Unwin, 1966.

_____. *A New Life of Anton Chekhov*. New York: Alfred A. Knopf, 1976.

Lafitte, Sophie. *Chekhov 1860-1904*. Trans. M. Budberg and G. Latta. London: Angus and Robertson, 1974.

Magarshack, David. *Chekhov: A Life*. 1953; rpt. Westport, Conn.: Greenwood Press, 1970.

Nemirovsky, Irene. *A Life of Chekhov*. Trans. E. de Mauny. London: Grey Walls Press, 1950.

Priestley, John B. *Anton Chekhov*. London: International Textbook, 1970.

Saunders, Beatrice. *Tchehov the Man*. London: Centaur Press, 1960.

Simmons, Ernest J. *Chekhov: A Biography*. Boston: Little, Brown, 1962.

Toumanova, Nina. *Anton Chekhov, The Voice of Twilight Russia*. New York: Columbia University Press, 1960 c. 1937.

Memoirs (Books)

Anton Tchekhov: Literary and Theatrical Reminiscences. Trans. and ed. S. S. Koteliansky. 2d ed., 1927; rpt. New York: Benjamin Blom, 1965.

Avilova, Lidiia. *Chekhov in My Life: A Love Story*. Trans. D. Magarshack. Westport, Conn.: Greenwood Press, 1971.

Reminiscences of Anton Chekhov by M. Gorky, A. Kuprin, and I. A. Bunin. Trans. S. S. Koteliansky and L. Woolf. New York: B. W. Huebsh, 1921.

Books and Collections of Essays on Chekhov's Prose and Drama

Abrams, Doris C. *Reflections in a Lake: A Study of Chekhov's Four Greatest Plays*. London: Weidenfeld and Nicolson, 1976.

Barricelli, Jeane-Pierre, ed. *Chekhov's Great Plays: A Critical Anthology*. New York and London: New York University Press, 1981.

Bitsilli, Petr M. *Chekhov's Art: A Stylistic Analysis*. Trans. T. W. Clyman and E. J. Cruise. Ann Arbor, Mich.: Ardis Press, 1983.

Bruford, Walter H. *Chekhov and His Russia: A Sociological Study*. 2d. ed., London: Routledge and Kegan Paul, 1948; rpt. Hamden, Conn.: Archon Books, 1971.

Chudakov, Alexander P. *Chekhov's Poetics*. Trans. E. Cruise and D. Dragt. Ann Arbor, Mich.: Ardis Publishers, 1983.

Debreczeny, Paul, and Thomas Eekman, eds. *Chekhov's Art of Writing: A Collection of Critical Essays*. Columbus, Ohio: Slavica Publishers, 1977.

Eekman, Thomas, ed. *Anton Čechov, 1860-1960: Some Essays*. Leiden: E. J. Brill, 1960.

Elton, Oliver. *Chekhov*. The Taylorian Lecture,. 1929. Oxford: Clarendon Press, 1929.

Emeljanow, Victor, ed. *Chekhov: The Critical Heritage*. London, Boston and Henley: Routledge and Kegan Paul, 1981.

Gerhardi, William. *Anton Chekhov: A Critical Study*. New York: Duffield, 1923.

Gottlieb, Vera. *Chekhov and the Vaudeville: A Study of Chekhov's One-Act Plays*. Cambridge: Cambridge University Press, 1982.

Hahn, Beverly. *Chekhov: A Study of the Major Stories and Plays*. London: Cambridge University Press, 1977.

Hulanicki, Leo, and David Savignac, eds. and trans. *Anton Čexov As a Master of Story-Telling*. The Hague: Mouton, 1976.

Jackson, Robert L., ed. *Chekhov: A Collection of Critical Essays*. Englewood Cliffs, N.J.: Prentice-Hall, 1967.

Katzer, Julius, ed. *A. P. Chekhov: 1860-1960*. Moscow: Foreign Languages Publishing House, 1960.

Kirk, Irene. *Anton Chekhov*. Boston: Twayne, 1981.

Kramer, Karl D. *The Chameleon and the Dream: The Image of Reality in Čexov's Stories*. The Hague: Mouton, 1970.

Llewellyn Smith, Virginia. *Anton Chekhov and the Lady with the Dog*. London: Oxford University Press, 1973.

Magarshack, David. *Chekhov the Dramatist*. New York: Hill and Wang, 1960.

_____. *The Real Chekhov: An Introduction to Chekhov's Last Plays*. London: George Allen and Unwin, 1972.

Melchinger, Siegfried. *Anton Chekhov*. Trans. E. Tarcov. New York: Frederick Ungar, 1972.

Nilsson, Nils Ake. *Studies in Čechov's Narrative Technique: "The Steppe" and "The Bishop."* A Univ St. Stockholm: Almqvist and Wiksell, 1968.

Peace, Richard A. *Chekhov: A Study of the Major Plays*. New Haven: Yale University Press, 1983.

Pitcher, Harvey. *The Chekhov Play: A New Interpretation*. London: Chatto and Windus, 1973.

Rayfield, Donald. *Chekhov: The Evolution of His Art*. New York: Barnes and Noble, 1975.

Styan, J. L. *Chekhov in Performance: A Commentary on the Major Plays*. Cambridge: Cambridge University Press, 1971.

Tulloch, John. *Chekhov: A Structuralist Study*. New York: Macmillan, 1980.

Valency, Maurice. *The Breaking String: The Plays of Anton Chekhov*. New York: Oxford University Press, 1966.

Van der Eng, Jan, Jan M. Meijer, and Herta Schmid, eds., *On the Theory of Descriptive Poetics: Anton P. Chekhov As Story-Teller and Playwright*. Lisse: Peter de Ridder Press, 1978.

Winner, Thomas. *Chekhov and His Prose*. New York: Holt, Rinehart and Winston, 1966.

Articles and Chapters in Books, General and Miscellaneous

Aldanov, Marc. "Reflections on Chekhov." *RusR* 14 (1955): 83-92.

Atchity, Kenneth J. "Chekhov's Infernal Island." *Research Studies* 36 (1968): 335-340.

Beeson, B. "Anton Tchekhov: A Resume of His Works and of His Career." *Annals of Medical History*, NS 3 (1931): 603-618.

Berdnikov, Georgi. "Chekhov and Our Time." *SovL* 1 (1980): 3-11.

Bill, Valentine T. "Nature in Chekhov's Fiction." *RusR* 33 (1974): 153-156.

Bitsilli, Petr. "From Chekhonte to Chekhov." In V. Erlich, ed. *Twentieth-Century Russian Literary Criticism*. New Haven: Yale University Press, 1975, pp. 212-218.

Bogayevskaya, Ksenia. Introd. "Tolstoy on Chekhov: Previously Unknown Comments." *SovL* 1 (1980): 40-44.

Bondarev, Yuri, et al. "Chekhov Through the Eyes of the Writers of the World." *SovL* 1 (1980): 91-103.

Bunin, Ivan. "Chekhov." *Atlantic Monthly* 188 (1951): 59-63.

Chizhevsky, Dmitri. "Chekhov in the Development of Russian Literature." In R. L. Jackson, ed. *Chekhov: A Collection of Critical Essays*, pp. 49-61.

Chudakov, Alexander P. "Newly-Discovered Works by the Young Chekhov." *SovL* 10 (1975): 134-142.

Chukovsky, Kornei. "Chekhov." In J. Katzer, ed. *A. P. Chekhov: 1860-1960*, pp. 56-112.

Cicerin, A. A. "The Role of Adversative Intonation in Čexov's Prose." In L. Hulanicki and D. Savignac, eds. and trans. *Anton Čexov As a Master of Story-Telling*, pp. 187-192.

Clarke, Chavanne C. "Aspects of Impressionism in Chekhov's Prose." In P. Debreczeny and T. Eekman, eds. *Chekhov's Art of Writing: A Collection of Critical Essays*, pp. 123-133.

Clyman, Toby W. "Chekhov's Victimized Women." *RLJ* 28 (1974): 26-31.

Collins, H. P. "Chekhov: The Last Phase." *ContempR*, 186 (1954): 37-41.

Conrad, Joseph L. "Anton Chekhov's Literary Landscapes." In P. Debreczeny and T. Eekman, eds. *Chekhov's Art of Writing: A Collection of Critical Essays*, pp. 82-99.

_____. "Sensuality in Čexov's Prose." *SEEJ* 24 (1980): 103-117.

_____. "Unresolved Tension in Čexov's Stories, 1886-1888." *SEEJ* 16 (1972): 55-64.

Curtis, Penelope. "Meditations on Chekhov." *Quadrant* 77 (1972): 24-39; 78 (1972): 31-45.

Derman, A. "Structural Features in Čexov's Poetics." In L. Hulanicki and D. Savignac, eds. and trans. *Anton Čexov As a Master of Story-Telling*, pp. 107-118.

Dobin, E. S. "The Nature of Detail." In L. Hulanicki and D. Savignac, eds. and trans. *Anton Čexov As a Master of Story-Telling*, pp. 39-58.

Eekman, Thomas A. "Anton Čechov and the Classical Languages." *Slavia* 40 (1971): 48-60.

_____. "Čechov and the Europe of His Day." In T. Eekman, ed. *Anton Čechov, 1860-1960: Some Essays*, pp. 13-38.

_____. "Chekhov—An Impressionist." *RusL* 15 (1984): 203-222.

_____. "The Narrator and the Hero in Chekhov's Prose." *California Slavic Studies* 8. Berkeley, Los Angeles, London: University of California Press, 1975, pp. 93-130.

_____. "A Recurrent Theme in Chekhov's Works." *Scando Slavica* 8 (1962): 3-25.

Eichenbaum, Boris. "Chekhov at Large." In R. L. Jackson, ed. *Chekhov: A Collection of Critical Essays*, pp. 21-31.

Ermilov, Vladimir. "A Great Artist and Innovator." In J. Katzer, ed. *A. P. Chekhov: 1860-1960*, pp. 113-162. [Anal. "Van'ka," 113-123.]

Farrell, James T. "On the Letters of Anton Chekhov." *University Review* (Kansas), 9 (1943): 167-173.

Flemming le, L.S.K. "The Structural Role of Language in Chekhov's Later Stories." *SEER* 48 (1970): 323-340.

Fodor, A. "In Search of a Soviet Chekhov." *JRS* 21 (1971): 9-19.

Frost, Edgar L. "The Search for Eternity in Čexov's Fiction: The Flight from Time as a Source of Tension." *RLJ* 31 (1977): 111-120.

Gassner, John. "The Duality of Chekhov." In R. L. Jackson, ed. *Chekhov: A Collection of Critical Essays*, pp. 175-183.

Glad, John. "Chekhov Adapted." *CSP* 16 (1974): 99-111.

Golubkov, V. V. "Čexov's Lyrico-Dramatic Stories." In L. Hulanicki and D. Savignac, eds. and trans. *Anton Čexov As a Master of Story-Telling*, pp. 135-168. [Anal. "Anna of the Neck," 148-158; "The Grasshopper," 141-148; "In the Cart," 160-167.]

Gorky, Maxim. "Anton Chekhov." In J. Katzer, ed. *A. P. Chekhov: 1860-1960*, pp. 5-30.

_____. "What Chekhov Thought of It." *English Review* 8 (1911): 256-266.

Gotman, Sonia K. "The Role of Irony in Čexov's Fiction." *SEEJ* 16 (1972): 297-306.

Graham, R. G. "Anton Chekhov: The Myth of Objectivity." *Socialist Review* (December 1927): 47-49.

Grossman, Leonid. "The Naturalism of Chekhov." In R. L. Jackson, ed. *Chekhov: A Collection of Critical Essays*, 1967, pp. 32-48.

Gruber, William E. "Chekhov's Illusions of Inaction." *CLAJ* 20 (1977): 508-520.

Hagan, John. "Chekhov's Fiction and the Ideal of Objectivity." *Publications of the Modern Language Association of America* 81 (October 1966): 409-417.

_____. "The Tragic Sense in Chekhov's Earliest Stories." *Criticism* 7 (1965): 52-80.

Hichliffe, Arnold. "Chekhov As I See Him: A Letter from England." *SovL* 1 (1980): 196-199.

_____. "Chekhov's Early Tales." *Literary Review* (Teaneck), 15 (1972): 253-255.

Hodgson, Peter. "Metaliterature: An Excerpt from the Anatomy of a Chekhovian Narrator." *Pacific Coast Philology* 7 (1972): 36-42. [Anal. "Boring Story."]

Ignatyeva, N. "Chekhov Films" *SovL* 1 (1980): 164-170.

Ivask, George. "Čechov and the Russian Clergy." In T. Eekman, ed. *Anton Čechov, 1860-1960: Some Essays*, pp. 83-92.

Jackson, Robert L. "Introduction: Perspectives on Chekhov." In R. L. Jackson, ed. *Chekhov: A Collection of Critical Essays*, pp. 1-20.

Jones, W. Gareth. "Chekhov's Undercurrent of Time." *MLR* 64 (1969): 111-121.

Karlinsky, Simon. "Chekhov, Beloved and Betrayed." *Delos: A Journal on and of Translation* 3 (1969): 192-197.

Kataev, Vladimir. "Understanding Chekhov's World." *SovL* 1 (1980): 171-183.

Katsell, Jerome H. "Character Change in Čexov's Short Stories." *SEEJ* 18 (1974): 377-383.

_____. "Mortality: Theme and Structure of Chekhov's Later Prose." In P. Debreczeny and T. Eekman, eds. *Chekhov's Art of Writing: A Collection of Critical Essays*, pp. 54-67.

Kitchin, Laurence. "Chekhov Without Inhibitions." *Encounter* 11 (1958): 68-72.

Klitko, Anatoli. "Chekhov and the Short Story in the Soviet Union today." *SovL* 1 (1980): 143-148.

Knipper-Chekhova, Olga. "The Last Years." In J. Katzer, ed. *A. P. Chekhov: 1860-1960*, pp. 31-55.

Korovin, Konstantin. "My Encounters with Chekhov." *Tri-Quarterly* (Evanston), 28 (1973): 561-569.

Kramer, Karl D. "Chekhov and the Seasons." In P. Debreczeny and T. Eekman, eds. *Chekhov's Art of Writing: A Collection of Critical Essays*, pp. 68-81.

_____. "Chekhov at the End of the Eighties: The Question of Identity." *Etudes Slaves et Est-Europeennes* 11 (1966): 3-18.

_____. "Cycles in Chekhov Criticism: Impressionism Refurbished." In W. C. Kraft, ed. *Proceedings: Pacific Northwest Conference on Foreign Languages. Twenty-third Annual Meeting April 28-29, 1972*. Corvallis: Oregon State University Press, 1973: 268-272.

Lakšin, V. "An Incomparable Artist." In L. Hulanicki and D. Savignac, eds. and trans. *Anton Čexov As a Master of Story-Telling*, pp. 91-106.

MacDonald, Alexander. "Anton Chekhov: The Physician and Major Writer." *JAMA* 22 (1974): 1203-1204.

Mann, Thomas. "Anton Chekhov." *Mainstream* 12 (1959): 2-21.

_____. "Chekhov." In Donald Davie, ed. *Russian Literature and Modern English Fiction: A Collection of Critical Essays*. Chicago and London: University of Chicago Press, 1965, pp. 214-235.

McConkey, James. "In Praise of Chekhov." *HudR* 20 (1967): 417-428.

Marshall, Richard H. "Čexov and the Russian Orthodox Clergy." *Slavonic and East European Journal* 7 (1963): 375-391.

Martin, David W. "Figurative Language and Concretism in Čechov's Short Stories." *RusL* 8 (1980): 125-150.

_____. "Historical References in Chekhov's Later Stories." *MLR* 71 (1976): 595-606.

Mathewson, Rufus, W., Jr. "Intimations of Mortality in Four Čexov Stories." In W. E. Harkins, ed. *American Contributions to the Sixth International Congress of Slavists*. Vol. II: *Literary Contributions*. The Hague: Mouton, 1968, pp. 261-284. [Anal. "Gusev," "Ionych," "The Kiss," and "The Lady with a Lapdog."]

Matlaw, Ralph. "Čechov and the Novel." In T. Eekman, ed. *Anton Čechov, 1860-1960: Some Essays*, pp. 148-167.

Matley, Ian M. "Chekhov and Geography." *RusR* 31 (1972): 376-382.

Meijer, Jan M. "Čechov's Word." In J. Van der Eng, J. M. Meijer, and H. Schmid, eds. *On the Theory of Descriptive Poetics: Anton P. Chekhov As Story-Teller and Playwright*, pp. 99-143.

Mirković, Damir. "Anton Pavlovich Chekhov and the Modern Sociology of Deviance." *CSP* 18 (1976): 66-72.

Mirsky, D. S. "Chekhov and the English." *Monthly Criterion* 6 (1927): 292-304.

Mudrick, Marvin. "Boyish Charmer and Last Mad Genius." *HudR* 27 (1974): 33-54. [Anal. "The Black Monk," 48-51.]

Murry, J. Middleton. "Chekhov Revisited." *Adelphi* (October 1937): 19-23.

Nagibin, Yuri. "Chekhov as an Editor." *SovL* 1 (1980): 112-119.

Nazarenko, Vadim. "Imagery in Čexov." In L. Hulanicki and D. Savignac, eds. and trans. *Anton Čexov As a Master of Story-Telling*, pp. 131-134.

O'Bell, Leslie. "Čexov's 'Skazka': The Intellectual's Fairy Tale." *SEEJ* 25 (1981): 33-46.

Ober, William B. "Chekhov Among the Doctors: The Doctor's Dilemma." *Boswell's Clap and Other Essays: Medical Analyses of Literary Men's Afflictions*. Carbondale: Southern Illinois University Press, 1979, pp. 193-205.

O'Brien, Edward Joseph. *The Short Story Case Book*. New York: Farrar, Rinehart, 1935. [Anal. "The Black Monk," 113-129.]

O'Connor, Frank. "The Slave's Son," Ch. 3. In *The Lonely Voice: A Study of the Short Story*. Cleveland and New York: Meridian Books, World Publishing Co., 1965, pp. 78-98.

O'Faolain, Sean. "Anton Chekhov or 'The Persistent Moralist.' " *The Short Story*. London: Collins, 1948, pp. 76-100.

Paperny, Zinovi. "Truth and Faith: Reading Chekhov's Rough Drafts and Notebooks." *SovL* 1 (1980): 104-111.

Patrick, George Z. "Chekhov's Attitude Towards Life." *SEER* 10 (1932): 658-668.

Pauls, John P. "Chekhov's Humorous Names." *Literary Onomastics Studies* 1 (1974): 53-65.

_____. "Chekhov's Names." *Names* 23 (1975): 67-73.

Phelps, G. "Indifference in the Letters and Tales of Chekhov." *Cambridge Journal* 7 (1954): 208-220.

Pifer, Ellen. "Čexov's Psychological Landscapes." *SEEJ* 17 (1973): 273-278.

Polakiewicz, Leonard. "Crime and Punishment in Čexov." In L. Leighton, ed. *Studies in Honor of Xenia Gasiorowska*. Columbus, Ohio: Slavica Publishers, 1983, pp. 55-67.

Pospelov, G. N. "The Style of Čexov's Tales." In L. Hulanicki and D. Savignac, eds. and trans. *Anton Čexov As a Master of Story-Telling*, pp. 119-30.

Rossbacher, Peter. "Nature and the Quest for Meaning in Chekhov's Stories." *RusR* 24 (1965): 387-392.

Senderovich, Savely. "Chekhov and Impressionism: An Attempt at a Systematic Approach to the Problem." In P. Debreczeny and T. Eekman, eds. *Chekhov's Art of Writing: A Collection of Critical Essays*, pp. 134-152.

Shestov, Leo. "Anton Tchekhov: Creation from the Void." In L. Shestov. *Chekhov and Other Essays*. Ann Arbor: University of Michigan Press, 1966, pp. 1-60.

Sholton, M. H. "Chekhov." In J. Fennell, ed. *Nineteenth-Century Russian Literature: Studies of Ten Russian Writers*. Berkeley and Los Angeles: University of California Press, 1973, pp. 293-346.

Sklovskij, Victor. "A. P. Čexov." In L. Hulanicki and D. Savignac, eds. and trans. *Anton Čexov As a Master of Story-Telling*, pp. 59-90.

Sokolova, Maya. "Chekhov's Unknown Humorous Sketches in *Budilnik*." *SovL* 1 (1980): 120-127.

Stowell, H. Peter. "Chekhov and *Nouveau Roman*: Subjective Objectivism." In P. Debreczeny and T. Eekman, eds. *Chekhov's Art of Writing: A Collection of Critical Essays*, pp. 180-191.

Struve, Gleb. "Chekhov in Communist Censorship." *SEER* 33 (1955): 327-342.

Templeton, N. "Chekhov in Wellington." *Landfall* 19 (1965): 174-185.

Thoms, H. "Anton Chekhov: Physician and Literary Artist." *JAMA* 3 (1931): 1631-1632.

Timmer, Charles B. "The Bizarre Element in Čexov's Art." In T. Eekman, ed. *Anton Čechov, 1860-1960: Some Essays*, pp. 277-292.

Trautmann, Joanne. "Doctor Chekhov's Prison." In Joanne Trautmann, ed. *Healing Arts in Dialogue: Medicine and Literature*. Carbondale: Southern Illinois University Press, 1981, pp. 125-137.

Vinogradov, V. V. "On Čexov's Style." In L. Hulanicki and D. Savignac, eds. and trans. *Anton Čexov As a Master of Story-Telling*, pp. 169-186.

Wilson, Edmund. "Seeing Chekhov Plain." *New Yorker* 22 (November 1952): 180-198.

Winner, Thomas G. "Čechov and Scientism. Observations on the Searching Stories." In T. Eekman, ed. *Anton Čechov, 1860-1960: Some Essays*, pp. 325-335.

______. "Myth as a Device in the Works of Chekhov." In B. Slote, ed. *Myth and Symbol: Critical Approaches and Applications*. Lincoln: University of Nebraska Press, 1963, pp. 71-78.

______. "Syncretism in Chekhov's Art: A Study of Polystructured Texts." In P. Debreczeny and T. Eekman, eds. *Chekhov's Art of Writing: A Collection of Critical Essays*, pp. 153-166.

Chekhov and Others, Comparative Studies of His Prose (Books, Articles and Chapters in Books)

Belgion, M. "Verisimilitude in Chekhov and Dostoevsky." *Criterion* 16 (1936): 14-32. [Anal. "Ward No. 6," 17-23.]

Berthoff, A. E. "Marvell's Stars, Schubert's Suns, Chekhov's Pipe-Recognizing and Interpreting Metaphor." *SR* 89 (1981): 57-82. [Anal. "Gooseberries," 75-82.]

Calder, Angus. "Literature and Morality: Leskov, Chekhov, Late Tolstoy." Ch. 8, *Russia Discovered: Nineteenth-century Fiction from Pushkin to Chekhov*. New York: Barnes and Noble Books, 1976, pp. 238-275.

Debreczeny, Paul. "The Device of Conspicuous Silence in Tolstoj, Čexov, and Faulkner." In Victor Terras, ed. *American Contributions to the Eighth International Congress of Slavists. Vol. II: Literature*. Columbus, Ohio: Slavica, 1978, pp. 125-145. [Anal. "In the Ravine," 128-137.]

Delp, W. E. "Goethe's 'Tasso' in the Light of Chekhov." *Comparative Literature Studies* 12 (1944): 5-8.

Doyle, P. A. "Chekhov in Erin: The Short Stories of Sean O'Faolain." *DubR* 241 (1967): 263-269.

Durkin, Andrew R. "Chekhov's Response to Dostoevskii: The Case of 'Ward Six'." *SlavR* 40 (1981): 49-59.

_____. "Trifonov's 'Taking Stock': The Role of Čexovian Subtext." *SEEJ* 28 (1984): 32-41.

Gordon, Caroline. "Notes on Chekhov and Maugham." *SR* 57 (1949): 401-410.

Jackson, Robert L. "The Garden-of-Eden in Dostoevsky's 'A Christmas Party and a Wedding' and Chekhov's 'Because of Little Apples'." *RLC Revue de Literature Comparee* 55 (1981): 331-341.

Karlinsky, Simon. "Frustrated Artists and Devouring Mothers in Čechov and Annenskij." In J. T. Baer and N. W. Ingham, eds. *Mnemozina: Studia Literaria Russica in Honorem Vsevolod Setchkarev*. Munich: Fink, 1974, pp. 228-231.

_____. "Nabokov and Chekhov: The Lesser Russian Tradition." *Tri-Quarterly* 17 (1970): 7-16.

Kauz'muk, V. A. "Vasilii Shukshin and the Early Chekhov: An Essay in Typological Analysis." *Soviet Studies in Literature* 14 (1978): 61-78.

Lau, Joseph. "The Peking Man and Ivanov: Portrait of Two Superfluous Men." *Contemporary Literature* 10 (1969): 85-102.

Lavrin, Janko. "Chekhov and Maupassant." *SEER* 5 (1926): 1-24.

_____. "Chekhov and Maupassant." *Studies in East European Literature*. London: Constable, 1929, pp. 156-192.

Lomunov, Konstantin. "Tolstoy, Chekhov, The Moscow Art Theatre." *SovL* (1980): 149-156.

McConkey, James. "Two Anonymous Writers: E. M. Forster and Anton Chekhov." In G. K. Das and J. Beer, eds. *E. M. Forster: A Human Exploration: Centenary Essays*. New York: New York University Press, 1979, pp. 231-244.

Mathewson, Rufus W. "Thoreau and Chekhov: A Note on 'The Steppe'." *UlbanR* 1 (1977): 28-40.

Matual, David. "Chekhov's 'Black Monk' and Byron's 'Black Friar'." *International Fiction Review* 5 (1978): 46-51.

Nagle, John J. "Idealism: The Internal Structure in Gogol's 'Nevsky Prospect' and Chekhov's 'An Attack of Nerves'." *West Virginia University Philological Papers* 19 (1972): 20-28.

Newcombe, J. M. "Was Čexov a Tolstoyan?" *SEEJ* 18 (1974): 143-152.

Pomorska, Krystyna. "On the Structure of Modern Prose: Chekhov and Solzhenitsyn." *PTL: A Journal of Descriptive Poetics and Theory of Literature* 1 (1976): 459-465.

Robinson, K. E. "Anton Chekhov and Henry James." *ISE* 2 (1970): 182-197.

Rossbacher, Peter. "The Function of Insanity in Čexov's 'The Black Monk' and Gogol's 'Notes of a Madman'." *SEEJ* 13 (1969): 191-199.

Rubenstein, Roberta. "Virginia Woolf, Chekhov, and 'The Rape of the Lock'," *Dalhousie Review* 54 (1974): 429-435.

Rukalski, Zygmunt. "Anton Chekhov and Guy Maupassant: Their Views on Life and Art." *SEES* 5 (1960): 178-188.

_____. "Fin-de-siècle in France and Russia." *SEES* 12 (1967): 124-127.

_____. "Human Problems in the Works of Maupassant and Chekhov." *SEES* 3 (1958): 80-89.

_____. "Maupassant and Chekhov: Differences." *CSP* 13 (1971): 374-402.

_____. "Maupassant and Chekhov: Similarities." *CSP* 11 (1969): 346-358.

———. "Maupassant's and Chekhov's Views on Spiritual Freedom in Relation to Creative Writing." *SEES* 5 (1960): 95-97.

———. "Russian and French Writers on Politics and Public Opinion." *Etudés Slaves et Est-Européennes* 6 (1961): 103-108.

Schneider, Elisabeth. "Katherine Mansfield and Chekhov." *Modern Language Notes* 50 (1935): 394-397.

Senanu, K. E. "Anton Chekhov and Henry James." *ISE* 2 (1970): 182-197.

Simmons, Ernest J. "Tolstoy and Chekhov." *Midway* 8 (1968): 91-104.

Smernoff, Susan S. "The Irony of the Doctor as Patient in Chekhov's 'Ward No. 6' and in Solzhenitsyn's *Cancer Ward.*" In P. Debreczeny and T. Eekman, eds. *Chekhov's Art of Writing: A Collection of Critical Essays*, pp. 167-179.

Speirs, Logan. "Tolstoy and Chekhov: *The Death of Ivan Ilych* and 'A Dreary Story'." *Oxford Review* 8 (1968): 81-93.

———. *Tolstoy and Chekhov.* Cambridge: Cambridge University Press, 1971.

Stephenson, R. "Chekhov on Western Writers." *Texas University Studies in English* 30 (1951): 235-242.

Stern, J. "*Dr. Zhivago* and Chekhov." *LonM*, 6 (1959): 60-63.

Stewart, Maaja A. "Scepticism and Belief in Chekhov and Anderson." *SSF* 9 (1972): 29-40.

Stowell, H. Peter. *Literary Impressionism: James and Chekhov.* Athens: University of Georgia Press, 1980.

Winner, Anthony. *Characters in the Twilight: Hardy, Zola, and Chekhov.* Charlottesville: University Press of Virginia, 1981.

Winner, Thomas G. "Čexov's 'Ward No. 6' and Tolstoyan Ethics." *SEEJ* 17 (1959): 321-334.

Articles on Individual Stories

"An Attack of Nerves"

Conrad, Joseph L. "Čexov's 'An Attack of Nerves'." *SEEJ* 13 (1969): 429-443.

Duncan, Phillip A. "Chekhov's 'An Attack of Nerves' As 'Experimental' Narrative." In P. Debreczeny and T. Eekman, eds. *Chekhov's Art of Writing: A Collection of Critical Essays*, pp. 112-122.

Senderovich, Marena. "The Symbolic Structure of Chekhov's Story 'An Attack of Nerves.' " In P. Debreczeny and T. Eekman, eds. *Chekhov's Art of Writing: A Collection of Critical Essays*, 1977, pp. 11-26.

"A Visit to Friends"

Clyman, Toby W. "Chekhov's 'Visiting Friends': A Satiric Parody." *Melbourne Slavonic Studies* 13 (1978), 9-18.

"Aniuta"

Lelchuk, Alan. "An Analysis of Technique in Chekhov's 'Anyuta'." *SSF* 6 (1969): 609-618.

"The Bet"

Childs, J. Rives. "Chekhov's 'The Bet': Its Source in Lord Cecil's Wager." *South Atlantic Quarterly* 40 (1941): 397-400.

"The Bishop"

Curtin, Constance. "Bridging Devices in Chekhov's 'The Bishop'." *Canadian Slavic Studies* 3 (1969): 705-711.
Stowell, H. Peter. "Chekhov's 'The Bishop': The Annihilation of Faith and Identity Through Time." *SSF* 12 (1975): 117-126.

"The Black Monk"

O'Toole, L. M. "Chekhov's 'The Black Monk': Semiotic Dimensions of Character, Social-Role and Narrative Function." *Essays in Poetics* 6 (1981): 39-66.
_____. "Chekhov: 'The Black Monk,' 1894; ('Chernyi monakh')." In *Structure, Style and Interpretation in the Russian Short Story*. New Haven and London: Yale University Press, 1982, pp. 161-179.

"The Bride"

Maxwell, David. "Chekhov's 'Nevesta': A Structural Approach to the Role of Setting." *RLT* 6 (1974): 91-100.
Winner, Thomas G. "Theme and Structure in Čechov's 'The Betrothed'." *Indiana Slavic Studies*, Vol. 3. Bloomington, Ind.: Indiana University Publications, 1963, pp. 163-172.

"The Darling"

Bayuk, Milla. "The Submissive Wife Stereotype in Anton Chekhov's 'Darling'." *CLAJ* 20 (1977): 533-538.
Poggioli, Renato. "Storytelling in a Double Key." *The Phoenix and the Spider*. Cambridge, Mass.: Harvard University Press, 1957, pp. 109-130. [Anal. "The Darling," pp. 124-130.]
Sperber, Michael A. "The 'As If' Personality and Chekhov's 'The Darling'." *Psychoanalytic Review* 58 (1971): 14-21.
Tolstoy, Leo. "An Afterword to Chekhov's Story 'Darling'." *The Works of Leo Tolstoy*. Trans. A. Maude. London: Oxford University Press, 1929, pp. 323-327.

"The Death of a Government Clerk"

Hamburger, H. "The Function of the Verbum Dicendi in Čexov's 'Smert' činovnika'." In A.G.F. van Holk, ed. *Dutch Contributions to the Sixth International Congress of Slavists*. The Hague: Mouton, 1968, pp. 98-122.

"Enemies"

Frydman, Anne. " 'Enemies': An Experimental Story." *UlbanR* 2 (1979): 103-119.

"For Stealing Apples"

Jackson, Robert L. "Chekhov's Garden of Eden, or, The Fall of the Russian Adam and Eve: 'Because of Little Apples'." *Slavica Hierosolymitana* 4. L. Fleishman et al., eds. Jerusalem: Magnes Press. Hebrew University, 1979, pp. 70-78.

"The Grasshopper"

Freling, Roger. "A New View of Dr. Dymov in Chekhov's 'The Grasshopper'."
    SSF 16 (1979): 183-187.

"Grisha"

Hamburger, H. "The Function of the Viewpoint in Čechov's 'Griša'." *RusL* 3
    (1972): 5-15.

"Gusev"

Ehre, Milton. "The Symbolic Structure of Chekhov's 'Gusev'." *UlbanR 2 (1979):
    76-85.*
Lantz, Kenneth A. "Chekhov's 'Gusev': A Study." *SSF* 15 (1978): 55-61.

"In the Cart"

Hamburger, H. "The Function of the Time Component In Čechov's 'Na podvode'."
    Dutch Contributions to the Seventh International Congress of Slavists. The
    Hague: Mouton, 1973, pp. 237-270.

"In the Ravine"

Harrison, John William. "Symbolic Action in Chekhov's 'Peasants' and 'In the
    Ravine'." *MFS* 7 (1961): 369-372.
McLean, Hugh. "Čexov's 'V ovrage': Six Antipodes." *American Contributions
    to the Sixth International Congress of Slavists, Vol. II: Literary Contribu-
    tions*. The Hague and Paris: Mouton, 1968, pp. 285-305.

"The Kiss"

Rosen, Nathan. "The Life Force in Chekhov's 'The Kiss'." *UlbanR* 2 (1979): 175-185.

"The Lady with a Lapdog"

Van der Eng, Jan. "The Semantic Structure of 'Lady with Lapdog.' " In J. Van
    der Eng. J. M. Meijer, and H. Schmid, eds. *On the Theory of Descriptive
    Poetics: Anton P. Chekhov As Story-Teller and Playwright*, pp. 59-94.

Little Trilogy—("The Man in the Shell," "Gooseberries," "On Love")

Conrad, Joseph L. "Čexov's 'The Man in the Shell': Freedom and Responsibility."
    SEEJ 10 (1966): 400-410.
Maxwell, David E. "The Unity of Chekhov's ' Little Trilogy.' " In P. Debreczeny
    and T. Eekman, eds. *Chekhov's Art of Writing: A Collection of Critical
    Essays*, pp. 35-53.
Mays, Milton A. " 'Gooseberries' and Chekhov's Concreteness." *Southern Hu-
    manities Review* 6 (1972): 63-67.
Wear, Richard. "Chekhov's Trilogy: Another Look at Ivan Ivanych." *RBPH*
    55 (1977): 897-906.

"Misery"

Brooks, Cleanth, and Robert Penn Warren. "Anton Chekhov: 'The Lament'."
    Ch. 3. *Undestanding Fiction*. New York: Appleton-Century-Crofts, 1959,
    pp. 203-210.

Winslow, Joan D. "Language as Theme in Chekhov's 'Misery'." *AL*, 4 (1978): 1-7.

"On The Road"

Senderovich, Savely. "The Poetic Structure of Čexov's Short Story 'On The Road' " In A. Kodjak, M. J. Konnolly, and P. Pomorska, eds. *Structural Analysis of Narrative Texts*, pp. 44-81.

"Peasants"

Harrison, John W. "Symbolic Action in Chekhov's 'Peasants' and 'In the Ravine'." *MFS* 7 (1961): 369-372.

"Rothschild's Fiddle"

Jackson, Robert L. " 'If I Forget Thee O Jerusalem': An Essay on Chekhov's 'Rothschild's Fiddle'." *Slavica Hierosolymitana* 3 L. Fleishman et al., eds. Jerusalem: Magnes Press. Hebrew University, 1978, pp. 55-67.

"The Shooting Party"

Hagan, John. "The Shooting Party: Čexov's Early Novel: Its Place in His Development." *SEEJ* 9 (1965): 123-140.

"Sleepy"

Curtin, Constance. "Čexov's 'Sleepy': An Interpretation." *SEEJ* 9 (1965): 390-399.
Rosen, Nathan. "The Unconscious in Čexov's 'Van'ka' (With a Note on 'Sleepy')." *SEEJ* 15 (1971): 441-454.
Stowell, H. Peter. "Chekhov's Prose Fugue: 'Sleepy'." *RLT* 11 (1975): 435-442.
Struve, Gleb. "On Chekhov's Craftmanship: The Anatomy of a Story." *SlavR* 20 (1961): 465-476.

"Solomon"

Rossbacher, Peter. "Čexov's Fragment 'Solomon'." *SEEJ* 12 (1968): 27-34.

"The Steppe"

Katsell, Jerome H. "Čexov's 'The Steppe' Revisited." *SEEJ* 22 (1978): 313-323.
Maxwell, David. "A System of Symbolic Gesture in Čexov's 'Step'." *SEEJ* 17 (1973): 146-154.
Stowell, H. Peter. "Čexov's 'Steppe': A Journey Through Endless Change." In W. C. Kraft, ed. *Proceedings: Pacific Northwest Conference on Foreign Languages. Twenty-Fourth Annual Meeting, May 4-5, 1973*. Western Washington State College. Vol. 24. Corvallis: Oregon State University, 1973, pp. 264-269.

"The Student"

Martin, David W. " 'Realia' and Chekhov's 'The Student'." *Canadian-American Slavic Studies* 12 (1978): 266-273.
O'Toole, L. M. "Structure and Style in the Short Story: Chekhov's 'The Student'." *SEER* 49 (1971): 45-67.

"Terror"

Leong, Albert. "Literary Unity in Chekhov's 'Strakh'." *JRS* 27 (1974): 15-20.

"Three Years"

Reeve, F. D. "Tension in Prose: Chekhov's 'Three Years'." *SEEJ* 16 (1958): 99-108.

"Typhus"

Polakiewicz, Leonard. "Čexov's 'Tif': An Analysis." *RLJ* 32 (1979): 92-111.

"Vanka"

Rosen, Nathan. "The Unconscious in Chekhov's 'Van'ka' (With a Note on 'Sleepy'.)" *SEEJ* 15 (1971): 441-454.

"Verochka"

Conrad, Joseph L. "Čexov's 'Veročka': A Polemical Parody." *SEEJ* 14 (1970): 465-474.

"Ward No. 6"

Basu, A., and S. Basu. "Author's Voice in 'Ward No. 6'." *Journal of the School of Languages* 7 (1980 Monsoon-1981 Winter): 41-47.

Articles and Chapters in Books (Mostly on Chekhov's Drama)

Bentley, Eric. "Chekhov As Playwright." *Kenyon Review* 7 (1949): 226-250.

Borker, David, and Olga K. Garnica. "Male and Female Speech in Dramatical Dialogue: A Stylistic Analysis of Chekhovian Character Speech." *Language and Style* 13 (1980): 3-28.

Brustein, Robert. "Anton Chekhov." *The Theatre of Revolt: An Approach to the Modern Drama*. Boston: Little, Brown, 1964, pp. 135-179.

Citron, A. "The Chekhov Technique Today." *DramR* 27 (1983): 91-96.

Corrigan, Robert W. "The Drama of Anton Chekhov." In T. Bogard and W. I. Oliver, eds. *Modern Drama: Essays in Criticism*. New York: Oxford University Press, 1965, pp. 73-98.

_____. "Some Aspects of Chekhov's Dramaturgy." *EThJ* 7 (1955): 107-114.

Croyden, Margaret. " 'People Just Eat Their Dinners: The Absurdity of Chekhov's Doktors." *TQ* 11 (1968): 130-137.

Egri, Petr. "The Dramatic Function of the Mosaic Design in Chekhov's Late Plays." *ALitASH* 21 (1979): 45-68.

Fludas, John. "Chekhovian Comedy: A Review Essay." *Genre* 6 (1973): 333-345.

Freedman, Morris. "Chekhov's Morality of Work." *MD* 5 (1962): 83-93.

Ganz, Arthur. "Arrivals and Departures: The Meaning of the Journey in the Major Plays of Chekhov." *DS* 5 (1966): 5-23.

Goodliffe, John D. "Time in Chekhov's Plays." *New Zealand Slavonic Journal* 7 (1971): 32-41.

Grecco, S. "A Physician Healing Himself: Chekhov's Treatment of Doctors in the Major Plays." In E. R. Peschel, ed. *Medicine and Literature*. New York: Watson, 1980, pp. 3-10.

Harris, W. B. "Chekhov and Russian Drama." *Annual Reports and Transactions of Plymouth Institution and Devon and Cornell Natural History Society* 21 (1947-1949): 141-150.

Heim, Michael H. "Chekhov and the Moscow Art Theatre." In J. P. Barricelli, ed. *Chekhov's Great Plays: A Critical Anthology*, pp. 133-143.

Holland, Peter. "Chekhov and the Resistant Symbol." In J. Redmond, ed. *Drama and Symbolism*. Cambridge: Cambridge University Press, 1982 (Themes in Drama), pp. 227-242.

Hubbs, Clayton A. "Chekhov and the Contemporary Theatre." *MD* 24 (1981): 357-366.

_____. "The Function of Repetition in the Plays of Chekhov." *MD* 22 (1979): 115-124.

Kovitz, Sonia. "A Fine Day to Hang Oneself: On Chekhov's Plays." In J. P. Barricelli, ed. *Chekhov's Great Plays: A Critical Anthology*, pp. 189-200.

Kuhn, Reinhard. "The Debasement of the Intellectual in Contemporary Continental Drama." *MD* 7 (1965): 454-462.

Lawson, John H. "Chekhov's Drama: Challenge to Playwrights." *Masses and Mainstream* 7 (1954): 11-26.

McDonald, Jan. "Production of Chekhov's Plays in Britain Before 1914." *TN* 34 (1980): 25-36.

Martin, David. "Philosophy in Chekhov's Major Plays." *Die Welt der Slaven: Halbjahresschrift fur Slavistik* (Munich) 23 (1978): 122-139.

Meyerhold, Vsevolod. "Naturalistic Theater of Mood." In R. L. Jackson, ed. *Chekhov: A Collection of Critical Essays*, pp. 62-68.

Moravcevich, Nicholas. "Chekhov and Naturalism: From Affinity to Divergence." *CompD*, 4 (1970): 219-240.

_____. "The Dark Side of the Chekhovian Smile." *DS* 5 (1967): 237-51.

_____. "Scène-à-faire and the Chekhovian Dramatic Structure." In P. Debreczeny and T. Eekman, eds. *Chekhov's Art of Writing: A Collection of Critical Essays*, pp. 100-111.

_____. "Women in Chekhov's Plays." In J. P. Barricelli, ed. *Chekhov's Great Plays: A Critical Anthology*, pp. 201-217.

Morgan, V. "Chekhov's Social Plays and Their Historical Background." *Papers of the Manchester Literary Club* 64 (1939): 96-114.

Nabokoff, C. "Chekhov on the English Stage." *ContempR* 129 (1926): 756-762.

Nag, Martin. "On the Aspects of Time and Place in Anton Chekhov's Dramaturgy." *Scando-Slavica* 16 (1970): 23-34.

Nilsson, Nils Ake. "Intonation and Rhythm in Chekhov's Plays." In R. L. Jackson, ed. *Chekhov: A Collection of Critical Essays*, pp. 161-174.

Pedrotti, Louis. "Chekhov's Major Plays: A Doctor in the House." In J. P. Barricelli, ed. *Chekhov's Great Plays: A Critical Anthology*, pp. 233-250.

Risso, Richard D. "Chekhov: A View of the Basic Ironic Structures." In J.-P. Barricelli, ed. *Chekhov's Great Plays: A Critical Anthology*, pp. 181-188.

Saint-Denis, Michel. "Chekhov and the Modern Stage." *DS* 3 (1965): 77-81.

Savvas, Minas. "Chekhov's Tragicomedy: Some Typical Examples." *Language Quarterly* 9 (1970): 54-56.

Seymour, Alan. "Summer Seagull, Winter Love." *LonM* 4 (May 1964): 63-67.

Skaftymov, A. "Principles of Structure in Chekhov's Plays." In R. L. Jackson, ed. *Chekhov: A Collection of Critical Essays*, pp. 69-87.

Smith, J. Oates. "Chekhov and the 'Theater of the Absurd'." *Bucknell Review* 14 (1966): 44-58.

States, Bert O. "Chekhov's Dramatic Strategy. *Yale Review* 56 (1967): 212-224.

Stein, Walter. "Tragedy and the Absurd." *DubR* 233 (1959-1960): 363-382.

Styan, J. L. "The Idea of a Definitive Production: Chekhov In and Out of Period." *CompD*, 4 (1970): 177-196.

Walton, Michael. " 'If Only We Knew' " (Chekhov Productions). *New Theatre Magazine* 8 (1968): 29-35.

Winner, Thomas G. "The Chekhov Centennial Productions in the Moscow Theatres." *SEEJ* 5 (1961): 255-262.

Wright, A. Colin. "Translating Chekhov for Performance." *Canadian Review of Comparative Literature—Revue Canadienne de Literature Comparee* 7 (1980): 174-182.

Comparative Studies of Chekhov's Plays
(Articles and Chapters in Books)

Adler, Jacob H. "Two *Hamlet* Plays: *The Wild Duck* and *The Seagull*. *Journal of Modern Literature* 1 (1970-1971): 226-248.

Beckerman, Bernard. "The Artifice of 'Reality': Chekhov and Pinter." *MD* 21 (1978): 153-161.

Cross, A. G. "The Breaking Strings of Chekhov and Turgenev." *SEER* 47 (1969): 510-513.

Egri, Peter. "The Reinterpretation of the Chekhovian Mosaic Design in O'Neill's *Long Day's Journey Into Night*." *AlitASH* 22 (1980): 29-71.

———. "The Short Story in the Drama: Chekhov and O'Neill." *ALitASH* 20 (1978): 3-28.

Erlich, Victor. "Chekhov and West European Drama." *Yearbook of Comparative and General Literature* 12 (1963): 56-60.

Gassner, John. "Chekhov and the Russian Realists." Ch. 25 in *Masters of the Drama*. New York: Random House, 1940, pp. 495-525.

Katsell, Jerome H. "Chekhov's *The Seagull* and Maupassant's *Sur l'eau*." In J.-P. Barricelli, ed. *Chekhov's Great Plays: A Critical Anthology*, pp. 18-34.

Kernan, Alvin B. "Truth and Dramatic Mode in the Modern Theatre: Chekhov, Pirandello and Williams." *MD* 1 (1958): 101-114.

Kleine, Don W. "The Chekhovian Source of 'Marriage a là Mode'." *Philological Quarterly* 42 (1963): 284-288.

Lahr, John. "Pinter and Chekhov: The Bond of Naturalism." *DramR* 13 (1968): 137-145.

Lau, Joseph S. M. "Ts'ao Yu, The Reluctant Disciple of Chekhov: A Comparative Study of *Sunrise* and *The Cherry Orchard*." *MD* 9 (1966): 358-372.

Mendelsohn, Michael J. "The Heartbreak Houses of Shaw and Chekhov." *Shaw Review* 6 (1963): 89-95.

Nilsson, Nils Ake. "Two Chekhovs: Mayakovskiy on Chekhov's 'Futurism.' " In J.-P. Barricelli, ed. *Chekhov's Great Plays: A Critical Anthology*, pp. 251-262.

Porter, Robert. "*Hamlet* and *The Seagull*." *JRS* 41 (1981): 23-32.

Quintus, John A. "The Loss of Dear Things: Chekhov and Williams in Perspective." *English Language Notes* (18 (1981): 201-206.

Reed, Walter. "*The Cherry Orchard* and *Hedda Gabler*." In M. Seidel and E. Mendelson, eds. *Homer to Brecht: The European Epic and Dramatic Traditions.* New Haven: Yale University Press, 1977, pp. 317-335.

Rinear, David L. "Day the Whores Came out to Play Tennis: Kopit's Debt to Chekhov." *Today's Speech* 22 (1974): 19-23.

Schwartz, Kessel. "La gringa and *The Cherry Orchard.*" *Hispania* 43 (1958): 51-55.

Senelick, Laurence. "Chekhov's Drama, Maeterlinck, and the Russian Symbolists." In J.-P. Barricelli, ed. *Chekhov's Great Plays: A Critical Anthology*, pp. 161-180.

Seyler, Dorothy U. "*The Seagull* and *The Wild Duck*: Birds of a Feather?" *MD* 8 (1965): 167-173.

Stroud, T. A. "*Hamlet* and *The Seagull.*" *Shakespeare Quarterly* 9 (1958): 367-372.

Styan, J. L. "The Delicate Balance: Audience Ambivalence in the Comedy of Shakespeare and Chekhov." *Costerus* 2 (1972): 159-184.

True, Warren R. "Ed. Bullins, Anton Chekhov, and the Drama of Mood." *CLAJ* 20 (1977): 521-532.

Vanholk, A.G.F. "Thematic Composition in Russian Drama: The Theme of Envy in Pushkin's "Mozart and Salieri,' Turgenev's *A Month in the Country* and Chekhov's *Uncle Vanya.*" *EP* 8 (1983): 53-73.

Wegener, Adolph. "Harold Pinter: Chekhov's Heir Apparent. In W. H. Sokel et al., eds. Bonn: Bouvier, 1978, pp. 296-315. *Probleme der Komparatistik und Interpretation: Festschrift fur André von Gronicka zum 65. Gebrutstag am 25.5.1977.*

Wilson, A. "The Influence of *Hamlet* Upon Chekhov's *The Seagull.*" *Susquehanna University Studies*, May 1952, pp. 309-316.

Winner, Thomas G. "Chekhov's *The Seagull* and Shakespeare's *Hamlet*: A Study of a Dramatic Device." *American Slavic and East European Review* 15 (1956): 103-111.

_____. "Speech Characteristics in Chekhov's Ivanov and Čapek's Loupežnik." *American Contributions to the Fifth International Congress of Slavists. Vol. II Literary Contributions*. The Hague: Mouton, 1963, pp. 403-441.

Articles on Individual Plays

The Cherry Orchard

Baehr, Stephan L. "Who Is Firs? The Literary History of a Name." *UlbanR* 2 (1979): 14-23.

Balukhaty, S. D. "*The Cherry Orchard*: A Formalist Approach." In R. L. Jackson, ed. *Chekhov: A Collection of Critical Essays*, pp. 136-146.

Barricelli, Jean-Pierre. "Counterpoint of the Snapping String: Chekhov's *The Cherry Orchard.*" *California Slavic Studies*. Berkeley, Los Angeles, London: University of California Press, 10 (1977): 121-136.

Beckerman, Bernard. "Dramatic Analysis and Literary Interpretation: *The Cherry Orchard* as Exemplum." *New Literary History* 2 (1971): 391-406.

Bely, Andrei. "*The Cherry Orchard.*" In L. Senelick, ed. and trans. *Russian Dramatic Theory from Pushkin to the Symbolists: An Anthology*. Austin: University of Texas Press, 1981, pp. 89-92.

Deer, Irving. "Speech as Action in Chekhov's *The Cherry Orchard.*" *EThJ* 10 (1959): 30-34.

Fagin, N. Bryllion. "In Search of an American *Cherry Orchard.*" *TQ* 1 (1958): 132-141.

Fergusson, Francis. "The Plot of *The Cherry Orchard*"/"Chekhov's Histrionic Art: An End and a Beginning." In his *The Idea of a Theatre: A Study of Ten Plays. The Art of Drama in Changing Perspective.* Princeton, N.J.: Princeton University Press, 1968, pp. 161-177.

Frost, E. L. "Characterization Through Time in the Works of Chekhov, with an Emphasis on *The Cherry Orchard.*" In C. Nelson, ed. *Studies in Language and Literature. Proceedings of the 23rd Mountain Interstate Foreign Language Conference.* Richmond: Eastern Kentucky University, 1976, pp. 169-173.

Gerould, Daniel C. "*The Cherry Orchard* as a Comedy." *Journal of General Education* 11 (1958): 109-122.

Hahn, Beverly. "Chekhov's *The Cherry Orchard.*" *CR* 16 (1973): 56-72.

Hubs, Clayton A., and J. T. Hubs. "The Godess of Love and the Tree of Knowledge: Some Elements of Myth and Folkore in Chekhov's *The Cherry Orchard.*" *South Carolina Review* 14 (1982): 66-77.

Kelson, John. "Allegory and Myth in *The Cherry Orchard.*" *Western Humanities Review* 13 (1959): 321-324.

Landesman, Rocco. "Comrade Serban in *The Cherry Orchard.*" *Yale Theater* 8 (1977): 136-141.

Latham, Jeagueline E. M. "*The Cherry Orchard* as Comedy." *EThJ* 10 (1958): 21-29.

Nichols, J. R. "*The Cherry Orchard*: The Fallacy of the Bourgeoisie Hero." *Studies in the Twentieth Century* 9 (1972): 77-82.

Remaley, Peter B. "Chekhov's *The Cherry Orchard.*" *South Atlantic Bulletin* 38 (1973): 16-20.

Silverstein, Norman. "Chekhov's Comic Spirit and *The Cherry Orchard.*" *MD* 1 (1958): 91-100.

Szewcow, M. "Anatolij Efros Directs Chekhov's *The Cherry Orchard* and Gogol's *The Marriage.*" *ThQ* 7 (1977): 34-47.

Ivanov

Berdnikov, G. "*Ivanov*: An Analysis." In R. L. Jackson, ed. *Chekhov: A Collection of Critical Essays*, pp. 88-98.

Dickstein, Morris. "Gielgud's *Ivanov*, or Chekhov Without Tears." *Salmagundi*, 2 (1967): 88-93.

Shakh-Azizova, Tatiana. "A Russian Hamlet: *Ivanov* and His Age." *SovL* 1 (1980): 157-163.

The Seagull

Bryden, R. "Chekhov: Secret of *The Seagull.*" *Observer Magazine* (May 31, 1970): 10-20.

Chances, Ellen. "Chekhov's *Seagull*: Ethereal Creature or Stuffed Bird." In P. Debreczeny and T. Eekman, eds. *Chekhov's Art of Writing: A Collection of Critical Essays*, pp. 27-34.

Curtis, James M. "Spatial Form in Drama: *The Seagull.*" *Canadian-American Slavonic Studies* 6 (1972): 13-37.

Hollosi, C. "Chekhov's Reaction to Two Interpretations of Nina." *Theatre Survey* 24 (1983): 117-126.
Jackson, Robert L. "Chekhov's *Seagull*: The Empty Well, the Dry Lake and the Cold Cave." In J. P. Barricelli, ed. *Chekhov's Great Plays: A Critical Anthology*, pp. 3-17.
Jones, W. G. "*The Seagull's* Second Symbolist Play-Within-the-Play." *SEER* 53 (1975): 17-26.
Kendle, Burton. "The Elusive Horses in *The Seagull*." *MD* 13 (1970): 63-66.
Sagar, Keith. "Chekhov's Magic Lake: A Reading of *The Seagull*." *MD* 15 (1972-1973): 441-447.
Scott, Virginia. "Life in Art: A Reading of *The Seagull*." *EThJ*, 30 (1978): 357-367.
Senelick, Laurence. "Lake-Shore Bohemia: *The Seagull's* Theatrical Context." *EThJ* 29 (1977): 199-213.
Strongin, Carol. "Irony and Theatricality in Chekhov's *The Seagull*." *CompD* 15 (1981): 366-380.

Tatiana Repina

Racin, J. "Chekhov's Use of Church Ritual in *Tatiana Repina*." *Drama and Religion. Themes in Drama*, No. 5. J. Redmond, ed. Cambridge: Cambridge University Press, 1983, pp. 1-19.

Three Sisters

Babula, William. "*Three Sisters*, Time, and the Audience." *MD* 18 (1975): 365-370.
Bennett, John L. "An Examination of Chekhov's Presentation of Characters and Themes in Act I of *Three Sisters*." *Proceedings: Pacific Northwest Conference on Foreign Languages. Twentieth Annual Meeting, April 11-12, 1969.* Vol. 20. Ed. J. L. Mordaunt, Victoria, B.C.: University of Victoria, 1969, pp. 94-102.
Bristow, Eugene K. "Circles, Triads, and Parity in *The Three Sisters*." In J.-P. Barricelli, ed. *Chekhov's Great Plays: A Critical Anthology*, pp. 76-95.
Hahn, Beverly. "Chekhov: *The Three Sisters*." *CR* 15 (1972): 3-22.
Karlinsky, Simon. "Huntsmen, Birds, Forests, and *Three Sisters*." In J. P. Barricelli, ed. *Chekhov's Great Plays: A Critical Anthology*, pp. 144-160.
Kramer, Karl D. "*Three Sisters* or Taking a Chance on Love." In J.-P. Barricelli, ed. *Chekhov's Great Plays: A Critical Anthology*, pp. 61-75.
LeMaster, J. R. "The Condition of Talk in Chekhov's *Three Sisters*." *New Laurel Review* 4 (1975): 9-16.
Moss, Howard. "*Three Sisters*." *HudR* 30 (1977-1978): 525-543.
Parker, David. "Three Men in Chekhov's *Three Sisters*." *CR* 21 (1978): 11-23.
Paul, Barbara. "Chekhov's 'Five Sisters'." *MD* 14 (1971): 436-440.
Purdon, Liam. "Time and Space in Chekhov's *The Three Sisters*." Publications of the Arkansas Philological Association 2 (1975): 47-53.
Stroyeva, Mariana. "*The Three Sisters* at the MAT." *Tulane Drama Review* 9 (1964): 42-56.
Tovstonogov, Georgii. "Chekhov's *Three Sisters* at the Gorky Theatre." *DramR* 13 (1968): 146-155.
Valency, Maurice. "Vershinin." In J. P. Barricelli, ed. *Chekhov's Great Plays: A Critical Anthology*, pp. 218-232.

Uncle Vania

Bentley, Eric. "Craftsmanship in *Uncle Vanya.*" In his *In Search of Theater.* New York: Alfred A. Knopf, 1953, pp. 342-364.

Bordinat, Philip. "Dramatic Structure in Chekhov's *Uncle Vanja.*" *SEEJ* 16 (1958): 195-210.

Ermilov, Vladimir. "*Uncle Vanja*: The Play's Movement." in R. L. Jackson, ed. *Chekhov: A Collection of Critical Essays*, pp. 112-120.

Gilman, R. "Broadway Critics Meet *Uncle Vanya.*" *ThQ*, 4 (1974): 67-72.

Singleton, Katrina. "A Translator's Note on *Uncle Vanya.*" *Drama & Theatre* 12 (1975): 127-129.

Vitins, Ieva. "Uncle Vanja's Predicament." *SEEJ* 22 (1978): 454-463.

IN RUSSIAN

Chekhov's Works

A. P. Chekhov. *Polnoe sobranie sochinenii i pisem.* Ed. N. F. Bel'chikov et al. 30 vols. Moscow, 1974-1983.

_____. *Polnoe sobranie sochinenii i pisem.* Ed. S. D. Balukhatyi et al. 20 vols. Moscow, 1944-1951.

Bibliographies

For a selected bibliography of secondary sources on Chekhov in Russian, see the bibliography in Victor Terras, "Chekhov at Home: Russian Criticism" in this volume.

Alexandrov, B. I. *A. P. Chekhov: seminarii.* 2d ed. Moscow, 1964.

Archiv A. P. Chekhova. Moscow: Publichnaia biblioteka, 1939-1941.

Gitovich, N. I. *Letopis' zhizni i tvorchestva A. P. Chekhova.* Moscow: 1955.

Iz arkhiva A. P. Chekhova: publikatsii. Moscow: 1960.

Masanova, I. F. *Chekhoviana—Vyp. I: sistematicheskii ukazatel' literatury o Chekhove i ego tvorchestve.* Ed. A. B. Derman. Moscow, 1929.

Muratova, K. D. *A. P. Chekhov: bibliograpfia.* Leningrad, 1944.

Osharova, T. V. *Bibliografia literatury o A. P. Chekhove.* Saratov, 1979.

Polotskaia, E. A. *Anton Pavlovich Chekhov: rekomendatel'nyi ukazatel' literatury.* Moscow, 1955.

Rukopisi A. P. Chekhova: opisanie. Moscow: Publichnaia biblioteka. Otdel rukopisei. 1938.

INDEX

Chekhov's work and collections of his works are listed under his name. Films based on his works are listed separately. The titles of his works are listed in English with the Russian titles in parentheses. Titles of the Russian films based on his works are given in English translation followed by the Russian titles in parentheses. The collections also appear under the names of their translators.

Abramova's Theatre, 209, 210
Academy of Sciences, 21
Actor's Studio (New York), 221-22, 242
Adamov, Arthur, 142, 143
Adelphi Play Society (London), 215
Adler, Luther, 222
Agate, James, 194
Aiken, Conrad, 148, 163
Aikhenwald, Iurii, 182 n.49
Aleichem, Sholem, 222
Aleksandrovna, Natalia, 260
Alexander II (Tsar), 5, 11
Alexander III (Tsar), 5, 10
Alexandra Theatre (St. Petersburg), 26, 170, 210, 212, 224
Alston, Patrick, 12
Altmann, Robert, 142
American Repertory Theatre (Cambridge, Mass.), 223
Anderson, Judith, 217
Anderson, Robert, 221
Anderson, Sherwood, 149, 158, 161, 162; "Death in the Woods," 158

Antonioni, Michelangelo, 142
Antonov, Sergei, 177, 178
Apollonskii, Roman, 210
Arestrup, Niels, 225
Artaud, Antonin, 141
Aseev, N. N., 171
Ashcroft, Peggy, 141, 216
Astangov, M., 219
Atkinson, Brooks, 195, 196
Avilova, Lidiia, 28, 32 n.21, 172

Bagnold, Enid, 141
Balukhatyi, S. D., 172, 173, 179
Balzac, Honore de, 37; *La comedie humaine*, 72; *The Stepmother*, 38-39
Baring, Maurice, 185, 187, 188
Barnes Theatre (London), 140, 216
Barrault, Jean-Louis, 221
Barth, John, 156, 162
Barthelme, Donald, 162
Bates, A., 188
Batiushkov, Konstantin, 43
Baudelaire, Charles-Pierre, 48

Bauer, Wolfgang, 145
Beckett, Samuel, 142, 143; *Waiting for Godot*, 142, 143
Bennett, Arnold, 188-89, 190
Berdnikov, G. B., 173, 179
Berlioz, Hector: *Symphonie Fantastique* 240
Bernard, Claude, 200
Bilibin, Viktor, 21
Bitsilli, Peter, 173, 174, 175, 177, 178-79, 182 n.50
Bjørnson, Bjørnstjerne, 50, 174
Bloom, Claire, 224
Boborykin, P. D.: *The Divide*, 174
Bogart, Paul, 242
Bolshoi Dramatic Theatre (Leningrad), 219
Bolshoi Theatre (Moscow), 224
Bond, Edward, 145, 201
Borges, Jorge, 156
Borodin, Aleksander, 4
Boruzescu, Radu, 223
Bouffes du Nord (Paris), 225
Bourget, Paul: *Le disciple*, 48, 173
Brecht, Bertolt, 141, 142, 144, 199
Brik, Osip, 171
Brinton, Christian, 185, 186, 187
Bristow, Eugene K., 302-4
Briusov, Valerii, 186
Brodskii, N. L., 177
Brook, Peter, 225
Brooks, Jeffrey, 12-13
Brown, Ivor, 216
Bruford, Walter, 6, 10, 11; *Chekhov and His Russia: A Sociological Study*, 9, 10, 12
Budilnik (*Alarm Clock*), 35, 100, 259
Buechner, George, 141
Bulgakov, S. N., 175
Bunin, Ivan, 88
Bushnell, John, 11

Cahan, Abraham, 185, 187
Calderon de la Barca, Pedro, 145
Calderon, George, 189, 215
Cambridge Theatre, 224
Cannan, Gilbert (translator), 292; *The House with the Mezzanine, and Other Stories*, 293

Carne, Marcel, 142
Carroll, Lewis, 87
Carver, Raymond, 149, 161, 162; "What We Talk About When We Talk About Love," 160; "Why Don't You Dance," 160-61
Chaadaev, Peter, 43
Chaikin, Joseph, 223
Chaikovskii, Petr, 4
Chayefsky, Paddy, 221
Chekhonte, Antosha (pseud. Anton Chekhov), 19, 88, 91, 95, 97, 101-2, 214
Chekhov, Alexander (Chekhov's oldest brother), 17, 23, 109, 110, 114, 255, 256, 257-66; *Christmas Stories*, 265; *History of Fire Fighting*, 258
Chekhov, Anton Pavlovich: collected works of: *The Bet, and Other Stories*, 293; *The Black Monk, and Other Stories*, 293; *Chekhov: The Early Stories, 1883-1888*, 297-98, 299; *Collected Works*, 171, 173; *Complete Works and Letters*, 255; *The House with the Mezzanine, and Other Stories*, 293; *The Image of Chekhov*, 299; *In the Twilight*, 126; *The Kiss, and Other Stories*, 292-93; *Lady with Lapdog, and Other Stories*, 299; *The Lady with the Dog, and Other Stories*, 295; *Motley Tales*, 126, 167; *The Schoolmaster, and Other Stories*, 295; *Selected Stories*, 294, 299; *Select Tales of Tchehov*, 295, 299; *Tales of Melpomene*, 19; *Tchekov's Plays and Stories*, 293, 296
Chekhov, Anton Pavlovich: works of: "Abolished" (Uprazdnili), 76; "About Love" (O liubvi), 45, 63, 65, 72; "Actor's Edge, An" (Akaterskaia givel'), 78; "Agafia" (Agafia), 59, 127; "Aniuta" (Aniuta), 19, 151, 156, 286 n.15; "Anna on the Neck" (Anna na shee), 63, 64, 72-73, 96, 99, 103 n.27; *The Anniversary* (*Iubilei*), 96, 103 n.21, 109, 171, 212-13; "An Anonymous Story" (Rasskaz neizvestnogo cheloveka), 39, 41, 63, 67; "Ariadna"

Chekhov, works of (continued)
(Ariadna), 39, 41, 49, 63; "Art" (Khudozestvo), 38; "At Home" (V rodnom uglu), 21, 27, 58, 63, 64, 67-68, 81, 126, 131; "At the Mill" (Na mel'nitse), 127-28, 129; "An Attack of Nerves"/"A Nervous Breakdown" (Pripadok), 43, 61, 73, 124, 178, 287 n.22; "Autumn" (Osen'), 21; "An Avenger" (Mstitel'), 176; *The Bear* (*Medved*), 21, 96 109, 137, 171, 209, 213, 214 (*see also* Meierkhold, Vsevolod, *33 Fainting Fits*); "The Beauties" (Krasavitsy), 60, 130; "The Beggar" (Nishchyi), 32 n.21; "Belated Flowers" (Tsvety zapozdalye), 240, 241; "The Bet" (Pari), 32 n.21, 293; "Big Volodia and Little Volodia" (Volodia bolshoi i Volodia malenkii), 21; "The Bishop" (Arkhierei), 30, 38, 39, 63, 67, 74, 79, 153-54; "The Black Monk" (Chernyi monakh), 26, 43, 128; "The Boarding House" (V pansione), 234; "A Boring Story" (Skuchnaia istoria), 298-99 (*see also* "A Dreary Story" [Skuchnaia istoria]); "The Bride" (Nevesta), 30, 40, 43, 83, 130, 131; "A Case from the Lawyer's Practice" (Sluchai iz sudebnoi praktiki), 93-94; "A Chameleon"/"The Chameleon" (Khemeleon), 72, 93, 97, 127, 129; *The Cherry Orchard* (*Veshnevyi sad*), 30, 38, 43-44, 57-58, 62, 68, 74, 77-78, 81, 83, 89, 99-102, 109-11, 111-14, 116-17, 119, 120-21, 130, 140, 169, 171, 179, 190, 200-202, 224-25, 227 n.16, 228-32 (*see also* Logan, Joshua, *Wisteria Trees*); "The Chorus Girl" (Khoristka), 46, 286 n.15; "Cold Blood" (Kholodnaia krov'), 176; "The Darling" (Dushechka), 29, 83, 96, 124, 131, 135, 168, 169; "The Daughter of Albion" (Doch' Albiona), 94-95; "Death of a Government Clerk" (Smert' chinovnika), 72, 95, 99; "Difficult People" (Tiazhelye liudi),

Chekhov, works of (continued)
17, 59; "A Doctor's Visit (Sluchai iz praktiki), 44, 62, 63, 69, 73, 295; "Dreams" (Mechty), 60, 74, 124, 126, 130; "A Dreary Story" (Skuchnaia istoria), 23, 42, 61, 74, 77, 154, 155, 156, 167, 168, 173, 175, 293 (*see also* "A Boring Story"); "The Duel (Duel'), 25, 37, 38, 47, 56, 60, 63, 65, 83-84, 130, 131, 168; "Easter Eve" (Sviatoiu noch'iu), 156-57, 158; "Enemies" (Vragi), 68, 126, 295; "Excellent People" (Khoroshye luidi), 32 n.21, 42, 50 n.7, 59, 127; "Fat and Thin"/"The Fat and Thin One" (Tolstyi i tonkii), 72, 93, 174; *Fatherlessness* (*Bezotcovshchina*), 18, 259; "From the Diary of a Violent-Tempered Man" (*Iz zapisok vspyl' chivogo cheloveka*), 91-92; "The Fugitive," (Beglets), 234; "A Gentleman Friend" (Znakomyi muzhchina), 46, 76-77; "Gooseberries" (Khryzhovnik), 40-41, 59, 62, 63, 65, 73, 103 n.27, 125, 128; "The Grasshopper (Popryguniia), 59, 99, 131, 156; "Grief" (Gore), 19; "Grisha" (Grisha), 80; "Gusev" (Gusev), 24, 57, 124, 125-26, 175; "Happiness" (Schast'e), 60, 283; "A Helpless Creature" (Bezzashchitnoe sushchestvo), 103 n.21; "Home" (Doma), 80-81; "Horse Thieves" (Vory), 99 (*see also* "Thieves"); "The House with an Attic" (Dom s mezoninom), 26, 63, 77, 98, 156; "The Huntsman" (Eger), 19, 59; "An Inadvertence," (Neostorozhnost'), 77; "In Exile" (V sylke), 24, 64, 74, 293; "In the Cart" (Na podvode), 27, 62, 64, 67, 73, 75, 83; "In the Ravine" (V ovrage), 24, 38, 43, 48, 62, 63, 74, 84, 124-25, 171; "Ionych" (Ionych), 21, 35, 58, 63, 64-65, 81-82, 83, 99-100; *The Island of Sakhalin* (*Ostrov Sakhalin: Iz putevykh zapisok*), 24, 25, 130, 273-84; *Ivanov* (*Ivanov*), 20-23, 44, 49, 72, 110, 167, 172, 209, 210,

Chekhov, works of (continued)
214-16, 229, 232, 265; "The Kiss"
(Potselui), 60, 173-74, 293, 300-301;
"The Lady with the Lapdog"/"The
Lady with the Dog" (Dama s sobachkoi), 29, 45, 47, 59, 64, 65-66, 82,
100, 126, 128, 131, 151, 173, 180
n.5, 203, 247 n.6, 286 n.13, 295-97;
"Late Flowers" (Tzvety zapozdalye),
55; "The Letter" (Pis'mo), 43;
"Lights" (Ogni), 21, 56, 126, 174,
286 n.13; "Man in the Case" (Chelovek v futliare), 40-41, 59, 64, 65,
73, 77, 88, 96, 97-98, 99, 103 n.21,
175; "A Marriage of Convenience"
(Bark po raschotu), 103 n.21; "Marriage Season" (Svadebnyi sezon),
103 n.21; "Mayonnaise" (Maenez),
92; "The Meeting" (Vstrecha), 32
n.21; "Mire" (Tina), 22, 45, 49, 51
n.22; "Misery" (Neschast'e), 19-20,
59, 74, 149-50, 163 n.9; "Misfortune" (Neschast'e), 41, 126, 129;
"The Mistress" (Barynia), 55; "The
Murder" (Ubiistvo), 24, 38, 73; "My
Life" (Moia zhizn'), 21, 42-43, 45,
58, 59, 63, 64, 66, 85 n.6, 98, 258,
293; "My Nana" (Moia Nana), 47;
"Name-Day"/"The Name-Day"
(Imeniny), 42, 56, 59, 61, 78-79, 126,
167, 168; "A Nervous Breakdown"
(Pripadok) (see "An Attack of
Nerves" [Pripadok]); "A Nightmare"
73, 127; "One of Many" (Ogin iz
nmogikh), 103 n.21; On the High
Road (Na bol'shoi doroge), 21; "On
the Road" (Na puti), 22, 40, 130;
"The Orator (Orator), 90-91, 94;
"Peasants" (Muzhiki), 26, 38, 43,
62, 74, 125, 171, 174, 176; "Peasant
Women" (Baby), 24, 58, 99 (see also
"Women'"); "Pecheneg" (Pecheneg),
27, 58, 72; "The Phosphorous
Match" (Shvedskaia spichka), 45;
Platonov (Platanov)/Play Without a
Title (Bez nazvaniia), 21, 31 n.9, 38,
49, 137, 221 (see also Fireworks on
the James); Play Without a Title (see

Chekhov, works of (continued)
Platonov); "The Post" (Pochta), 60;
"The Privy Councillor" (Tainyi
sovetnik), 72; "Problems of a Mad
Mathematician" (Zadachi suma
shedshego matematika), 90; "The
Professional Pianist" (Taper), 92-93;
The Proposal (Predlozhenie), 21, 96,
109, 137, 171, 209, 210, 214 (see also
Meierkhold, Vsevolod, 33 Fainting
Fits); "The Requiem" (Panikhida),
59; "Revenge" (Mest'), 234; "Rothschild's Fiddle" (Skripka Rotshilda),
63, 67, 73-74, 158-60; "The Schoolmaster" (Uchitel'), 295; The Seagull
(Chaika), 25, 26, 27, 28, 31 n.9, 32
n.22, 32 n.23, 36, 39, 40, 44, 47, 48,
49, 51 n.15, 67, 80, 81, 84, 108,
111-15, 118-19, 137, 140, 144, 170,
172, 178, 191, 194, 199, 210, 212,
214-24, 228-32; "Sergeant Prishibeev"
(Unter Prishibeev), 58, 59, 60, 77,
93, 97, 98, 127; "The Shepherd's
Pipe" (Svirel'), 60; "The Shoemaker
and the Devil" (Sapozhnik i ne chis-
taia sila), 32 n.21; "The Shooting
Party" (Drama na okhote), 45, 47;
"Sleepy" (Spat' khochetsia), 126,
129, 153, 154, 234, 235, 297-98;
"The Steppe" (Step'), 21, 28, 30,
60, 74, 80, 85 n.8, 126, 130, 167,
168, 176, 177, 182 n.46, 283; "A
Story Without a Title" (Bez
zaglavia), 45, 94; "The Student"
(Student), 26, 38, 67, 68, 126,
156-58, 300; "Surgery" (Khirurgia),
56, 57; Swan Song (Levedinnaia
pesnia), 21; "Teacher of Literature"
(Uchitel' slovestnosti), 21, 58, 72,
75, 78; "Terror" (Koshmar), 76, 77;
"Thieves" (Vory), 213 (see also
"Horse Thieves"); Three Sisters (Tri
sestry), 28, 29, 38, 40, 44, 56, 63, 64,
73, 88, 98-101, 109, 110, 114-16,
117, 119-21, 130, 143, 144, 169, 178,
179, 195, 201, 211-12, 214, 216-25,
228-32; "Three Years" (Tri goda),
18, 26, 37, 38, 47, 56-57, 58, 59, 63,

Chekhov, works of (continued)
64, 65-66, 73, 85 n.6, 128, 131, 174;
A Tragic Role (*Tragik po nevole*),
21, 96, 103 n.21, 109; "Two in
One" (Dvoe v odnom), 72; *Uncle
Vania* (*Diadia Vania*), 21, 28, 44, 49,
59, 62-68, 72, 74, 88, 98, 109, 110,
113, 115-20, 140, 143, 170, 193, 202,
211, 213-17, 222-23, 228, 230-31;
"An Upheaval" (Pereplokh), 127;
"Van'ka" (Van'ka), 74; "Verochka"
(Verochka), 40; "Visiting Friends"
(U znakomykh), 27; "Volodia"
(Volodia), 234, 235-36; "The
Wallet" (Bumazhnik), 51 n.15, 234;
"Ward No. 6" (Palata No. 6), 26,
38, 48, 63-64, 73, 76, 77, 99, 131,
168; *The Wedding* (*Svad'ba*), 21, 96,
103 n.21, 109, 213 (*see also* Meier-
khold Vsevolod, *33 Fainting Fits*);
"The Wedding Season" (Svadebnyi
sezon), 260; "A Wedding with a
General" (Svad'ba s generalom), 103
n.21; "What Does One Most Find in
Novels, Short Stories, Etc.?" (Chto
chashche vsevo vstrechayetsya v
romanakh, povestyakh, i t.p.?), 123;
"The Wife" (Zhena), 172; "The
Witch" (Ved'ma), 22; "A Woman's
Kingdom" (Bab'e tsarstvo), 26, 37,
41, 46, 47, 48, 63, 73, 75, 131;
"Women" (Baby), 293 (*see also*
"Peasant Women" [Baby]); *Wood
Demon* (*Leshyi*), 21, 167, 170, 172,
210, 211, 219; "A Work of Art"
(Proizvedenie iskusstva), 128, 234
Chekhov, Ivan (brother), 18
Chekhov, Michael (brother), 18, 23
Chekhov, Michael (cousin), 213-14
Chekhov, Nikolai (brother), 18, 20,
23, 257, 260
Chekhov, Pavel (father), 17-18
Chekhova, Evgeniia (mother), 17, 18
Chekhova, Mariia (Masha) (sister), 18,
21, 25, 28, 255, 256, 257
Chichester Festival, 223
Chirico, Giorgio de, 221
Christie, Julie, 222

Chudakov, Aleksandr, 173, 175, 176,
177, 178, 179, 182 n.45
Chukovsky, Kornei, 303; *A High Art*,
303
Circle in the Square Theatre (New
York), 222
Civic Repertory Theatre, 217
Cocteau, Jean, 142
Comedy Theatre (Leningrad), 171
Compagnie Barrault-Renaud (Paris),
221
Conrad, Joseph, 192; *Heart of Dark-
ness*, 148
Coover, Robert, 156, 162
Corneille, Pierre, 145
Cornell, Katharine, 217
Cort Theatre (New York), 217

Dali, Salvador, 221
Darwin, Charles, 200
Davydov, V. H., 209
Demidova, Alla, 220
Derman, Avram, 171-72, 173, 174,
175, 176, 177, 178, 179-80; *On
Chekhov's Craftsmanship*, 172
Descaves, Lucien, 214
Dewey, John, 148
Dickens, Charles, 36
Dillon, E. J., 185, 186, 187
Dostoevskii, Fedor, 4, 35, 36, 37, 41,
185, 214; "Bobok," 169; *Crime and
Punishment*, 41; "The Gambler,"
41; *The Idiot*, 41
Dreiser, Theodore, 190
Dreyfus, Alfred, 27, 43, 45, 48
Duboisgobey, Fortune Hippolyte
Auguste, 45
Duerrenmatt, Friedrich, 143
Duke of York Theatre, 215-16
Dunnigan, Ann (translator), 292, 299,
300-302, 304; *Selected Stories*, 294,
299

Efremov, Oleg, 220
Efros, Dunia, 21, 31 n.11, 220
Eliot, T. S., 150
Eng, Jan van der, 202-3
Erisman, F. F., 198

Ermilov, V. V., 173, 175
Ermolova, Maria, 137
Ervine, St. John, 194
Ethel Barrymore Theatre (New York), 217
Evans, Edith, 216

Fagan, J. B., 140
Fasquel, Maurice, 234, 235
Faulkner, William, 161
Fell, Marian, 303
Ferguson, Suzanne C., 155-56
Fet, Afanasii, 48
Films based on Chekhov's works: *The Anniversary* (*Iubilei*), 248; *Belated Flowers* (*Tzvety zapozdalye*), 250; *The Boor*, 248; *Desire to Sleep*, 235, 251; *The Fugitive*, 237, 251; *The Grasshopper* (*Popryguniia*), 236-38, 248; *Lady with the Dog* (*Dama s sobachkoi*), 236, 238-40, 247, 249; *Revenge*, 251; *Rothschild's Violin*, 251; *The Seagull* (*Chaika*), 242, 243-44, 249, 250; *The Shooting Party* (*Drama na okhote*), 241, 250; *Three Sisters* (*Tri sestry*), 237, 242, 244, 249, 250; *Uncle Vania* (*Diadia Vania*), 242, 244-46, 247, 250; *Volodia*, 251; *The Wallet*, 251; *The Wedding* (*Svad'ba*), 248; *A Work of Art* (*Khudozhestvo*), 237, 249
Fireworks on the James, 221. See also Chekhov, Anton Pavlovich: works of: *Platonov* (Platonov)
Flaubert, Gustave, 35, 37, 45, 50, 192
Fontanne, Lynn, 217
Fortune Theatre (England), 216
Foss, Kenelm, 215
Friche, V. M., 171
Frieden, Nancy, 11
Fuller, H. de, 193
Fyfe, Hamilton, 194

Gaboriau, Emil, 45
Garland, Patrick, 224
Garnett, Constance (translator), 292, 294-96, 298, 302, 303, 304, 306; *The Lady with the Dog, and Other Stories*, 295; *The Schoolmaster, and Other Stories*, 295; *Select Tales of Tchehov*, 295, 299
Garnett, David, 295
Garnett, Edward, 195
Garshin, Vsevolod, 43, 173
Genet, Jean, 142, 143
Georgievskaia, A., 218
Gerhardie, William, 192
Gerschenkron, Alexander, 6
Gershenzon, M. O., 175
Gialyi, G. A., 173
Gielgud, John, 140, 141, 216, 251
Giovangigli, Orazio Costa, 220
Gish, Lillian, 217
Gitovich, Nina, 26, 27; *Chronicle of Chekhov's Life and Work*, 173
Glama-Meshcherskaia, 209
Glasgow Repertory Theatre, 215
Glassby, Lily, 89
Gogol, Nikolai, 35, 37, 40-41, 58, 173, 214; *Dead Souls*, 40; *The Inspector General*, 92; "Sorochintsy Fair," 40; "Taras Bulba," 18
Golcev, Viktor, 267
Goldsmith, Raymond, 7
Golike, P. P., 24
Golubkov, V. V., 236
Goncharov, Ivan, 185
Gordimer, Nadine, 155
Gordon, Ruth, 217
Goreva's Theatre (Moscow), 209
Gorkii, Maksim, 37, 43, 87, 94, 140, 168-69, 191, 213; *Reminiscences*, 168-69
Gornfeld, A. G., 176
Gottlieb, Vera, 96
Greene, David, 294, 295
Greenstreet, Sydney, 217
Gregory, Andre, 222
Gregory, Paul, 7
Grierson, John, 116
Griffiths, Trevor, 201-2, 224
Grigorovich, Dmitrii V., 20, 37, 40, 75-76, 167, 178
Grillparzer, Franz: *Sappho*, 266
Gromov, Leonid, 173, 174, 175, 177
Guinness, Alec, 141, 216

Guroff, Gregory, 12
Gushchin, M., 174
Guthrie, Tyrone, 216, 222, 292, 304, 305
Guthrie Theatre (Minneapolis), 223
Gwenn, Edmund, 217

Hacket, Francis, 194
Hagen, Uta, 217
Hahn, Beverley, 197
Hankin, St. John, 188, 189
Hardy, Thomas, 192
Harris, Jed, 217
Hauptmann, Gerhart, 36, 141, 172, 174; *Einsame Menschen*, 49
Hawthorne, Nathanial, 161
Hayes, Helen, 221
Heifitz, Joseph, 238, 247
Hemingway, Ernest, 149, 152-53, 161; "Big, Two-Hearted River," 153; "Hills Like White Elephants," 152, 153
The Herald of Europe, 173
Hingley, Ronald, 21-22, 97, 203, 292, 300, 302, 304, 305, 306; *The Oxford Chekhov*, 294, 299
Hippius, Zinaida, 169
Hoare, S., 192
Hofmannsthal, Hugo von, 142
Holland, Peter, 201, 202
Houston Grand Opera, 224
Howarth, Herbert, 193
Howe, George, 224
Hugo, Victor, 45
Hunter, N. C.: *Waters of the Moon*, 141

Iakovleva, Olga, 219
Iavorskaia, Lidiia, 26
Ibsen, Henrik, 49, 112, 136, 140, 141, 142, 145, 172, 174, 187; *Ghosts*, 112; *Hedda Gabler*, 112; *Rosmersholm*, 136; *The Wild Duck*, 49, 112
Inge, William, 141, 221
International Chekhov Society, vii
Ionesco, Eugene, 142, 143
Iunovich, S., 219
Ivanov-Razumnik, V. I., 169

Jackson, Robert L., 196, 202
James, Emrys, 224
James, Henry, 148, 149
Jameson, Margaret, 190-91
Jarrell, Randall, 222
Johnson, Robert, 9
Johnson, Samuel, 122
Joyce, James, 149, 158, 161, 162; "Clay," 151; "The Dead," 155; *The Dubliners*, 158; "Eveline," 151; "The Sister," 158
Julia, Raul, 222

Kafka, Franz, 149, 153, 154; "The Judgement," 153; "Metamorphosis," 154
Kamernyi Theatre (USSR), 218
Karasik, Juli, 242, 243-44
Karlinsky, Simon, 22, 97, 258, 267
Karpov, Evtikhii, 210
Keeton, A., 187
Kennedy Center (Washington, D.C.), 224
Khinkis, Viktor, 294
Kilroy, Thomas, 224
King, Dennis, 217
Kingston-Mann, Esther, 8
Kipnis, Leonid, 292, 304
Kirsh Theatre, 21, 26
Kiseleva, Mariia, 22, 47, 113, 117
Kleines Theatre (Berlin), 213
Knight, Shirley, 222
Knipper, Olga, 27, 28-30, 87, 90, 211, 212, 218, 255, 256, 257, 266, 269
Koltsov, M. E., 171
Komisarjevsky, Theodore, 140, 215-16
Kommissarzhevskii, Fedor. *See* Komisarjevsky, Theodore
Kommissarzhevskaia, Vera, 210
Konchalovskii, Andrei, 242, 244-46, 247
Koonen, Alisa, 218-19
Korolenko, Vladimir, 169
Korsh Theatre (Moscow), 209
Koteliansky, S. S. (translator), 196, 215, 292, 293, 302; *The Bet, and Other Stories*, 293, 299; *Chekhov's Notebooks*, 196; *The House with the Mezzanine, and Other Stories*, 293;

Tchekhov's Plays and Stories, 293, 296
Kracauer, Siegfried, 233
Krainii, Anton. *See* Hippius, Zinaida
Kramer, Karl, 197
Krejča, Otmar, 219, 227 n.25
Kroetz, Franz Xaver, 145
Kucherov, Samuel, 12
Kuprin, Aleksandr, 169
Kurkin, P. I., 198

La Mama (New York), 223
Lanchester, Elsa, 216
Laughton, Charles, 216
Lavrov, Vukol, 246
LeGallienne, Eva, 217
Lebedev-Polianskii, P. I., 171
Lee, Ming Cho, 222
Lef, 171
Leikin, Nikolai, 19, 20, 23, 37, 72, 167, 256-57, 259
Lelevich, G., 171
Leningrad Comedy Theatre (Teatr Komedii), 171
Lenin-Komsomol Theatre (Moscow)
Lenin Library, 256, 258
Leontev, Ivan, 17, 22, 24, 256, 273
Lermontov, Mikhail, 37, 267
Leskov, Nikolai, 37-38, 173; *Cathedral Folk*, 38; "Enchanted Wanderer," 38; "Hare Park," 38; "The Sealed Angel," 38
Levental, Valerii, 220, 224
Levin, Iu. D., 291
Levitan, Isaak, 267
Libedinskii, Iu. M., 171
Linkov, V. Ia., 81-82
Lintvareva, Natalia, 24
Liubimov, Iurii, 225
Livanov, Boris, 220
Logan, Joshua: *The Wisteria Trees*, 221. *See also* Chekhov, Anton Pavlovich: works: *The Cherry Orchard*
Long, R.E.C. (translator), 186, 187, 188, 292, 293, 298, 302; *The Black Monk, and Other Stories*, 293, 297; *The Kiss, and Other Stories*, 292-93

Loquasto, Santo, 223
Loteanu, Emil, 241
Lovell, Terry, 189-90
Lukačs, Georg, 149
Lumet, Sidney, 242, 243-44
Lunacharskii, Anatolii, 170, 171, 177
Lunt, Alfred, 217
Lynd, Robert, 195

McCarthy, Kevin, 222
McClintic, Guthrie, 217
McConkey, James: *To a Distant Island*, vii
Maeterlinck, Maurice, 36, 142, 172, 174; *Les aveugles*, 48
Magarshack, David, ix, 200, 202, 203, 292, 294, 295, 303, 304; *Lady with Lapdog, and Other Stories* (translated by), 299; *The Real Chekhov*, 198-99
Maiakovskii, Vladimir, 181 n.20; *Mystery-Bouffe*, 213
McKay, John, 9
Malaia Bronnaia Theatre (Moscow), 219
Malamud, Bernard, 149, 158-59, 161; "The Jewbird," 159; "The Loan," 160; "The Mourners," 160
Maliugin, Leonid: *My Bantering Happiness*, vii
Mamet, David, 144
Mamuna, Countess, 267
Manhattan Project, 222
Mann, Thomas, 203
Mansfield, Katherine, 149, 151, 161, 215; "The Fly," 150
Marks, Adolf F., 27, 32 n.24, 87
Martin Beck Theatre (New York), 221
Massey, Anna, 224
MAT. *See* Moscow Art Theatre
Matlaw, Ralph E., 294, 295, 298
Maupassant, Guy de, 35, 36, 37, 45-47, 173; *Bel-Ami*, 47; "Boule de Suif," 46; *Pierre et Jean*, 46-47; *Sur l'eau*, 46, 47
Meierkhold, Vsevolod, 144, 171, 178, 201, 211, 212; *33 Fainting Fits*, 171, 178, 214, 230. *See also* Chekhov,

Anton Pavlovich: works of: *The Bear*; *The Proposal*; *The Wedding*
Mendeleev, Dmitrii, 4
Merezhkovskii, D. S., 169, 177, 180 n.4
Mikhailovskii, Nikolai, 47-48, 168, 169, 174, 176
Miles, Patrick (translator), 292, 299, 300-302, 304-5; *Chekhov: The Early Stories: 1883-1888*, 297-98, 299
Milestone, Lewis, 218
Miller, Arthur, 141, 221
Miller, Jonathan, 223, 224
Minneapolis Repertory Theatre, 222
Mirsky, D. S., 148, 174, 175, 177, 291
Mizinova, Lidiia (Lika), 25, 32 n.20, 96-97, 257, 266-69
Moliere, Jean Baptiste Poquelin, 145
Mordvinov, Nikolai, 219
Moscow Art Theatre, 27, 28, 30, 108, 112, 140, 144, 170, 171, 178, 210, 213, 214, 216, 220, 225, 226 n.5
Moscow Art Theatre Third Studio, 213
Moscow Art Theatre 2, 171
Moskovskie vedomosti (*Moscow News*), 168
Moskvin, Ivan, 212
Mossovet Theatre (USSR), 219
Murry, John Middleton (translator), 191-92, 195-96, 215, 292, 293; *The Bet, and Other Stories*, 293, 299
Murry, Middleton. *See* Murry, John Middleton
Musorgskii, Modest, 4

Nabokov, Vladimir, 58, 89
Nadson, Semën, 44
Nazimova, Alla, 217
Nemirovich-Danchenko, Vladimir, 27, 50, 112, 140, 170, 178, 210-11, 218
New Theatre (England), 223
New Times. See Novoe vremia
New York Tribune, 193
Nicholas II, 5, 117
Nichols, Mike, 222
Nikolaev, Iurii, 168
Novoe vremia (*New Times*), 20, 27, 37, 131, 256, 259, 261-62, 263-64

O'Connor, Flannery, 161
Odets, Clifford, 141, 221
Old Vic Theatre (London), 216
Olivier, Laurence, 141, 223, 237, 242-43
Olminskii, M. S., 171
On Guard Group, 171
Orlov, I. I., 84
Ortega y Gasset, Jose: *The Dehumanization of Art*, 161
Oskolki (*Fragments*), 19, 35, 37, 45, 131, 167, 256, 259
Ostroumov, A. O., 198
Ostrovskii, Aleksandr, 116
Ovsianiko-Kulikovskii, D. N., 170
Owen, Thomas, 9
Oxford Playhouse (England), 140
Ozerov, Vladislav, 43
Ozu, Yasujiro, 234

Page, Geraldine, 222
Palmarini-Campa-Capodgalio Company (Italy), 217
Parker, R. A., 191
Parry, Natasha, 225
Pasatiri, Thomas: *The Seagull* (opera), 224
Patrick, G. Z., 193
Pavlov, Ivan, 4
Pavlova, Tatiana, 218
Payne, Robert (translator), 292, 295-96, 298, 300, 302, 304-5; *The Image of Chekhov*, 299
Pennington, Michael: *Anton Chekhov*, vii
Perkins, Osgood, 217
Piccoli, Michel, 225
Piccolo Teatro del Milano, 221
Pinter, Harold, 143, 144
Pintilie, Lucian, 223
Pirogov, N. I., 168
Pitcher, Harvey, 292, 299, 300-302, 304-5; *Chekhov: The Early Stories: 1883-1888* (translated by), 297-98, 299; *Olga Knipper, Chekhov's Leading Lady*, vii
Pitoëff family, 140
Pitoëff, Georges, 214, 215

Pitoëff, Sacha, 215
Pleschev, Aleksei N., 23, 37, 75, 84, 256
Plisetskaia, Mariia: *The Seagull* (ballet), 224
Poe, Edgar Allen, 148, 153
Pomialovskii, Nikolai, 173
Popov, Aleksandr, 4
Porter, Katherine Anne, 149, 153, 154, 161; "The Jilting of Granny Weatherall," 154; "Pale Horse, Pale Rider," 153
Potapenko, Ignatii, 25, 266, 267
Prague Narodni Divadlo, 219
Provincetown Playhouse, 221
Przhevalskii, Nikolai: *From Kiakhta to the Sources of the Yellow River*, 37; *Journey in the Ussuri District*, 37
Publick Theatre (New York), 222
Pushkarev, Sergei, 6
Pushkin Prize for Literature, 21, 264
Pushkin, Aleksander, 37, 40, 43, 44, 83, 131, 177; *Eugene Onegin*, 39, 40; *Gypsies*, 40; *The Hero*, 40

Queen's Theatre, 216

Racine, Jean, 145
Radzinskii, Eduard, 219
Rascoe, Burton, 195
Rattigan, Terence: *The Browning Version*, 141; *Separate Tables*, 141
Rayfield, Donald, 197
Redgrave, Michael, 141, 216, 223
Reinhardt, Max, 213
Renoir, Jean, 142
Richardson, Ralph, 141, 223
Rieber, Alfred, 9
Rimskii-Korsakov, Nikolai, 4
Robbins, Richard, 8
Robinson, Geroid Tanquary, 6
Roksanova, M. I., 211
Room, Abram, 240
Roosevelt, Theodore, 193-94
Rose, Marilyn, 292
Rossolimo, Grigorii, 256
Royal Court Theatre (London), 224
Rozanov, Vasilii, 181 n.14
Rozov, Viktor, 219

Russkaia mysl' (*Russian Thought*), 24, 256, 267, 273

Sacher-Masoch, Leopold, 39, 49; *Venus in Furs*, 49
St.-Denis, Michel, 216, 218, 221
St. Petersburg Gazette, 263
Sakhalin Island, 23-24, 273-84. See also *The Island of Sakhalin*
Sakharova, E. K., 21
Salle Privee (Paris), 214
Samsonov, Samson, 236-38, 242, 244
Sand, George, 263
Schnitzler, Arthur, 141
Schopenhauer, Arthur, 39, 48; *Parerga and Paralipomena*, 48-49
Schultz, Michael, 222
Scott, Clement, 136-37
Scott, George C., 222
Serban, Andrei, 222, 223
Severnyi vestnik (*Northern Herald/ Northern Messenger*), 21, 256
Shakespeare, William, 44, 51 n.15 135, 140, 145, 263; *Hamlet*, 44, 90; *Macbeth*, 44
Shakh-Azizova, T. K., 173, 174
Shavrova, Elena, 266
Shaw, George Bernard, 187, 190, 191, 194, 215; *Heartbreak House*, 140
Shaw, Irwin, 221
Shchedrin, P., 224
Shchegelov. *See* Leontev, Ivan
Shchepkina-Kupernik, Tatiana, 95
Sherman, S. P., 194
Shestov, Lev, 169-70, 176
Shubert Theatre (New York), 217
Simmons, Ernest J., 266
Simms, James, 7, 8
Simon, Neil: *The Good Doctor*, 222
Simonov, R. N., 171
Sinel, Allen, 12
Skabichevskii, A. M., 168, 169
Smirnitskii, V., 219
Smith, Virginia Llewellyn: *Anton Chekhov and the Lady with the Dog*, 32 n.27, 203
Sobolev, Iurii V., 171; *In the Ravine*, 171

Sobolshchikov-Samarin, N. I., 213
Sologub, Fëdor, 43
Sovremennik Theatre, 220
Sperr, Martin, 145
Srizhenov, O., 220
Stalin, Joseph, 214
Stanislavskii, Konstantin, 89, 102, 108, 111-12, 119, 138, 139, 140, 141, 144, 170, 178, 198-99, 211, 212, 215, 217, 220
Stanislavskii, Lilina, 211
Stanley, Kim, 222
Starr, Frederick, 12
State Alexandra Theatre. See Alexandra Theatre (St. Petersburg)
State Society (London), 215
Steiner, George, 291, 304
Stenberg, Enar, 220
Stowell, H. Peter, 155, 200, 202; Literary Impressionism: James and Chekhov, 189, 198
Strasberg, Lee, 221
Streep, Meryl, 222-23
Strehler, Giorgio, 221
Strindberg, August, 36, 49-50, 141, 145 174; Miss Julie, 49-50, 117-18
Struve, Pëtr, 169
Studio Theatre (USSR), 171
Styan, J. L.: Chekhov in Performance, 198, 199-200
Suvorin, Aleksei, 19, 20, 22, 23, 24, 25, 26, 27, 28, 37, 41, 42, 43, 72, 256, 257, 260, 274
Svoboda, Joseph, 219
Szeftel, Marc, 12

Taganka Theatre (Moscow), 220, 224-25
Tairov, Aleksandr, 218
Tchaikovsky, Petr. See Chaikovskii, Petr
Teatro Eliseo (Rome), 221
Teatro Quirino (Rome), 221
Theatre Hebértot (France), 221
Theatre des Champs-Elysees (Paris), 214
Tolstoi, Aleksei: Tsar Fedor Ioanna-vich, 211

Tolstoi, Dmitrii, 12
Tolstoi, Lev, 4, 25, 36, 37, 39, 41-43, 50, 50 n.9, 83, 118, 129, 130, 168, 169, 173, 175, 177, 180 n.5, 185, 191, 214; Anna Karenina, 39, 41, 42, 48, 129; Confession, 48; "Death of Ivan Il'ich," 42; "The Kreutzer Sonata," 41, 42; Resurrection, 41
Tovstonogov, Georgii, 219
Tretiakov, S. M., 171
Turgenev, Ivan, 4, 36, 37, 38-40, 50, 126, 173, 185, 267; Fathers and Sons, 39; "Hamlet and Don Quixote," 39, 44; A Month in the Country, 38; On the Eve, 39; Rudin, 40; Smoke, 39, 48; Torrents of Spring, 39
Turrini, Peter, 145

Vakhtangov, Evgenii, 213, 214
Valency, Maurice, 196
Varlamov, Konstantin, 210
Vega, Lope de, 145
Vengerov, S. A., 170, 175
Veresaev, V. V., 169
Veselitskaia, L. I.: "Mimochka Taking the Waters," 173
Visconti, Luchino, 221
Vishnevskii, A. L., 211
Vivian Beaumont Theatre (New York), 222
Volchek, Galina, 220
Volin, Lazar, 6
Voltaire, François-Marie Arouet de, 44-45; Candide, 45
Vysotskii, Vladimir, 220

Wagner, Geoffrey: The Novel and the Cinema, 235
Wagner, William, 12
Washington Square Players, 216
Webster, Margaret, 217
Wedekind, Frank, 141
Welty, Eudora, 148, 161
Werth, A., 194
Whelan, Heide, 10
Wilbur, Elvira, 7-8

Wilde, Oscar, 87
Willcocks, M. P., 194, 196
Williams, Raymond, 197, 201
Williams, Tennessee, 141
Williamson, Nicol, 222
Wilson, Edmund, 190, 294
Woolf, Janet, 202
Woolf, Leonard, 189
Woolf, Virginia, 190, 202
Worth, Irene, 222, 224
Wortman, Richard, 11-12
Wright, Ralph, 194

Yarmolinsky, Avrahm, 292, 294, 299, 304
Young, Stark, 217, 292, 303, 304

Zaika (*Stammerer*), 18
Zakharin, G. A., 198
Zamiatin, Evgenii, 29
Zavadskii, Iurii, 219
Zola, Emile, 36, 37, 47-48, 136, 138,
    190, 200, 261-62; *Germinal*, 47, 48;
    Nana, 47; *Therese Raquin*, 47
Zozulia, E. D., 171
Zritel' (*The Spectator*), 260

CONTRIBUTORS

TOBY W. CLYMAN, Associate Professor of Slavic Languages and Literatures at the State University of New York at Albany, has published studies on Chekhov, Gogol, Babel, and on Russian autobiography. She is co-translator of P. M. Bitsilli, *Chekhov's Art: A Stylistic Analysis* and is currently completing a work on women in Chekhov's fiction.

JOSEPH L. CONRAD, Professor of Slavic Languages and Literatures at the University of Kansas at Lawrence, has written, among other studies, numerous articles on Chekhov. His present research is on traditional Russian folklore in Chekhov's works.

ANDREW R. DURKIN, Associate Professor of Russian Literature at Indiana University, Bloomington, writes on nineteenth- and twentieth-century Russian literature. He is the author of *Sergei Aksakov and Russian Pastoral* and is currently at work on a study of Chekhov's fiction.

THOMAS EEKMAN, Professor of Slavic Languages and Literatures at the University of California, Los Angeles, has written widely in the field of Slavic literature. He is the author of *The Realm of Rime: A Study of Rime in the Poetry of the Slavs, Thirty Years of Yugoslav Literature: 1945-1975*, and is the editor of *Anton Chekhov, 1860-1960: Some Essays*. He is also co-editor of several books, among them *Chekhov's Art of Writing: A Collection of Critical Essays*, and *Juraj Križanič (1618-1683): Russophile and Ecumenic Visionary, A Symposium*.

MARTIN ESSLIN, Professor of Drama at Stanford University, has published extensively in the field of modern and contemporary drama. His books include *Brecht: A Choice of Evils*; *The Theatre of the Absurd; Pinter: The Playwright*; *Artaud*; and *The Age of Television*.

RALPH T. FISHER JR., Professor of History and Director of the Russian and East European Center at the University of Illinois at Urbana-Champaign, is the author of *Pattern for Soviet Youth*. His interest in the Chekhov period was stimulated by his work with Vernadsky and Pushkarev on the three-volume *Source Book for Russian History*.

KENNETH A. LANTZ, Associate Professor of Russian at the University of Toronto, is the author of *Nikolay Leskov* and editor and translator of *The Sealed Angel and other Stories* by Nikolay Leskov. He is currently completing work on *Anton Chekhov: A Reference Guide*.

LAUREN G. LEIGHTON is Professor of Russian Literature at the University of Illinois at Chicago and former editor of the *Slavic and East European Journal*. He is the author of *Alexander Bestuzhev-Marlinsky and Russian Romanticism: Two Essays*, and the translator of *The Art of Translation: Kornei Chukovsky's "A High Art,"* and is currently completing a critical-comparative study of *The High Art in the Two Worlds: Translation in Russia and America*.

RALPH LINDHEIM, Associate Professor of Slavic Languages and Literatures at the University of Toronto, has published studies on Chekhov, Gogol, and modern Slavic drama and is presently engaged in research on nineteenth-century Russian fiction and drama.

CHARLES E. MAY, Professor of English at California State University, Long Beach, is editor of *Short Story Theories* and the author of over 100 articles and chapters in books primarily on the subject of short fiction. He is currently working on a six-volume theoretical/historical study of short fiction in Europe, England, and America since 1800.

HARVEY PITCHER established the Russian Department at the University of St. Andrews in Scotland and is presently writing full time. He is the author of *The Chekhov Play: A New Interpretation*, *Chekhov's Leading Lady: A Portrait of the Actress Olga Knipper*, *Understanding the Russians*, *When Miss Emmie was in Russia*, and is co-translator of *Chuckle with Chekhov: A Selection of Comic Stories*, and *Chekhov: The Early Stories*.

LEONARD POLĄKIEWICZ is Assistant Professor of Slavic Languages and Literatures at the University of Minnesota-Twin Cities. He has published works on Chekhov and is currently engaged in research on studies of Dostoevsky and of Czesław Milosz.

DONALD RAYFIELD, Senior Lecturer and Head of the Russian Department at Queen Mary College, University of London, has published numerous articles on nineteenth- and twentieth-century Russian literature. He is the author of *Chekhov: The Evolution of His Art* and *The Dream of Lhasa: Life of Przhevalsky.*

LAURENCE SENELICK, Professor of Drama at Tufts University, is a member of the Russian Research Center at Harvard University and a Fellow of the John Simon Guggenheim Foundation. His books include *Anton Chekhov* (Macmillan Modern Dramatists Series), *Russian Dramatic Theory from Pushkin to the Symbolists, Gordon Craig's Moscow Hamlet, Russian Satiric Comedy* and *Serf Actor: The Life and Art of Mikhail Shchepkin.* He is also co-author of *British Music Hall 1840-1923* and translator of several Chekhov plays.

H. PETER STOWELL, Professor of English and Director of Film Studies at Florida State University at Tallahassee, has published in the fields of English, Russian, Comparative Literature, and Film. He is the author of *Literary Impressionism, James and Chekhov*, and is presently writing a book on interdisciplinary film theory.

J. L. STYAN, Franklyn Bliss Snyder Professor of English Literature at Northwestern University, is the author of *The Elements of Drama, The Dark Comedy, The Dramatic Experience, Shakespeare's Stagecraft, Chekhov in Performance, The Challenge of the Theatre, Drama, Stage and Audience, The Shakespeare Revolution, Modern Drama in Theory and Practice*, and *Max Reinhardt.* His current research is on Restoration comedy.

VICTOR TERRAS, Professor of Slavic Languages and Comparative Literature at Brown University, has written extensively in the field of Russian, German, Estonian, and Comparative Literature. His books include *The Young Dostoevsky, Belinskij and Russian Literary Criticism, A Karamazov Companion, Mayakovsky, A Handbook of Russian Literature.*

JOHN TULLOCH is Associate Professor at the School of English and Linguistics and Head of Mass Communication at Macquarie University, in Australia. His books include *Chekhov: A Structuralist Study, Doctor Who: the Unfolding Text, Australian Cinema: Industry, Narrative and Meaning*, and *Legends on the Screen: The Narrative Film in Australia, 1919-1929.*